Jewish Guide to Practical Medical Decision-Making

מדריך לענייני רפואה והלכה למעשה

JEWISH GUIDE
TO PRACTICAL MEDICAL
DECISION-MAKING

Rabbi Jason Weiner

Urim Publications
Jerusalem • New York

Book design by Ariel Walden

Printed in USA

First Edition

ISBN 978-965-524-278-2

Urim Publications
P.O.B. 52287
Jerusalem 9152102 Israel
www.UrimPublications.com

Library of Congress Cataloging-in-Publication Data

Names: Weiner, Jason, author.
Title: Jewish guide to practical medical decision-making / Rabbi Jason Weiner.
Description: First edition. | Jerusalem ; New York : Urim Publications, [2017]
Identifiers: LCCN 2017031026 | ISBN 9789655242782 (hardcover : alk.
  paper)
Subjects: LCSH: Medicine—Religious aspects—Judaism. | Medicine in
  rabbinical literature. | Medical ethics. | Jewish ethics. | Medical laws and
  legislation (Jewish law)
Classification: LCC BM538.H43 W47 2017 | DDC 296.3/642—dc23 LC
  record available at https://lccn.loc.gov/2017031026

אשר זעליג וייס

כגן 8

פעיה"ק ירושלם ת"ו

בע"ה   כסלו תש'

הן הגיע את ספרי גדול א' יען הרב היקר הרב יהונתן ליב נרו אלי'ו מאריך וינני

רגשיו ונאמנה אמ''ר כנין. אשר גין לו קלא אם שמחה וסב לא האנן גרד הביות גמולד

אנכי תין" דלום וונגלם, ואגו שמגד לא קשוע (נהי וא היוונ דשמבת קקול, ובעל ני.

ואן היא סוק רבי לעוד גל שמחר גדל מן הגאנן קלחנין ובין הגברים

אגונב בכוד שאש וקעת וכאמין, קמזיו הוא תוטא רבה.

כשני לנוד וינו אלינו קשקין לגש ש' שמע ולומק'ל חשוה ולוטעזיה

ולבושם לו וא קנרד מגנב.

          דצעדה

RABBI Z. N. GOLDBERG

Abbad Badatz & Bies Horaa'h "Hayashar Vehatov"
Member Of Supreme Rabbinical Court

הרב זלמן נחמיה גולדברג

אב"ד בד"ץ ובית הוראה לדיני ממונות "הישר והטוב"
חבר בית הדין הרבני הגדול

ב"ה, יום ___ ___ תשע"ו

המרכז הרפואי שערי צדק, ירושלים   **Shaare Zedek Medical Center, Jerusalem**

מסונף לפקולטה למדעי הבריאות אוניברסיטת בן-גוריון בנגב   Affiliated with the Faculty of Health Sciences Ben-Gurion University of the Negev

הרב פרופ' אברהם שטינברג
מנהל היחידה לאתיקה רפואית

דורנו זכה לראות בהתקדמות אדירה של מקצוע הרפואה בכל התחומים, הן במצד האחבוני והן בצד הטיפולי, הן בידע המדעי והן ביכולות הטכנולוגיות. קידמה עצומה זו חלה בתוך זמן קצר, באופן חסר תקדים, ובדרך שלא קרה בכל שנות ההיסטוריה האנושית.

קידמה מבורכת זו הביאה לשיפור ניכר באיכות החיים ולהארכת תוחלת החיים. אכן, יחד עם זאת עוררה התפתחות אדירה זו סוגיות הלכתיות ומוסריות חסרות תקדים בהיקף ובעומק.

במקביל לקידמה המדעית-טכנולוגית הזו חל שינוי דרמטי ביחסי חולה-רופא. העולם המערבי עבר ממערכת יחסים פטרנליסטית, שעל פיה הרופא הוא הקובע באופן בלעדי כיצד יטופל החולה, למערכת יחסים אוטונומיסטית, שעל פיה החולה הוא הקובע מה ייעשה או לא ייעשה בגופו ובנפשו. היישומים העיקריים של הקידמה הרפואית מחד גיסא, והמתחים הנובעים מהבעיות ההלכתיות והאתיות של הקידמה הזו מתרחשים ברובם בתוך כותלי בתי החולים. זה המקום בו מאושפזים חולים קשים, זה המקום בו מבוצעים אבחונים מורכבים וטיפולים עם פוטנציאל גדול אך גם עם סיכונים רבים, ועל כן זה המקום בו בא לידי ביטוי בולט הדיון ההלכתי והאתי.

זכינו בדורנו לקבוצה מרשימה של גדולי תורה והלכה שהתמחו – וממשיכים להתמסר - למציאת פתרונות והדרכה הלכתיים לכל הבעיות שהרפואה המודרנית מציבה בפנינו. גדולי הפוסקים – הנערכים ברופאים ובחוקרים שהם גם תלמידי חכמים ויראי שמים – עוסקים בכל הסוגיות הרלוונטיות מתחילת החיים ועד סוף החיים וכל מה שביניהם. היבול הספרותי-הלכתי בשנים האחרונות בתחומי הרפואה וההלכה הוא רב, מפורט ומעמיק.

דבר גדול עשה ידידי הרב ג'ייסון ויינר, המשמש כרב בית החולים Cedar-Sinai בלוס אנג'לס, בהוציאו לאור חוברת בשם "עניני רפואה – הלכה למעשה". חוברת זו משמשת הדרכה מעשית לסוגיות ההלכתיות מן החמורות ביותר עבור החולים והרופאים בבית חולים. הן הצוות הרפואי והן החולים ובני משפחותיהם "הולכים לאיבוד" בסבך הבעיות ההלכתיות המבצעות מההישגים של הרפואה המודרנית, ובמקורות הרבים והמורכבים של ספרות ההלכה בנושאים אלה. לרובם בודאי יקשה מאד לא רק לחפש את תשובות המורכבות לשאלות החמורות שלפניהם אלא שלעתים אף אינם מודעים שיש בעיה הלכתית הדורשת תשומת לב והתייחסות. סבורני שהמדריך המעשי שלפנינו יהא לאחיסמך ולאחיעזר לכל מי שעומדת ההלכה חשובה לו.

מפאת עיסוקי הרבים לא עלה בידי לעיין כראוי בדברים הכתובים כאן, אך חזקה על תלמיד חכם כמו הרב ויינר שלא תצא תקלה תחת ידו.

יחד עם זאת יש לזכור שהכרעות הלכתיות תלויות פעמים רבות בדיוקים של פרטי המקרה, והתוצאה ההלכתית יכולה להשתנות בהתאם לנתונים הספציפיים והייחודיים של כל מקרה ומקרה. המדריך ההלכתי שלפנינו בודאי ישמש נאמנה את הצוות הרפואי ואת החולים ומשפחותיהם, אך אין הוא מייתר כמובן התייעצות עם פוסק מובהק הבקי בנושאים אלה ככל שהפרטים הרפואיים בכל מקרה מסובכים וייחודיים לו.

הנני מברך את המחבר, הרב ג'ייסון ויינר, בהמשך הצלחה בתפקידו החשוב, ויפוצו מעיינותיו חוצה.

בברכה ובידידות רבה,

אברהם שטינברג

ת.ד. 3235 ירושלים 91031 טל. 5111 02-655 פקס. 02-651 3946
P.O.B. 3235 Jerusalem 91031 Tel: 972-2-655 5111 Fax: 972-2-651 3946
www.szmc.org.il

749700002   580007557 ע'

CONTENTS

Introduction   11
Acknowledgements   25

1. FACILITATING SHARED DECISION-MAKING
   A. Understanding Terminology: Key Concepts to
      Facilitate Collaborative Decision-Making   29
   B. Truth-Telling: When Painful Medical Information
      Should and Should Not Be Revealed   44
   C. Mental Illness: Determining Capacity and Proper
      Treatment in Accordance with Jewish Law   51

2. HOW MUCH TREATMENT?
   A. Risk and Self-Endangerment: Determining the
      Appropriateness of Attempting Various Levels of
      Dangerous Medical Procedures   69
   B. Making Decisions on Behalf of an Incapacitated Patient   73
   C. Pediatrics: Jewish Law and Determining a Child's
      Consent and Treatment   77
   D. Palliative Care and Hospice in Jewish Law and Thought   86

3. PRAYER
   A. Is Prayer Ever Futile? On the Efficacy of Prayer for
      the Terminally Ill   93
   B. Viduy: Confessional Prayers Prior to Death   105

4. AT THE END OF LIFE
   A. Advance Directives and POLST Forms   113

B. End-of-Life Decision-Making: DNR, Comfort
Measures, Nutrition/Hydration, and Defining
"Terminal" in Accordance with Jewish Law   121
C. Withholding vs. Withdrawing: Deactivating a
Ventilator and Cessation of Dialysis and Cardiac
Defibrillators at the End of Life   137
D. Case Study: Deactivating a Total Artificial Heart   154
E. Supporting Patients Who Request Physician-Assisted
Suicide: Towards a Nuanced Approach   169
Appendix: Triage: Determining Which Patients to
Prioritize in an Emergency According to Jewish Law   178

5. AFTER DEATH
A. Definition of Death in Jewish Law   185
B. Jewish Customs at the End of Life and After One Dies   195
C. Organ Donation   203
D. Jewish Guidance on the Loss of a Baby or Fetus   217
E. Autopsy and Jewish Law   236
F. Cremation and Jewish Law   250
Appendix: Ethical Issues in the Sale of Organs   258
Appendix: Burial in a Mausoleum and Jewish Law   266

6. REPRODUCTIVE QUESTIONS
A. Genetic Testing, Disclosure of Results, and PGD   285
B. Assisted Reproductive Technology: Fertility Issues,
Artificial Insemination, IVF   304
C. Abortion, Pregnancy Reduction, and Stem Cell Research 319
D. Surrogacy and Egg Donation   335
E. Labor and Delivery: Some Jewish Customs and Issues
that Arise upon the Birth of a Baby   349

APPENDIX
Stories from the Front Lines: Confronting Complex
Ethical Scenarios and Dilemmas   355

INDEX   363

INTRODUCTION

The Challenge

Jewish Law, Halakhah, is a massive corpus that deals with a tremendous range of situations, events, and areas of life. For centuries, it has guided Jews in their every decision – both minor and significant – including medical decisions. To some, Halakhah may mistakenly seem like an outdated method of approaching medical issues. Indeed, medical technology has advanced to heights not thought possible even in the recent past. We can now create and prolong life in ways previously unimaginable, and it is sometimes difficult to apply classical Jewish sources to these contemporary dilemmas.[1] However, Halakhah is actually a tremendous resource in approaching and responding to the numerous challenges presented by modern medicine.

Judaism certainly encourages technological advancement and the potential it holds. The Torah does not accept the approach that insists on "natural law" alone, but rather encourages humanity to manipulate nature, in partnership with God, to make the world a better place.[2]

At the same time, technological advancement comes with many costs. Much of the precedent for medical decisions in Talmudic literature relates to the pain and suffering that Roman torturers inflicted on our great sages as they killed them as punishment for teaching Torah. Ethicist Dr. Benjamin Freedman notes that despite all of the incredible good that modern medicine has to offer, an unpleasant side effect of medical advances is the fact that the modern hospital also has the potential to inflict even more pain and suffering than any Roman master of torture could dream of. This is because today we can keep people alive – oftentimes in excruciating agony – who in the past would have necessarily died of their illness or injuries.[3] This leads to a critical question: Just because something *can* be done, *should* it be done?

Instead of asking this question, many people today make medical decisions based on guilt. People often cannot bear the thought that they might be responsible for ending the life of a loved one. As a result, they make decisions based on avoidance of feeling guilty rather than on what is best for the patient. Unfortunately, this can have the unwanted consequence of prolonging pain and suffering.

On the other hand, Jewish values related to healthcare and the value of life frequently encourage Jewish patients to be more aggressive in the pursuit of lifesaving or life-prolonging therapies and interventions, which sometimes leads to conflicts. There are also the very pressing contemporary issues of cost, scarcity, and accessibility of resources. Some patients may not be offered certain curative or therapeutic options, because they simply do not have anyone knowledgeable, concerned, or assertive enough to advocate for them or to help research and navigate all potential options. Others may lack the financial or insurance resources to qualify them for possible medications or procedures. All healthcare professionals today wrestle with the justice of such disparity in accessibility.

Most challenging issues that arise in hospitals today cannot truly be categorized as "problems." Problems have answers. The challenges we face in medical care in the modern age are more accurately classified as "dilemmas," as there is generally no one simple solution, but rather a number of difficult alternatives. This often forces us to compromise and/ or simply choose the "least bad" path. How can Jewish Law provide practical guidance on these very complex contemporary challenges and questions? The answer comes in the eternal relevance of the Torah and the adaptability of the Talmudic legal system.

A Solution

One of the basic principles of Jewish faith is that there is an Oral Torah in addition to the written one, and that both are essential.[4] The Oral Torah was passed down from God to Moses, and then from generation to generation.[5] There are numerous reasons suggested for God's method of giving the Torah in writing as well as via oral tradition, some of which are especially relevant for this discussion. For example, the teachings of the Torah must be conveyed orally because it is essential for the subtle concepts to be fully explained by living Torah scholars, not only texts. In this way, each student can learn from a teacher who lives according to those concepts, and who can therefore explain subtleties and answer any questions that arise. This avoids ambiguities inherent in the use of text alone.[6] Furthermore, the Torah includes both a written and an oral element so that it can be understood by both adults and children, sophisticated and unlearned alike. The Oral Torah is entrusted to the great sages in each generation, so that they can transmit it to everyone in a relevant manner, in accordance with each person's capacity for understanding.[7] A great teacher is required to pass on traditions; textbooks cannot provide answers to dynamic questions.

Although much of the Oral Torah has now been recorded in the form of the Mishnah and the Talmud, the oral tradition is designed to withstand the test of time by being adaptable. Written Law can never fully encompass all situations and eras. God orally transmitted to Moses principles and general rules (some of which are hinted at in the Torah, others available by tradition alone) because in writing they could be misinterpreted by different readers. The Rabbinic leaders of every generation are thus able to apply the principles of the Oral Torah to contemporary situations, allowing the Torah to remain relevant even in circumstances that were unimaginable a millennium ago.[8]

The job of Talmudists and halakhic decisors is thus to identify and interpret the relevant material in Rabbinic literature and to apply it to the case at hand.[9] The oral tradition imbues their opinions with authority that becomes binding on their followers and future generations.[10] However, properly identifying parallels between the modern world and ancient Rabbinic writings and principles is no simple task. Today, this is sometimes accomplished by authorities who have advanced training and experience in Rabbinic literature and are able to carefully compare different circumstances to practical situations in order to arrive at an approach to modern dilemmas (*medamin milta le-milta*).[11] Our sages taught, "Turn it [the Torah] over and over, for everything is in it."[12] When a sage delves deeply into the Torah, it is possible to find everything in it, including some sort of precedent for or approach to contemporary challenges. The Chazon Ish, one of the greatest recent authorities on Jewish Law, famously writes, "There is no such thing as a law that is not explicated in the Torah; everything is in the Torah."[13]

In attempting to explain and elaborate upon the general principles that it establishes, the Talmud often discusses hypothetical examples, some of which must have seemed hopelessly far-fetched to the students of previous generations. Yet these examples often provide relevant case material for contemporary rabbis to apply to modern dilemmas, often through intricate cross-category comparisons, as mentioned above.[14] In presenting an example of this type of abstract case material, Tosafot (one of the classic Talmudic commentaries) suggests the case of a fetus that is drawn out of a womb and then reinserted.[15] The Talmud refers to this as a hypothetical scenario that may never occur, but nevertheless encourages us to study it. Today we see how such an unlikely case could, in fact, be relevant. The greatness of Talmudic jurisprudence is that nearly every type of case that can arise is dealt with in some way through general paradigms that establish useful principles.[16] There is almost always some precedent that can be drawn upon.

As we will see in this volume, however, some modern questions are so challenging that even the greatest Rabbinic scholars have difficulty finding any precedent in classical Rabbinic literature.[17] Some maintain that even in these cases, the great rabbis must still use this methodology to creatively draw analogies from similar laws, or sometimes even an anecdote. Others, however, concede that there may indeed be no precedent in Rabbinic literature; qualified rabbis must instead apply more general Torah values and principles in order to develop an approach to the issue.[18] In more extreme cases, when clear precedent is completely unavailable, we simply rely on the reasoning and intuition of the greatest Rabbinic thinkers to provide guidance.[19]

It is important to note that Jewish Law must be applied by experienced and knowledgeable individuals who have achieved expertise in these matters. Specifically, as Rabbi Joseph B. Soloveitchik explained, complex cases in Jewish Law cannot be ruled on by anyone who simply has a Rabbinic degree,[20] but rather only by a rabbi who is a scholar with a mastery of Jewish Law, accepts the sacredness and totality of Jewish Law, is pious and God-fearing, and interprets it in accordance with traditional methods.[21] In addition to knowledge and discernment, the person applying Jewish Law must also be someone who is accepted by the people.[22] This expertise is achieved not only through intensive study of classical texts, but also through extensive practical experience, guided by experts (*shimush chachamim*).[23]

These conditions obviously limit the number of those who can be viewed as competent authorities in Jewish Law to provide guidance in modern bioethical dilemmas. This is all the more true given that even very competent rabbis often do not have particular experience or expertise in the rapidly changing medical field, and therefore must either consult with someone who does or pass the question on to a more appropriate address. As Rabbi Aharon Lichtenstein explained in the context of warning that "only a Rav of eminent stature may render a decision regarding abortion." Just as a general internist would not perform a liver transplant simply because he or she is an "MD," not every rabbi is qualified to render decisions regarding many major questions of Jewish Law. This is especially true of questions that relate to modern medicine, which require an expertise of their own.[24]

Even when appropriate Rabbinic guidance is sought, the human factor in working out these complicated cases frequently results in differences of opinion on various matters. As long as these views are all faithfully working within the same traditional assumptions and methodology, multiple approaches can be legitimate.[25]

The Role of the Rabbi and the Importance of Halakhah

Although many people recognize the role of clergy in providing pastoral support and spiritual care, the role of a rabbi in a traditional community is often also to issue rulings about proper observance of Jewish Law. It is essential for medical practitioners to understand this central and influential legal role of the rabbi in the decision-making process for many observant Jews, particularly when facing critical situations. Jewish Law places many obligations upon an observant Jew and often restricts a patient's autonomy.[26] Furthermore, Jewish medical ethics emphasize different primary values than some other ethical systems, as will be described in the next chapter.

One of the most frequent questions medical professionals ask after hearing presentations on the very detailed and nuanced Jewish laws related to medicine is, "Why do people have to follow these rules? What will happen if they don't?"

At its most basic level, these decisions can often be excruciatingly difficult and fraught with tremendous guilt and uncertainty. Receiving guidance from a wise, ancient, and trusted belief system can be very comforting, as it provides specific advice and structure, allowing one to feel that he or she is doing what is proper and in harmony with their tradition, community, and ultimately God's will. It is very important for a religious person to know that he or she is acting with integrity in accordance with the will of God. Indeed, in order for an individual to be able to preserve his or her integrity while interacting with others, it is crucial that medical professionals do not impose their own values on them.

Furthermore, Judaism teaches that there are obligations that we must live by and that there is divine reward and punishment for our actions. Although Judaism does not have one central Rabbinic authority and we do not coerce observance of Jewish Law, the eleventh principle of Maimonides's famous thirteen fundamental principles of faith is that God "grants good to those who observe God's commands and causes those who transgress God's commands to be punished."[27] The traditional belief is that this reward and punishment does not usually take place during one's lifetime, but rather in the World to Come.[28] While this might not be the primary reason a Jew observes the commandments of the Torah,[29] it is an important factor in the observance of Jewish Law.[30]

Goal and Scope of This Work: Principles and Questions

As has been explained in this introduction, the active participation of rabbis, along with medical professionals, is essential in medical decision-making for observant Jews. To produce a book that would undermine the need for Rabbinic involvement would thus be counterproductive – and, indeed, impossible. Rabbinic rulings involve various complex nuances and often vary from case to case based on numerous personal circumstances in each situation. Codification of such issues thus rarely succeeds. Furthermore, many of the topics discussed in this volume are highly sensitive and involve some of the most serious prohibitions and requirements in the Torah.

The purpose of this book is thus to increase Rabbinic involvement and to make it more efficient. To that end, this book will not provide exhaustive treatment of topics, nor final conclusions on the various issues. My goal is to provide an introduction to the *general principles* relevant to each issue and the *essential questions* that must be asked by laypeople in order to productively move towards a resolution to each situation. It is also my hope that the information in this book will assist medical professionals in being understanding and accommodating of religious needs and sensitivities.

Methodology

The goal of this work is to be as useful to as many types of individuals as possible. The body of the work is therefore written in a concise and basic manner. It is intended to be useful to patients and clinicians, those familiar with Rabbinic literature and those unfamiliar with it. In addition, I have cited each point with in-depth end notes for those interested in the scholarly aspects of the discussions, primarily focusing on the Rabbinic literature and debates, but often also on the relevant discussions in secular bioethical thought. I have also included appendix chapters to some of the sections with less practical, but nevertheless often relevant, deeper discussions and analyses related to the topics referenced within that section.

There are many wonderful books on Jewish medical ethics, most of which are cited in the end notes of this book. As a hospital chaplain, my focus is on the real-life scenarios that I face along with patients and their families. The focus of this work is thus more on concrete guidance than on philosophical or conceptual analysis. This is not intended to be an exhaustive academic scholarly study, but rather a practical, real-world guidebook dealing with the most frequent and challenging health-related dilemmas that arise. Indeed, the topics were chosen specifically based on what I have encountered in my work as a chaplain and regarding which I have practical advice to offer. Other topics, although interesting and useful, were not included, as I have not personally encountered them in real-life situations. I believe that the topics dealt with in this book cover virtually all of the most common challenges that arise in contemporary healthcare.

I must point out that while I have shared many true anecdotes in this book in order to help illustrate some of the real life applications of the principles discussed therein, I have altered any details that could possibly reveal the actual identity of the people involved.

In addition to my work as a chaplain, I am an ordained rabbi with great interest in Rabbinic literature. I frequently consult with Rabbinic experts much greater than myself, and pursue further study on medically relevant fields whenever possible. For example, I have completed Yeshiva University's Continuing Rabbinic Education course, "Confronting End-of-Life Issues: The Rabbi's Role," as well as Agudath Israel's Chayim Aruchim Rabbinic training seminars, and I participated in a Jewish Medical Ethics summer internship at Shaare Zedek Medical

Center in Jerusalem. I also have advanced graduate level training in clinical bioethics, with a master's degree in Bioethics and Health Policy from Loyola University (Chicago), where I am currently pursuing a doctorate in Clinical Bioethics. Since I work in a clinical setting, this book attempts to address the most accurate and up-to-date medical realities, as well as the most recent Rabbinic rulings on each topic.

I serve as a chaplain and a rabbi for all Jews, and indeed all people, regardless of denomination, background or belief system, and I try to write that way as well. Nevertheless, it is important to recognize my own perspective. I am an Orthodox rabbi, and while I try to draw upon a very wide variety of sources and opinions in this work, the primary authority I have chosen to follow in Jewish Law in this book is the great Rabbi Shlomo Zalman Auerbach (1910–1995) of Jerusalem, particularly as his opinions were explained to me by Profs. Abraham S. Abraham and Avraham Steinberg, both in their numerous writings and our extensive personal meetings and correspondence. I follow the rulings of R. Auerbach because they have achieved very broad acceptance amongst contemporary Rabbinic leaders, particularly his guidance relating to medical decision-making, and I find them to be quite compelling, well-grounded, and compassionate. For similar reasons, in addition to R. Auerbach, in particular when he did not issue a ruling on a given topic, I have attempted to follow the published rulings of Rabbi Moshe Feinstein (1895–1986), one of the greatest rabbinic decisors in American history. For guidance from a living authority and for more contemporary issues, I rely on the writings of and my frequent correspondence with Rabbi Asher Weiss, the *posek* (Jewish legal authority) for Shaare Zedek Medical Center in Jerusalem.

I never intended to become a chaplain or work in a hospital. However, once I got a taste of it, I fell in love with the profundity and intensity of my encounters, as well as the opportunity to play a meaningful role in people's lives during difficult times. It is my hope and prayer that this book will serve as another method through which I can provide support and guidance to patients and their support systems in their times of need. I also hope that this book can provide insight to professionals who are struggling to find clear and practical guidance for their patients, as I did when I first became a chaplain. I pray for the day when the topics discussed in this book will be only theoretical, and "there will be no more death forever, and the Lord God will wipe away tears from all faces" (Isaiah 25:8).

ENDNOTES

1. For example, in *Iggerot Moshe*, CM 2:74, R. Feinstein addresses the question of whether there is an obligation to prolong the life of a suffering patient who cannot be cured. In his answer, R. Moshe implies that there is no obvious or clear-cut answer in Rabbinic literature when he writes, *"Efshar ke-demistaber lechorah. . . ."* ("It seems on its face logical that perhaps. . . .") In the next responsum (75:3), he writes that since he is unaware of any classical precedent from within Rabbinic literature to answer this question, he must rely on logic. See also *Minchat Shlomo* 3:103(3), also quoted in *Nishmat Avraham*, EH 1:1 (p. 2 in 3rd ed.), for a similar statement of R. Shlomo Zalman Auerbach. See also fn. 17 below. This introduction will seek to demonstrate why these great Rabbinic scholars' answers are nevertheless binding (see fn. 18 for more examples).

2. The Midrash relates that R. Akiva once instructed an ill individual how to be healed. The person responded, "You are interfering in a matter that is not your concern! God afflicted me and you wish to heal?" R. Akiva asked the man his profession, and he responded that he was a tiller of the soil. R. Akiva then rhetorically asked how he could interfere with God's vineyard, and then explained, "Just as the tree, if not weeded, fertilized, and plowed, will not grow and bring forth its fruits . . . so it is with the human body. The fertilizer is the medicine and the healing the means, and the tiller of the earth is the physician."

Many similar stories are told of R. Akiva. See, for example, *Bava Batra* 10a, where R. Akiva is challenged by a Roman general that if God decrees that someone should be poor, to support them should constitute an act of rebellion against God's decree. R. Akiva responds that in our view, the opposite is true. Even when a king decrees suffering on his child, he does not desire it, and in fact appreciates it if someone helps his child despite the apparent decree. In the same way, we are all God's children and obligated to help each other despite God's decree. See also *Midrash Tanchuma* (*Tazria* 5), where another Roman general challenges R. Akiva that since God's deeds are greater than those of humans, we should leave the world as it is, and therefore leave boys uncircumcised. R. Akiva responds that God put humans in the world to complete creation. God created wheat and our job is to make it into bread. This is why we must cut the umbilical cord when a baby is born and circumcise baby boys.

Furthermore, the biblical command to conquer the earth (Gen. 1:26) is understood in the Jewish tradition as permitting people to modify – conquer, dominate, and control – nature to make it more amenable to humans. See R. Michael Broyde, "Pre-Implantation Genetic Diagnosis, Stem Cells, and Jewish Law," *Tradition* 38(1) (2004), 54. Similarly, R. Immanuel Jakobovits once wrote, "In the Jewish tradition, ['playing God'] is expressly sanctioned in the biblical words, 'And he [an attacker] shall surely cause him [his victim] to be healed.' The Talmud states: 'From here we see that the physician is given permission to heal'" ("Will Cloning Be a Disaster?" *The Wall Street Journal*, May 2, 1997). See also R. Judah Loew (Maharal) of Prague, *Be'er Ha-Golah* 38–39, and R. Eliyahu Dessler,

Mikhtav Mei-Eliyahu, vol. 1, 270–1, who emphasize that when developing technology, it is our responsibility not only to innovate, but also to make sure that there are safeguards that ensure that the technology will not be used improperly and that advances will be implemented productively. Similarly, the Midrash relates that Adam was told not only to master, but also to protect and not destroy the world (*Midrash Kohelet* 7:28). For more on the topic of natural law and Judaism, see R. J.D. Bleich, "Cloning: Homologous Reproduction and Jewish Law," in *Bioethical Dilemmas II* (Targum Press, 2006), 7–15. See also http://98.131.138.124/articles/tora/subject2.asp.

3. Benjamin Freedman, *Duty and Healing: Foundations of a Jewish Bioethic* (Routledge, 1999), 287–8.

4. See Rashi, Deut. 30:14: "The Torah was given to you in writing and accompanied by an oral explanation." See the Rambam's introduction to the *Mishnah Torah* for further elaboration.

5. *Avot* 1:1.

6. Rambam, *Hilkhot De'ot* 6:2, and introduction to *Mishnah Torah*; Ritva, *Gittin* 60b.

7. Maharal, *Tiferet Yisrael* 69.

8. *Sefer Ha-Ikarim* 3:23.

9. See R. Akiva Tatz, *Dangerous Disease and Dangerous Therapy in Jewish Medical Ethics: Principles and Practice* (Targum Press, 2013), 301–2.

10. *Chiddushei Ha-Ritva, Eruvin* 13b; *Derashot Ha-Ran* 7; Introduction to *Iggerot Moshe* 1.

11. When the Torah commands us to appoint Rabbinic leaders (Deut. 1:13), it says we must provide "men who are wise and understanding and well known to your tribes." Commenting on the word "understanding" (*nevonim*), Rashi explains

that they can logically derive one thing from another. See, for example, *Teshuvot Avraham Ben Ha-Rambam* 97 and *Nitei Gavriel, Hilkhot Yichud*, pp. 23–26, for a discussion and application of this concept to Jewish legal decision-making. See also the introduction to *Iggerot Moshe*, where R. Moshe Feinstein notes that the role of a decisor of Jewish Law is to study in depth and apply this process of comparing one area to another.

Cf. *Shulchan Arukh*, YD 242:9, who writes that comparing one case to another can be dangerous. There are particular areas of Halakhah (such as Rabbinic enactments) regarding which we are warned, "*Ein midamin milta le-milta*," "Do not compare one thing to another." In general, however, this is what the greatest Rabbinic sages have always done in order to arrive at rulings in Jewish Law regarding complex cases, especially when attempting to find precedent for issues involving new technology.

12. *Avot* 5:26.

13. Chazon Ish, *Likutim, Nezikin* 16: "But the words of the *Shakh* are difficult to match [with what we know to be true], as there is no difference between a law that is explicated and a law that is not explicated. Indeed, there is no such thing as a law that is not explicated, as everything is explicated in the Torah."

14. Tosafot, *Ketuvot* 4b, s.v. *ad she-yistom*, states, "The style of the Talmud is often to deal with unlikely cases so that we can expound [the Torah] and be rewarded."

15. *Chullin* 70a.

16. Another example may be the Talmudic passage regarding the creation of a Golem (*Sanhedrin* 65b), which has been used in the discussion of cloning. While this Talmudic story seemed fanciful for many generations, perhaps the entire reason that this passage is included in the Talmud was to provide precedents and insights many

generations later. For further discussion on this topic, see R. Hershel Schachter, http://www.yutorah.org/lectures/lecture .cfm/809040/Rabbi_Hershel_Schachter /Q_&_A.

17. See, for example *Nishmat Avraham*, EH 1 (37 in 3rd ed.), where R. Shlomo Zalman Auerbach is quoted as arguing that there is no clear proof in the entire Rabbinic corpus to be able to issue a ruling as to who is considered the mother when a surrogate mother is utilized. See *Nishmat Avraham* (English ed., vol. 3), 15, where Prof. Abraham writes the following regarding in vitro fertilization (IVF): "Rav Auerbach *zt"l* refused to give a ruling on the subject. He told me that since the basis of IVF was not discussed in the Torah, Talmud, or *Rishonim*, he would not discuss it." R. Auerbach begins his responsum about triage in Jewish Law (*Minchat Shlomo, Tinyana* 2–3:86) by stating, "I do not want to establish fixed rules with this, because these are very serious questions and I am unaware of clear proofs on the matter." R. Asher Weiss has also written that there is no clear proof in Rabbinic literature for determining who is the mother in cases of egg donation/ surrogacy, and the matter must therefore be determined based only on logic. We need greats the likes of the Ramban or the Rashba in order to do this, and we unfortunately do not have them. "Until then," he writes, "we must remain in doubt" (published in *Ratz KaTzvi* on EH, 95). Similarly, R. Aaron Rakeffet-Rothkoff, *The Rav: The World of Rabbi Joseph B. Soloveitchik* (Ktav Publishing, 1999), 60, quotes R. Joseph B. Soloveitchik in 1955: "I do not know how to be *posek* [how to decide] in this area. When it is a problem of AIH [artificial insemination from the husband], I can be lenient in my ruling. However, when it is AID [artificial insemination from a donor], I do not know how to decide the Halakhah on a practical level." See also Dr. John D. Loike and R.

Dr. Moshe Tendler, "Creating Human Embryos Using Reproductive Cloning Techniques," *Journal of Halacha and Contemporary Society* 67 (Spring 2014), 48, who conclude that there is no clear answer in Torah literature as to who is the parent when it comes to cloning. See also L.E. Newman, "Woodchoppers and Respirators: The Problem of Interpretation in Contemporary Jewish Ethics," *Modern Judaism* 10(2) (Feb. 1990), 17–42, as well as fn. 1 above.

18. This debate is generally conceptualized as a dispute between the Chazon Ish (cited in fn. 13 above), who believed that there is precedent within the Rabbinic corpus for any case that may arise, and the *Shakh* (CM 73:39), who assumes that there are sometimes situations that are not explicit in the halakhic system: "*Ein ha-din mefurash etzlaynu.*"

This dispute plays out in the realm of contemporary medical ethics in a debate between R. J.D. Bleich and R. Ezra Bick regarding determining the maternal identity of a donated ovum (initially published in the journal *Tradition* and republished in *Jewish Law and the New Reproductive Technologies* [Ktav Publishing, 1997], 46–114). Although classical Rabbinic sources could not have imagined such technology, R. Bleich (as well as the long list of contemporary Rabbinic scholars cited in his article) marshals various possibly relevant sources to build a case for his ruling (assuming the approach of the Chazon Ish). R. Bick argues, however, that the conceptual approach of analogy with existing halakhic rulings will not work in this case, because no halakhic sources exist that can serve as adequate precedent to allow us to draw conclusions in this situation (assuming the approach of the *Shakh*). R. Bick therefore attempts to analyze the Torah's general approach to the concept of parenthood, analyzing Talmudic assumptions and its worldview to tease out the sages' conceptual framework concerning conception in order to develop principles for determining maternity. R. Bleich retorts that when there are indeed questions for which conventional halakhic methodology provides no solutions, the answer is not to engage in desperate attempts to find one or construct conceptual models, but rather to confess ignorance and apply the Torah's various laws governing situations of doubt. For a summary of this topic, see R. Aryeh Klapper, "Stem Cell Research" (6/3/09), http://www.torahleadership.org /categories/stemcells.mp3. See also Alan Jotkowitz, "Nomos and Narrative in Jewish Law," *Modern Judaism* 33(1) (2013), 56–74 (esp. 69–71).

19. The Malbim (Prov. 24:3) explains that *"tevunah"* is the ability of great sages to understand one thing from another, *"meivin davar mitokh davar,"* once they have already amassed a great deal of Torah knowledge and wisdom. R. Ahron Soloveichik explained that this is a sense of Torah intuition that great Rabbinic scholars can develop after many years of study: http://www.yutorah.org /lectures/lecture.cfm/837727/Rabbi_Cha yim_Soloveichik/Torah_Ethics_in_a_Per ceived_Moral_World#. See also, for example, Haym Soloveitchik, "A Response to Rabbi Ephraim Buckwold's Critique of 'Rabad of Posquieres: A Programmatic Essay,'" *The Torah u-Madda Journal* 14 (2006/7), 193–214, where he points out the importance of intuition in *psak*, citing the Chatam Sofer, who maintained that the halakhic intuition of a *posek* in answering a question is more important than his actual arguments (see Shlomo Sofer, *Ha-Chut Ha-Meshulash*, 97–99).

20. Joseph B. Soloveitchik, *Community, Covenant, and Commitment: Selected Letters and Communications of Rabbi Joseph B. Soloveitchik*, ed. Nathaniel Helfgot (Ktav, 2005), 104.

21. Ibid., 147–8. See also *Teshuvot Ri Migash* 114, who writes that a decisor of Jewish law must be God-fearing, and the introduction to *Iggerot Moshe*, where R. Feinstein explains that in order to render a judgment in Jewish Law, one must study a topic in depth with seriousness and fear of God. See also R. J.D. Bleich, *Where Halakha and Philosophy Meet* (Brill, 2015), 27.

22. See, for example, the Rambam's introduction to the *Mishnah Torah*, where he writes that the Talmud *Bavli* (Babylonian Talmud) has become authoritative over the Talmud *Yerushalmi* (Jerusalem Talmud) because the *Bavli* was accepted by the Jewish People, and that grants it binding authority. R. Moshe Feinstein (introduction to *Iggerot Moshe* 1) also implies that Rabbinic authority is created through communal acceptance when he argues that a rabbi who is approached by questioners develops an obligation to respond to them. R. Moshe goes on to write that when there is a debate in Jewish Law about which it is difficult to find a conclusive ruling, we should always follow the majority. See also Ramban on Deut. 1:13.

23. *Pirkei Avot* 6:6; *Berachot* 7b. Indeed, the Talmud in *Yevamot* 109b (codified by the *Shulchan Arukh*, YD 242:9) criticizes a judge of Jewish Law who only uses his powers of logic to compare one case to another in order to arrive at a decision, instead of conferring with his teacher. The Talmud there concludes that one who rules in matters of Jewish Law should have tremendous fear of Divine retribution if they rule incorrectly, and must thus confer with those greater than them in order to ensure a correct ruling.

24. R. Howard Jachter, "Embryonic Stem Cell Research," http://www.koltorah.org /ravj/Embryonic%20Stem%20Cell%20 Research.htm.

25. For further discussion, see Dr. Alan Jotkowitz, "On the Methodology of

Jewish Medical Ethics," *Tradition* 43(1) (2010), 53.

26. One major principle of Jewish medical ethics is that we do not own our bodies. The Torah teaches that our bodies and our lives do not belong to us, but to God. See *Shulchan Arukh Ha-Rav*, CM, *Hilkhot Nizkei Guf Ve-Nefesh* 4: "One may not strike another, even if given permission to do so, because a person has no ownership whatsoever over his body, to strike it." See also Rambam, *Hilkhot Rotze'ach U-Shemirat Ha-Nefesh* 1:4. Radbaz (*Sanhedrin* 18:6) writes, "A person's soul [life] is not his possession, but rather the possession of the Holy One, Blessed be He, as it is written, 'And all the souls are Mine.'" *Shulchan Arukh*, CM 427:10, and *Be'er Ha-Golah* 90 explain that God put each individual in the world for a reason, and one who does not take his life seriously shows disregard for God's will and commandments. See also *Magen Avraham*, OC 328:6, and R. Yaakov Emden, *Mor U-Ketzia*, OC 328, for a classic example of a case in which a person must be compelled to undergo a medical procedure even if he or she does not want to. For a range of sources and discussion on personal autonomy in Jewish Law, see Yechiel Bar-Ilan, *Jewish Bioethics* (Cambridge University Press, 2013), 104 and 144 and *Nishmat Avraham*, CM 427:10(4), 251–2 in 3rd ed. For an interesting example of how this plays out in Israeli bioethics, see S. Glick, "Unlimited Human Autonomy – A Cultural Bias?," *New England Journal of Medicine* 336(13) (Mar. 1997), 954–6.

In secular bioethics literature, a distinction is sometimes made between "autonomy ethics" and "virtue ethics." Autonomy ethics is based on respect for the importance of individual self-governance, such that people should be able to act freely in accordance with a self-determined plan, and is not focused on distinguishing right from wrong. In contrast, virtue ethics does not prioritize patient autonomy, but instead is built on a fundamental moral code that governs human behavior and differentiates right from wrong. Some have argued that the emphasis on autonomy in contemporary medicine is an attempt to assert self-sufficiency and avoid the anxiety of losing control, based on the illusion of human self-determination and control over life and death. This approach reduces the sense of helplessness, uncertainty, and vulnerability that people face when making end-of-life decisions. See Megan-Jane Johnstone, "Bioethics, Cultural Differences, and the Problem of Moral Disagreements in End-Of-Life Care: A Terror Management Theory," *Journal of Medicine and Philosophy* 37 (2012), 190.

27. Even R. Yosef Albo, who narrows down the fundamentals of Jewish belief to just three roots instead of thirteen, includes the belief in Divine justice as one of these three core fundamentals of Jewish belief (*Sefer Ha-Ikkarim* 4:29). While this principle is found throughout the Torah, it is stated most explicitly in Exod. 20:5–6.

28. The *mishnah* teaches, "If you have studied much Torah, they will give you great reward, and your Employer can be relied upon to pay you the wage for your labor, but be aware that the reward of the righteous will be given in the World to Come" (*Avot* 2:16). This principle is discussed throughout the Talmud; see, for example, *Kiddushin* 39b and *Sanhedrin* 108a. As for why this system is not explicitly stated in Torah, see R. Sa'adia Gaon, *Emunot Ve-De'ot* 9, and *Chovot Ha-Levavot* 4:4, as well as Ibn Ezra, Deut. 32:39, and Abarbanel, Lev. 26. Nevertheless, the rabbis frequently found sources for this idea in the Torah. For example, the Torah states, "Your blood which belongs to your souls I will demand" (Gen. 9:5). How can someone who is already dead be punished? The Midrash claims that this verse refers to one who has committed suicide, and will thus be denied entry into the

World to Come (*Bereishit Rabbah* 34:5 and elsewhere; see citations and extended discussion in *Yalkut Yosef, Bikkur Cholim Ve-Aveilut*, 56, n. 1).

29. *Pirkei Avot* 1:3 teaches, "Do not be as slaves, who serve their master for the sake of reward. Rather, be as slaves who serve their master not for the sake of reward. And the fear of Heaven should be upon you."

30. See *Mesillat Yesharim*, chap. 1.

ACKNOWLEDGEMENTS

There are three people who have most profoundly influenced my thinking in the realm of Jewish Law and medicine, all of whom read the first draft of this manuscript and offered incredibly valuable feedback. Rav Nachum Sauer is the brilliant local *posek* whom I most frequently consult regarding very challenging questions. Dr. Irving Lebovics, Chairman of Agudas Yisroel of California and former Chairman of the Cedars-Sinai bioethics committee, has taken time to share his deep wisdom with me, to study with me, and to allow me to follow him in family meetings when I was new to the Intensive Care Units. Stuart Finder, Ph.D., the director of the Cedars-Sinai Center for Healthcare Ethics, has an incredibly sharp mind and is at the same time a deeply caring practitioner. He dedicated a remarkable amount of his time to guiding me through complicated situations and providing very thorough feedback on my work in the hospital, and on my writing.

I hasten to add that these three scholars and mentors of mine only read the first draft of this work. Some material has been added and changed since they reviewed it, and any mistakes should be assumed to be mine alone. *Ve-im shagiti, Hashem ha-tov yichaper be'adi* – If I have erred, may the merciful Lord forgive me.

This work benefited tremendously from the wonderfully insightful and thorough editors who offered excellent feedback on early drafts: Michal Alatin, Chaplain Miriam Berkowitz, R. Michael Broyde, Keenan Davis, Paula Van Gelder, Tzvi Mauer, Meira Mintz, and Batsheva Pomerantz. I would also like to thank R. Dr. Eddie Reichman for his kind friendship, guidance, and gracious sharing of his wealth of articles and resources related to Jewish medical ethics.

I would like to acknowledge the publications that have permitted me to republish articles of mine that were originally published in their journals. Each has been significantly modified and updated for this book since they were first published, but the opportunity to prepare them for publication and receive feedback has helped each chapter immensely: The *RJJ Journal of Halacha and Contemporary Society*, in which the chapter on burial in a mausoleum and the chapter on deactivating an artificial heart were first published; Yeshiva University's *Verapo Yerape*, in which the chapters on prayer and some of the chapter on end-of-life decisions were first published; the Torah Musings blog, where my thoughts on assisted suicide were first published; In the Light Urns blog, where my thoughts on cremation were first published; Kodesh Press, which published my first book, *Guide to Observance of Jewish Law in a Hospital*, and allowed me to republish updated versions of the chapters on "Death and Post-Mortem Care" and "Labor and Delivery"; *Ami Magazine*, in which the concluding chapter "Reflections of a Frum Hospital Chaplain" was first published; *Hakira*, in which the chapter on guidance upon the loss of a baby or fetus was published; *B'Or HaTorah*, in which the chapter on mental health issues in Jewish law was first published; Koren-Maggid Press's *Halakhic Realities – Collected Essays on Organ Donation*, where my introductory chapter on understanding terminology was published.

I am grateful to the entire staff of the Spiritual Care Department at Cedars-Sinai Medical Center. It is an honor to lead such a wonderful department and to have the opportunity to work alongside such dedicated, compassionate, and sophisticated practitioners, who re-inspire me every day (and occasionally cover for me so I can get some learning and writing done!).

From the depths of my heart, the most profound debt of gratitude and appreciation is owed to my loving wife, Lauren, who has been the rock of our family, my support, guide, and love, and without whom I could accomplish nothing.

CHAPTER 1

Facilitating Shared Decision-Making

A. UNDERSTANDING TERMINOLOGY: Key Concepts to Facilitate Collaborative Decision-Making

I once participated in a family meeting in the hospital during which a doctor tried to explain to the son of a dying patient that his mother was actively dying. The doctor concluded, "I'm afraid that we will have to withhold further aggressive interventions." "Absolutely not!" the imposing son responded. "My rabbi is out of town, but he left clear instructions for me to make sure they do everything possible to keep her alive at all costs." The doctor politely explained that given the mother's frailty and the aggressiveness of her cancer, resuscitation would only cause her to suffer more, and would be medically and ethically inappropriate. The son of the patient then stood up, got in the doctor's face, and declared, "You will resuscitate my mother or I will grab your hands and force you to!" Everyone in the room froze in shock and the tension mounted. The doctor then stood up and quickly walked out of the room, and as the door closed, he responded to the son, "Too bad you won't be able to be by your mother's side as she dies. I'm calling security. . . ."

In contrast, the father of a dying child I was supporting, once asked his rabbi for guidance in medical decision-making. The medical staff – who never spoke directly to the rabbi – was surprised by the rabbi's very aggressive requirements, but they were willing to abide. The father, however, couldn't bear to witness the invasiveness of the procedures that this would require. Instead, he threw his hands up and told us, "You do whatever you think is right. Don't ask my opinion, because I can't tell you to go against my rabbi, but I also can't tell you to follow his guidelines!" The overwhelmed father then left the hospital and couldn't bring himself to return, never seeing his young child again.

This sort of unfortunate dynamic and breakdown of communication is not uncommon in contemporary healthcare settings. Can it be avoided? Some of the concepts in this chapter may help to mitigate these challenges and help facilitate improved clinical collaboration.

INTRODUCTION

When seeking clarity on issues related to medical ethics, effective communication is essential; little progress can be made if the religious and medical communities are unable to communicate. In order for communication to be productive, our precise choice of words is critical. The Book of Proverbs teaches that "death and life are in the power of the tongue,"[1] and this is often literally true in discussions about patients at the end of life.

This chapter will highlight some key principles and distinctions in terminology, roles, and concepts that can be of great consequence for both spiritual caregivers (i.e., clergy and chaplains) and healthcare providers (i.e., physicians, nurses, and other medically trained clinicians). By improving their ability to communicate, members of both groups will be better able to articulate their positions, know their roles, and better understand each other's perspectives. Only then can they work together to face the challenging questions that arise in matters of healthcare and at or near the end of life.

1.   *Value vs. Sanctity, and Infinite vs. Relative Value*

While there is much discussion in our society about the *value* of life, Judaism focuses on the *sanctity* of human life. As opposed to "value," "sanctity" generally implies a basic duty to preserve life, however frail, and derives from theological perspectives that imply a profound respect for all human life.[2]

However, this sanctity is not necessarily unlimited. It is also possible to distinguish between viewing human life as possessing *infinite* value or as being of *relative* value.[3] Some Rabbinic sources regard all of life as possessing infinite, unlimited value. According to this school of thought, everything possible must be done to prolong every moment of life, no matter how much pain is involved. Since life is the ultimate value, these authorities argue, it must be prolonged at all costs.[4] In contrast, most contemporary Rabbinic authorities conceptualize life as being sacred, but of value relative to other values, such as adherence to certain *mitzvot*, and thus not of "infinite" value.[5] For this reason, many authorities limit the extent to which one is obligated to prolong life of a dying patient in the face of tremendous pain or suffering.[6]

2.   *Pain vs. Suffering*

In a hospital setting, many assumptions are frequently made about a patient's condition and the amount of pain and suffering he or she is enduring. However, as noted by R. Joseph B. Soloveitchik, not all pain is the same.[7] We can distinguish between physical pain, which he terms "pain," and emotional pain, which he calls "suffering." Although the two are often coupled together, there can be a fundamental experiential difference between them. R. Soloveitchik describes pain as a basic physiological sensation, whereas he describes suffering as psychological, emotional, spiritual, and existential.

To illustrate this point, R. Soloveitchik presents the contrast between a woman in labor and a person diagnosed with a terminal malady. A woman in labor may experience excruciating pain, but she rarely feels sorrow. She does not experience her pain as suffering because it is a meaningful prelude to a joyous event. On the other hand, a person who discovers that he or she is afflicted with a fatal illness, "even though he is free from pain, is a man of suffering, and his distress is overwhelming."

Because everyone interprets his or her pain and suffering subjectively, choosing the right intervention requires caution, sensitivity, and understanding. For instance, some patients have a higher pain threshold than others, but even this can vary from one situation to another. Every patient is unique and should be treated as such. Even if someone feels great pain, Dr. Eric Cassel has noted, "assigning meaning to the injurious condition often reduces or even resolves the suffering associated with it."[8] This meaning, Cassel argues, is most powerfully experienced via transcendence, which gives pain a meaning beyond the person. Cassel argues that lack of attention to the whole person – mind, body, and spirit – may theoretically lead to medical treatment that addresses pain management but actually increases suffering. Thus, for any given person there can be pain without suffering, pain with suffering, and suffering without pain. The challenge for all healthcare providers, both medical and spiritual, is to identify what *this* patient is experiencing at *this moment* and how to appropriately address it from every available angle.

Pain is usually addressed medically; suffering can be addressed through spiritual care. Positive religious and spiritual meaning-seeking behaviors can provide a patient with an unlimited Divine source of strength and a greater intensity of positive attitudes.[9] Indeed, numerous studies have concluded that as a result of "meaning making," a sense of purpose, hope, and openness to what lies beyond the ordinary, people who are "more religiously and spiritually open to seeking a connection to meaningful spiritual practice and/or the transcendent are more able to tolerate pain."[10] Thus, even spiritual care focused on relief of suffering can have positive effects on the physiological pain typically addressed through medical channels.[11]

Even the best spiritual care does not always alleviate all suffering. There are, of course, times when pain is accompanied by tremendous suffering, particularly at the end of life. While one may attempt to ameliorate suffering by helping to inculcate meaningfulness into patients' lives, Rabbinic authorities also advocate providing medical pain relief and palliative care when appropriate (see Chapters 4B and 2D). Traditional Jewish sources tend not to advocate enduring unnecessary pain.[12] Nevertheless, a number of sources highlight the fact that there are situations in which life can be worth living despite physical pain.[13] It is thus crucial to be sensitive to context and an individual's personal constitution.

There are times when those who recognize a spiritual dimension to life can find significant value to every stage of it, even for a patient who is in a coma or persistent vegetative state.[14] This may certainly be true for those who are able to continue performing *mitzvot* (Divine commandments), even at the most basic level.[15] If pain is infused with meaning that makes it worthwhile, it is not an experience of meaningless suffering.[16]

For this reason, there may be patients who are experiencing great pain, but who, due to embracing this worldview, do not see their lives as meaningless. Such patients may not be experiencing the same sort of suffering as other patients in their situation with a different worldview.[17]

This may be difficult for some medical practitioners to understand.[18] When chaplains or rabbis find themselves helping to advocate for treatment of patients who may be experiencing a great deal of pain, it is most effective if their arguments are couched in language that clearly explains some of Judaism's teachings about the preciousness of life and the distinction between pain and suffering.[19]

3.   *Definition vs. Criterion*

One of the most common and potentially painful miscommunications between spiritual care providers and healthcare providers occurs all too often during end-of-life treatment. It is often assumed that it is the physician's responsibility to define what it means to be dead and to determine whether the patient's state fits that biological or medical definition. However, death is more than simply a medical or scientific issue; death is a process, and the point at which a human being no longer retains the status of a living entity is the subject of complex religious, philosophical, and moral discussions.

Modern medicine has articulated its own definitions of death, and a barrage of medical tests has been designed to help determine when the patient's state matches the defined status. However, this definition itself simply represents a choice of a particular point in the dying process that the medical tests can isolate and test for. There is no purely "scientific" reason to have chosen that point in the process. Even the medical establishment must rely on meta-scientific considerations, whether ethical, social, philosophical, or some combination thereof, to justify their position.[20]

This is a very important point. The medical tests are valid, but only in order to determine whether certain criteria for meeting their predetermined definition have been met.

The distinction between articulating a definition, and testing for whether certain criteria have been met was articulated in 1981 in the *Annals of Internal Medicine*. Coincidentally – or perhaps not so coincidentally – this was the same year that a presidential commission issued the landmark report that became the basis for the Uniform Determination of Death Act (UDDA), using "brain death" as a legal definition of death. The authors of this oft-cited article made the case that:

> A proper understanding of the ordinary meaning of the word or concept of death must be developed before a medical criterion of death is chosen. We must decide what is commonly meant by death before physicians can decide how to measure it. . . . Providing the definition is primarily a philosophical task; the choice of the criterion is primarily medical; and the selection of the tests to prove that the criterion is satisfied is solely a medical matter.[21]

Based on this, one could argue that while implementing criteria and appropriate tests to determine death is best done by physicians based on contemporary science and technology, when it comes to religiously-oriented patients and their families, the process of determining death cannot end there. Rather, decisions about patients in such liminal states as brain death or PVS (Persistent Vegetative State) should be made in consultation with the patient's family and should be facilitated by the patient's spiritual care providers. Although the jargon and technology of a hospital can leave spiritual care providers feeling like confused outsiders, the realization that determining death is not purely a medico-scientific process can provide them with a sense of purpose and confidence in end-of-life discussions.

Unfortunately, healthcare professionals and spiritual leaders often talk right past each other, as if they were speaking different languages. This generally occurs without either side even realizing it, thus making effective communication extraordinarily difficult.[22]

4.   State vs. Status

Another important conceptual distinction is articulated by Dr. Naftali Moses, who observes that in the biomedical and legal view, death is understood as a "biological state," whereas Judaism views death as a "legal status."[23] In traditional Judaism, a person's status as it relates to various religious circumstances and obligations is not equivalent to biological fact. Jewish Law does not conceptualize death solely as a physical *state*, but also as a *status* that implies different obligations and repercussions than does being alive. Recognizing a patient's religious status requires seeing the world in a way that is different than the common medical or legal worldview. This status may be indicated by scientific tests, but for an observant Jew, it ultimately belongs to the specific parameters shaped by Judaism's legal reasoning and categories, produced by its own very specific rules and construction of reality. A patient may have a dismal medical prognosis and meet certain requirements to be defined by some of the medical establishment as dead, but in some religious worldviews, this patient may maintain the status of a completely living person. This distinction is often overlooked by medical healthcare professionals and not fully explained by spiritual care providers, resulting in miscommunication and misunderstanding.

R. Michael J. Broyde eloquently described this principle in the *New England Journal of Medicine* in defending New Jersey's "reasonable accommodation" statute for those who do not accept the neurological criteria of death:

> Reasonable people agree that human tissue loses its status as a person before there is complete cellular lysis, but cannot agree on whether "humanness" legally disappears when brain function ceases, cardiopulmonary function ceases, or some other criterion is met. The question is, at its core, not a medical question but a moral or religious one. To a religious person, death is the departure of the soul from the body. To a secular person, death is the point at which human rights no longer apply. Medicine cannot provide answers to either of these questions.[24]

5.   *Treatment vs. Care, Curing vs. Healing, and Hope vs. Expectation*

Once it has been decided that aggressive medical treatment will no longer continue and the focus of the medical attention for the patient turns toward symptom management and comfort measures only, it is important to emphasize that even when curative medical *treatment* has been withheld, patient *care* continues until the very end.[25] It is at this point, when some of the medical team begins to step back, that spiritual support becomes increasingly essential.

Thinking about this stage of care helps to crystallize the unique roles of medical healthcare providers on the one hand and spiritual care providers on the other. Although both work towards the improvement of the patient in all realms, the former group focuses on curing the patient's physical maladies, while the latter group works towards helping the patient experience spiritual and emotional healing. The significance of the distinction between curing and healing was stated most profoundly by R. Dr. Levi Meier: "Even when a cure is not possible, healing is always possible."[26]

At a certain point, the focus should shift from finding a specific *cure* for a patient's malady to helping the patient *heal*, whether this healing is emotional, spiritual, or relational. This healing involves finding a sense of wholeness despite (or because of) terminal illness, and it can involve repairing strained relationships (whether with family, friends, or God), thinking about one's legacy and writing an ethical will, or simply coming to terms with one's mortality. In this way, an incurable patient who is given appropriate care, space, and guidance can literally heal into death.

Although an interdisciplinary cooperative approach to taking care of patients is generally ideal, there is often a point at which the primary care for religiously oriented patients falls into the realm of those who specialize in spiritual care. At this point, it becomes the role of the chaplain or clergy to accompany patients through the end of their lives with dignity, compassion, and respect for their religious needs and values. The same sort of spiritual healing should be offered to the patient's family members as well. Members of this constituency are in need of no physical cure, but they nevertheless may be experiencing deep suffering as their loved ones pass into the next world.

Furthermore, it is clear that hope often gives patients and their families the courage to confront challenging circumstances and the ability to cope with them, and it can even alter neurochemistry, significantly aiding the healing process. Maintaining and fostering a sense of hope is essential for patients and their loved ones. However, it is crucial to gently ensure that this *hope* does not become false *expectation* or irrational optimism, which can result in unnecessary suffering and self-blame and leave people completely unprepared for adverse circumstances.

CONCLUSION –
AUTHORITY VS. AUTHORITARIAN

Providing end-of-life care for the whole person is a complex but indispensable task. We have explored the idea that many medical health-care professionals focus on pain reduction, seeking cures, and testing scientific criteria, while spiritual care providers can help ensure that suffering, healing, hope, and meaning are addressed in a way that make sense to the different value structures at work for a given patient or their surrogate.

Nevertheless, even when the process is optimal, decision-making about how to care for a particular patient at the end of life can be very complicated because there is rarely a clear right or wrong choice. While collaborative decision-making is always challenging, it becomes even more complex with the addition of universal human issues such as guilt, grief, ego, and trust, confusing new technologies and jargon, and social, legal, and financial pressures.

In order for progress to be made with compassion and integrity, internalizing the above distinctions and identifying each professional's specific role is crucial. Although healthcare professionals strive to incorporate patients' perspectives in the development of a plan of care, many patients and their surrogates describe feeling reluctant to speak openly. For example, participants in one study reported that "they did not feel respected or heard because their physician was often authoritarian, rather than authoritative."[27]

This situation presents an opportunity for spiritual care providers to share their own expertise, helping to explain and advocate for a patient's spiritual and religious values. Decisions influenced by religious faith or doctrines can sometimes be especially troubling for healthcare professionals.[28] However, sincere attention to a patient's religious beliefs, practices, culture, and spirituality shows respect for their autonomy and best interests, and it builds trust, enriching the physician-patient relationship.[29]

Unfortunately, patients' values are not always respected in this way, as demonstrated in one oft-cited study that recorded physicians' discussions about Do Not Resuscitate orders with patients. It found that physicians spent 75% of the time talking, missing opportunities to allow patients to discuss their own values and goals.[30]

Unfortunately, patients and their families do not always grasp what has been explained to them. Patients often need time to assimilate medical information and to work through complicated family dynamics. Sensitive professional spiritual care can help uncover, navigate, translate, and resolve many of these issues.

When the spiritual dimension in the care of patients is ignored, clinical settings risk becoming "biological garages," focusing only on fixing the shell and the machinery of the person, while diminishing their integrity, dignity, depth, and scope.[31] Once patients and/or their surrogates feel that the medical team has taken the time to understand them, has heard the input of clergy, and cares about their spiritual or religious values, they tend to be more willing to agree on medical goals and treatment decisions.[32]

At the same time, a spiritual care provider should not act in an authoritarian manner towards the staff or patient either. I have encountered a number of patients who, for various reasons, were unable to accept their clergy's stringent requirements, and as a result simply threw up their hands in confusion and despair. In order for spiritual care providers to be effective, it is essential for them to be familiar with the specifics of the situation that the patient is experiencing and in touch with his or her goals and values.

Furthermore, although clergy are sometimes wary of physicians, this mistrust can be to their own detriment. It is crucial to build trust and cooperation by recognizing and respecting the expertise of physicians. After all, they tend to have a tremendous amount of experience regarding the trajectory of various illnesses, in addition to guiding patients and their families through difficult decisions. As we attempt to work towards collaborative, patient-centered care, religiously oriented patients and spiritual care providers should seek to understand the deeply ingrained theories and practices central to the provision of medical care, as well as the medical value structures of a hospital, and how healthcare providers are attempting to navigate these intersecting values. We should respect the fact that religiously focused patients can often be very challenging to medical healthcare providers, who may have a difficult time accepting decisions that appear to be based solely on religious faith or doctrines that preclude any further discussion or negotiation.

By serving as an effective intermediary and advocate, those providing spiritual care can help uncover and translate the various issues for the patient and/or their surrogates, as well as for the medical team. When the entire team functions with this kind of collaboration, the patient can benefit from the *authoritative* input of various experts, without the imposition of *authoritarian* demands. In this way, all involved can work towards truly collaborative decision-making, a process that makes use of the medical, psychological, and spiritual expertise of the various team members in a way that profoundly respects the whole person.

ENDNOTES

1. Prov. 18:21.

2. On this concept, see Albert R. Jonsen, Mark Siegler, and William J. Winslade, *Clinical Ethics: A Practical Approach to Ethical Decisions in Clinical Medicine, Seventh Edition* (McGraw-Hill, 2010), chap. 3. In Jewish sources, many quote the fact that Jewish Law requires violating almost every commandment in order to save life, even if the likelihood of saving that life is very remote (*Shulchan Arukh*, OC 329:3), and even if the person being saved is mentally handicapped or will likely die within a short time (*Biur Halakhah* 329, s.v. *ela lefi*). See also R. Yechiel Michel Tucazinsky, *Gesher Ha-Chaim* 1:2 (2), n. 3, who makes the point that every moment of life has value, based on the Torah law that there is no difference between murdering a young and healthy individual and murdering an elderly *"gosses"* (dying person). See also Rambam, *Hilkhot Rotze'ach U-Shemirat Ha-Nefesh* 2:6–7. Some argue that this value stems from the fact that human beings are created in the image of God, which gives human life absolute value, independent of any external criterion; see R. Levi Meier, *Jewish Values in Health and Medicine* (University Press of America, 1991), 60.

3. The school of thought that posits "infinite value" to life and a more aggressive approach to end-of-life interventions often bases itself on the ruling in the Talmud (*Yoma* 85a, especially as codified by *Biur Halakhah* 329:4, s.v. *ela lefi sha'ah*) that obligates desecration of Shabbat to remove victims trapped in the rubble of a fallen building, even when they can only live for a short amount of time. On the other hand, the view that ascribes "relative value" to human life, and thus sometimes permits withholding interventions from a dying patient who is suffering, often bases itself on the Talmud's story of the passing of R. Yehudah Ha-Nasi (*Ketuvot* 104a, with the Ran's interpretation in *Nedarim* 40a, and *Arukh Ha-Shulchan*, YD 335:3). When R. Yehudah Ha-Nasi was dying, his students' prayers were preventing his passing. His maid noticed his great suffering and intentionally interrupted the students' prayers, thus causing his soul to depart (see discussion in *Refuah Ke-Halakhah*, 446–54).

R. Shilat (*Refuah, Halakhah, Ve-Kavanot Ha-Torah*, 48) presents this debate as follows: Perhaps the verses "You shall live by them" and "do not stand idly by" imply an absolute value to every moment of human life, independent of anything else, such that we are obligated to prolong life to the best of our ability no matter what. On the other hand, he suggests, perhaps these verses imply the need to protect life simply *in order to* enable us to serve God. If that is so, there might be times when the excruciating suffering of a dying patient not only does not permit them to serve God, but actually diminishes their ability to serve God, such that they are no longer obligated to guard such a life. As support for this second approach, R. Shilat (48, n. 40) quotes the verse (Deut. 4:9), "Guard yourself . . .," which concludes "lest you forget these things that I have taught you." One might argue that a dying person who is suffering to the extent that he or she is unable to think about anything else is no longer obligated in this commandment to guard his or her body. He argues that this applies both to the patient and those caring for the patient, since the commandment to not "stand idly by" is connected to the commandment to "love your neighbor as yourself" (based on a Rashi, *Sanhedrin* 84b). Therefore, in the case of a dying patient who is suffering and no longer wants to live, we are not obligated to prolong such a life and may even be forbidden from doing so (although it would be forbidden to actively shorten a life). "Do not stand idly by" does not apply to an act that does not actually help another person and may even cause him or her more suffering. Indeed, R. Z.N. Goldberg has written that in a situation in which death would be preferred to life because of a dying individual's suffering, there is no requirement to save such a life (*Assia* 5746, p. 72).

4. For example, R. J.D. Bleich writes (*Bioethical Dilemmas* [Ktav, 1998], 69), "Judaism regards human life as being of infinite and inestimable value. The quality of life that is preserved is thus never a factor to be taken into consideration. Neither is the length of the patient's life expectancy a controlling factor." See also J.D. Bleich, "The Infinite Value of Human Life in Judaism" in *The Value of Human Life* (Feldheim Publishers, 2010), 15–30. See also *Encyclopedia Hilkhatit Refu'it*, vol. 5, 131, for a summary of this position.

5. For example, there is an obligation to put one's life in danger by going to war, there are three transgressions that one may not violate even on pain of death, and one must kill a pursuer who is attempting to kill someone else.

6. See *Encyclopedia Hilkhatit Refu'it*, vol. 5, 132, for a summary of this position. Unlike R. Bleich, who conceptualizes life as being of "infinite value" and thus argues against ever taking "quality of life" into account, these authorities rule that quality of life may indeed be a factor in end-of-life decision-making, *but only as*

it relates to the patient's pain and not to other factors, such as age, finances, social circumstances, or any other aspects of life. Age would only be a factor if it is clinically relevant. See Tatz, *Dangerous Disease and Dangerous Therapy*, 24, 182.

Anyone who would ever permit forgoing any life-sustaining treatment, as many Rabbinic authorities do in certain situations, must recognize that making quality of life judgments is sometimes permissible. R. M.D. Tendler (*Responsa of Rav Moshe Feinstein: Care of the Critically Ill* [Ktav, 1996], 81–82) writes, "Quality of life decisions can only be made by the patient. A patient may decide to bear the pain rather than suffer the consequence of no treatment. . . . A physician is only obligated to heal when he has a medical treatment or modality to offer the patient. . . . Pain, unrelieved by medication, makes life unbearable. Under such conditions it may even be proper to withhold further therapeutic protocols that may prolong life but not cure the patient."

Indeed, some have argued that it is philosophically mistaken to claim that life has infinite value. They argue that since all people are mortal, life itself is finite. Furthermore, if life is in fact of infinite value, then one would perforce have to prioritize life over all other values, and even months of excruciating pain would not overrule the "infinite value" of even a few nanoseconds of life. If the value of life were indeed infinite, one could never forgo any treatment or ration any healthcare. It is possible to argue that while all life has equal, intrinsic value, the length of life is not what defines the value of life; valuing life and valuing life-extension are different. Therefore, some suggest that the value of life should not be referred to as "infinite," but rather as "beyond measure" (similar to other things that cannot be measured, such as love or justice). Accordingly, a better description of the value of life would be that it is "priceless." This implies that life is unlike most other values, which can be assigned a price, but that the value of life is not infinite. See D.P. Sulmasy, "Speaking of the Value of Life," *Kennedy Institute of Ethics Journal* 21(2) (2011), 188–93.

7. R. Joseph B. Soloveitchik, *Out of the Whirlwind: Essays on Mourning, Suffering and the Human Condition* (Toras HoRav Foundation/Ktav, 2003), 123. See also R. Jonathan Sacks, *The Koren Mesorat HaRav Siddur* (Koren Publishers, 2011), xxvi.

8. Eric J. Cassel, *The Nature of Suffering and the Goals of Medicine* (Oxford University Press, 1991), 45.

9. This is in contradistinction to "negative religious coping," such as feeling punished or abandoned by God, or using prayer as a means to relinquish control and responsibility for a person's health situation and how they seek solutions for their pain, which can negatively impact disability and suffering. See Jeffrey Ashby and Scott Lenhart, "Prayer as a Coping Strategy for Chronic Pain Patients," *Rehabilitation Psychology* 39(3) (1994), 205–9; George Fitchett, Bruce D. Rybarczyk, Gail A. De-Marco, and John J. Nicholas, "The Role of Religion in Medical Rehabilitation Outcomes," *Rehabilitation Psychology* 44(4) (Nov. 1999), 333–53; E.G. Bush, M.S. Rye, C.R. Brant, E. Emery, K.I. Pargament, and C.A. Riessinger, "Religious Coping with Chronic Pain," *Applied Psychophysiology Biofeedback* 24(4) (Dec. 1999), 249–60.

10. Carol Lysne and Amy Wachholtz, "Pain, Spirituality, and Meaning Making: What We Can Learn From the Literature," *Religions* 2 (2011), 1–16. Participation in religious activities, such as prayer services, has also been correlated with lower amounts and better tolerance of pain, as well as better relationships and psychological well-being and greater satisfaction with life. See H.G. Koenig, H.J. Cohen, L.K. George, J.C. Hays, D.B. Larson, and D.G. Blazer, "Attendance at Religious Services, Interleukin-6, and other Biological Parameters of Immune Function in Older Adults," *International Journal of Psychiatry in Medicine* 27(3) (1997), 233–50.

11. On this topic, see the work of Aaron Antonovsky, known as "Salutogenesis," which is a model of well-being focusing on the relationship between health, stress, and coping.

12. See, for example, *Sanhedrin* 43a, which states that even a person condemned to capital punishment is given an intoxicating drink to mitigate his pain and mental anguish and not prolong his agony. See also *Iggerot Moshe*, YD 2:174 (3), who writes that we may not keep someone alive simply in order to harvest his or her organs for transplantation, because "we must not artificially prolong a life of suffering."

13. See, for example, *Mesillat Yesharim*, chap. 19: ". . . in the same way that a doctor's cutting of flesh or of a limb to prevent infection from spreading to the rest of the body and killing the patient is a merciful deed, with the patient's good in mind, though on the surface it may appear to be an act of cruelty. . . ."

14. David Holzer, *The Rav Thinking Aloud: Transcriptions of Personal Conversations with Rabbi Joseph B. Soloveitchik* (Holzer Seforim, 2009), 103; R. Joseph B. Soloveitchik, *The Emergence of Ethical Man* (Ktav, 2005), 27–29. See also *Biur Halakhah* 329, s.v. *ela lefi*, who states that Judaism confers value to life even if one is not able to perform *mitzvot*.

15. See, for example, Meiri, *Yoma* 85a, who writes that one should violate Shabbat to save the life even of a person who would only survive for a very short time, because "during that time one is able to mentally repent and confess his wrongdoings."

16. In this regard, the Talmud teaches that

if the suspected adulterous wife (*sotah*) who drank from the "bitter waters" (Num. 6:11–31) had special merits, she would be rewarded with a gradual death as a result of severe illness and slow deterioration, rather than an immediate death (*Sotah* 22a; Rambam, *Hilkhot Sotah* 3:20). Similarly, R. Chaim Shmulevitz quotes the Talmudic statement in *Sotah* 11a that Balaam was punished with immediate death for advising Pharaoh, while Job was punished with a life of pain for his silent acquiescence to Pharaoh. R. Shmulevitz notes that Balaam's crime was worse, and we thus see that his punishment of a swift death is considered more severe than Job's punishment of a life of terrible pain. See also *Sefer Chasidim* 236. See, however, Rashi, Exod. 15:5, s.v. *kemo even*.

17. This is why R. Moshe Feinstein and R. Shlomo Zalman Auerbach rule (*Iggerot Moshe*, CM 2:75 (1) and *Minchat Shlomo* 1:91) that if terminal patients so desire, they may pursue treatment to prolong their lives, despite being in excruciating pain, "if they prefer a life of pain to death."

18. Indeed, I have encountered well-meaning, compassionate healthcare providers who have expressed concern that they were being asked to contribute to the pain of a compromised individual by continuing aggressive treatment. Sometimes they are correct, but in situations in which the patient has expressed willingness to endure his or her pain for various reasons, my response has been that this may be a case in which the patient is not *suffering*, despite his or her *pain*.

19. Additionally, for elderly patients, the perspective on aging taken by the patient and his or her family members may make an enormous difference in their attitudes towards treatment. The commandment to honor the elderly may be understood as a consequence of the idea that the later years are those in which a person has gained unique wisdom and a true perspective on the world, which confers the highest "quality of life" on these years, and particularly the last days of life, when this "true perception" of reality is especially heightened. See R. Yitzchak Zilberstein, *Shoshanat Amakim*, 80, and *Shiurei Torah Le-Rofim*, vol. 3, 316–7.

20. For further discussion on death as a process, see Dr. Joseph Isaac Lifschitz's article in *Halakhic Realities – Collected Essays on Brain Death* (Maggid Press, 2015). For a more positivistic look at the role of medicine in defining death, see Dr. Noam Stadlan's article, ibid. On defining death based solely on medical criteria, not religious, see *Siach Nachum*, 271.

21. James L. Bernat, Charles M. Culver, and Bernard Gert, "On the Definition and Criterion of Death," *Annals of Internal Medicine* 94(3) (1981), 389–94. See also Bleich, *Where Halakha and Philosophy Meet*, 74, for discussion of this issue. R. Bleich argues that the "Time of Death Statute" should actually be called the "Withholding Treatment Statute," since it is really about whom should be provided treatment and whom should not be – which is actually a value judgment, not a medical decision.

22. Benjamin Freedman, *Duty and Healing: Foundations of a Jewish Bioethic* (Routledge, 1999), 17. Dr. Freedman points out that secular bioethics often concerns itself with the procedure of deciding and *who* will decide, whereas Jewish writers on bioethics concentrate on *how* to decide – which decisions should be made and for what reason. These two approaches do not have to be in contradiction; each fills in for the other's deficiency. Similarly, it is often thought that one must believe in either science or religion – one cannot believe in both. However, the two can live quite comfortably side by side. Religion teaches us *why*; science teaches *how*. Religion and medicine work together because they are

answering different questions and serving different purposes.

23. Naftali Moses, *Really Dead? The Israeli Brain–Death Controversy 1967–1986* (Israel, 2011), 277.

24. *New England Journal of Medicine* 345 (2001), 617.

25. *Nishmat Avraham*, YD (English ed., 324 [#1]), makes the point that even in those circumstances in which a DNR (Do Not Resuscitate) order is permissible by Jewish Law, all nursing care necessary for the patient's comfort must be provided. A DNR must never be seen as a DNT (Do Not Treat).

26. R. Levi Meier, *Second Chances* (Urim Publications, 2005), 106. Similarly, Dr. Shimon Glick stressed to this author the reality that until the mid-twentiety century, physicians could do little curing, and they therefore emphasized caring. With the introduction of antibiotics and other medical advances, physicians began to emphasize curing and began to neglect caring, which has caused a great deal of poor performance on the part of physicians. Francis Peabody of Harvard University, in an article entitled "The Care of the Patient" (*JAMA*, Mar. 1927), included a famous and often quoted line: "The secret of the care of the patient is in caring for the patient."

27. Dominick L. Frosch, Suepattra G. May, Katharine A.S. Rendle, Caroline Tietbohl, and Glyn Elwyn, "Authoritarian Physicians and Patients' Fear of Being Labeled 'Difficult' among Key Obstacles to Shared Decision-Making," *Health Affairs* 31(5) (2012), 1030–38.

28. Several studies and surveys have shown that physicians and mental health workers on the whole are significantly less "religious" than the general American public, and they are thus often less "religious" than their patients as well. See A.B. Astrow, C.M. Puchalski, and D.P. Sulmasy, "Religion, Spirituality, and Health Care: Social, Ethical, and Practical Considerations," *The American Journal of Medicine* 110(4) (2001), 283–7. How can we hope to achieve the objective of patient-centered care when patients feel that their spiritual needs are being ignored in the clinical environment? Indeed, this type of neglect often drives patients away from effective medical treatment. See Steven G. Post, Christina M. Puchalski, and David B. Larson, "Physicians and Patient Spirituality: Professional Boundaries, Competency, and Ethics," *Annals of Internal Medicine* 132(7) (2000), 578–83 (esp. 578).

29. Thomas L. Delbanco, "Enriching the Doctor-Patient Relationship by Inviting the Patient's Perspective," *Annals of Internal Medicine* 116(5) (1992), 414–8.

30. James A. Tulsky, Margaret A. Chesney, and Bernard Lo, "See One, Do One, Teach One?: House Staff Experience Discussing Do-Not-Resuscitate Orders," *Archives of Internal Medicine* 156(12) (1996), 1285–89.

31. Larry VandeCreek and Laurel Burton, "Professional Chaplaincy: Its Role and Importance in Healthcare," *The Journal of Pastoral Care* 55(1) (2001), 81–97 (esp. 82–83).

32. B. Lo, D. Ruston, and L. W. Kates, "Discussing Religious and Spiritual Issues," *JAMA* 287 (2002), 749–54 (esp. 752); Allan S. Brett and Paul Jersild, "Inappropriate Treatment Near the End of Life: Conflict Between Religious Convictions and Clinical Judgment," *Archives of Internal Medicine* 163(14) (2003), 1645–49 (esp. 1648).

B. TRUTH-TELLING:
When Painful Medical Information Should and Should Not Be Revealed

R. Levi Meier, Ph.D., of blessed memory, my predecessor at Cedars-Sinai Medical Center, relates the following anecdote in his book, *Second Chances*: Dr. Mark, a psychiatrist on staff at a hospital, was diagnosed with a terminal illness. His attending physician felt that it would not be in Dr. Mark's best interest to know how much time he had left to live. But Dr. Mark persisted, saying, "I'm a psychiatrist. I can handle any news you're going to give me. I want the whole truth, and I want it now." So his physician told him, "You know you've got cancer, and it's stage 4. I don't think you have more than six or seven months left." Dr. Mark thought he assimilated all this information well and that he could grasp it intellectually. But he was wrong. Soon after hearing this news, he fell into a severe depression. Soon after that, he died. Another patient, herself not a physician, told me that she was shocked beyond words at the way her surgeon communicated with her. "You won't believe what he said to me as I was coming out of anesthesia after surgery," she told me. "His very first words to me were, 'The tumor was inoperable.' Can you believe that? If he had just presented his findings at the right time, in the right place, after some words of encouragement, I wouldn't have lost hope."[1]

Truth-telling, including revealing painful medical information to patients, poses a common and very challenging issue in healthcare. How much medical information should be revealed to patients? What if the patient is frail and the information is potentially very frightening? While there was a time in American society when it was standard practice to avoid disclosing a serious diagnosis to a patient, as medical practice has moved away from paternalism to a focus on patient autonomy,[2] it has become generally accepted in contemporary healthcare that patients have a right to know all relevant information related to their health condition.[3] Does Jewish Law support such a stance of complete disclosure, or does it advocate limiting truth-telling in certain situations?

JEWISH VALUES

Truth is a core Jewish value. The Torah requires one to stay away from any false matter,[4] and the Talmud describes the seal of God as truth.[5] However, truth is not an absolute ethical imperative in Jewish Law, as some deviations from the truth are permitted in certain specific circumstances.[6] Furthermore, there is a Jewish version of the cliché "ignorance is bliss," as described by Ecclesiastes: "For in much wisdom is much vexation, and one who increases knowledge increases sorrow."[7] Indeed, many biblical stories[8] and traditional Jewish sources[9] recognize the fact that very painful or shocking information can have a significant impact on one's physical health and well-being.[10]

Similarly, there is a fundamental concept in Jewish Law known as "*tiruf ha-da'at*," acute mental anguish. Jewish Law sometimes permits violation of even biblical commandments in order to put a patient's mind at ease if the patient is in a life-threatening situation.[11] For this reason, the *Shulchan Arukh* (code of Jewish Law) rules that if a close family member of a dangerously ill patient has died, the patient should not be informed of this bad news, since it may cause great anguish and exacerbate their illness.[12] This holds true even if it means that the patient will not be able to engage in any of the traditional acts of mourning and that healthy family members will have to avoid mourning practices while in the presence of the patient. Others are even permitted to lie about the situation if asked directly by the patient.[13]

RULINGS

Based on these values and rulings, some contemporary Rabbinic authorities have argued that medical professionals may not reveal to a patient that he or she is afflicted with terminal cancer[14] or that there is no cure for a dangerously ill patient's illness, out of concern that disclosing this news may hasten the patient's death.[15]

However, other Rabbinic authorities note that nowadays, concealing such diagnoses from a patient may be impossible and sometimes even counterproductive, particularly since most patients will receive some form of therapy, whether surgery, chemotherapy, radiotherapy, or a combination of these. Such treatments cannot be administered without the patient realizing that they are being treated for cancer or a serious illness. Therefore, if such patients are not told the truth, they may develop unnecessary and unjustified despair as they begin to imagine and possibly exaggerate the type of serious illness that they do have.[16] Furthermore, medicine now has much more to offer these patients than it used to – not only in prolonging life, but even in providing a complete cure.

Therefore, some suggest that doctors should first reveal the information to very close relatives. Only then, together with these relatives, should doctors present the information to the patient in the most sensitive and appropriate manner possible, as they build rapport and together determine the proper treatment regimen for the specific individual, with an understanding of his or her goals, values, and clinical condition.[17]

Many Rabbinic authorities also emphasize the need for all medical information to be conveyed in a way that is carefully individualized for the specific patient and situation,[18] and shared in a positive, supportive, and encouraging manner if possible, attempting to focus on the helpful treatment options so that a patient does not lose hope.[19] Obviously, there is not always hope for recovery or cure, and some patients may legitimately be suffering and may not respond well to constant emphasis only of the positive. Nevertheless, medical information should always be shared in the most sensitive, supportive, and appropriately optimistic manner.

However, if a disease is so widespread that nothing can be done other than reduce the patient's suffering, Rabbinic authorities rule that in the vast majority of situations, one *should not tell* the patient either the diagnosis or the seriousness of the situation. Rather, the patient should be encouraged to maintain some level of hope, even as the focus of the treatment may shift from curative to comfort measures.[20]

CONCLUSION

Like the contemporary secular approach, Jewish Law usually requires truth-telling and revelation of details to patients, but for different reasons. From a traditional Jewish perspective, the importance of disclosure of medical information is not based on the value of complete sharing of truth or the patient's right to autonomy, but rather on what will ultimately be best for the well-being of the patient on a case-by-case basis.[21] Sometimes that may mean sensitively sharing much or all relevant information with a patient, but sometimes it may mean concealing certain things if that promotes the best interests of the patient,[22] as Jewish Law recognizes pain, anguish, depression, and hopelessness as relevant factors affecting survival. These decisions must be made very carefully, with the thoughtful input of experienced medical practitioners (including mental health professionals), expert Rabbinic guidance, and the input of those who know the patient best.

ENDNOTES

1. R. Levi Meier, *Second Chances* (Urim, 2005), 102.

2. For a discussion of paternalism in medical ethics, its decreased utilization over time, and scenarios in which even contemporary secular ethicists still justify it, see Beauchamp and Childress, *Principles of Biomedical Ethics* (Oxford University Press, 2013), 7th ed., 216–22.

3. Beauchamp and Childress, ibid., 304, note that a dramatic shift has occurred in many countries regarding physicians' policies of disclosure of a serious diagnosis to patients. In the United States in 1961, 88% of physicians avoided disclosing such a diagnosis to patients, whereas by 1979, 98% disclosed all information.

4. Exod. 23:7.

5. *Shabbat* 55a.

6. For example, deviations from truth are permitted in order to preserve peace between individuals (*Yevamot* 65b), to protect a person's dignity or personal privacy (*Bava Metzia* 23b), and when there is danger to life (*Ketuvot* 19a). See R. Prof. A. Steinberg, *Encyclopedia of Jewish Medical Ethics* (Feldheim Publishers, 2003), 322, for discussion.

7. Eccl. 1:18. See the commentary of Ibn Ezra on this verse, where he explains that if one seeks excessive information and wisdom, he or she will not be able to enjoy their life.

8. For example, Rashi (Gen. 23:2) writes that Sarah's death is juxtaposed with the story of the binding of Isaac because she died simply through hearing the news that her son was readied for slaughter and was nearly sacrificed. This may also result from hearing good news. As the Ramban writes (45:26), when Yaakov heard the report that Yosef was still alive, "His heart ceased beating and his breathing stopped . . . his heart stopped as if he were dead. This is a well-known phenomenon that occurs when joy comes suddenly. . . ."

9. The Midrash (*Kohelet Rabbah* 5:6) describes a conversation between the prophet Isaiah and King Hezekiah (see II Kings 20:1–11). God sent Isaiah to inform Hezekiah that the latter's illness was fatal. The Midrash describes Hezekiah's criticism of Isaiah for delivering such a depressing message: "Customarily, when one visits the sick, the visitor says to the patient, 'May Heaven have mercy on you.' When a physician visits a sick individual, he tells him, 'This you may eat and this you may not eat. This you may drink and this you may not drink.' Even if the doctor sees that the patient is near death, he does not say to him, 'Write a will for your family,' lest this weaken the patient's resolve. But you are telling me, 'Go home because you will die and not live!?!'" For contemporary examples of this approach, see *Ta'am Ve-Da'at, Parashat Vayigash*, 244, which recounts how the Chatam Sofer went to great lengths to make sure that his elderly father-in-law, R. Akiva Eiger, did not find out about the death of his daughter, the Chatam Sofer's wife. Similarly, R. Menachem Mendel Schneerson, the Lubavitcher Rebbe, concealed the news of his younger brother's death from his mother for twelve years, out of fear that it would shock and hurt her too much. See J. Telushkin, *Rebbe* (Harper, 2014), 376–9.

10. Indeed, contemporary secular scholars have also recognized this point. Some have described the "nocebo effect," the concept that negative thoughts can harm one's health. Specifically, researchers have determined that negative health beliefs and expectations lead to a worsening of symptoms. For example, when a cancer diagnosis is disclosed to a patient whose cultural values and beliefs render such frank discussions as immoral or taboo, it can be catastrophic, triggering deeply held negative beliefs and expectations, which in turn not only negatively impact a patient's will to live, but can even shorten life expectancy. See M. Johnstone, "Bioethics and Cultural Differences," *Journal of Medicine and Philosophy* 37 (2012), 187–8, and the studies about the power of hope cited in R. J.D. Bleich, *Judaism and Healing* (Ktav, 2002), chap. 4.

11. The classic example of this is a ruling in the Talmud that a lamp may be lit on Shabbat (thereby violating a biblical prohibition) for the sake of a woman who is giving birth, even if she is blind, since knowing the light is on will put her mind at ease (*Shabbat* 128b). See also *Iggerot Moshe*, OC 1:132, on permitting a passenger to ride in a taxi along with a woman who is going to the hospital to give birth if she is afraid to go alone.

There are many examples of this sensitivity in Jewish Law. For example, the *Mishnah Berurah* (328:38) rules that if an infant is locked in a room on Shabbat, the door must be broken down to let the child out, out of fear that the shock of being locked in the room will endanger the child. *Minchat Yitzchak* (4:8) rules that a person who is told that whatever he brings to the hospital will be burned when he is discharged – to prevent the spread of disease – may still bring *tefillin* with him because it would cause mental anguish to make him go without putting on *tefillin* for many days. Furthermore, the *Shulchan Arukh* (YD 339:1) rules that in

the presence of a dying patient, no matters relating to death may be performed until the patient has died, out of fear that such actions could scare the patient (see also *Beit Yosef*, YD 339). This entails continuing routine medical care, even if unnecessary, and sometimes even giving a patient priority in a triage situation, if not doing so or not touching the patient could cause him to realize that he is dying and to become frightened (*Nishmat Avraham*, YD 339:1; *Iggerot Moshe*, CM 2:73). At times, this approach is mandated even if the patient does not appear to be conscious. Conversations about the patient's imminent death should take place outside of the hearing of the unconscious patient (*Nishmat Avraham*, YD 337:4). See also *Nishmat Avraham*, 3rd ed.: EH 5:12(4), 153; 145:9(3), 339–40; CM 250:1(1), 65 and 425:1, 168 for more examples and a distinction between two different types of acute mental anguish in Jewish Law.

12. *Shulchan Arukh*, YD 337:1.

13. *Arukh Ha-Shulchan*, YD 337:2; *Nishmat Avraham*, YD 3337(2); *Kol Bo Aveilut*, 17; *Chazon Ovadia, Aveilut*, 38.

14. *Teshuvot Be-Tzel Ha-Chokhmah* 2:55. Similarly, R. Zilberstein has ruled that just as one should not tell people who cannot handle it about the death of their parent, one should not tell parents bad news about their baby in utero; when information is shared, it must be done in a positive manner (*Torat Ha-Yoledet*, 191–4 [2nd ed.]).

15. *Iggerot Moshe*, CM 2:73.

16. *Nishmat Avraham*, YD 338:1(4) (490–91 in 3rd ed.). Furthermore, some argue that a physician should disclose information to a patient who is experiencing mental anguish as a result of their condition, because he or she would like to leave instructions related to their death, such as one's wishes for their burial and funeral, etc. (*Sefer Chassidim*; see Steinberg, *Ency-*

clopedia of Jewish Medical Ethics, 324).

17. *Nishmat Avraham*, YD 338:1(4) (490–91 in 3rd ed.).

18. S. Glick, *Assia* 3, (5743/1983), 497–8; "*Divuach Emet Le-Choleh*," *Assia* 42–43 (5747/1987), 8–15.

19. The *Shulchan Arukh* requires that one broach the topic of reciting the confession before dying (*Viduy*) with the patient. *Shulchan Arukh* writes (YD 338:1) that one should begin by stating, "Many have recited the confession and did not die. . . ." See also *Nishmat Avraham*, YD 338:1(4) (491 in 3rd ed.); Bleich, *Judaism and Healing*, 33; Tatz, *Dangerous Disease and Dangerous Therapy*, 289–90. On a doctor or nurse informing people of the passing of one of their family members, see *Nishmat Avraham*, YD 402 (645 in 3rd ed.).

20. *Nishmat Avraham*, YD 338:1. He concludes that even if the doctor thinks that the patient's situation is hopeless, and that under natural circumstances, he or she cannot possibly recover, the doctor should nevertheless not accept this prognosis decisively and with absolute certainty. Certainly, one should not be so brash as to give a definitive opinion as to how long the patient will live. For who knows what medical breakthrough may come tomorrow?

21. R. Y. Shafran, *Assia* 42–43 (5747/1987), 16–23.

22. Indeed, many secular ethicists are beginning to argue that the pendulum may have swung too far against withholding any medical information from patients. In some cases, it may indeed be ethically appropriate not to disclose all painful medical information that may cause anxiety, destroy hope, and potentially have a negative impact on the therapeutic outcome. See *Principles of Biomedical Ethics*, 304–7, who suggest that a responsible approach would be to balance all of the patient's relevant welfare interests and informational interests, and, when possible, to ask the patient at the outset and as the illness progresses about the extent to which he wants to be informed and wants others involved.

C. MENTAL ILLNESS:
Determining Capacity and Proper Treatment in Accordance with Jewish Law

A patient who was trying to get admitted into an in-patient psychiatric unit told me that she was desperate to finally receive some help, but that the unit wouldn't accept her because she was pregnant. This patient confided in me that she had thus decided to have an abortion just to gain acceptance into the psych unit! This story highlights the level of desperation, urgency, and importance of effectively supporting and treating individuals suffering from various forms of mental illness.

Mental illness is a common and often debilitating struggle, and issues related to determining capacity and compelling treatment are challenging and crucial questions that frequently arise. A person's ability to live a meaningful life and observe Torah and mitzvot often hangs in the balance.

JEWISH ATTITUDES TOWARDS MENTAL ILLNESS

Jewish Law shows tremendous compassion and sensitivity towards individuals struggling with mental illness. For example, whenever a physical illness presents even a possible danger to human life, the Torah requires setting aside Torah prohibitions in order to do everything possible for the benefit of the sick person.[1] The very same halakhic rules that govern one who has a physical infirmity apply to one whose life is in danger – or who presents a danger to the lives of others – due to a psychiatric condition,[2] including depression.[3] Indeed, just as there is a commandment to attempt to heal those with a physical infirmity, it is also a mitzvah to attempt to heal those with mental illness.[4] Therefore, in numerous situations, Rabbinic authorities have overridden Torah prohibitions, in accordance with the circumstances and the severity of a person's mental illness, for the sake of helping such an individual.[5]

Furthermore, the fact that an individual suffering from severe mental illness is exempt from many commandments[6] may reflect an attempt to avoid unnecessarily burdening this individual with obligations that may add further stress to an already delicate state of mind. This is in recognition of the fact that in some situations, religious obligation might potentially exacerbate a patient's clinical state or impede recovery from a current disabling mental illness.[7]

In addition to categorizing such a patient as dangerously ill, our rabbis are sensitive to the fact that mental and emotional suffering is often much worse and more difficult to bear than physical pain.[8] Just like one should not be ashamed when they are stricken with a physical malady, mental illness is an illness like any other, which can be treated and for which there need not be a stigma. Indeed, Jewish tradition encourages the utmost respect for those suffering from any form of mental illness, calling upon us to go out of our way to support such individuals.[9] Moreover, Jewish tradition argues that such individuals are considered free of sin. Their merits thus protect the entire community, and God will ensure that they stand with the righteous in the World to Come.[10]

TREATMENT OPTIONS

In the course of treatment for various types of mental illness, an observant Jew may be asked to engage in activities that seem to compromise or challenge his or her commitment to practicing Jewish Law. There are many such examples, and each case should be dealt with on a case-by-case basis in consultation with a knowledgeable and sensitive Rabbinic authority who knows the patient personally.[11] I will present some of the most common issues that arise and the approaches that some of the leading Rabbinic authorities have taken.

"Lashon Ha-Ra"

A common question relates to the permissibility of even speaking with a mental health professional, specifically because of concerns related to the prohibitions against *lashon ha-ra* (gossip about others), since this often includes the need to speak about others.[12] Rabbi Yisrael Meir Kagan, known as the Chafetz Chaim after his classic code on the laws of *lashon ha-ra*, rules that one may speak about others when there is a specific rationale or purpose in doing so (*to'elet*). He includes in this category the act of unburdening oneself to relieve oneself of worry.[13] This is only true, however, if one is relating information about another person in order to relieve one's concerns, not if it is said in order to hurt the other person or to enjoy relating their shortcomings.[14] Many understand this ruling as permission to speak about others to a therapist if necessary, as long as one does not exaggerate or cause undo damage to the one being spoken about.[15] Moreover, sharing information with a therapist does not necessarily constitute gossip or slander, since the therapist does not "accept and believe" disclosures as fact, but rather views them in the framework of the patient's expression and perception of their subjective distress.[16]

The additional requirement to honor one's parents complicates this issue when an individual's concerns are related to their parents and when, in the course of treatment, they are asked to describe or express anger about their parents. While authorities of Jewish Law have more reservations about permitting this activity, some permit it if it is done with the intention of ultimately ridding the patient of their negative feelings towards their parents in order to be able to honor them properly.[17] Ideally, such therapy should not be creating anger towards one's parents, but rather attempting to help the patient get through it, since a lack of a cathartic outlet may mean that the existing anger will remain and contribute to the patient's mental condition.[18]

"Yichud"

Another common issue pertains to the halakhic prohibition for men and women to be secluded alone together (*yichud*). This prohibition promotes modesty and helps avoid improper conduct or any accusations of such. Many rule that this requirement limits one's choice of a therapist to those of the same gender,[19] and they discourage observant Jews from being admitted to a psychiatric hospital with co-ed wards.[20] Some permit a patient to see a therapist of the opposite gender in a professional context such as this, as long as the door remains unlocked.[21] However, most authorities argue that even if the specific rules are observed to avoid the prohibition of *yichud*, when it comes to intensely personal interventions, such as "dynamic psychotherapy," the deep emotional attachment and closeness that is developed in the psychotherapeutic relationship – which is in and of itself part of the treatment – is prohibited between individuals of different genders. Therefore, in most circumstances, one should attempt to find a therapist of the same gender.[22]

Obsessive Compulsive Disorder

Another issue that presents challenges in the treatment of observant Jews relates to obsessive compulsive disorder (OCD).[23] Religious observance does not cause OCD[24] or increase the incidence of it.[25] Indeed, classical Jewish teachings may in fact mitigate it.[26] However, religion can sometimes be used to legitimize one's obsessions[27] or contribute to the challenges of treating OCD.[28]

In addition to medication and psychotherapy, there are two common therapies for OCD, one proactive and the other passive. The proactive intervention is known as Exposure and Response Prevention (ERP), in which a patient must confront his or her fears but avoid their problematic responses. This can present significant challenges for an observant Jew. For example, ERP might theoretically force a patient who has fears about mixing meat and milk in the kitchen to put butter onto a meat knife. This would be problematic for any observant Jew and would likely lead to their discontinuing the therapy altogether. It is thus ideal if a professional can avoid recommending that such a patient engage in treatment that will violate his or her religion, especially a Torah prohibition.[29] However, if a professional is aware of these issues, it is possible to engage in ERP without forcing a patient to actually commit a religious transgression.[30]

The more passive therapy requires never indulging one's OCD. For example, many patients with OCD desire to constantly repeat blessings or correct their prayers. This may, in fact, be required by Jewish Law under some circumstances if a mistake was indeed made. Nevertheless, Rabbinic authorities tend to be lenient in this regard,[31] permitting an OCD patient to passively violate Jewish Law by not repeating their prayers, in order to follow this treatment.[32]

To properly treat OCD in observant Jews, it is therefore important to work with a professional who has knowledge of the patient's religion and culture[33] and does not blame religion,[34] but rather understands the patient's values and what is important to him or her, and is able to show how treatment is, in fact, virtuous.[35] It is often crucial to include a knowledgeable and sensitive rabbi in the treatment as well.[36]

Compelling Treatment

Secular law often governs and mandates when certain patients must be detained and admitted to a psychiatric hospital, even against their will, or when they may be protected from compulsory treatment, such as from being compelled to take a certain medication. According to Jewish Law, individuals suffering from mental illness who may hurt themselves or others must be treated and admitted to a hospital even against their will.[37] However, people whose illness does not present any threat to their own life should not be forced into treatment unless they are so confused that they are not able to make reasonably levelheaded decisions. In the latter case, one may unilaterally initiate any treatments that are for the patients' benefit, with the assumption that if the patients were able to think rationally, they themselves would choose to undergo such treatment.[38]

CAPACITY AND HALAKHIC STATUS

Degree of mental capacity or competence is an issue that may arise regarding individuals suffering from various forms of mental illness.[39] The fact that an individual simply makes bad decisions does not render an individual incapacitated,[40] but Jewish Law recognizes certain categories of people who are considered incapable of giving consent, and are thus also not obligated to perform *mitzvot*, do not receive punishment for transgressions, and cannot perform business transactions.[41] There are a number of categories that identify different types of incapacity:

- The term "*shoteh*" (often translated as "a fool") focuses on a patient's *irrationality* and refers to an individual who consistently behaves irrationally in one area of his life.[42]
- The term "*peti*" (often translated as "naïve" or "gullible") focuses on a patient's *inability for comprehension*. A *peti* is a person who has exceptionally poor comprehension and difficulty understanding things and making decisions.[43] The difference between a *peti* and a *shoteh* is that a *shoteh*'s mind is entirely confused and dysfunctional in one area, such that we must extrapolate to all areas of their

decision-making process, whereas the *peti*'s mind is not necessarily entirely dysfunctional in any one matter; he or she is simply unable to properly comprehend the matter at hand or is generally very weak-minded.[44]

- The term "*nechpaz*" ("hasty") focuses on a patient's *thought process*. A *nechpaz* is someone who is especially impatient and makes rash decisions, hastily and without rationally considering the ramifications or goals of their actions.[45]

It is impossible to give general guidelines to assist in determining how to classify any given patient, as such a determination must be based on the subjective, case-by-case evaluation of the expert Rabbinic authority who assesses the person and attempts to understand their nature.[46] These determinations should also be made with the expert input of a skilled and experienced mental health diagnostician, who can perform a mental status examination and obtain a psychosocial history to help the rabbi determine the significance of various behaviors and verbalizations in reflecting levels of wellness, sanity, mental health, cognitive functioning, and so on.

(Regarding the obligation to inform others about one's mental illness, such as in the case of prospective marriage partners, see Chapter 6A.[47])

ENDNOTES

1. *Shulchan Arukh*, OC 328:2.

2. *Kol Kitvei Ha-Ramban*, vol. 2, 43; *Nezer Matai* 1:8; *Nishmat Avraham*, OC, introduction to 328(6:2) (421 in 3rd ed.); *Lev Avraham* 13:9. *Encyclopedia Hilkhatit Refu'it*, vol. 7, 570–1, demonstrates that according to some authorities, the reason prohibitions may be overridden to save someone from mental illness is out of fear that they may hurt someone else or themselves (either intentionally or accidentally), while other authorities argue that prohibitions may be overridden in order to simply relieve the mental illness and prevent its spread so that the individual will be able to function normally and fulfill the commandments, even without a specific danger to life. For a discussion of the various sorts of psychiatric danger and halakhic responses to them, see Moshe Halevi Spero, *Handbook of Psychotherapy and Jewish Ethics* (Feldheim, 1986), 21–27, 251–6.

3. *Nishmat Avraham*, vol. 5, 159(7) (1st ed.) (subsequently published in *Dinei Ha-Rofeh Be-Shabbat Ve-Yom Tov*, 7) rules explicitly that one suffering from deep depression is classified as dangerously ill, a "*choleh she-yesh bo sakanah*." See *Chelkat Yaakov*, OC 64(6). One may thus violate a Torah law for the sake of a patient with severe depression, or even for one who is not currently manifesting dangerous symptoms but is likely to manifest them if not treated (*Nishmat Avraham*, OC 328:2(2) [434 in 3rd ed.]; *Encyclopedia Hilkhatit Refu'it*, vol. 7, 576, in the name of R. Elyashiv and R. Feinstein). See also forthcoming responsum of R. Asher Weiss on fasting on Yom Kippur

for patients with mental illness, where he rules that depression can be considered a life-threatening illness in some cases, and thus, in consultation with professionals, they can be permitted to violate certain prohibitions such as taking medication on Yom Kippur, if necessary.

Diagnosing the severity of a patient's depression is very difficult and should be performed on a case-by-case basis, with the input of an experienced Rabbinic authority and a qualified mental health professional. Many rule that even in the case of mild depression and anxiety, if the patient has another illness and is already weakened, Torah law may be violated to help them. If the patient is suffering from mild depression or anxiety but nothing else, then Rabbinic laws may be violated. See R. M. Torczyner, "Treating Anxiety and Depression," available at: http://www.yutorah.org/sidebar/lecture.cfm/79 3289/rabbi-mordechai-torczyner/medic al-halachah-treating-anxiety-and-depres sion/. On depression in Halakhah, see also *Encyclopedia Hilkhatit Refu'it*, vol. 7, 562–3. See also *Siach Nachum* 1:23, where R. Nachum Rabinovitch rules that one suffering from psychological trauma after a terrorist attack should be categorized as dangerously ill, and psychiatric professionals may therefore violate Torah prohibitions in order to help him (see also *Techumin*, vol. 23, 73–88). Similarly, R. Asher Weiss has written (currently unpublished responsum on fasting on Yom Kippur for patients with mental illness, cited above) that mental health professionals may violate the Sabbath, ideally only rabbinic prohibitions but even Torah prohibitions if necessary to be with people in a traumatic situation, in order to try to prevent PTSD, such as after a terrorist attack.

4. *Encyclopedia Hilkhatit Refu'it*, vol. 7, 574. In *Masorat Moshe*, 359, R. Moshe Feinstein is quoted as ruling that just as a name may be changed for a patient suffering from a severe physical illness, one may change a name for a person suffering from severe mental illness.

5. See *Tzitz Eliezer* (8:15 [3:1]); *Iggerot Moshe*, OC 1:127; *Nishmat Avraham*, EH 145:9(3) (339–40 in 3rd ed.). See also *Jewish Medical Ethics*, vol. 1, 306–7 (*Assia* 4:1 [Feb. 2001], 30–34). For example, some authorities permitted eating non-kosher food in order to prevent mental anguish in certain circumstances (*Responsa Pri Ha-Aretz* 3:2), if that would be necessary in order to be treated as an inpatient in the best mental health clinic (*Iggerot Moshe*, YD 2:59) or if it is a component of a proven treatment (*Encyclopedia Hilkhatit Refu'it*, vol. 7, 578). Authorities also sometimes permit eating on Yom Kippur and birth control for a woman with serious mental health issues (*Iggerot Moshe*, EH 1:65, 3:22; *Minchat Yitzchak* 1:115, 3:25). See *Nishmat Avraham*, EH 5:7(4), (152–3 in 3rd ed.) for discussion of birth control in these situations, as well as issues related to postpartum depression.

When Torah prohibitions cannot be violated, Rabbinic authorities still show compassion and find ways to help the patient. For example, there was a case of a child with severe autism who could only be calmed and put to sleep at night by being taken for a drive in a car. Prof. Abraham, with the agreement of R. Neuwirth, ruled that the parents may not drive him on Shabbat, since it is not necessary to do so in order to save his life. However, since such a child can be categorized as a "*choleh kol ha-guf*," on whose behalf a non-Jew may be asked to violate even Torah prohibitions, the parents may arrange for a non-Jewish driver to take the child

and his parents for a drive; see *Nishmat Avraham*, OC, introduction to 328 (6:2) (421 in 3rd ed.). On autism in Halakhah, see *Encyclopedia Hilkhatit Refu'it*, vol. 7, 558–9.

6. See extensive discussion of this issue in *Encyclopedia Hilkhatit Refu'it*, vol. 7, 567–8.

7. *Jewish Medical Ethics*, vol. 1, 302 (*Assia* 4:1 [Feb. 2001], 30–34). Similarly, Jewish Law protects this individual from harm by providing certain exemptions and protections in the laws of damages; see n. 9 below.

8. *Tzitz Eliezer* 13:102.

9. For example, a Beit Din (religious court) appoints a guardian for such individuals to protect them (*Ketuvot* 48a; Rambam, *Hilkhot Mekhirah* 29:4; *Shulchan Arukh*, CM 235:20, 290:34). Furthermore, if such an individual damages someone else, they are not held accountable, but if someone damages them, the offender is held accountable, since people are expected to defend him or her (Rambam, *Hilkhot Chovel U-Mazik* 4:20; *Shulchan Arukh*, CM 424:8). See *Encyclopedia Hilkhatit Refu'it*, vol. 7, 569–70.

Moreover, in a related ruling, though not specifically dealing with mental illness, a community is obligated to provide *tzedakah* in order to see to it that there are special schools, classes, or programs for children with learning disabilities, Down syndrome, or mental retardation. Synagogues must be welcoming to them and they should be encouraged to participate in *mitzvot* and communal life to the extent possible (*Iggerot Moshe*, YD 4:29; *Nishmat Avraham*, YD 245:15(1) [302–5 in 3rd ed].)

10. *Nishmat Avraham*, YD 81:7(4:1) (35–36 in 3rd ed.), in the name of R. Neuwirth and R. Wosner; R. Zilberstein, *Shiurei Torah Le-Rofim*, vol. 3, 510. Our sages make it clear that even someone

halakhically categorized as a *"shoteh"* for legal purposes, was created by God and is needed in the world, and salvation comes through their merits (*Encyclopedia Hilkhatit Refu'it*, vol. 7, 570, based on *Beit Yosef*, EH 1).

11. See also *Encyclopedia Hilkhatit Refu'it*, vol. 7, 606–7, for discussion of issues in Jewish Law related to psychotherapy, neuropsychiatry surgery (such as frontal lobectomy), and hypnotism; see vol. 6, 491, for discussion of the "facilitated communication" technique. On the topic of the permissibility of psychotherapy, see R. Naftali Bar-Ilan, *"Rabbanim Ve-Yei'utz Psychologi,"* *Techumin* 29, 323–8. See also S. Hoffman, *Psycholog: Aseh Lekha Rav* (Golden Sky, 2016), 1, 20–25, 38, 60 regarding the obligation of a therapist to rebuke his or her sinning patients; see p. 26 regarding concerns related to "arousing the Satan" in Cognitive Behavioral Therapy. On the topic of arousing inappropriate thoughts or fantasies in the course of psychotherapy, see Moshe Halevi Spero, *Judaism and Psychology: Halakhic Perspectives* (Ktav, 1980), chap. 10. For a summary and discussion of opinions regarding sending a child with severe intellectual disability to an institution where they will have to eat non-kosher food, see *Nishmat Avraham*, YD 81:7(4) (32–34, 37 in 3rd ed.) and EH 121:3 (325–8 in 3rd ed.); *Teshuvot Minchat Asher* 2:47. Regarding treatment of a child with Down syndrome, see *Nishmat Avraham*, YD 81:7(4:1) (34–5 in 3rd ed.); *Teshuvot Minchat Asher* 2:48.

12. Jewish Law demands purity of thought (*hirhur assur*) and especially speech (i.e., prohibition against *lashon ha-ra*), which could potentially pose a problem for many forms of psychoanalysis. Prof. Moshe Halevi Spero has developed a theoretical method of dealing with these issues in therapy by conceptualizing therapy as *viduy* (confession). The process of repentance for any sin requires one to fully recognize all aspects of the sin, which includes both an internal and a verbal experience. In this way, argues Prof. Spero, some psychotherapy can potentially be accepted by Jewish Law as a form a *viduy*, thus permitting certain thoughts or speech about whatever is therapeutically necessary for behavior modification. See Spero, *Judaism and Psychology*, 151–2, and *Handbook of Psychotherapy and Jewish Ethics*, 18–20, 48–50, 199.

13. Chafetz Chaim, *Issurei Lashon Ha-Ra*, gloss to 10:14. For a thorough discussion of this concept in Jewish Law, see R. Daniel Feldman, *False Facts and True Rumors* (Maggid Press, 2015), 93–119.

14. R. Shlomo Rosner, *Shut Le-Chafetz Chaim* 2:1, quoted in *Ha-Ma'ayan* (Nissan 5774), vol. 54, 2 [209], 53. Since the permission to speak about others only applies when there is a specific rationale to relieve one's burdens, one must make sure that this is indeed his intention and focus. If one is publicizing this information to many people, it may be a sign that he or she is doing so only to hurt the person being spoken about, not to relieve one's own anxiety.

15. R. Zilberstein, *Shiurei Torah Le-Rofim* 4:266, 383, 406; *Encyclopedia Hilkhatit Refu'it*, vol. 7, 608.

16. This point was noted to me by Dr. David Fox.

17. R. Zilberstein, *Shiurei Torah Le-Rofim* 4:266, 393–400. R. Zilberstein adds the proviso that the parent has given approval for such treatment and there is no effective alternative (397), and in certain cases (fn. 3) he distinguishes between situations in which the parent has repented for the pain they caused their child (in which case it can be assumed that the parent would be supportive of such therapy) and when the parent has not repented (and thus the parent's express permission would be required). See also R. Naftali

Bar-Ilan, quoted in S. Hoffman, *Reader for the Orthodox Jewish Psychotherapist*, 104; R. Nachum Rabinovitch, quoted in S. Hoffman, "Halacha and Psychological Treatment Dilemmas and Conflicts," in *Jewish Medical Ethics*, vol. 1, 320–21 (*Assia* 12:2 [2004], 36–38). R. Rabinovitch adds that if this is done for a constructive goal and in an effective manner, it can also serve as atonement for the parents, although one may never curse their parents, even if they were "wicked." See also Benzion Sorotzkin, "Honoring Parents Who Are Abusive," in *Rabbis and Psychologists* (Mondial Press, 2014), 61–83, for discussion of the many limitations on the requirement to honor parents who negatively impact one's mental health, including the ruling that one is not obligated to honor an abusive parent. Similarly, R. Moshe Feinstein is quoted as ruling that even though one should not contradict their parents, in the setting of psychological therapy, it is permissible to do so since it is done for the sake of healing, as long as it is not done in a disgraceful or humiliating manner (R. Aaron Felder, *Rishumei Aharon,* vol. 1, 61). In contrast, R. Nissan Kaplan has written that the permission to speak *lashon ha-ra* when there is a specific rationale or purpose (*to'elet*) does not apply to speaking about one's parents (*Kol Ha-Torah* 50 [5761]: 25). R. Eliezer Melamed also rules that speaking *lashon ha-ra* about one's parents is always forbidden, even in the context of psychotherapy and reducing one's suffering (http://www.yeshiva.org.il/midrash/3182). For a thorough discussion of the various rulings and classical source material on this topic, see R. Naftali Bar-Ilan, "*Tipul Psychologi Ve-kavod Horim*" in S. Hoffman, *Psycholog: Aseh Lekha Rav*, 7 and *Assia* 95–96 (5775), 111.

18. This point was noted to me by Dr. David Fox.

19. R. Zilberstein, quoted in S. Hoffman, *Reader for the Orthodox Jewish Psycho-* therapist, 108; Prof. Moshe Halevi Spero, "*Dinei Yichud Be-Tipul Psychoterapoiti*," *Assia* 47–48 (Kislev 5750), 32–39. Prof. Spero analyzes the various sources relating to the laws of *yichud* and their application to psychotherapy, and he points out that it is more difficult to be lenient in this case than regarding visits to other types of doctors. This is because such meetings engender very personal, intimate discussions, and because of their inherently private nature, it is difficult to truly ensure that other people will always be around and may enter the room at any time. See also *Encyclopedia Hilkhatit Refu'it*, vol. 3, 828.

20. *Encyclopedia Hilkhatit Refu'it*, vol. 7, 583, in the name of R. Shlomo Zalman Auerbach. For a thorough discussion of the pros and cons of mixed gender wards, see the articles culled from *Assia* presented in *Jewish Medical Ethics*, vol. 1, 337–64.

21. R. Naftali Bar-Ilan and R. Michael Broyde, quoted in S. Hoffman, *Reader for the Orthodox Jewish Psychotherapist*, 107, 109. R. Bar-Ilan adds the caveat that if a professional feels that a certain patient arouses inappropriate thoughts or feelings, the professional must refer the patient to another therapist. See also Dr. Nachum Klafter, "Psychotherapy with Patients of the Opposite Sex," in *Rabbis and Psychologists*, 32–60, for an analysis of the lenient position permitting therapists to treat patients of the opposite sex based on the principles of professionals being mentally preoccupied with their professional work and due to their fear of being caught. Klafter cites R. Gedalia Dov Schwartz and R. Shmuel Fuerst as permitting psychotherapy between members of the opposite sex as long as the laws of *yichud* are followed (43–46). When a therapist of the opposite gender is the most competent and qualified choice, that may also be taken into account. However, R. Asher Weiss told this author that as long as another therapist is qualified, it is

better not to permit this simply because one psychotherapist has a better reputation. R. Weiss maintains that it is always best to choose a therapist of the same gender, unless there is some reason not to be concerned, such as in the case of a very elderly patient (personal communication, winter 2016).

22. This ruling was issued to Dr. Michael Bunzel (Chairman of the Department of Psychiatry and former Medical Director of the Chiba Clinic at Ma'ayanei HaYeshua Medical Center in Bnei Brak) by R. Yitzchak Zilberstein, and it was signed by a broad spectrum of leading Rabbinic authorities in Israel and America, including R. Ovadia Yosef, R. Shmuel Wosner, R. Yaakov Ariel, R. Dov Lior, R. Yisroel Belsky, R. Shmuel Kaminetsky, R. Dovid Cohen, and many others. The ruling states that such a formation of emotional bonds between men and women who are not married is prohibited because of the possibility that it could lead to illicit relations. Moreover, the emotional closeness that is created is itself prohibited, even if there is no concern that it will lead to an illicit act. This ruling challenges the leniency that is based on the principle that professionals are mentally preoccupied with their professional work and are afraid of being caught (see previous note). Since the psychiatric discipline includes developing an emotional closeness and dependence, it is different than leniencies that have been issued in other areas, including the practice of medicine, and necessitates more caution. This ruling did, however, leave a certain flexibility in unique cases that necessitate a cross-gender setting, with case-by-case input from a rabbinic authority.

23. The primary areas in which OCD expresses itself in Orthodox Jews are prayer (concentration and devotion, as well as cleanliness before prayer), cleanliness in *kashrut*, and menstrual purity. See D. Greenberg and E. Witztum, *Sanity*

and Sanctity (Yale Press, 2001), 128. For an excellent summary of many of these issues, see R. Mordechai Torczyner, "Judaism and Obsessive-Compulsive Disorder," http://www.yutorah.org/sidebar/lecture .cfm/810961/rabbi-mordechai-torczyner /judaism-and-obsessive-compulsive-disor der/.

24. Greenberg and Witztum, *Sanity and Sanctity*, 128–30. They point out that if observance of Jewish law induced OCD, we would expect all areas of Jewish practice to be involved in the disorder. However, this is not the case. OCD symptoms of a religious nature are not found in all areas of ritual, nor necessarily in the most important areas. Jews who suffer from OCD may spend hours carefully cleaning the perianal region before prayer (at the expense of properly fulfilling the requirement to pray on time), but they do not display such scrupulousness in other very important laws and rituals, such as Shabbat. It is thus clear that while religious practices may sometimes be the setting, they are not the catalyst for the disorder. Indeed, all people who suffer from OCD, across cultures and amongst both religious and secular people, tend to focus on the same types of issues, such as cleanliness and orderliness. These obsessions are simply expressed in different manners, which mirror the prevalent habits and values of the person's culture. This has led researchers and psychiatrists to conclude that "religion is the context for the presentation of OCD, rather than the reason."

25. Greenberg and Witztum, *Sanity and Sanctity*, 130, 132–3, cite studies that have concluded that not only do the types of compulsive behaviors found in ultra-Orthodox Jews match the same category/ type of OCD in other populations, but they do so in the identical proportions of their societies. In fact, studies have shown that all cultures, regardless of how religious or irreligious they are, show a

remarkably similar prevalence of OCD, even two societies (Chinese and Indian) that are considered to be at opposite poles of obsessionality in everyday life.

26. For example, many observant Jews who suffer from OCD go overboard cleaning obsessively for Passover, but the *mishnah* rules (*Pesachim* 1:2), "We are not concerned that a rodent may have dragged leaven from house to house or place to place, for then [we would have to be concerned that leaven was dragged] from yard to yard and city to city – there would be no end to the matter!" Similarly, others who suffer from OCD clean their perianal region excessively before prayer, yet the Talmud states (*Yoma* 30a) that before reciting the *Shema*, one need not be concerned that there is feces on his body that is not visible, as "the Torah was not given to the ministering angels!" Moreover, Judaism emphasizes serving God with joy and knowing the difference between law and stringency.

27. Many who suffer from OCD deal with what is known as "Thought-Action Fusion," in which they treat thoughts as if they are an action. While some view this as a sign of illness, in Jewish Law, thought is indeed viewed seriously (for example, in the case of blasphemous thoughts or accepting Shabbat upon oneself on Friday afternoon). Since this is a legitimate issue in Judaism, a therapist cannot simply say, "Since you only thought it, it doesn't matter." Furthermore, religions that focus on minutiae of religious observance, the concept of a God who punishes, or statements about flawed humanity present valid religious ideas, but they can contribute to the challenges of those who struggle with living up to exacting standards. While Jewish Law presents a healthy and balanced system of belief and practice, someone struggling with OCD focuses only on those sources that confirm their obsessions and anxiety. (These issues are all discussed thoroughly in R. Torczyner's lecture, cited above, n. 23.)

28. It can be very difficult to properly distinguish between healthy religious fervor/scrupulousness and obsessive-compulsive behavior, and many observant Jews are uncomfortable turning to secular mental health professionals for guidance in this regard. One of the ways professionals assess whether a person who is very scrupulous about certain religious matters has a mental illness or is simply being very pious is by determining if that person experiences a sense of religious growth or feels frustrated and depressed by a self-imposed imprisoning ritual, in which case it is likely a mental dysfunction (see http://www.ohelfamily.org/?q=content/totally-engrossed-extreme-piousness-or-obsessive-compulsive-disorder).

29. R. Asher Weiss told this author (personal communication, winter 2016) that because of the tremendous burden and suffering involved, one could, in this case, apply the logic that it is "better to violate one Shabbat in order to be able to observe many." He ruled that it would thus be permissible to violate a custom or even a Rabbinic prohibition in order to engage in ERP (as long as it is proven to be effective in the case at hand), but not a Torah prohibition. See n. 32 below regarding R. Weiss's responsum on OCD. In most situations, a competent therapist would not actually force a patient to do something like putting butter on a meat knife, but might instead instruct the patient to place a package of butter and a package of meat in one bag at the supermarket, which would not contravene Jewish Law; see n. 30 below.

30. The mental health concern is the fear and anxiety that leads to obsessive behavior, not the act itself. Experts have thus concluded, "When treating religious patients, we believe it is not necessary or appropriate to include exposure to actual sin. . . . Exposures do not usually require

individuals actually to experience the ultimate negative consequences, but rather to tolerate risk, ambiguity, and uncertainty. Similarly, scrupulous patients need not actually sin or tell themselves that they are doing so; instead, they need to allow for slightly greater risk than others normally would, without actually making the violation occur" (Huppert, Siev, and Kushner, "Treating Scrupulosity in Orthodox Jews," *Journal of Clinical Psychology* 63(10) (2007), 933. Thus, for example, one who engages in obsessive cleaning before handling meat or dairy dishes can be asked to handle a dairy tray and then touch meat silverware without washing his hands. This does not require engaging in any forbidden meat and milk mixtures, but it may trigger the same anxieties, so it can nevertheless be beneficial. Similarly, some "OCD patients ritualize by praying to prevent bad things from happening after doing an exposure. Some therapists would encourage patients to 'spoil' or undo this ritual by praying for bad things to happen. However, given that religious patients believe in the efficacy of prayer, they may be reluctant to engage in such an act. An alternate approach is to ask them to undo the ritual by praying instead to "allow God's will." This suggests that if the person is to die, then allow that, and if not, then not. It inserts ambiguity and removes active attempts to prevent the negative outcome" (ibid., 936). Of course, all of this requires a therapist to be sensitive and to understand the patient's ingrained religious beliefs and practices.

31. For example, R. Yisrael Ganz (*Rosh Ha-Yeshiva* of Yeshivat Kol Torah in Jerusalem) has stated, "In cases that come before you regarding sufferers of religious compulsions, I think it is important to recall that which the *Gedolei Yisrael*, such as the Steipler Rav, *ztvk"l* and the Gaon Rav Shlomo Zalman Auerbach, *ztvk"l*, and others, have opined on this matter – that in every case of doubt in the Halakhah, one is to decide on the lenient side of the question. Likewise, even if it is unclear whether there is a doubt, one is also to be lenient" (cited in A. Bonchek, *Religious Compulsions and Fears*, 132, and in Hebrew in S. Hoffman, *Psycholog: Aseh Lekha Rav*, 50).

32. R. Asher Weiss (*Teshuvot Minchat Asher* 2:134) rules that the primary focus should be the patient's treatment, for which one may even passively violate a Torah prohibition or not fulfill a Torah requirement. Furthermore, R. Weiss rules that one should not attempt to mitigate these concerns by, for example, eating only a small amount of bread in order to not become obligated to recite the blessings after a meal, because this will only indulge the illness and can lead to thousands of similar applications, which would not help the individual. Instead, one should simply eat the normal amount and only allow themselves to recite the blessings afterwards once. See extensive discussion of this ruling in D. Lichtenstein, *Headlines 2* (OU Press, 2017), chp. 15.

R. Yaakov Yisrael Kanievsky similarly rules leniently on this matter and does not permit such an individual to repeat prayers, even if they are sure they made a mistake (*Kreina De-Igrata* 373; *Eitzot Ve-Hadrakhot*, 45, 48). R. Kanievsky also writes that someone who is obsessed with wiping himself before leaving the restroom must use a maximum of only 5 or 6 pieces of toilet paper and may wash himself, but he is forbidden from using any more than that (*Eitzot Ve-Hadrakhot*, 48, 53, based on *Divrei Chaim* 2:9). Similarly, R. Nachman of Breslov, clearly referring to those suffering from OCD, writes strongly that one should not spend excessive amounts of time on the toilet or cleaning themselves because this is a misunderstanding of the law and interferes with Torah study (*Sichot Ha-Ran*, 30), nor should one become overly obsessed with Passover cleaning (ibid., 235). See also Hoffman, *Reader for the Orthodox Jewish Psychotherapist*, 56–64. For more advice for treating mental illness in the name of R. Kanievsky, see *Shiurei Torah Le-Rofim*, vol. 4, 415–16.

33. A therapist must understand what is considered normal behavior and thinking in a given culture or religion; otherwise, he or she may assume that a person's appropriate religious behavior is OCD. See Huppert, Siev, and Kushner, "Treating Scrupulosity in Orthodox Jews," 927–8. It is also crucial to understand the patient's religious beliefs and behaviors in order to help the patient identify the core fear. For example, is the core fear mixing meat and milk, or is it God's punishment if they do so? If the therapist does not understand the patient's religion, it can be very challenging to help the patient identify his or her core fear. Furthermore, many treatment modalities can be supported by classical Jewish texts and teachings. If a therapist is able to reference them, this can help to gain the patient's trust and compliance (ibid., 934).

34. To ensure compliance, a therapist should build an alliance with their patients by ensuring that they understand that the therapist is not against or blaming their religion, and by otherwise providing a sensitive rationale so that the patients will value the therapist's approach and intervention (ibid., 933). For example, "A number of patients have articulated, 'If I just weren't religious, I wouldn't have this problem.' Although not necessarily intended to test the therapist, a statement such as this creates an opportunity for psychoeducation and alliance building. One response might be, 'You might not have OCD about Halakhah, but you would likely have it about something else instead. You cannot run away from OCD.' Such statements dispel concerns that the therapist believes that religion is part of the problem" (ibid., 933).

Another part of the rationale for treat-ment that should be conveyed early on is that OCD is likely a barrier to the spiritual connection religious patients want to have with God, and that ERP can be a way to help them rebuild that relationship.

35. Many patients will not want to engage in treatment that may reduce their religiosity, but if they can sense that the treatment will help them to be better Jews, they may feel that it is good for them. Prof. David Greenberg thus writes, "OCD is NOT being very *frum*; it is a distortion of everything spiritual. Improving the OCD improves one's spirituality. Removing the OCD does not remove religiousness" (Hoffman, *Reader for the Orthodox Jewish Psychiatrist*, 105). Similarly, Huppert, Siev, and Kushner write, "Another part of the rationale for treatment that should be conveyed early on is that OCD is likely a barrier to the spiritual connection religious patients want to have with God, and that EX/RP can be a way to help them rebuild that relationship" ("Treating Scrupulosity in Orthodox Jews," 933).

36. Hoffman, *Reader for the Orthodox Jewish Psychiatrist*, 68. In addition to guiding the treatment, a rabbi can help provide guidance on the tradition (*mesorah*) for what is considered within the normal bounds of behavior (see *Eitzot Ve-Hadrakhot*, 49). R. Kanievsky advises that a rabbi dealing with an individual who asks numerous questions as a result of their OCD should not respond with reasons or explanations for his answer, since the OCD patient will attempt to undermine every reason given in order to contradict and reject completely whatever he or she was told (ibid., 45, 48; see also *Religious Compulsions and Fears*, 135–6, and Greenberg and Shefler, "Ultra-Orthodox Rabbinic Responses to Religious Obsessive-Compulsive Disorder," *Israel Journal of Psychiatry Related Sciences* 45(3) (2008), 185. However, a rabbi cannot expect to be able to solve these problems without the involvement of mental

health professionals. As R. Dr. Abraham Twerski writes, "[A]n OCD sufferer may not necessarily be reassured by the opinion of the *poskim*. One woman with OCD threw out three sets of dishes because she could not accept the Rav's ruling that the dishes were perfectly kosher, saying, 'The Rav did not understand my *she'eilah*'" (foreword to *Religious Compulsions and Fears*, 16).

37. *Encyclopedia Hilkhatit Refu'it*, vol. 7, 574, based on R. J.D. Bleich (see also pp. 602, 618–9). See also *Shiurei Torah Le-Rofim* 4:270, 417–8, regarding force-feeding someone suffering from anorexia. R. Asher Weiss has permitted women suffering from eating disorders to eat on Yom Kippur when necessary for their treatment.

38. *Encyclopedia Hilkhatit Refu'it*, vol. 7, 575, quoting *Mishpatei Ha-Da'at*, 195.

39. For an excellent discussion of these issues and the relevant sources, see *Encyclopedia Hilkhatit Refu'it*, vol. 7, 551–66; R. Mordechai Torczyner, "Patient Capacity to Consent," http://www.yutorah.org /sidebar/lecture.cfm/783340/rabbi-morde chai-torczyner/medical-halachah-patient -capacity-to-consent/.

40. Rambam, *Hilkhot Nachalot* 10:8.

41. Rashi, *Chagigah* 3b, s.v. *eizehu*.

42. The Talmud (*Chagigah* 3b) lists dangerous behaviors that a *shoteh* engages in, such as traveling alone at night, sleeping in a cemetery, and tearing his clothing. The Beit Yosef (EH 121) rules, based on the Rambam's understanding of the Talmudic discussion, that a *shoteh* is defined as anyone who is of perpetually irrational and confused intelligence in any given area of his life, even if this person is rational in many other areas of his life. He is considered a *shoteh* until he becomes competent in that area (*Shulchan Arukh*, CM 35:8; *Iggerot Moshe*, YD 4:29; see *Encyclopedia Hilkhatit Refu'it*, vol. 7,

556, fn. 130, 601; *Nishmat Avraham* CM 35:10(1), 28–9 in 3rd ed.; *Teshuvot Minchat Asher* 2:47).

43. Rambam, *Hilkhot Eidut* 9:10. The Rambam writes that a *peti* is one who cannot recognize contradictory statements and does not understand matters as other people do. However, one who understands basic things, even if others need to explain to him or her, and even without an in-depth comprehension of the reasons, is not classified a *peti* in those areas that he or she understand (*Teshuvot Maharit* 2, EH 16; see also *Encyclopedia Hilkhatit Refu'it*, vol. 6, 486, n. 42). R. Moshe Feinstein defines a *peti* as one who may be rational, but who does not intellectually understand things. An adult *peti* is one with such weak understanding and inability to make distinctions that his comprehension level is like that of a young child, such as a 6-year-old or younger (*Iggerot Moshe*, YD 4:29). This is the halakhic category assigned to one who is mentally retarded (R. Z.N. Goldberg, *Techumin* 7 [5746], 231). See also *Encyclopedia Hilkhatit Refu'it*, vol. 6, 478–94.

44. *Sma*, CM 35:21; *Oneg Yom Tov*, 153; *Encyclopedia Hilkhatit Refu'it*, vol. 6, 486; *Nishmat Avraham* CM 35:10(1), pp. 27–9 in 3rd ed.

45. *Sma*, CM 35:22. A *nechpaz* is someone with an especially poor decision-making process who changes his or her mind under stress. Part of determining this state may entail asking them to explain how they arrived at a given decision.

46. Chatam Sofer, EH 2:2, based on Rambam, *Hilkhot Eidut* 9:9–10. Some have noted that this process of determining mental competence is primarily a legal, rather than a clinical concept. Thus, the evaluation and diagnosis is primarily rendered by a Rabbinic court of Jewish Law (*beit din*), although a clinician such as a psychiatrist, physician, or psychologist should certainly provide input. See Dr.

Rael Strous, "Halachic Sensitivity to the Psychotic Individual: The *Shoteh*," in *Jewish Medical Ethics*, vol. 1, 307 (*Assia* 4:1 [Feb. 2001], 30–34). The halakhic process of diagnosis generally includes questioning to determine if the individual can answer questions logically or not (*Gittin* 16b), as well as determining if a specific action has been done that demonstrates incapacity, and not simply intellectual inability (*Pitchei Teshuvah*, EH 121:2). See also *Encyclopedia Hilkhatit Refu'it*, vol. 7, 556, n. 132.

47. See also *Encyclopedia Hilkhatit Refu'it*, vol. 7, 580; *Shiurei Torah Le-Rofim* 4:269, 414.

CHAPTER 2

How Much Treatment?

A. RISK AND SELF-ENDANGERMENT: Determining the Appropriateness of Attempting Various Levels of Dangerous Medical Procedures

One of the most common questions faced by patients is if they should take a risk by undergoing an optional procedure. The answer to this question generally depends on the patient's current condition, prognosis and the amount of risk involved in the procedure in question.

Although Jewish Law forbids self-endangerment,[1] and all medical procedures involve some risk, the Torah grants permission to assume such risk in order to attempt to cure a medical problem.[2] However, the question is more complicated when it involves a particularly risky procedure on a very ill or terminal patient, which may shorten his or her life if it is unsuccessful. The primary source for the discussion of this issue is the biblical story of the four *metzora'im*, who risked their lives to find food because they would certainly die without it.[3] This implies that one may forfeit short-term survival (*chayei sha'ah*) if there is a hope for a normal lifespan (*chayei olam*).[4] (For definitions of terminal/short-term and long-term lifespan, see Chapter 4A.)

Indeed, authorities in Jewish Law generally conclude that if a seriously ill, terminal patient has the option to undergo a procedure or treatment that may extend their life beyond the terminal period, even though the procedure is risky and may in fact shorten their life substantially if it is unsuccessful, it is permitted (but not obligatory) to attempt that intervention, as long as the patient consents.[5] According to some, this is true even if the procedure is done not to extend the patient's life, but only to relieve intense pain, even if the patient is not dangerously ill.[6]

However, there must be acceptable likelihood that the given intervention will be successful.[7] Furthermore, there must be sufficient certainty amongst the medical staff of the need for the intervention.[8] (For discussion of the propriety of entering low-, moderate-, and high-risk situations in the pursuit of healing others, see the section entitled "Living Donors" in Chapter 5C on organ donation.[9])

SUMMARY

A terminally ill patient is not obligated to, but may choose to attempt risky interventions intended to cure and prolong his or her life, even if there is a chance that these interventions may shorten their life (as long as it is certain that the suggested intervention can indeed be helpful to this particular patient). If most experts agree that in the majority of cases the given intervention would certainly be successful, then it must be attempted. However, if the intervention is not even intended to be curative, but just to reduce the immediate danger of the patient, it should not be attempted if the intervention itself may hasten death (unless it can significantly reduce the patient's pain).

EXPERIMENTAL AND ALTERNATIVE MEDICINE

A dangerously ill individual is obligated to pursue accepted, scientifically tested medical treatment and not simply rely on God to miraculously heal him or her.[10] This obligation includes engaging in safe therapeutic procedures of known efficacy (*refuah bedukah*).[11] Indeed, one of the reasons that the authorities in Jewish Law cited above permit a terminal patient to engage in dangerous therapy is that the patient is pursuing standard, accepted medicine.[12] Nevertheless, authorities in Jewish Law conclude that one is permitted (but not obligated) to:

* Engage in *experimental treatment* that may endanger their life, provided that the odds that it will be beneficial to that patient are better than the odds that it will be detrimental.[13]
* If there is no remaining hope in any known medical therapies, one may try *alternative, non-conventional treatments* (assuming there is no violation of Jewish Law entailed in utilizing them) in place of or as a supplement to conventional therapies.[14] However, one may also legitimately refuse therapy of unproven value.[15]

ENDNOTES

1. Deut. 4:15 warns us to be "exceedingly watchful with regard to your lives," and the Talmud thus rules that a person should never stand in a place of danger (*Shabbat* 32a; *Ta'anit* 20b); see also *Shulchan Arukh*, YD 116.

2. Ramban, *Torat Ha-Adam, Inyan Ha-Sakanah* (*Kitvei Ha-Ramban*, Chavel edition, vol. 2, 41); Ran, *Sanhedrin* 84b. See also *Tur*, YD 336; *Tzitz Eliezer* 4:13(1–3); *Nishmat Avraham*, YD 155(2:5) (p. 88 in 3rd ed.). Furthermore, even risky procedures performed on people who are not dangerously ill are permitted, invoking the principle that "God protects the simple" (*Nishmat Avraham*, YD 155(2:5) (87 in 3rd ed.).

3. II Kings 7:1–20.

4. Ibid., 7:3–4; *Avodah Zarah* 27b; *Shulchan Arukh*, YD 155:1; *Shevut Yaakov* 3:75; *Teshuvot Minchat Asher* 1:115; *Chokhmat Adam, Binat Adam* 73 (93). See discussion in Bleich, *Bioethical Dilemmas* (1998), vol. 2, 246–50. Furthermore, R. Eliyashiv ruled that one should even attempt a risky procedure on a child who is imminently dying, and the risky procedure can only prolong their life for another month (*Shiurei Torah Le-Rofim* 2, 131).

5. *Shulchan Arukh*, YD 155:1; *Ketuvot* 8a; *Iggerot Moshe*, YD 3:36, *Tzitz Eliezer* 4:13 (5–8) and 10:25(17) and many more sources cited by *Encyclopedia Hilkhatit Refu'it*, vol. 5, 746, n. 51; *Nishmat Avraham*, YD 155(2) (81–90 in 3rd ed.) and YD 28:18(2) (14 in 3rd ed.). However, if the patient is not considered to have a terminal illness and a given procedure carries a substantial risk of killing him, such a procedure would be forbidden (*Tzitz Eliezer* 4:13 [8]). If a dying patient has an option to either pursue partial treatment that will prevent his or her death, but will require further repeated interventions and a life of suffering, or to attempt one very risky major surgery which can remedy the entire situation without requiring any more interventions, the one major surgery should be preferred over the multiple minor interventions (*Minchat Yitzchak, Likkutei Teshuvot*, 120).

6. *Iggerot Moshe*, CM 2:73(9); *Nishmat Avraham*, YD 28:18(2) (p. 14 in 3rd ed.). See also *Encyclopedia Hilkhatit Refu'it*, vol. 5, 750. See also comment at the very end of *Tzitz Eliezer* 10:25(17) and discussion in *Refuah Ke-Halakhah*, 436–7.

7. Some allow this risk only if the chances of success are at least 50% (*Tzitz Eliezer* 10:25[5:5]). Others only require the success rate to be at least 30% (R. Elyashiv, cited in *Encyclopedia Hilkhatit Refu'it*, vol. 5, 747, n. 54, and in *Shiurei Torah Le-Rofim* 3, 128 and 152, although R. Zilberstein notes there that if the patient wants to take these risks to possibly save his or her life, they may do so, since they are already terminal). Still others rule that as long as there is even a slim chance of prolonging life, it is permissible (*Iggerot Moshe*, YD 2:58, 3:36). R. Feinstein allows this only if the treatment is for the patient's benefit and is curative, not when the treatment will merely postpone the danger and death. *Teshuvot Ve-Hanhagot* (2:739, 3:362) requires only a 5% chance in this case, although the patient cannot be compelled; if one refuses the intervention,

we respect that option. Some authorities also require Rabbinic approval before initiating any dangerous therapy (*Achiezer*, 2:16[5]). See also Bleich, *Bioethical Dilemmas*, vol. 2, 250–8, and *Nishmat Avraham*, YD, p. 83, who write that there must be more than a 20–25% chance.

8. The permission to put oneself in danger to undergo a procedure is only given if the physicians have certainty about the need for the surgery and that the patient will certainly die without it. Some authorities maintain that if it is uncertain if there is a need for the procedure and the patient may survive without it, and there is a chance that the patient will die as a result of the surgery, it is forbidden for patients to put themselves into such danger (*Binyan Av* 1, 50:1; *Encyclopedia Hilkhatit Refu'it*, vol. 5, 749).

If a patient will die from his or her disease, but physicians are divided about the benefit of a given dangerous procedure, the patient may still choose to have it done, although others require a majority of medical opinion and Rabbinic approval (*Encyclopedia Hilkhatit Refu'it*, vol. 5, 751).

9. See also Tatz, *Dangerous Disease and Dangerous Therapy*, 45–54. On the parameters of the principle of "*shomer peta'im Hashem*" and "*dashu bah rabbim*,"

see *Encyclopedia Hilkhatit Refu'it*, vol. 5, 762–7; Bleich, *Bioethical Dilemmas*, vol. 2, 239–46.

10. See the detailed discussion in *Teshuvot Minchat Asher* 1:120(1).

11. *Mor U-Ketziah*, OC 328. R. Feinstein rules that a terminal patient should attempt a therapy of even doubtful efficacy if it is safe (*Iggrerot Moshe*, CM 2:74).

12. *Tzitz Eliezer* 10:25(17). The other reason that it is permitted is because even without the treatment, the patient is going to die in any case.

13. *Nishmat Avraham*, YD 28:18(2) (p. 14 in 3rd ed.). Regarding participating in a medical trial in which one may receive a placebo, *Nishmat Avraham* (p. 16) rules that it is permitted as long as the patient consents and will also receive all standard treatments for his illness, even if he is chosen to receive a placebo. See also Bleich, *Judaism and Healing*, 150.

14. *Teshuvot Minchat Asher* 1:120(2). "Alternative therapies" are generally defined as medicine that has not undergone adequate testing or government approval, or that does not function via normal, natural, discernable means.

15. Bleich, *Judaism and Healing*, 151.

B.   MAKING DECISIONS ON BEHALF OF
   AN INCAPACITATED PATIENT

While incredible advances in medical technology often help save lives, these same medical advances also frequently give rise to challenging ethical dilemmas. This is especially true when people face the prospect of making irreversible life and death decisions on behalf of patients, decisions that can lead to tremendous uncertainty, guilt, and conflict both for the patient's family and the healthcare providers.[1] Exacerbating the challenge, data shows that most people reach the end of their lives cognitively impaired, and thus unable to make their own decisions about their care. Most people have not had advance planning conversations with their family or medical providers.[2] Indeed, one of the most challenging ethical issues that arise in hospitals is determining the appropriate care for a patient who lacks the capacity to participate in the decision-making process regarding their own medical care.[3]

In contemporary bioethics, there are generally two standards for making decisions on behalf of such patients (otherwise known as "surrogate decision-making"). One is known as "Substituted Judgment." Following this approach, the goal is to derive the correct course of action from advance healthcare directives or from others who know the patient and are familiar with the patient's values or preferences and have insight about what the patient would have said or thought if he or she had capacity and could participate in the decision-making at hand. The aim is to reasonably infer from past statements or actions what the patient would choose for him or herself if he or she could do so.[4] The other standard is referred to as the "Best Interest Standard." With this approach, there is an attempt to decide for patients what is in their best interest, promoting their welfare and making choices that a reasonable person in a similar circumstance would be likely to choose.

Contemporary bioethicists generally favor substituted judgment over the best interest standard if it is practically plausible to know what the patient would indeed want.[5]

In Jewish Law, precedent can be found for both approaches,[6] but Rabbinic authorities generally encourage substituted judgment by the patient's family members, who should attempt to determine what the patient's wishes would be. This is because people normally rely on the opinion of close relatives,[7] who are assumed to be most intimately aware of the patient's overall situation[8] and able to determine what the patient would have wanted if they were able to speak for themselves.[9] However, the family of the patient has no independent status per se in making medical decisions for a patient.[10] The final decision must involve detailed investigation and full consultation between medical staff, the family, and experienced and knowledgeable rabbis to ensure that Jewish Law is being followed appropriately.[11]

When a family is unable to determine what the patient would have wanted, they may assume that the patient would not want pain to be prolonged when it is of such intensity that most people would not want it, if the patient is at the end of life and the treatment being offered will merely prolong a painful life with additional suffering.[12] On the other hand, if there is a clearly indicated way to save the patient's life that does not involve excessive pain or risk, the procedure is obligatory, even if the patient may not want it.[13] It thus seems that in Jewish Law, just as in much of contemporary bioethics, if substituted judgment cannot be obtained, we turn to the best interest standard.

Of course, if a patient has previously expressed his or her personal desires, it makes the process much easier. These instructions should be followed as long as they do not violate Jewish Law and there is no reason to think that the patient's decision may have changed. An Advance Directive can be very helpful in this regard (see Chapter 4A).[14]

ENDNOTES

1. See discussion in Kenneth R. Mitchell and Herbert Anderson, *All Our Losses, All Our Griefs: Resources for Pastoral Care* (Westminster John Knox Press, 1983), 76.

2. A. Gawande, "Quantity and Quality of Life," *JAMA* 315:3 (Jan. 2016), 267.

3. For discussion of these issues, see Beauchamp and Childress (eds.), *Principles of Biomedical Ethics*, 188; Benjamin Freedman, *Duty and Healing: Foundations of a Jewish Bioethic* (Routledge, 1999), 68; R.J. Ifrah, "The Living Will," *Journal of Halacha and Contemporary Society* 24 (1992), 121.

4. Many studies have shown that surrogates often mistakenly believe that they know what their family member would have wanted. Nevertheless, the studies also show that the family members do know more often than the physician does. See A.R. Jonsen, M. Siegler, W.J. Winslade, "Patient Preferences," in *Clinical Ethics: A Practical Approach to Ethical Decisions in Clinical Medicine* (McGraw-Hill, 2010), chap. 2.

5. Ibid; Beauchamp and Childress, *Principles of Biomedical Ethics*, 227 (see also 190–3).

6. For example, an argument can be made in favor of the best interest standard based on *Gittin* 52a, which rules that a legal guardian acting on behalf of orphans is expected to evaluate what is best for them, and *Bava Batra* 8a, which rules that since it is in an orphan's best spiritual interest, one can draw upon the orphan's estate to support charity funds. On the other hand, the principle of substituted judgment can be supported by *Ketuvot* 48a (based on the explanation of the *Kesef Mishneh, Hilkhot Nachalot* 11:11), which rules that if a man becomes insane, the court can use his property to support his wife and children, and even to give to charity, because it is assumed that in his right mind, the husband would have been in favor of contributing as a meritorious deed (even if it is not in his best interest to do so, due to his poor financial situation). These sources were suggested by R. Mordechai Torzcyner and discussed in his presentation on this topic, http://www.yutorah.org/lectures/lecture.cfm/752500/Rabbi_Mordechai_Torczyner/Medical_Halachah:_Acting_on_behalf_of_an_incapacitated_patient.

7. *Iggerot Moshe*, CM 2:74 (2, 5). R. Feinstein writes that we can presume that the family's decision will match the patient's wishes, and the fact that people rely on their family members tacitly empowers family members as de facto proxies.

8. R. Zalman Nechemia Goldberg, *Jewish Medical Ethics*, vol. 2, 346, based on R. David Zvi Hoffman's *Melamed Le-Ho'il* 2:104. R. Z.N. Goldberg argues that a patient's family does not have an inherent right to decide for a patient what their treatment should be, and relying on them alone can be dangerous because: (1) They are not permitted to choose to violate Jewish law, and (2) There are circumstances in which the family may prefer the patient's death. Nevertheless, he argues, we should listen to the family's opinion because they are most likely to know the patient's general situation better than others (*Assia* 16:3–5 [63–64] 5759:8).

9. R. Shlomo Zalman Auerbach, *Shulchan*

Shlomo, Erkhei Refuah, vol. 1, 75; *Assia* 3 (5743), 325 (republished in *Brakha Le-Avraham*, 135). R. Feinstein (*Iggerot Moshe*, CM 2:74) also writes that the family's authority is based on the fact that they care about the patient's best interest, which implies an element of the best interest standard when the family is unaware of the patient's specific desires. On the other hand, R. Hershel Schachter argues, based on *Melamed Le-Ho'il* 2:104, that when the patient's wishes are unknown, the opinion of family members of the patient is meaningless according to Torah Law. Instead, one should rely on the recommendation of the doctors, as long as they do not violate Halakhah (R. Schachter, "*Eilav Hu Nosei et Nafsho*," in *Beit Yitzchak* (Yeshiva University, 1985–1986), 104. R. Asher Weiss (*Teshuvot Minchat Asher* 1:116[3]) similarly argues that according to the reasoning that the family is presumed to be able to determine what the patient would have wanted, when the family is unable to determine what the patient would want, their suggestion regarding the patient's treatment is of no import. However, according to R. Feinstein's other reasoning (mentioned above) – that the family can make decisions for the patient since the patient would generally want what their family suggests – we can rely on the family even if they do not know what the patient would have wanted.

10. R. Zalman Nechemia Goldberg, *Jewish Medical Ethics*, vol. 2, 346. Furthermore, a family has no right to ask the doctors to act contrary to Halakhah in their treat-ment of a Jewish patient; in some cases, the family has an interest in the patient's demise, which is neither "best interest" nor appropriate "substituted judgment." See also *Nishmat Avraham*, YD 28:18(2) (15 in 3rd ed.), who writes that parents may subject a child to painful treatment as long as the child benefits from it and it is not too painful, but if it causes excessive pain and there is no direct benefit to the child, it is forbidden. However, according to Halakhah, parents do not own their children and thus may not subject a child to experimental research procedures, for example, even if medical personnel are already drawing blood and simply want to take a little bit more for research purposes (see also *Melamed Le-Ho'il* 2:104).

11. Zalman Nechemia Goldberg, *Jewish Medical Ethics*, vol. 2, 346; *Iggerot Moshe*, CM 2:74(2, 5).

12. *Nishmat Avraham*, YD 339(1) (p. 498, col. 2 in 3rd ed.), with clarifications from Prof. Abraham in a personal communication (Summer 2015); *Iggerot Moshe*, CM 2:74(2); A. Tatz, *Dangerous Disease and Dangerous Therapy in Jewish Medical Ethics* (Targum, 2010), 110.

13. *Iggerot Moshe*, CM 2:74(5); *Mor U-Ketzia*, OC 328.

14. *Nishmat Avraham*, YD 339:4 (2:10) (511 in 3rd ed.). Prof. Abraham recommends that a person should ideally appoint a proxy in the family who will consult with the family's rabbi and appoint an authority in Jewish Law who should be consulted if such questions arise.

C. PEDIATRICS:
Jewish Law and Determining a Child's Consent and Treatment

While many of the principles addressed throughout this book are intended to be applied as widely as possible, there are frequently different principles and approaches when it comes to the treatment of children. Proper treatment of children is a very complex and nuanced matter, which often differs based on the various specific ages and stages of development, and how severely ill a particular child is. I will not delve fully into all of the complexities of this issue here, but will instead provide some of the basic key principles that are necessary to be aware of, with many citations and references in the notes for those desirous of further study on this matter.

CONSENT

Making decisions on behalf of a minor is more complex than doing so for an incapacitated adult. In American Law, substituted judgment is usually applied for adults who are unable to make their wishes known, meaning that clinicians rely on a surrogate of the patient, who can represent the patient's voice and respond as the patient would if he or she could speak for themselves (see previous chapter).[1] However, in the case of children, the "best interest standard" is usually applied. This means that instead of someone with authority to make decisions for the child attempting to speak for what the child would want, they should rather try to determine what is in the child's best interests.[2] Typically, this authority is a parent, assuming that they are competent and do not have conflicts of interest.[3] However, the "harm principle" must also be taken into consideration, meaning that if a decision-maker makes choices that are deemed to be harmful to the child, their decision-making power is revoked.[4]

When it comes to Jewish Law and the issue of whether or not a minor child who is alert can play any role in decision-making about his or her care, many Rabbinic authorities rule that since Jewish Law does not attribute full responsibility or decision-making status of any kind for a minor until after age 12 for a girl and age 13 for a boy,[5] we should not take a child's wishes into account at all before that age.[6] Other Rabbinic authorities, and many secular ethicists, don't completely disregard a minor's preferences or responses regarding treatment or treatment options, but do partially take them into account in certain situations, especially once minors have reached an age at which they can be considered somewhat competent.[7] Even though Jewish Law grants certain responsibilities to a child once they have become Bar or Bat Mitzvah, such a child is still usually not capable of making very significant and complex decisions on their own (they are likely still categorized as a "*peti*," often translated as "naïve" or "gullible" – see Chapter 1D on mental illness for further discussion).[8] Therefore, as a child ages and matures, he or she can gradually be given more and more decision-making responsibilities and autonomy based on that particular child and the situation.

While both Jewish Law and American Law recognize the "best interest standard,"[9] there are differences regarding who can make that decision for the child. Within the American legal context, many ethicists debate who is best positioned to make such decisions (sometimes it may be the doctor, other times the parents, at still other times an independent third party, etc.), while Jewish Law generally dictates that it must be the rabbi – likely in consultation with the parents – because the "best interest" is what will benefit the child from a religious point of view. Indeed, Jewish Law assumes not only that a child cannot decide for him or herself, but also that the parents' duty is simply to carry out the mandates of Jewish Law. For this reason, some rabbis have ruled that if Jewish Law deems a given surgery to be in the best interests of a child, the parents must consent to the procedure.[10]

Another important point that distinguishes Jewish Law from American legal perspectives is that even those rabbis who grant greater decision-making authority to the parents do not do so because the parents are legal guardians of the child; rather it is as a result of the principle that one may do something for someone that is ultimately in the other person's best interest, even if that individual is not able to consent to it.[11] Parents may thus decide what is in the best interest of the child.[12] This sometimes includes compelling a minor to undergo a procedure that is determined to be in the child's best interest, even without the child's assent.[13]

There are times when we might go beyond determining only what is in the children's best interest and seek to determine what they would in fact desire if they were competent to decide (the principle of "substituted judgment").[14] However, Jewish Law usually does not base substituted judgment on what that *individual* would want, but the presumed desire of *humankind* in general. This approach presents an additional layer of complexity, since it is usually not clear if an individual would be willing to undergo the risks involved in a given procedure.[15]

FORCING A MINOR TO DONATE TISSUE OR ORGANS

Donations of blood, bone marrow, kidneys, etc., are not medically beneficial for the donor (and may even be dangerous for him or her), but they are very positive altruistic deeds. However, using the "best interest standard," one could argue that a minor may be encouraged to donate because saving another person's life is considered one of the highest religious good deeds.[16] Thus, a parent is acquiring religious merit on the child's behalf, which would be permitted even without consent. Indeed, even applying "substituted judgment," some rule that a minor can donate bone marrow to a family member,[17] and in certain cases even undergo a more dangerous procedure, such as a kidney donation.[18] Some rabbis rule that helping others in such a manner may be included in the parents' obligation to educate their children to do the right thing.[19] Especially when it involves an action that we can assume most adults would also consent to, in such a situation we may be able to accept a minor's consent (assuming that they understand what they are doing).[20]

However, many authorities challenge the very possibility of allowing a minor to endure any sort of a wound in order to make a donation. Even though the command of "do not stand idly by" may obligate a person to donate, minors are not obligated to fulfill any commandments,[21] and thus cannot be compelled to endure a wound to make such a donation. Furthermore, since consent is so limited by Jewish Law,[22] their donations should not be compelled.[23]

It is important to note that although there are a range of opinions on this issue, since blood and bone marrow donations carry minimal risk to the donor, Jewish Law is much more likely to mandate such donations if they are needed to help people in life-threatening situations.[24] Kidney donation, however, being medically more dangerous for the donor, would likely not be regarded as obligatory.[25] (See further discussion of this issue in Chapter 5C.)

The conclusion of most authorities is that a minor can be used as a donor to save a family member's life if the minor is able to understand what he or she is doing and assents to it.[26] If children do not yet fully understand what they are doing, but they are the only fitting match for a relative in life-threatening danger, there is uncertainty if they may be compelled. The matter must therefore be dealt with by an expert in Jewish Law on a case-by-case basis.[27]

TREATMENT OF VERY ILL MINORS

Similar to Rabbinic rulings for a terminally ill adult, most Rabbinic authorities do not require aggressive interventions or surgeries to extend the life of a baby who is born extremely ill with minimal chances of survival, but they do require routine biological maintenance, such as nutrition and pain relief medications.[28] Likewise, it is forbidden to do anything to hasten the death of such a baby. However, most Rabbinic authorities do not require artificially prolonging a baby's life of suffering, and thus permit signing a DNR (Do Not Resuscitate) order for him or her (pursuant to the prerequisites stipulated in Chapter 4B).[29] Regarding a baby who is born very prematurely – when the numerous interventions needed to sustain his or her life carry severe side effects, such as blindness and permanent brain damage – there is a difference of opinion amongst Rabbinic authorities as to whether aggressive interventions are required (even against the will of the parents) or if it is preferable to passively allow such a baby to die.[30] Qualified guidance should thus be sought on a case-by-case basis. It should be pointed out that I have found in my clinical experience that babies and children can sometimes show incredible resilience and the ability to recover despite horrible odds. One should thus occasionally consider giving them more time and possibilities to recover than might be the norm in other situations.

ENDNOTES

1. D. Micah Hester, "Ethical Issues in Pediatrics," in *Guidance for Healthcare Ethics Committees* (Cambridge Press, 2012), 116. See chap. 2B, where we discuss the different options in general surrogate decision-making.

2. Ibid., Lew Hester Swota, "When Rights Just Won't Do," *Perspectives in Biology and Medicine* 58(3) (Summer 2015), 23.

3. D. Diekema, "Parental Refusals of Medical Treatment: The Harm Principle as Threshold for State Intervention," *Theoretical Medicine* 25 (2004), 244, notes a number of reasons that parents are generally selected as surrogates for their children: (1) Most parents care about their children and understand their unique needs better than others, so they are most likely to make decisions that are beneficial to the child. (2) Parents can weigh competing interests within the family better than outsiders. (3) Parents should be allowed to raise their children according to their own standards and values. (4) In order for a family to flourish, it needs space and freedom from intrusion by others. However, when parents act contrary to the child's best interests, the state may intervene.

4. Hester, "Ethical Issues in Pediatrics," 119. In addition to considering "what is best for the child," we must keep in mind "what decisions exceed parental decision-making authority." We take both into account: parental authority to decide what is in the child's best interest, but limit that authority by ensuring that no harm is being caused to the child setting a threshold below which we cannot allow parents to go. Above that we can try to persuade, but must allow the parents freedom.

5. *Avot* 5:21; Rambam, *Hilkhot Ishut* 2:1, 10; *Hilkhot Shevitat Asor* 2:11; *Shulchan Arukh*, OC 616:2; EH 155:12, 167:3; CM 35:1. This age is derived from the oral tradition; see Rashi and Bartenura, *Avot* 5:21; *Teshuvot Ha-Rosh* 16:1; *Teshuvot Maharil* 51. See also *Nishmat Avraham* CM 427:10 (264–5 in 3rd ed.). It should be noted that whereas the business dealings of a child are generally considered null and void, from age 6 on, many of a minor's transactions become binding if he knows what he is doing (Rambam, *Hilkhot Mekhirah* 29:1, 6). From ages 6–10, we need to know that the minor understands what he is doing; after age 10, we can assume that he knows what he is doing and many of his transactions are considered valid (*Shulchan Arukh*, CM 235:1). Interestingly, some studies have shown that it is around the age of 12 or 13 that children begin to develop increased intellectual ability and volition to give informed, voluntary, and rational consent. See Tara Kuther, "Medical Decision-Making and Minors: Issues of Consent and Assent," *Adolescence* (Summer 2003), 350–1.

6. R. Avigdor Nevenzahl, *Assia* 53–54, 208, writes that a minor's consent is completely invalid. See also R. Shneur Zusha Reiss, *Choveret Ha-Me'or*, vol. 240, 15–16; *Ma'aseh Choshev* 4:26.

7. R. Shlomo Zalman Auerbach permitted bone marrow transplants from a minor as long as he or she gave consent and was mature enough to understand (*Nishmat Avraham* CM 243:1, [64 in 3rd ed.]). See R. J.D. Bleich, "May Tissue Donations Be Compelled?," in *Contemporary Halakhic*

Problems IV (Ktav Publishing, 1995), n. 76, for challenges to this view.

R. Y. Zilberstein discusses the case of a woman who wanted an orthodontist to fix her son's teeth for cosmetic reasons. The procedure required removing permanent, healthy teeth, and the child strongly objected, but he wanted to honor his parents. R. Zilberstein ruled that as long as the child had reached the age of being able to be educated to perform *mitzvot* and was mature enough to have basic understanding, the child was not obligated to undergo the surgery and the orthodontist should not follow the mother's instructions against the patient's will (*Halakha U-Refuah*, vol. 4, 156). Secular ethicists also frequently argue that as children mature, they become more accountable for their decisions and should have more authority in their decision-making; see Hester, "Ethical Issues in Pediatrics," 119.

Many bioethicists argue that as minors age, they develop more of a need for an independent relationship with physicians, and they can have more input about medical decisions as they gradually become the primary guardians of their personal health. Therefore, instead of seeking their *consent* while they are still a minor, as they age, they can be turned to for *assent*, as a means of involving them in treatment decisions. Setting a lower standard of competence than full "informed consent," "assent" does not require the depth of understanding or demonstration of reasoning ability that informed consent does. See Kuther, "Medical Decision-Making and Minors," 350–1.

Some have argued that patients should participate in their medical decision-making commensurate with their development, and their parents or other surrogates can provide informed *permission*. Thus, in cases involving medical interventions for infants and young children, physicians should seek "the informed permission of the parents," and when working with older children, they should seek not their consent, but the "assent of the patient as well as the informed permission of the parents" (Commission on Bioethics, "Informed Consent, Parental Permission, and Assent in Pediatric Practice," *Pediatrics* 95(2) (Feb. 1995), 316.

8. See also brief discussion of child's decision-making capacity in *Nishmat Avraham* CM 35:10(1) (30 in 3rd ed.).

9. R. Bleich, "May Tissue Donations Be Compelled?," 296. R. Bleich bases this on the ruling that guardians are to be appointed for mentally incompetent persons to provide for their needs (Rambam, *Hilkhot Nachalot* 10:4, 8, based on *Gittin* 52b and *Bava Batra* 8a), and that if they have sufficient assets, the guardian may distribute charity on behalf of an orphaned minor so that the minor will acquire a "good name" (*Shulchan Arukh*, CM 290:15).

10. R. David Zvi Hoffman, *Melamed Le-Ho'il* 2, YD 104, was asked if a doctor may perform a curative operation (or one whose benefits may be doubtful but without which the child would certainly die) on a minor if the parents do not want it. Based on *Shevut Yaakov* 3:75, who writes that such a possibly lifesaving surgery is obligatory even though it is dangerous, R. Hoffman rules that as long as most doctors agree with the necessity of the surgery, the doctors are obligated to carry it out regardless of the parents' opposition, and if they do not they could be considered complicit in the death of the child.

Another example of acting in the child's best interest is found in a ruling of R. Zilberstein (*Halakhah U-Refuah*, vol. 4, 156) responding to a query as to whether a child can be forced to undergo diagnostic tests that he does not want to undergo (specifically for digestive problems). R. Zilberstein rules that since it is important to be healthy, and this often requires painful procedures, and since such procedures are being done for the benefit of the child, the parents may compel the child to undergo them even if he does not want to. (For this reason, R. Zilberstein states that it could also be argued that if the procedure in the teeth-fixing case cited in n. 7 above will help the child in the long run, e.g., to find a suitable marriage partner, the minor could in fact be compelled to undergo the procedure, since he would appreciate it later in life.)

11. *Ma'aseh Choshev* 4:26. See also Rambam, *Hilkhot Mekhirah* 29:11. R. Moshe Hershler, *Halakhah U-Refuah*, vol. 2, 126, writes that since a mentally incompetent donor would derive no benefit from his or her organ or tissue donation and it is dangerous, it is not in his or her best interest. R. Bleich notes ("May Tissue Donations Be Compelled?," 297) that if the recipient is a family member who can help care for him or her, the halakhic ruling might be different.

12. *Iggerot Moshe*, CM 2:74(5) rules that parents or other family members may decide for a child (or an adult who is unable to decide on his own) because most people rely on their parents or family, whom we can assume want what is best for the patient. If there is no family, one should rely on a *beit din* (religious court). See also R. S.Z. Auerbach, *Minchat Shlomo* 2:82(1) fn. Of course, according to Jewish Law, the family has a say only when they follow the Torah and their desire is indeed only for the benefit of the patient.

R. Zilberstein (*Shiurei Torah La-Rofim*, vol. 3, 372) quotes R. Elyashiv as arguing that when evaluating what is in the child's best interest considering the amount of pain involved in a given procedure, we should take into account the fact that children may suffer somewhat less than adults do, since they are less cognizant of the implications of their pain and have less memory of past pain. This consideration is coupled with R. Elyashiv's assumption that prolonging a child's life is usually for his benefit. See

also *Refuah Ke-Halakhah*, 435.

13. *Lev Avraham* 70:33, quoting *Iggerot Moshe*, CM 2:74, s.v. *u-ve-em ha-choleh*;" *Tzitz Eliezer* as quoted in *Nishmat Avraham*, CM 427:4 (7), (264–5 in 3rd ed.) and R. Shlomo Zalman Auerbach, who all rule that we can assume that a child will rely on his parents or family to decide what is best for him since they know what the child would want and are concerned for his benefit, and if there is no family available, the religious court may decide for them. If the question relates to using a minor to conduct human research, if it carries any risks and will not directly benefit the child, it is forbidden regardless of the child's consent (*Nishmat Avraham*, YD 155).

14. Some authorities would support this process, while others would not. R. Bleich, "May Tissue Donations Be Compelled?," quotes Tosafot, *Bava Metzia* 22a, who argue that we need explicit consent to eat others' food without their knowledge, even if it is certain that one would be able to achieve such consent, whereas *Ketzot Ha-Choshen* 358:1 disagrees, ruling that children can be supported by an incompetent father, even if they are past the age of support, because we can assume that he would consent if he were capable.

15. R. Bleich, "May Tissue Donations Be Compelled?," 298.

16. See, for example, *Sanhedrin* 37a, which states that saving one life is like saving an entire world, as well as biblical commandments such as "you shall return it to him" (Deut. 22:2) and "you shall not stand idly by" (Lev. 19:16). *Sanhedrin* 73a even requires spending money to help others in need.

17. R. Naftali Bar-Ilan (*Sefer Assia*, vol. 9, 364–66) rules that a child can be compelled to donate bone marrow for a family member based on the ruling of the *Shulchan Arukh*, CM 235:1, that a

guardian can take from an orphan's funds to give charity in order to give the orphan a good name and prevent disgrace. R. Bar-Ilan rules that a child should similarly be compelled to donate, even to non-relatives, if he or she is the only match, since there would be no worse disgrace than not donating in such a situation. R. Shlomo Zalman Auerbach rules that a child may be used as a bone marrow donor if he or she is old enough to comprehend and assents to the procedure, but if this child is not old enough to comprehend, R. Auerbach was not certain if he or she could be compelled to be a donor (*Nishmat Avraham* CM 243:18(1), 64 in 3rd ed.).

18. R. Hershler, *Halakhah U-Refuah*, vol. 2, 127, and R. Moshe Meiselman, ibid., 121. R. Hershler argues that a guardian must make decisions only in accordance with the best interests of the minor. He cannot agree on the minor's behalf to give away an organ, regardless of the minor's consent or lack thereof, since a minor's consent is invalid. This is especially true when the procedure causes damage to the minor. While an adult may put him or herself in this danger because of the commandment to save another's life, a minor is not obligated in the commandments. However, in a case in which a family member needs an organ (such as a kidney) and a minor is the only match, and he or she wants to donate it (despite the invalidity of a minor's consent), we can assume that the minor is indeed able to consent to such a case.

19. R. Naftali Bar-Ilan (*Sefer Assia*, vol. 9, 361) rules that since an adult may be forced to donate bone marrow to save a life, we can argue that just as a parent is obligated to educate a child to perform commandments that involve pain, such as fasting, a parent is obligated to teach a child to donate bone marrow, which can save a life.

20. Ibid., 362–3. R. Bar-Ilan rules that a parent should try to convince the child to do this, but should not compel him or her (although perhaps a religious court can force the child). He goes on to write that although a minor's consent is invalid, that is only in a case in which we can assume that an adult would not have consented. When we can assume that an adult would also agree, a child's assent is binding according to Jewish Law, and a child can therefore certainly decide that he wants to help save someone's life. Furthermore, argues R. Bar-Ilan, this would be true not only to save a life, but in any case in which it is clear that the child understands what he or she is doing and an adult would make a similar decision. The child should then be permitted to behave accordingly, even if there is some element of danger involved.

21. *Arakhin* 22a.

22. *Pesachim* 50b, which states that minors lack the capacity for "forgiveness" (*lav bnei mechilah ninhu*).

23. R. Bleich, "May Tissue Donations Be Compelled?," 299–300. R. Zilberstein, *Halakhah U-Refuah*, vol. 4, 156, ruled in a case in which a 12-year-old needed a new kidney and his 11-year-old brother was a perfect match that even if the parents want the child to donate, he may not.

24. R. Moshe Meiselman, *Halakhah U-Refuah*, vol. 2, 118; *Shevet HaLevi* 5:119; R. Bleich, "May Tissue Donations Be Compelled?," 285.

25. R. Bleich, ibid., 315.

26. *Lev Avraham* 70:26, quoting R. Shlomo Zalman Auerbach.

27. Ibid., R. Auerbach entertains the possibility that this could be permitted in certain situations, based on the principle that we can acquire merit for someone without their consent, but he does not issue a definitive permissive ruling. See also *Nishmat Avraham*, CM 243:1.

28. R. Shlomo Zalman Auerbach, quoted in *Ve-Aleihu Lo Yibol*, vol. 2, 136–7; R. Eliyahu Bakshi Doron, *Binyan Av* 5:67 (also published in *Sefer Binyan Av: Refuah Be-Halakhah*, 13). The case that both R. Auerbach and R. Doron's rulings refer to is a baby born with trisomy 13 or 18, which includes severe cardiac deformities, no skull bone, and only 50% odds of surviving for 3 months, and less than a 5% chance of surviving for a year.

29. Ibid. On the other hand, R. Zilberstein quotes his father-in-law, R. Elyashiv, as ruling that everything possible should be done to prolong the life of a baby (especially if interventions can enable the baby to live for a year or more), because life is of inestimable value. Even though we do not require a terminally ill patient who is suffering to do everything to prolong his or her life (particularly if the interventions are known to inflict much pain), we cannot assume that a baby is suffering unbearably and no longer wants to live (because we cannot know for sure what a baby would want and must therefore err on the side of prolonging life). Indeed, it is possible that babies suffer much less than adults (*Shiurei Torah Le-Rofim* 3:196, 370–9). R. Doron, however, argues in his responsum that it is apparent that these babies are in severe pain. Even if they are not, while R. Elyashiv assumed that a comatose patient is not suffering and must therefore have his life prolonged, R. Auerbach and many other authorities did not require prolonging such a life artificially (although they forbid actively hastening such a patient's death). A baby can be compared to a comatose patient for whom we are not required to aggressively prolong life artificially.

30. See the summary in *Encyclopedia Hilkhatit Refu'it*, vol. 3, 905. See also ibid., vol. 5, 151.

D.   PALLIATIVE CARE AND HOSPICE IN JEWISH LAW AND THOUGHT

I was once asked to visit the family of a patient who was dying, and who was unfortunately suffering very much. The family couldn't bear to witness the prolonged agony of their loved one's final hours, and they asked me for advice on how to cope with this situation. In the course of our conversation, the family members mentioned to me that hospice seemed like it would have been an excellent option, but, "Of course, we know it is forbidden by Jewish Law." I then asked if they had discussed this with their rabbi, and they said, "No, but we've heard that many times." I suggested that we call their rabbi right away to discuss this with him. We did so, and the rabbi indeed encouraged them to put the patient into hospice care. In hospice, her pain was fully controlled, and she was able to die a peaceful and dignified death at home a few days later.

Unfortunately, misconceptions like those of this family are common and cause much unnecessary pain and suffering.

Palliative Care and Hospice are two different fields of medicine that are presently undergoing substantial growth and change. Because these terms are commonly used but frequently misunderstood, I will define what they are, describe the differences between them, and discuss if and when they are permitted by Jewish Law, as well as note some issues concerning these interventions that Jewish patients should be aware of.

DEFINITIONS AND DIFFERENCES

Palliative care is interdisciplinary care that entails sophisticated co-ordination of medical and nursing experts along with social workers, chaplains, and other professionals. This team focuses on decreasing pain (both physical pain and emotional suffering) and improving quality of life in order to provide additional support to patients. Palliative care can be initiated at any point during the course of illness, including at the time of diagnosis, and for patients of any age who are living with any serious illness. In addition, palliative care may be provided along with all life-prolonging and disease-directed interventions. Thus, palliative care should not be viewed as only pertaining to end-of-life care, nor should it be assumed that palliative care implies that there is no hope for recovery or improvement in a patient's condition. Palliative care is most frequently utilized in hospitals, but it can also be part of the care for patients in other settings, such as clinics, cancer centers, and nursing homes, and increasingly as part of home care.

In contrast, hospice care is a service specifically designed for patients who have received a prognosis of survival of six months or less. Hospice focuses on the management of pain and symptoms associated with dying, and patients being cared for by hospice must generally forgo all major curative treatments. However, hospice patients may in most cases still receive routine maintenance care, such as nutrition and hydration, as well as antibiotics and other minor medical interventions. Hospice commonly takes place in a patient's home, but a hospice patient can also be in a setting such as a nursing home, residential hospice facility, or inpatient hospice unit in a hospital.[1]

PERMISSIBILITY OF PALLIATIVE CARE AND HOSPICE IN JEWISH LAW

According to Jewish Law, palliative care for a patient who is in pain or suffering is a permissible, and indeed laudatory medical intervention when appropriate. While the permissibility of hospice is more complex, it is also permitted in the appropriate context. (See Chapter 4B for a detailed description of circumstances in which Palliative Care and Hospice are permitted.) However, it should be ensured that an observant Jewish patient is treated by a hospice provider that is willing and prepared to accommodate specific religious needs. For an observant Jew on hospice, this entails that the hospice must be willing to provide the patient with nutrition and hydration (unless it will be detrimental; see Chapter 4B). Patients should also discuss with their rabbis and hospice providers, on a case-by-case basis, if a particular hospice is willing to treat medical complications that may arise during hospice care.

Furthermore, the patient must be one who truly qualifies for hospice (i.e., terminal), for whom there are no accepted curative interventions that can bring the patient out of the terminal status. If the patient's life can be prolonged, but only through unconventional procedures and/or with much pain and suffering, such aggressive intervention may not be required. One should attempt to determine if the patient wishes to undergo such treatment, and also seek rabbinic guidance. If a patient does not have a clear terminal diagnosis, even if a hospice would admit them, they may not be appropriate for hospice care under Jewish Law.

It is important to note that outside of the hospice context medical professionals sometimes use the term "comfort care" in a misleading or imprecise manner.[2] For example, when medical professionals discuss comfort care with patients or their surrogates, they may sometimes assume that this automatically means that the patients should be made DNR (see Chapter 4B) and have various interventions withheld, even without having an open discussion about these specific matters. While "comfort measures" are usually permissible, withholding potentially life-sustaining measures may not be, and one should make sure that the precise definitions and goals of care are made absolutely clear.

CONCLUSION

In the past, hospice care was treated with great suspicion in the observant Jewish community, perhaps based on the concern that it was akin to "giving up," or even intentionally shortening life. However, when done appropriately, hospice should not be viewed as stopping treatment, but rather as continuing to engage in fulfilling the commandment to heal – merely changing the emphasis from cure to comfort. In fact, it can even be seen as "aggressive" medical treatment, but it is specifically aggressive in terms of pain management and care for the whole person, rather than in emphasis on inappropriate interventions.

When it comes to palliative care, numerous studies have shown that it not only reduces symptom distress, but also significantly enhances quality of life and mood, and can even prolong life.[3] Patients receiving palliative care tend to live longer than patients with similar diagnoses who are not receiving palliative care or hospice.[4] Furthermore, studies have shown that concerning care for terminally ill patients, those who opt for a very aggressive approach to artificially prolonging life during the final week of a patient's life are three times more likely to suffer from major depression than those caring for patients who do not opt for such interventions.[5]

Adherents of Jewish Law will most frequently choose to do whatever is possible to prolong life, but there are limits. Knowing when hospice or palliative care is appropriate according to Jewish Law is delicate and requires much case-by-case expert rabbinic consultation. Thankfully, today there are many hospices willing to accommodate religious needs and considerations, and they can assure patients and families that they will not do anything to intentionally hasten death. For these reasons, hospice is becoming much more acceptable in the observant community.

ENDNOTES

1. These definitions are based primarily on the discussion in A. Kelley and R. Morrison, "Palliative Care for the Seriously Ill," *New England Journal of Medicine* 373(8) (2015), 747–55.

2. C. Blinderman and J. Billings, "Comfort Care for Patients Dying in the Hospital," *The New England Journal of Medicine* 373(26) (2015), 2550.

3. Kelley and Meier, "Palliative Care: A Shifting Paradigm," *New England Journal of Medicine* 363(8) (2010), 781–2; J.S. Temel, J.A. Greer, A. Muzikansky, et al., "Early Palliative Care for Patients with Metastatic Non-Small Cell Lung Cancer," *New England Journal of Medicine*, 363 (2010), 733–42. It should be noted that these studies refer to patients who received both palliative care and standard medical/curative interventions.

4. According to one study, patients receiving palliative care may live up to 25% longer. See discussion in Atul Gawande, *Being Mortal* (Metropolitan Books, 2014), 177–8. See also Kelley and Morrison, "Palliative Care for the Seriously Ill," 751; S.R. Connor, B. Pyenson, K. Fitch, C. Spence, K. Iwasaki, "Comparing Hospice and Non-Hospice Patient Survival Among Patients Who Die Within a Three-Year Window," *Journal of Pain Symptom Management* 33(3) (2007), 238–46; Temel, et al., "Early Palliative Care for Patients with Metastatic Non-Small Cell Lung Cancer," 733–42.

5. 2008 National Coping with Cancer project, cited by Atul Gawande, "Letting Go: What Should Medicine Do When it Can't Save Your Life?" *The New Yorker* (Aug. 2, 2010), http://www.newyorker.com/reporting/2010/08/02/100802fa_fact_gawande?printable=true#ixzz0vppUXmX7.

CHAPTER 3

Prayer

A.   IS PRAYER EVER FUTILE?
On the Efficacy of Prayer for the Terminally Ill

As I sat with the parents of a very sick young patient who was in emergency surgery, I knew that the patient's chances of survival were not good. "Can we say some prayers for her speedy recovery?" the patient's father inquired. "Of course!" I responded, and we proceeded to recite *Tehillim* (Psalms) and a *Mi She-Be-rach* (healing prayer). No sooner had we finished praying than I received a call letting me know that the parents were about to receive the worst news possible. We grieved together. When I went to visit them during *shiva* the following week, the father of the patient intently made his way through the throngs of people gathering to offer their condolences, pointed right at me, and cried, "Rabbi, your prayers didn't work!"

This incident brings up crucial questions. In addition to examining the efficacy and goals of prayer in general, we must specifically address the question of prayer in this situation. How should we approach prayer for an end-stage dying patient, for whom medical professionals predict no chance of recovery? It is precisely at these moments that families of patients frequently ask their rabbis to hold "*Tehillim* rallies" (gatherings to recite Psalms) or to recite other prayers in the hope that they will contribute to a miraculous recovery. Are such activities encouraged by classic Jewish texts and Rabbinic scholars? I will examine three recent leading Rabbinic authorities' approaches to this issue, along with some of the sources that support each of their opinions.

R. SHLOMO ZALMAN AUERBACH

R. Shlomo Zalman Auerbach takes a very cautious approach to this issue, ruling that prayer for an end-stage terminal patient who is suffering
and for whom there is no known medical cure is forbidden under the
prohibition against praying for a miracle.[1] This prohibition is based on
a *mishnah* (rabbinic teaching):

> To cry out over an occurrence that has passed is to utter a prayer
> in vain. [For example,] if a man's wife is already pregnant and
> he says, "May it be Your will that my wife give birth to a male,"
> this is a prayer in vain. Similarly, if one is coming along the road
> and he hears the sound of screaming in the city, if he says, "May
> it be Your will that this is not taking place within my house,"
> this is a prayer in vain.[2]

This ruling is codified by the *Shulchan Arukh* (code of Jewish Law).[3] R.
Auerbach cites the comment of R. Akiva Eiger there: "It is forbidden for
a person to pray that God perform a miracle that includes a deviation
from the natural order."[4]

Furthermore, R. Auerbach writes that it is best to avoid public
prayer gatherings for a person whose physicians have already given
up on curing. R. Auerbach was concerned that if people's prayers are
frequently not answered and the patients do not recover, this will lead
to a weakening of their faith. Thus, in such a case, one should not
specifically pray for the patient to be cured, but rather that "it should
be good for the ill person and their family," that the patient not suffer,
and that God mercifully do that which is right in God's eyes.[5]

R. Auerbach would counsel teachers to instruct their students not to
become accustomed to thinking that all prayers are answered the way
they want them to be. Rather, he would tell students to view themselves
as children standing before a parent; each child asks for something
different, and the compassionate parent makes their own accounting of
how to respond. A person should pray for his or her needs, not expect
an immediate answer, and rely on the fact that God – Who knows all
of the specific accountings of the world – will do the right thing.

R. Auerbach notes that even when circumstances are bleak, one
should never lose hope in God's capability of bringing a cure, should
God so choose. However, argues R. Auerbach, even as we maintain hope

and trust in God, we should not engage in numerous, persistent prayers for a miraculous cure, for the reasons mentioned above.[6]

This approach recognizes the pitfalls of false hope and seeks to protect us from the dangers of excessively irrational optimism. In my case, then, perhaps it would have been better not to have acquiesced to the father's request for healing prayers, but rather to have found some other way to support him in a compassionate but realistic manner.

THE STEIPLER GAON

R. Yaakov Yisrael Kanievsky, known as the Steipler Gaon (1899–1985, Israel), takes a different approach to this issue. He is quoted as arguing that it is a mistake to ever lose hope in the value of prayer, even for a desperately ill patient who has no chance of recovery according to the laws of nature.[7]

R. Kanievsky offers five reasons for this view. First, even if the patient is not cured, it is possible that his or her suffering will be slightly diminished as a result of our prayers. Second, the patient may live a little bit longer than they would have otherwise, and this also has tremendous value. A third reason is based on the Talmudic statement, "Even if a sword is placed on one's neck, one should not despair of God's mercy."[8] Even if it seems impossible, R. Kanievsky points out, there are numerous stories about people who have been miraculously cured, and we should thus never give up. Fourth, even if the prayers do not result in any change at all in the patient's condition, they are nevertheless a source of merit for him or her. All of those who prayed aroused Heavenly compassion through their prayers, which were uttered specifically because of this individual. These merits will stand by the individual in the World to Come and may also protect his or her offspring in the future, and they thus have incredible value.[9] Finally, argues R. Kanievsky, these prayers can bring recovery to other individuals and to the community as a whole.[10]

R. Kanievsky thus concludes that one should always engage in prayer, no matter how desperate the situation seems. In the End of Days, when all will be revealed, we will learn how every prayer uttered by each individual somehow did indeed bring about great goodness and salvation.

Perhaps we can suggest that this outlook is supported by the Talmud, which quotes R. Pinchas bar Chamah's teaching: "Whoever has a sick person in his house should go to a sage and have the sage plead for mercy on his behalf."[11] Based on this statement, Meiri writes, "A person should always be confident that if he prays properly, it will nullify the bad decree."[12]

Indeed, R. Kanievsky notes elsewhere that one is not only encouraged to pray in such circumstances, but this is the ideal time to pray. Although reciting daily prayers is a Rabbinic enactment according to most opinions, prayer during an *eit tzarah* (a time of distress) is obligated by the Torah.[13]

What about R. Auerbach's concern that this falls under the prohibition against praying for a miracle? R. Kanievsky quotes the Chazon Ish (his brother-in-law), who was asked this precise question. The Chazon Ish responded that he knew of a rabbi who was told by his physicians that he would live only a short while longer, but who then went on to live another thirty years. Sometimes, despite a dire prognosis, a person can indeed live much longer. We are thus not praying for a miracle, but simply that the doctors are wrong.[14]

This approach maintains the crucial value of hope, and affirms that there are often ways of finding optimism and courage even in the bleakest of situations. According to this worldview, it was certainly appropriate for me to engage in prayer with the patient's father. Although the father did not perceive that these prayers were answered, we are called upon to maintain faith that the prayers did have some impact, even if it is beyond us to know exactly how.

R. JOSEPH B. SOLOVEITCHIK

An entirely different perspective on this issue was offered by R. Joseph B. Soloveitchik (often referred to as "the Rav"). In the Rav's view, the goal of prayer is not to receive God's sympathetic answers to our requests, but rather to develop a supportive relationship between a human being and God:

> When man is in need and prays, God listens. One of God's attributes is *shome'a tefillah*, "He who listens to prayer." Let us note that Judaism has never promised that God accepts all prayer. The efficacy of prayer is not the central term of inquiry in our philosophy of *avodah she-balev*. Acceptance of prayer is a hope, a vision, a wish, a petition, but not a principle or a premise. The foundation of prayer is not the conviction of its

effectiveness, but the belief that through it we approach God intimately and the miraculous community embracing finite man and his Creator is born. The basic function of prayer is not its practical consequences, but the metaphysical formation of a fellowship consisting of God and man.[15]

Similarly, the Rav summarizes his view as follows:

> We have the assurance that God is indeed a *shome'a tefillah*, One who *hears* our prayers, but not necessarily that He is a *mekabel tefillah*, One who *accepts* our prayers and accedes to our specific requests. It is our persistent hope that our requests will be fulfilled, but it is not our primary motivation for prayer. In praying, we do not seek a response to a particular request as much as we desire a fellowship with God.[16]

In the view of the Rav, it is always essential to pray, even when there appears to be no chance of recovery or any hope that our prayers will be answered (although the wording of these prayers may have to be adjusted at times to avoid "prayer in vain"). The emphasis of our faith is not on God's answer, but that God hears our prayers, which forces us to expand what we mean by prayer being "effective." Truly effective prayer is not that which results in our desired ends, but that which brings about a change in the one offering the prayer, specifically in creating a meaningful relationship and providing true comfort. After all, the experience of being in God's caring presence throughout our time of need can be the best possible comfort, as the Midrash says:

> It is the way of a father to have mercy, as it says, "As a father is merciful towards his children, so has the Lord shown mercy to those who fear Him" (Psalms 103:13). It is the way of a mother to give comfort, as it says, "Like a man whose mother consoles him, so will I console you" (Isaiah 66:13). God says: "I will do that of the father; I will do that of the mother," as it says, "I, only I, am He Who comforts you" (ibid., 51:12).[17]

Profound comfort can be experienced as a result of prayer, since it can ultimately bring us closer to God; the comfort itself is the effectiveness of prayer. According to this view, the goal of contact with the Almighty is not only to get our needs fulfilled, but also to be ennobled, to deepen our relationship with God, and to be brought to heights that we could not otherwise reach. Even if we do not receive what we prayed for, prayer that uplifts us and brings us to a closer relationship with God is certainly not uttered in vain. The value of prayer lies not in the response to our prayer from God, but rather in our response to intimately experiencing God's presence.[18]

Not surprisingly, the perspective of the Rav seems to find support in the thought of the Rambam.[19] There appears to be a contradiction within the Rambam's writings regarding prayer. On the one hand, he suggests certain philosophical problems with the notion that our prayers can change God's mind. Foremost among them, God is not like humans and does not experience human emotions or change His mind.[20] At the same time, the Rambam certainly rules that we must pray and supplicate for all of our needs.[21] One profound resolution of these concepts is based on the way that the Rambam categorizes the mitzvah of prayer, placing prayer among the "actions prescribed to remind us continually of God and of our duty to fear and to love Him, to keep all His commandments, and to believe concerning God that which every religious person must believe."[22] Based on this and the Rambam's ruling that during prayer one must view himself as though he were literally standing before the Divine presence,[23] some maintain that the Rambam does affirm the import of petitionary prayer, but it can be conceptualized as follows:

> Just as the Temple code with its laws of purity is intended to create an awe of the Divine presence, so is prayer of supplication intended to sustain a loving awareness of the presence of God, rather than to satisfy a human need. Prayer presents the humanity of the worshipper – including its needfulness that is expressed in petition – before God, but it is not intended as means to satisfy those needs. . . .[24]

Kiryat Sefer, one of the commentators on the Rambam, explains in the same spirit:

> A person should not consider that the primary purpose of prayer is to have his requests answered. This principle is found in the Talmud in *Berakhot* 32b that a person who expects to

have his prayers answered will simply end up heartbroken and that one whose prayers are not answered should keep trying. . . . The purpose of prayer is to show that there is no one other than God to whom to pray and one should realize that he is inherently lacking in this world and only God can rectify the awareness of reality. . . . We want to acknowledge that we are lacking many things, which we mention in prayer before Him to show that there is no one who can fulfill our needs and to save us from our suffering except for God. . . . God does what is good in His eyes as to whether to accept our prayers if they are appropriate or not.[25]

The essence of prayer is thus the sense of accessibility, that we can turn to God and develop the crucial comforting experience of being in God's presence. This does not deny the possibility of Divine acceptance of prayers, but it does view prayer primarily as a mode of worship that inculcates essential beliefs and emotions in the worshipper. This perception recognizes the crucial need for hope within the realistic limits of expectations, encouraging us to maintain faith as we refocus our expectations on something more attainable, and possibly even more crucial.

As individuals offering support to patients and their families in a clinical setting, our job is not only to pray for whatever people want, but also to facilitate the deepest spiritual healing possible for those individuals in order to enable them to deal with adversity. After all, even if we pray for an unlikely outcome and the patient miraculously recovers, that miracle will necessarily be impermanent; life is fraught with suffering and everyone eventually dies. According to this view, it was indeed highly appropriate to pray with the anxious father of the critical patient, but imperative to couch the focus of those prayers in a desire for God's proximity and support during those trying times and the difficult days ahead, more than in specific pleas for a miraculous recovery.

CONCLUSION

We have seen three very different, although related, approaches to prayer in bleak circumstances. Each works for different people at different times. The position of R. Shlomo Zalman Auerbach is an important reminder that there may be limits to what it is appropriate to pray for and that we must be sensitive to the ramifications of "unanswered prayers" for many individuals. On the other hand, the Steipler's points serve as a powerful reminder that we can always turn to prayer in times of need and that we must think more broadly about the unfathomable ways in which the Almighty might, in fact, respond to our heartfelt prayers. The Rav offers a nuanced middle approach that affirms the efficacy of prayer and the necessity to pray during trying and seemingly impossible circumstances, while encouraging us to reconceive the ultimate multifaceted impact of our prayers on both God and ourselves.

Every individual must develop a philosophy of life and prayer – ideally well before a critical situation arises[26] – that can be integrated into his or her life and help inoculate against total despair. It is my fervent prayer that one or all of the approaches presented here will help others strike a balance between maintaining hope and managing appropriate expectations under trying circumstances.

ENDNOTES

1. *Nishmat Avraham*, YD 335:4(12). Similarly, it has been reported that when R. Yosef Shalom Elyashiv was asked whether one should pray for the recovery of someone who was brain dead, he answered, "This is a vain prayer!" See Moshe Halbertal, "The Limits of Prayer," *Jewish Review of Books* (Summer 2010). In a personal communication with the author, it was explained that the context of the question was actually even broader; R. Elyashiv said that praying for any patient whom the doctors say has no chance of survival is considered a prayer in vain. See *Assia* 93–94 (vol. 24 a–b), 111, for a similar ruling by R. Ram Hacohen. R. Zilberstein also rules that if one sees in an ultrasound that a fetus does not have a brain and there is no natural hope for the child to live other than by a miracle, it is forbidden to pray that the fetus heal and live (*Torat Ha-Yoledet* 61:8, 2nd ed.). He writes that in a case in which an individual sustained significant brain trauma and the doctors determine that he or she will certainly be a "vegetable," one should not pray for a miracle that goes against nature, but may pray for the person in the hope that it will at least lessen the suffering (ibid., n. 10).

2. *Berakhot* 9:3. A similar point is made in *Rosh Hashanah* 17b–18a regarding prayer for an ill person or for someone in other dangerous situations. In such cases, the *gemara* states, prayer recited before the Divine decree is issued can be answered, but prayer said after the determination of a Divine decree cannot be answered. R. Sa'adia Gaon (*Emunot Ve-De'ot* 5:6) seems to incorporate these rulings into his systematic presentation of Jewish belief when he writes that there are seven things that prevent prayer from being accepted, the first of which is "prayer after a Divine decree has been issued." He bases this view on God's rejection of Moshe's prayer to enter the Land of Israel after it had been decreed that he could not go in (Deut. 3:23). *Sefer Chassidim* (95) strengthens this point by quoting the *mishnah* in *Berakhot* and arguing that it is forbidden to pray for anything that is improper (*eino ra'ui*). Even though it is indeed possible for God to do these things ("*af al pi she-yesh yekholet be-yad Ha-Kadosh Barukh Hu la-asot ken*"), it is still considered a prayer said in vain. Similarly, the Gra comments on the *mishnah* that even though God is capable of answering our prayers with a miracle, asking God to do so still qualifies as a prayer said in vain (*Shenot Eliyahu, Berakhot* 9:4).

3. *Shulchan Arukh*, OC 230:1.

4. *Hagahot Rabbi Akiva Eiger, Shulchan Arukh*, ad loc. R. Auerbach quotes this source in *Halikhot Shlomo, Hilkhot Tefillah*, chap. 8, n. 56. Interestingly, R. Auerbach conflates prayer for a miracle with prayer in vain.

There are many more sources and nuances related to the issue of praying for (and benefiting from) miracles, as well as regarding the issue of when it is permitted to pray for a patient to die (which R. Auerbach mentions in the context of our discussion in *Minchat Shlomo* 91:24). These sources are beyond the focus of this chapter. For a summary of approaches and exceptions to this ruling against prayer for a miracle, see R. Yehuda Turetsky, "Prayer and the Terminally Ill Patient," *Verapo*

Yerape 4 (Yeshiva University Press, 2012), 146–9.

5. *Halikhot Shlomo, Hilkhot Tefillah,* chap. 8, n. 56. Similarly, R. Moshe Feinstein is quoted as ruling that one should not change the name of an individual who is very ill with little chance of recovery and who may be dying shortly, because if he does not recover, it will cause people to lose faith in the sages, who suggested changing the name of a sick person (*Masorat Moshe,* 359; *Rishumei Aharon,* vol. 1, 70).

6. Ibid. It is possible that R. Ovadia Yosef was of the same opinion as R. Auerbach, as the prayer he suggests to use in situations in which it is permissible to pray for someone to die is: "Have mercy on this patient and revive him, but if the decree has already been issued, remove his suffering and do what is right in your eyes" (*Chazon Ovadia, Aveilut* 1:39).

7. *Sefer Toledot Yaakov,* 118.

8. *Berakhot* 10a. R. Bachya ben Asher (*Kad Ha-Kemach,* "*Tefillah*") also quotes this Talmudic source as encouraging one to pray in a case exactly like the one we have described – that of a dying patient (*choleh noteh la-mut*). In contrast, the *Minchat Chinukh* points out that the Talmud tells one not to give up hope only when the sword is on (*al*) his neck; it is not referring to when the sword is actually penetrating his neck (*mamash be-tzavaro*). See *Ke-Motzei Shalal Rav: U-Refuah Kerovah La-Vo,* 203, for this quote, and 203–8 for the opinions of some of the authorities who disagree with it. The latter include R. Bentzion Rabinowitz, the Biala Rebbe, himself a descendant of *Minchat Chinukh.* The Biala Rebbe argues (*Mevaser Tov: Ma'amar Techiyat Ha-Meitim*) that one should pray for mercy no matter how bleak the situation is, even if one's physician has told him that there is no medical cure for his illness. He bases his opinion on the statement of Ritva (*Bava*

Metzia 85b) concerning the two mentions of the resurrection of the dead recited in the second blessing of the daily *Amidah.* Ritva writes that the first mention of resurrection alludes to the request to "revive sick people who have reached the gates of death." Abudraham similarly comments that the prayer refers to a patient whom the "doctors consider as if dead." The Biala Rebbe concludes that since the sages established one prayer in the *Amidah* for the deathly ill to recover in addition to another prayer for all other ill people (*Refa'einu*), it is clearly appropriate to pray that such a critically ill patient recover.

9. This point seems to be based on *Sefer Chassidim* 378.

10. This point finds support in *Nefesh Ha-Chayim, Sha'ar* 2:10 (based on *Zohar, Toledot* 137a), which states that God desires prayers because they increase holiness and Godly influence in the world, benefitting all those in need of that prayer. I thank R. Yaakov Siegel for bringing this source to my attention.

11. *Bava Batra* 116a.

12. Meiri, *Bava Batra* 116a, s.v. *la-olam.* Similarly, the statement in *Rosh Hashanah* 18a that prayer said after the determination of a Divine decree cannot be answered (see n. 2 above) also records an opinion that although *tefillah* (prayer) said too late cannot be answered, "crying out in prayer (*tza'akah*) is beneficial for a person both before and after a decree is issued." See also *Berakhot* 32b: "Although the gates of prayer have been locked, the gates of tears have not been locked, as the verse states, 'Hear my prayer, God, give ear to my outcry; to my tears, be not silent.'" Similarly, the Talmud *Yerushalmi* (*Ta'anit* 8b) states: "Three things cancel a bad decree (*mevatlin et ha-gezeirah ha-kashah*) – prayer, charity, and repentance." Moreover, the *Midrash Tanchuma* (*Vayeitzei* 8) quotes the *mishnah* in *Berakhot* that crying out over an occurrence that has

passed constitutes uttering a prayer in vain, but contends that "even until the moment a woman is giving birth, one may still pray about the gender of the child, for it is not difficult for God to transform females into males or males into females." *Bereishit Rabbah* (*Vayeitzei* 6) also quotes this idea in the context of the claim of the Targum Yonatan ben Uziel (*Bereishit* 29:22) that Dina was originally conceived in Rachel's womb but God transferred her to Leah's womb because Rachel prayed to give birth to Yosef instead. See also Rabbeinu Bechayei (Deut. 11:13): "The strength of prayer is so great that it can even change nature and save a person from danger, nullifying a decree."

Another support for the appropriateness of prayer even after a divine decree has been issued may be the fact that King David prayed for the recovery of his sick baby despite the prophecy that he would die (II Sam. 12:16–22 and Radak there). However, *Metzudat David* (II Sam. 12:22) argues that King David was not praying to nullify the decree, but simply praying in the hope that the decree had not yet been made. For a summary of perspectives on how some heartfelt prayers nevertheless appear to go unanswered, see R. Yehuda Turetsky, "Prayer and the Terminally Ill Patient," 142–4.

13. *Peninei Rabbeinu Ba'al Ha-Kehillat Yaakov*, vol. 1, 118.

14. *Sefer Toledot Yaakov*, 118. Similarly, *Nishmat Avraham*, YD 338:1(4), quotes R. Avraham Yitzchak Ha-Kohen Kook (*Da'at Kohen* 140) as claiming that most terminal predictions made by doctors cannot be considered certainties (*torat vadai*), but must be categorized as only possibly true (*anu machzikim rak le-safek*). Another approach, offered by R. Yaakov Kaminetsky, is that since prayer for a terminally ill person to be cured is a forbidden prayer for a miracle, "Rather than praying that the patient be miraculously cured, one should pray that a cure be found for the disease;" see Yonason Rosenblum, *Reb Yaakov* (Mesorah Publications, 1993), 368. Such a prayer would be permitted, as it does not beseech God to alter the natural order, but rather assumes the cure must already exist in nature and is just waiting to be discovered. I thank R. Yaakov Siegel for bringing this source to my attention.

Similarly, R. Chaim Kanievsky reportedly ruled that rather than prayer for a miracle, one can pray for something that is currently impossible by praying for a new medicine to be discovered (*Torat Ha-Yoledet* 61:8, fn. 10). Rabbi Dr. David Fox shared with me his approach, which is to pray to God by saying, "I am not sure what to ask for, I don't know whether to ask for relief from suffering or a for a miracle, but I will accept Your will, whatever it is, please give me the strength to align my contradictory emotions in congruence with your Ultimate Will."

15. R. Joseph B. Soloveitchik, *Worship of the Heart* (Ktav, 2003), 35. In the same essay (29), the Rav refers to prayer that is not accompanied by distress and anxiety as the only "futile" prayer.

16. Abraham R. Besdin, *Reflections of the Rav* (Ktav, 1993), vol. 1, 78.

17. *Pesikta De-Rav Kahana* 19, s.v. *anochi anochi*. There are many verses in the Bible that emphasize the comforting role that God can play, such as "I am with him in distress" (Psalms 91:15). Similarly, Psalms 147:3 describes God as "the Healer of shattered hearts" and 118:6 states, "God is with me; I have no fear." Along these lines, *Sefat Emet* (*Va'etchanan* 5632) writes that God is close to a person to the extent that he has *kavanah* (intent) in prayer. He homiletically interprets the concept of *semikhat geulah le-tefillah* (the proximity of the prayer for redemption to the *Amidah* prayer) as the ability of a person to achieve personal redemption through his understanding of – and con-

nection to – the Divine, which is achieved through prayer.

18. It should be noted that according to the Rav, we cannot expect to achieve this connection through prayer alone, but rather through an entire Godly way of life: "Any kind of injustice, corruption, cruelty or the like desecrates the very essence of the prayer adventure. . . . If man craves to meet God in prayer, then he must purge himself of all that separates him from God. The Halakhah has never looked upon prayer as a separate magical gesture in which man may engage without integrating it into the total pattern of his life. . . ." (*The Lonely Man of Faith*, 65).

19. The Rav's view of prayer as "worship of the heart" (*avodah she-balev*) is motivated by his halakhic/existential perspective. The Rav's concern tends to be with human religious consciousness as we direct ourselves to God. The Rambam's view, on the other hand, is a more philosophical/theological consideration, focusing on the world as seen from God's vantage point. I thank Professor Lawrence Kaplan for pointing out this distinction.

20. *The Guide of the Perplexed* 1:36, 56; *Yesodei Ha-Torah* 1:11–12.

21. Commentary to the Mishnah, *Berakhot* 4:2; *Hilkhot Tefillah* 1:2, 8:1; *Hilkhot Teshuvah* 7:7; *Hilkhot Matanot Le-Evyonim* 10:16; *Hilkhot Ta'aniot* 1:3–4.

22. *The Guide of the Perplexed* 3:44.

23. *Hilkhot Tefillah* 4:16. The Rav similarly defines prayer as "an awareness of man finding himself in the presence of and addressing himself to his Maker, and to pray has one connotation only: to stand before God" (*The Lonely Man of Faith*, 35).

24. Ehud Benor, *Worship of the Heart* (SUNY Press, 1995), 85. This is not to say that God cannot or does not respond to prayer according to the Rambam, but simply that the *intention* of prayer is the awareness of God's presence, not God's answer.

25. R. Moshe Di-Trani, *Beit Elokim, Sha'ar Ha-Tefillah*, 2. Variations of this theme are found in many works. For example, R. Shlomo Breuer (*Hokhmah U-Mussar*, vol. 1, 110) asks why we have to ask God for what we need if it would be given to us by God in any event if it is in fact necessary. R. Breuer explains that the primary purpose of prayer is clearly for us to be reminded of our dependence on God.

26. R. Shlomo Breuer (*Hokhmah U-Mussar*, vol. 2, 1) makes the point that prayer is meant to inculcate trust in God's omnipotence and compassion, which should optimally be done before a crisis, not in the midst of one, based on the Talmudic statement (*Sanhedrin* 44b), "One should always offer prayers in advance of trouble (*le-olam yakdim adam tefillah le-tzarah*)."

B.   *VIDUY:*
Confessional Prayers Prior to Death

Referrals frequently come to my office to perform "last rites" for a dying Jewish patient. On one such occasion, as I arrived in the patient's room, I asked the gathered family to explain exactly what sort of prayers they were hoping I would say with them. At the exact same moment, the daughter of the patient said, "A *Mi She-Berach* (healing prayer)" and the son said, "*Viduy* (end-of-life confessional)"! The confused look on my face alerted the family to the fact that there may be somewhat of a contradiction between these two requests. As we stepped back to discuss their goals and understanding of the situation, everyone in the room agreed that the patient was dying; they simply held differing views on the need to maintain hope for a miracle and had varying degrees of concern about not scaring the patient. We eventually concluded that it was indeed appropriate to recite *Viduy* with this patient, while taking their important concerns into account. The points in this chapter will attempt to elucidate the importance of this prayer and how this balance can be navigated.

Some are under the impression that the concept of "last rites" is not a Jewish one. However, despite concerns that this might cause distress, Jewish tradition in fact mandates that when someone is dying, they should recite the *Viduy* (confessional prayers).[1] By reciting *Viduy* before death, one leaves the world in a state of purity[2] and proclaims one's faith in God and God's justice.[3] In particular, *Viduy* is viewed as a way to repent, make amends, and get one's affairs in order before dying.[4] Traditional sources thus refer to reciting *Viduy* while still alive as a source of tremendous merit that assists a person in obtaining a share in the World to Come.[5]

WHEN SHOULD *VIDUY* BE RECITED?

Although Judaism teaches that one who repents as they are dying attains a special merit and Divine connection,[6] it must be stressed that it is ideal for a person to sincerely repent and make amends while they are still clear-minded and able to focus on what they are saying, well before they begin to lose consciousness.[7] For this reason, many suggest not to wait until one is actually actively dying to recite *Viduy*, but to do so any time one is ill[8] or in some sort of danger.[9]

Part of the *Viduy* text includes the hope that the patient will recover, such that *Viduy* may be recited again at a later point when necessary, and even many times throughout one's life. However, care must be taken not to frighten a patient unnecessarily by mentioning *Viduy* at the wrong time, thus causing them to think that they are dying or more seriously ill than they really are.[10] This can be avoided by wording the purpose of *Viduy* very carefully. It should be emphasized that it is a custom that brings merit and that reciting it does not indicate that one is necessarily dying.[11] One can explain to a patient that reciting *Viduy* may give him or her the opportunity to relieve some of the emotional burden of unresolved conflicts or unrealized hopes, so that they can experience lightness of spirit and removal of regret. Rather than a depressing statement, *Viduy* can be said as a beautiful and intimate prayer in which one affirms their beliefs, hopes, and values as they reach a potential crossroads in their life and focus on making peace above and below.[12] *Viduy* can also be part of a person's ethical will, through which he or she ensures that their values and hopes are articulated and passed on.

Nevertheless, because of the concern of frightening sick individuals, some authorities suggest limiting the recitation of *Viduy* only to those who are actually dying and who we are concerned will die very soon, without having said *Viduy*.[13] As stated above, it is important to explain *Viduy* in a sensitive manner, making it clear that it does not necessarily mean that the person will die soon, and emphasizing that it is a merit to recite this prayer.

Viduy may be recited on Shabbat or festivals, if necessary.[14] It may be recited even in an unclean environment, but without mentioning God's name.[15]

SAYING *VIDUY* ON BEHALF OF ANOTHER PERSON

Since it is essential for the person reciting *Viduy* to understand what they are saying so that they can truly repent, it is ideal for the patient to say it themselves.[16] If that is difficult, one may recite *Viduy* "in their heart"[17] or have someone recite it for them while they listen intently.[18] Even if a patient is not alert, it is customary to recite *Viduy* on their behalf, as they may nevertheless have some cognizance of what is being said in their presence[19] and it may be possible for one person to pray for the atonement of another.[20] When reciting *Viduy* on behalf of another person, one should still speak in the first person (i.e., "my death," "my sins," etc.).[21]

ENDNOTES

1. *Shulchan Arukh*, YD 338:1; *Arukh Ha-Shulchan*, YD 338:1.

2. See, for example, *Bava Metzia* 86a; *Avodah Zarah* 27b. These two Talmudic stories imply that it is ideal to die in the midst of reciting words of prayer, or even the word "pure."

3. See, for example, *Berakhot* 61b.

4. See, for example, *Sanhedrin* 43b; *Shabbat* 153a; *Shulchan Arukh*, YD 335:7.

5. *Sanhedrin* 43b; *Arukh Ha-Shulchan*, YD 338:1; Rambam, *Hilkhot Teshuvah* 7:1–2.

6. *Derekh Chaim* on *Pirkei Avot* 2:10 (quoted in *Oz Ve-Hadar Metivta Pirkei Avot*, vol. 2, 114).

7. *Tzitz Eliezer* 5, *Ramat Rachel* 27:1, in the name of the Shelah; *Nishmat Avraham*, YD 338:1, in the name of the *Sefer Zikhronot*.

8. *Gesher Ha-Chaim*, vol. 1, 1:5 (4).

9. *Tzitz Eliezer* 5, *Ramat Rachel* 27:1. The *Chokhmat Adam* (151:11) records a practice of always reciting *Viduy* on the third day of one's illness. This was done in particular so that people would not be frightened at the thought of reciting *Viduy*, as it was standard practice that everyone said it on that day.

10. *Nishmat Avraham*, YD 338:1 (a).

11. *Shulchan Arukh*, YD 338:1.

12. This phraseology was shared with me by Rabbi Dr. David Fox.

13. *Shakh*, YD 338:1; *Nishmat Avraham*, YD 338:1–2. This would not preclude reciting *Viduy* when one is still generally healthy and clear-minded, but it may restrict *Viduy* from being recited by a person who has a life-threatening illness but who is not yet approaching the very end of their life. However, some have noted that since reciting *Viduy* is for the benefit of the ill, it should not be withheld from them unless there is strong basis for the concern that the particular patient's condition will suffer as a result of fears brought about by reciting *Viduy*. See R. Rabinovitz, *Halakhah U-Refuah*, vol. 3, 102–5.

14. *Shemirat Shabbat Ke-Hilkhatah* 2:64(1).

15. Ibid.

16. *Arukh Ha-Shulchan*, YD 338:3. See also *Bereishit Rabbah* 53:17: "When an ill person prays for himself, it is better than when others prayer on his behalf." For this reason, *Viduy* can be said in any language that one understands.

17. *Shulchan Arukh*, YD 338:1; *Torat Ha-Adam*, *Sha'ar Ha-Sof*, *Inyan Viduy*.

18. *Gesher Ha-Chaim*, vol. 1, 1:5(2); *Me-Olam Ve-Ad Olam* 5:7.

19. R. Chaim Jachter, *The Final Vidui*, http://www.koltorah.org/ravj/The_Final _Vidui_1.html. However, R. Asher Weiss told this author that in his opinion it is not appropriate to recite *Viduy* for a patient who is not alert, since he cannot actually engage in repentance (similar to the ruling of the *Arukh Ha-Shulchan*, YD 338:3, cited above). In R. Weiss's view, it is better to simply recite the *Shema* for the patient as he dies so that he will die in

an atmosphere of holiness. Similarly, R. Moshe Feinstein (*Masorat Moshe*, vol. 2, 278) is quoted as ruling that it does not make sense to recite *Viduy* for a dying patient who is in a coma, as it is not possible to repent for another person. However, *Masorat Moshe* notes that nevertheless it has become customary to recite *Viduy* for such patients.

20. As in Num. 14:19–20.

21. As heard from R. Elhanan Zohn. This is because we are relying on the principle of *shome'a ke-oneh* in the hope that the patient is hearing our words and thinking them as we recite them.

CHAPTER 4

At the End of Life

A. ADVANCE DIRECTIVES AND POLST FORMS

THE NEED

One of the most challenging ethical issues that arise in hospitals is determining the appropriate interventions for a patient who lacks the capacity to participate in the decision-making process regarding their own medical care (see Chapter 2B). Over the past thirty-plus years, it has been suggested that one of the ways to prevent such challenging situations from arising is to complete an advance directive ahead of time, while one is of sound health and mind. Completing an advance directive allows one to give expression to one's goals, values, and preferences in relation to becoming ill, or to appoint others to speak on one's behalf and participate in medical decision-making whenever one lacks the capacity to do so, not only at the end of life. Completing an advance directive is thus an opportunity to better ensure that others caring for a patient have a clearer understanding of what matters to that patient.

Furthermore, such documents may also help protect one's family from unnecessary stress and guilt, as well as enable healthcare providers to better serve the patient. Without such a document, healthcare providers, who are often strangers and lack long-term relationships with their patients, may have little to rely upon for understanding the deeply held values of their patients. The necessity of having an advance directive is thus especially acute for observant Jews, who will want to ensure that Jewish Law is followed when determining their course of treatment.[1]

CONCERNS RELATED TO ADVANCE DIRECTIVES

When the concept of an advance directive for the sake of healthcare decision-making was first introduced in American society, some Rabbinic authorities expressed concerns, since these documents are based on the belief that honoring personal autonomy is the highest form of demonstrating respect for another person, whereas Jewish Law is based on a different set of commitments rooted in specific obligations that do not grant complete individual autonomy.[2] However, within the traditional set of obligations and basic guidelines dictated by Jewish Law, there is sometimes some room for personal values/choices regarding certain clinical decisions.[3] Therefore, as long as an advance directive is filled out in accordance with Jewish Law and the patient appoints a knowledgeable rabbi to be contacted, not only is it *not* problematic to complete an advance directive, but it may *help ensure* that a person is treated in accordance with Jewish Law.[4]

Furthermore, it may be that the initial opposition of some religious leaders was caused by the fact that early "living wills" only included the option for patients to list which medical interventions *not* to utilize.[5] However, today the focus of these documents tends to be on how to best treat the patient in accordance with their own goals, values, and preferences – those matters that give one's life meaning and purpose – and thus address both what *should not* and what *should* be done when caring for the person, who is unable to participate in his or her own medical decision-making.

Independent of the overall concern about the status of advance directives in general, there has also been concern about ambiguous instructions in advance directives, which thus do not provide sufficient guidance. For this reason, in addition to putting something in writing, it is crucial to also have conversations with one's family, rabbi, and other surrogates whom one wishes to appoint in an advance directive. Furthermore, it is essential that whomever one appoints as a surrogate will be available when needed. It is therefore often best to list multiple surrogates and Rabbinic authorities or organizations, preferably in sequential order, such that there is a recognized first preference, second preference, etc., in order to avoid disputes between listed surrogates.

It is also crucial to ensure that this document can be easily located and is on file with one's healthcare provider, rabbi, and family members mentioned in the document. Similarly, as years go by after one has completed an advance directive, one's preferences and/or medical technologies and outcomes may change drastically. For this reason, these documents should be reviewed and updated every few years, particularly if an individual receives a new diagnosis.[6]

It is important to recognize that it is impossible to accurately predict every scenario ahead of time and to know the exact path that one would wish to pursue in every situation. It is therefore important to be familiar with the different types of documents, as well as some specific recommendations.

TYPES OF ADVANCE DIRECTIVES

There are generally two types of written advance directives used in healthcare: the "living will" and the "proxy" or "durable power of attorney." Each fulfills a different role, and hence a different need.

- *Living Will*: This type of advance directive document includes specific instructions regarding one's goals, values, and preferences as they relate to various treatment options and circumstances. This was the very first kind of advance directive, and it is what many people think of when they hear the phrase "advance directive." This document has traditionally generated the most negative response within the Jewish community, since this kind of document has been primarily promoted within secular society as emphasizing individual autonomy and personal rights, as previously discussed. However, as the Jewish community has become more familiar with what such a document can be used to capture regarding a person's fundamental commitments and values, formats appropriate for Jewish patients have become available.
- *Proxy/Durable power of attorney*: This is a document in which an individual assigns another person(s) the authority to serve as his or her surrogate – that is, to speak on one's behalf when one lacks the capacity to do so – and hence to represent the patient when medical decisions need to be made and values-based input from and about the patient is crucial.
- *Combined "living will" and "proxy/durable power of attorney" documents*: Often referred to as "advance healthcare directives," these documents combine the two above types into a single document. Most documents nowadays are of this type, including those encouraged by various state laws. The current Rabbinical Council of America and Agudath Israel forms are both this type of document; their primary goal is to simply appoint a proxy, but they also include some mention of the patient's values.[7]

Whether a single "living will" or "proxy/durable power of attorney" form or a combined "advance healthcare directive," these are more than simply statements of preference; when completed in accordance with state law, these are legal documents. While every state has applicable statutes describing the procedures necessary to establish the legal legitimacy of such documents, it is fairly standard that they must either be signed by two witnesses or notarized. Nevertheless, even if an advance directive does not completely satisfy the requirements of a given state's law, it can still be valuable in providing healthcare providers with insight into how best to proceed in medical decision-making.

Because there may be concerns about what to enter into a "living will" (or in the similarly-structured section of an "advance healthcare directive"), and how it will be interpreted, it may be best to simply appoint a proxy by filling out a proxy/durable power of attorney form, appointing people whom one knows well and one's rabbi (and alternates in case that rabbi is unavailable). But one must also make sure to talk, directly and explicitly, with those whom one has appointed, about what gives value and meaning to one's life, and what preferences one might have in the face of challenging illness or injury. This provides the proxy with valuable insight that can help them serve as a surrogate, and thus to pursue decisions that best reflect who the patient is. One may then provide these individuals with (or append to one's proxy form) an unofficial living will that details some of one's preferences, while making it clear that healthcare providers should defer only to one's proxy to make all decisions based on the given circumstances, in accordance with Jewish Law.[8]

CONCLUSION

Although decision-making for patients who lack the capacity to participate in that decision-making can be very challenging, for the halakhically observant Jew, having an experienced rabbi involved helps to relieve what might otherwise be experienced as an overwhelming burden, enabling a patient's family to feel comforted by the fact that their loved one is treated in accordance with the dictates of their faith. Similarly, when an individual is able to state important goals, values, and/or preferences and what kind of life is meaningful and worthwhile to them, and has made the effort to appoint people to speak for him or her when capacity is lost, it can mitigate many of the emotional and practical challenges that frequently accompany medical decision-making.

Indeed, Jewish Law requires a patient to put his or her affairs in order.[9] As the *midrash* points out, a person cannot tell the Angel of Death to wait for them while they organize their accounts and leave a testament for their family.[10] For this reason, it was the custom in some Jewish communities that whenever anyone became ill, on the third day of their illness, a community representative would tell them, "It is our custom to visit all sick people at this time, so do not let our visit cause you any concern. We advise you to prepare a directive delineating your wishes, including any outstanding obligations you have toward others or vice versa."[11]

Many people have a difficult time discussing these matters while they are healthy, or think it is some sort of a bad omen (*ayin hara*). However, there is a traditional Jewish belief that purchasing a burial plot while one is young and healthy is a charm (*segulah*) for a long life.[12] It can be argued that completing an advance directive is one as well. After all, even if it does not actually cause a person to live longer, people who think seriously about the fragility of life are more likely to focus on things that really matter and live their lives to the fullest.[13] It may well be suggested, therefore, that it is an imperative that every observant Jew complete some form of an advance directive to ensure that they will be treated in accordance with Jewish Law.[14] Some halakhic authorities have also argued that every responsible rabbi should have one, in order to serve as a role model.[15]

POLST FORMS

"POLST" ("Physician Orders for Life-Sustaining Treatment") is a physician order outlining the medically indicated plan of care for a patient who, based on best medical judgment, is nearing the end of his or her life. In general, POLSTs are appropriate for patients with a life-expectancy of twelve months or less. The aim of a POLST is to ensure that the patient receives care consistent with both medical judgment and patient preferences. It is most typically used to prevent unwanted or ineffective treatments, reduce patient and family suffering, and ensure that a patient's wishes are honored.

A POLST differs from an advance directive in that advance directives are based solely on a patient's preferences – be it identifying the person the patient wants to make decisions when the patient cannot make his or her own, or providing a general guide as to what the patient wants in terms of medical care. A POLST, in contrast, is a physician's order that the healthcare team can act upon, akin to any other physician order found in a patient's medical record. A doctor or patient can reevaluate and change a POLST form at any time. In fact, it should be reevaluated as the patient's condition changes, just as any other medical order should be reassessed based on the patient's condition.

ENDNOTES

1. See Chaim Dovid Zwiebel, "The 'Halachic Health Care Proxy': An Insurance Policy With Unique Benefits," in *The Ethical Imperative* (Artscroll, Mesorah Publications).

2. See Bleich, *Bioethical Dilemmas*, 75. On autonomy in Judaism, see the introduction to this book, n. 26.

3. For example, in *Minchat Shlomo* 1:91(24:2), R. Shlomo Zalman Auerbach rules that even though some argue that a dying patient has no autonomy whatsoever to forgo even a moment of life, in his opinion if such a patient is suffering, they must receive routine nutrition, hydration, and oxygen, even against their will, but may decline medications that contribute to their suffering *if he makes such a request*. For more examples of R. Auerbach's rulings that medical decisions should be made with the consent of the patient, see *Assia* 3 (5743), 323–5 (republished in *Bracha Le-Avraham*, 135).

4. *Nishmat Avraham*, YD 339:1(10) (511 in 3rd ed.) and CH 252:2(1) (67 in 3rd ed.); R. J. Ifrah, "The Living Will," *Journal of Halacha and Contemporary Society* 24 (1992), 129, n. 25.

5. See Luis Kutner, "Due Process of Euthanasia: The Living Will – A Proposal," *Indiana Law Review* (1969), 539–54.

6. A. Steinberg and C.L. Sprung, "The Dying Patient: New Israeli Legislation," *Intensive Care Med* 32 (2006), 1236. The Israeli Dying Patient Law establishes a detailed mechanism to verify that an advance directive reflects the most current wishes of the now incompetent patient, including "renewal of the statement ev-ery 5 years; reevaluation of the statement when diagnosed with a serious illness, with the aid of an expert physician; and establishment of a national pool of advance medical directives. Every 5 years, reminders are sent to the owners of the advance directives to verify whether or not they have changed their minds about the directives. . . ." Similar concerns have been raised related to POLST forms; see Moore, Rubin, and Halperin, "The Problems with Physician Order for Life-Sustaining Treatment," *JAMA* 315(3) (Jan. 2016), 259–60.

7. These documents are primarily proxy forms, but they also affirm certain religious values. It should be noted that a number of states have enacted healthcare proxy laws, providing specific guidelines as to the formal requirements of the proxy. One should ensure that the document that they are signing, whether it is a proxy or a living will, meets the standards of their state. Agudath Israel forms have been created for a number of different states.

8. R. Chaim Jachter writes, "One might also consider the option of merely filling out a healthcare proxy and subsequently writing a document that is addressed to the proxy and one's Rav in which one would express his feelings regarding the extension of life in case of enormous suffering and no hope for cure. One must be exceedingly careful in regards to the writing of a living will to insure that it does not create the potential to prevent one from receiving proper medical care. Each document should specify that healthcare decisions are to be applied in a manner consistent with Orthodox

Jewish law (Halacha). One should clarify that a particular Rabbi, a Rabbi selected by his agent, or a Rabbi appointed by an organization is authorized to resolve any Halachic issues" (http://www.kolto rah.org/ravj/Estate_Planning_Health_Ca re_Proxies_and_Living_Wills.html). For example, one can simply attach a sheet a paper to the proxy form, with a paragraph stating, "Although this is not binding, I wish to express my wishes concerning x and y." Alternatively, one can fill out a pre-existing living will form, such as the "5 wishes" document, and not have it witnessed or notarized (making it clear that the proxy takes precedence). This can then be given to one's proxy for use in informing the decisions he will make on the patient's behalf.

9. *Shulchan Arukh*, YD 335:7.

10. *Devarim Rabbah* 9:3.

11. *Chokhmat Adam* 151:11.

12. *Kol Bo Aveilut* 1, p. 174, based on *Vayikra Rabbah* 5:5. See also *Mishmeret Shalom* in the back of *Yoreh Deah* (90:9), which argues that it is not *"tiftach peh la-satan"* (opening one's mouth to the accuser) if one writes a will at age 50 or later. The same age is quoted in the name of R. Shlomo Kluger, who based it on the verse, "During this Jubilee year, you shall return, each man to his property" (Lev. 25:13), as well as the *Tiferet Yisrael* (end of *Nezikin*, *"Derush Ohr ha-Chaim"* 4), based on the verse, "And you shall sanc-

tify the fiftieth year")Lev. 25:10). See also *Ma'avar Yabok*, *"Siftei Tzedek,"* 8. R. Herschel Schachter reports that when R. Mordechai Gifter celebrated his 50th birthday, he told his family that he had just finished putting together his will. Nevertheless, many recommend filling out an advance directive at a much younger age.

13. A. Twerski, *Light at the End of the Tunnel* (Shaar Press, 2003), 18.

14. The Chafetz Chaim writes (*Shem Olam* 1:7) that the *mishnah*, "If I am not for myself, who will be for me?" is a command to write a will, for if one does not choose for himself, others will not choose properly for them. Some have argued that the model of King David preparing the nation and his son Solomon for his impending death (I Kings 2:1–12) is a precedent for the need for everyone to set their affairs in order and not assume that one's children will simply act as one expects. Others cite the model of Jacob's requests and wishes for his children as additional precedent (Gen. 47:28–49:33). See also *Pirkei D'rebbi Eliezer* 52 that Jacob prayed to God to create illness so that people could receive a warning before dying in order to afford them the opportunity to share their desires with their family.

15. R. Feivel Cohen, quoted by R. Chaim Jachter, in http://www.koltorah.org/ravj /Estate_Planning_Health_Care_Proxies _and_Living_Wills_1.html.

B. END-OF-LIFE DECISION-MAKING: DNR, Comfort Measures, Nutrition/Hydration, and Defining "Terminal" in accordance with Jewish Law

Having discussed Advance Directives and POLST forms, we will now discuss three of the primary categories of medical intervention that these documents frequently cover, as well as general guidance regarding approaches to them in Jewish Law.

DNR

A DNR (Do Not Resuscitate) order indicates that if the patient's heart stops beating (cardiac arrest), the medical staff will not initiate CPR (cardiopulmonary resuscitation) through chest compressions or electronic defibrillation, but will instead allow death to occur naturally. Similarly, a DNR order usually indicates that if the patient stops breathing (respiratory arrest), the medical staff will not initiate artificial (mechanical) respiration by inserting a tube into the lungs (intubation) and then connecting that tube to a mechanical ventilator. In this case as well, natural death is allowed to occur (this is sometimes referred to as a DNI – Do Not Intubate).

As discussed previously, Jewish Law strongly emphasizes and often requires the preservation of life. The general principle is that we must do everything we can to prolong life; however, it is not obligatory to initiate medical interventions that prolong suffering at the end of life.[1] It is forbidden to do anything to hasten a patient's death, even by a moment and even if the patient is already dying, but it is not obligatory to *actively* administer interventions that briefly prolong a life of pain and suffering.[2]

Patients who adhere to Halakhah often do not accept a DNR order.

However, there are circumstances in which it would be halakhically appropriate to withhold CPR and intubation in order to *passively* allow nature to take its course.[3] There are generally three conditions under which a DNR may be permissible (or possibly even obligatory),[4] under the guidance of an experienced expert in Jewish Law and as long as *all three criteria are met*:[5]

1. Expert medical opinion has determined that the patient is terminally ill (as per the definition of terminal discussed later in this chapter):
    a. There is no chance of a cure.
    b. The patient is heading towards death (and as such, medical interventions can only minimally prolong life).[6]
2. The patient is suffering very much – physically or emotionally – even though he or she is receiving medication to control the pain.[7]
3. The patient does not want to undergo resuscitation.[8]

We can thus say that the halakhic imperative is that as long as we can keep a person alive, we must do so, unless the benefit of such actions is counterbalanced by the fact that they cause extreme pain and suffering. At that point, the Torah permits a compassionate response of allowing the death process to occur with appropriate palliative care, if this is what the patient or their surrogate desires and a competent rabbi has ruled accordingly for that specific case.

It is crucial to ensure that even if a DNR order has been initiated, as long as the patient is still alive, we must continue to provide attentive care and all the basic necessities of life, and make certain that the patient does not suffer.[9] Oxygen is usually considered a basic necessity and one that can reduce suffering, and it should therefore be provided to all patients for whom it is medically indicated. Therefore, even if artificial respiration (intubation) is withheld, basic oxygen supplementation and/or a noninvasive positive pressure airway device should still be provided to alleviate discomfort, such as via a face mask or a nasal prong (nasal cannula).[10]

Furthermore, it should be noted that although Jewish Law sometimes permits, and may demand, that a dying patient forgo resuscitation or intubation, there is much debate concerning when a tube may be removed from the patient's lungs (extubated) once the patient has already been placed on the respirator.[11] As discussed in the next chapter, Jewish Law generally only permits *withholding* life-sustaining interventions, but it is usually forbidden to *withdraw* them once they have begun (even if they are not basic, essential treatments).[12] It is important to consider this when the decision is made whether or not to intubate.

Accordingly, when consulting a Rabbinic authority on DNR questions, it is essential to clarify if:

- there is a plausible cure or possibility for remission in the patient's underlying illness
- if the patient is in severe pain
- what his or her desires and goals of care are
- if the resuscitation procedures are likely to inflict severe discomfort in this patient[13]

OPTIONS: COMFORT MEASURES, LIMITED INTERVENTIONS, OR FULL TREATMENT

Establishing the halakhically acceptable level of treatment for a given patient in many ways hinges on the approach to the first issue discussed above. In a situation in which a DNR would be permitted, "comfort measures" may be permitted as well. This usually means that aggressive medical interventions will not be pursued at the end of life and the patient will be allowed to die a natural death. The patient will, however, receive medication to ensure that he or she does not experience overwhelming pain or other significant distress associated with death. Narcotic pain medications, such as morphine, are often prescribed for patients with terminal diseases to alleviate suffering near the end of life.

The alleviation of pain and suffering is a mitzvah[14] and should not be withheld out of concern for potential adverse effects.[15] It is halakhically permitted for patients to receive narcotic pain medication,[16] even when it may possibly hasten their death, provided that:

1. The *intent* is only to alleviate pain, not to shorten the patient's life.
2. The dose of medicine is gradually increased as necessary to alleviate the pain, but each dose on its own is not enough to certainly shorten the patient's life.[17]

However, an option of "limited interventions" should often be considered as well. Many authorities in Jewish Law distinguish between treatments that supply natural necessities and those that are considered "aggressive" and not routine. Basic treatments that are unrelated to the patient's primary illness and that simply constitute biological maintenance should generally *not* be ceased, as doing so may hasten death. These include:

- oxygen
- nutrition
- hydration
- treatments that any other patient would receive to prevent complications, such as insulin for a diabetic, antibiotics,[18] and blood transfusions

On the other hand, it is often not required to actively treat or initiate aggressive measures for a dying patient who is suffering and does not want them, if a competent rabbi has ruled accordingly.[19] This includes:

- surgery
- radiation
- chemotherapy with minimal projected benefit[20]

A patient who opts for limited interventions in an advance directive or POLST will be administered IV fluids and may choose to be respirated in a non-invasive fashion. Alternatively, a patient may record that he or she prefers full interventions to be made under all circumstances.

ARTIFICIALLY ADMINISTERED NUTRITION

Secular POLST documents include the option to refuse nutrition and hydration, reflecting the standard approach in American society, which views artificial nutrition as a medical treatment that can be withdrawn if necessary. In contrast, there is a strong consensus among Rabbinic authorities that artificial nutrition and hydration must be provided to all patients, whether conscious or comatose, even artificially[21] – such as via an NG (nasogastric tube) or PEG (percutaneous endoscopic gastrostomy)[22] – unless medically contraindicated.[23] This is based on the ruling, discussed above, that distinguishes between treatments that supply natural necessities or are accepted as routine, which are required, and those that are considered "aggressive," which are not always obligatory. Accordingly, when nutrition and hydration are unrelated to the illness that underlies the dying process, withdrawing them is viewed as a form of euthanasia.[24] Most halakhic authorities have further ruled that nutrition and hydration may not even be passively discontinued from dying patients to hasten their death.[25]

If a patient refuses to accept these feedings, one should encourage him or her to accept them. If they still refuse, however, they should not be forced,[26] nor should one utilize coercive methods such as tying down the patient's hands to prevent him or her from pulling out the tube.[27] If the patient is competent and expresses clear opposition to a feeding tube, their desire should be granted.[28]

There are some circumstances in which artificial nutrition and hydration may be discontinued in accordance with Halakhah. Patients nearing the end of life often lose interest in eating or have difficulty swallowing or absorbing their intake, which can lead to infections, choking, and aspiration. In such cases, it is sufficient to make the patient comfortable by providing minimal feeding by mouth, such as using menthol swabs or ice chips, instead of IV feeding.[29]

There are times when the provision of artificial nutrition and hydration very close to the time of death is not only dangerous for the patient, but also actually increases the patient's discomfort. Since some base the obligation to continue nutrition and hydration on the assumption that death by starvation or dehydration increases the intensity of the pain and suffering of a dying individual,[30] there may be situations in which the focus should instead be on providing comfort measures (as discussed above).[31] Rabbinic authorities thus rule that if a dying patient will likely die as a result of their underlying illness before dying of lack of nutrition, and the patient does not want nutrition, there is no obligation to initiate artificial nutrition.[32] Sometimes this is possible by providing some basic IV or subcutaneous infusion/hypodermoclysis (minimally invasive) hydration to ensure that the patient does not die of dehydration.[33] Similarly, if a patient's illness is so severe that placing a feeding tube could be harmful or the medical team is unwilling to do it, hydration via these minimally invasive methods can be a beneficial method for meeting the obligation of hydration without putting the patient at risk.[34] If a patient has no chance of survival and is suffering, one may also switch from total parenteral feeding (TPN) to nasogastric or even to IV feeding, and the IV content may be reduced from concentrated nutrients to basic glucose and electrolytes in water.[35]

DEFINING "TERMINAL ILLNESS" IN JEWISH LAW

In Jewish Law, it is frequently important to determine if a given patient can be classified as "terminal."[36] Jewish Law refers to the case of someone who has only a short time to live as one of "*chayei sha'ah*." However, the definition of this status is not entirely clear, and it is generally very difficult to know with certainty if a given patient can be classified as such, as even experienced clinicians often fail to make accurate prognoses.

There is no standard clinical definition of "terminal," although in contemporary medicine the word is often loosely used to refer to the prognosis of any patient with a lethal disease, and in hospice care it is often defined as one who is predicted to have six months or less to live. However, many clinicians suggest that "terminal" should be applied only to those patients whom experienced clinicians expect will die from a lethal, progressive disease despite appropriate treatment and in a relatively short period of time, measured in days, weeks, or at most several months.[37]

Although most Rabbinic authorities are reluctant to specify a predicted lifespan for this determination, many rule that anyone who will not survive for more than twelve months is considered "terminal."[38] Others argue that six months is a more precise definition of "terminal,"[39] and this is indeed the standard that was adopted by the Israeli Dying Patient Law.[40] However, categorization of a patient as "terminal" – particularly when that categorization may lead to a decision to refrain from treatment that would prolong the life of a patient who is suffering – must be based on fully competent expert medical opinion, utilizing the best medical information available.[41] Furthermore, if there is doubt on the matter, the more stringent view must be adopted (i.e., that the patient is not terminal), as this is a matter of life and death.[42]

If a patient is dying of a given illness such that they would die within a month or two if not treated, but with aggressive interventions he or she can be kept alive for more than a year longer, the patient cannot be considered terminal. If such a patient were considered terminal, for example, any case of serious pneumonia would be considered terminal, as without antibiotics the patient would die imminently.[43]

SUMMARY: MEDICAL INTERVENTIONS FOR DYING PATIENTS

The concise summary of the consensus view thus is that:

While everything must be done to prolong life, suffering and the dying process must not be prolonged. Nevertheless, even at the end of life, basic routine necessities must be provided, as well as comfort measures. Although certain aggressive medical interventions may be withheld in some cases, they may not be withdrawn when doing so may hasten death.

For a more detailed summary, see Table 1:

Intervention	*Permissibility*
Actively hastening death	Never

Withdrawal of life-sustaining treatment	• Consensus view: Forbidden, but sometimes distinguish between:
	   □ **Withholding** – sometimes permitted, i.e., not initiating new therapy or not renewing in between cycles – see next box.
	   □ **Withdrawing** – almost always forbidden if it leads to death.
	• Minority view: May (or must) remove external impediment to death, including respirator, *if patient is a gosses* (it is difficult to be certain if a patient is a *gosses*)

Passive Inaction (i.e., DNR)	Not obligated to *actively* administer interventions that briefly prolong life, and may withhold CPR and intubation in order to *passively* allow nature to take its course under (all three of) the following conditions: 1. Patient is terminally ill, there is no chance of a cure, and the patient is heading towards death, such that medical interventions can only minimally prolong life. 2. The patient is suffering very much – physically or emotionally – even though they are receiving pain medication. 3. The patient does not want to undergo resuscitation.

Table 1

The halakhic imperative is that everything possible must be done to prolong life, but one is not obligated to initiate medical interventions that prolong suffering at the end of life. In other words, we must do everything to prolong life, but we do nothing to prolong the dying process. As we can keep a patient alive, we must do so, unless the benefit of such actions is counterbalanced by their causing extreme pain and suffering. At that point, the Torah permits a compassionate response of allowing the death process to occur with appropriate palliative care, if this is what the patient or their surrogate desires and a competent rabbi has ruled accordingly for that specific case.

Comfort measures/hospice is usually permissible in situations in which "passive inaction" is permitted (as detailed above), in consultation with a rabbinic expert, if:

1. The *intent* is only to alleviate pain, not to shorten the patient's life.
2. The dose of medicine is gradually increased as necessary to alleviate the pain, but each dose on its own is not enough to certainly shorten the patient's life.

During this time of "passive inaction" a patient must still receive *routine basic treatments* that constitute biological maintenance that are unrelated to the patient's primary illness:

Must Provide	Not Always Required

• **Oxygen:** Must intubate if necessary, *unless*:
  ☐ Consensus view (R. Auerbach, R. Sternbuch): The patient is dying (not necessarily imminently) and is suffering, and there is no possibility of meaningful recovery.
  ☐ R. Schachter: In a situation in which it is normal for people to decline a ventilator.
  ☐ R. Zilberstein: Must intubate if it will relieve suffering, even if does not extend life.
	• **Aggressive/Extraordinary measures** (determined case-by-case and is always changing)
	  ☐ surgery
	  ☐ radiation
	  ☐ chemotherapy with minimal projected benefit
	  ☐ vasopressors (subject to dispute)

• **Basic nutrition and hydration** (even artificially such as via an NG tube or PEG)
  ☐ May not be required if it increases discomfort and patient will likely die of illness before dying of starvation. Ideal to provide basic IV or subcutaneous *hydration*, as a person will normally die much quicker without hydration than they will without food.
  ☐ A suffering patient with no chance of survival may also be switched from TPN to NG or even IV feeding, and content may be reduced from concentrated nutrients to basic glucose and electrolytes in water.
  ☐ Minority opinions: Nutrition/hydration need not be provided for a dying patient.
• **Routine Medications**: insulin for a diabetic, routine antibiotics, and blood transfusions
	• **Harmful nutrition** (inability to absorb, high likelihood of aspiration)
	  ☐ In such a case, it is sufficient to provide minimal feeding by mouth instead of IV (swabs or ice chips), if possible.

Table 2

ENDNOTES

1. *Nishmat Avraham*, YD 339:4 (7) (509 in 3rd ed.); *Lev Avraham* 32:11; *Encyclopedia Hilkhatit Refu'it*, vol. 5, 142, 146.

2. *Iggerot Moshe*, CM 2:73(1); *Minchat Shlomo* 1:91; *Lev Avraham* 32:11; *Shiurei Torah Le-Rofim*, vol. 3, 313.

3. *Nishmat Avraham*, YD 339:4 (2:V) (502–3 in 3rd ed.); *Lev Avraham* 32:10; *Iggerot Moshe*, YD 2:174; CM. 2:74. Based on these principles, R. Moshe Feinstein is quoted as ruling that if a patient's heart has stopped for an extended period of time and he or she can possibly be resuscitated, but will likely be severely debilitated and thus suffer, the patient should not be resuscitated unless we know that he or she would want to be despite the associated pain. However, when we do not know the patient's wishes, we assume that most people would not want to live that way (*Masorat Moshe*, 356).

4. *Iggerot Moshe*, YD 2:174(3) and CM 2:74(1); Tatz, *Dangerous Disease and Dangerous Therapy* (2010), 106. It is important to note that there is a difference in this regard between the rulings of R. Moshe Feinstein and R. Shlomo Zalman Auerbach. R. Feinstein (*Iggerot Moshe*, YD 2:174[3]; see also CM 2:74[1]) argues that it is *forbidden* to provide medications or interventions to a dying patient who is suffering and cannot be cured, since this will prolong the patient's suffering. In contrast, R. Auerbach writes (*Minchat Shlomo* 1:91[24:2]) that it is *permissible* to withhold medications that prolong the suffering of a dying patient, if that is the patient's desire, but it is *not obligatory* to do so, because there is a merit in enduring suffering and remaining alive to engage in repentance, if a patient wants to do so (although the goal should be to prolong life, not cause suffering).

5. *Nishmat Avraham*, YD 339:4(iii) (501, 511 in 3rd ed.); *Lev Avraham* 32:10 #6.

6. R. Auerbach's position as it relates to DNR, as explained to this author by Prof. Abraham and as cited in *Nishmat Avraham*, is that the patient must not only be terminal, but suffering from an end-stage disease, for whom nothing more can be done. There is no obligation to intervene to prolong this life of suffering. R. Feinstein's ruling is very similar, but his condition is simply that the patient cannot be cured to live a normal lifespan (*chayei olam*), but can only live a short time, such as a few months (*Iggerot Moshe*, CM 2:74[1]).

7. *Lev Avraham* 32:10 #6. The suffering of the family is not a factor (unless the patient is a child). Furthermore, we are concerned only with how much the patient is suffering, not their age, mental capacity, socio-economic status, etc. (*Encyclopedia Hilkhatit Refu'it*, vol. 5, 157). R. Moshe Feinstein rules that an unresponsive patient is considered to be suffering because the soul's inability to leave the body at the end of life is considered painful, even though it is unrecognizable to an observer (*Iggerot Moshe*, YD 2:174). R. Shlomo Zalman Auerbach similarly ruled that a comatose patient is considered to be suffering and may remain DNR (*Nishmat Avraham*, YD 339:4(iii) [p. 501 in 3rd ed.]). R. Elyashiv, on the other hand, ruled that an unconscious patient cannot be considered to be in pain and thus cannot be DNR (ibid., and p. 104).

8. When possible, we must ask the patient their opinion, explaining the value of a continued life of *teshuvah* (repentance) and *ma'asim tovim* (good deeds) (*Encyclopedia Hilkhatit Refu'it*, vol. 5, 155), and we must receive the opinions of multiple expert doctors that the patient is indeed dying (*Iggerot Moshe*, CM 2:75). If we are unable to determine the patient's wishes, we are not obligated to request aggressive interventions, because we assume that the patient would not want a life of suffering prolonged (*Teshuvot Ve-Hanhagot* 6:300).

9. *Encyclopedia Hilkhatit Refu'it*, vol. 5, 156. *Nishmat Avraham*, YD, (English ed., 325 [#6]), makes the point that even in those circumstances in which a DNR order is permissible by Jewish Law, all nursing care necessary for the patient's comfort must be given. A DNR must never be seen as a DNT (Do Not Treat).

10. Prof. Avraham Steinberg, personal communication, Summer 2015. See also *Iggerot Moshe*, CM 2:73(1) and *Nishmat Avraham* YD 339, (509 in 3rd ed.). However, it would not be permissible to extubate a patient who is respirator-dependent simply by switching them to a breathing mask, because the patient will still die very shortly after the extubation.

11. Extubation is desirable when the goal is to wean a patient off a ventilator so that he can survive without it; if he cannot survive without ventilation, he would have to remain intubated. See *Iggerot Moshe*, YD 3:132; *Nishmat Avraham*, YD 339:1(4) (602–6 in 3rd ed.); R. J.D. Bleich, *Time of Death in Jewish Law* (Z. Berman Publishing, 1991), 50.

12. *Encyclopedia Hilkhatit Refu'it*, vol. 5, 148.

13. R. Avraham Union, *Le-Eit Metzo* (VITAS Innovative Hospice Care/Rabbinical Council of California, 2015, 3rd ed.), 13. Although this was not mentioned as one of the conditions listed above, it is important to ask this question because in a case of a dying patient who is rapidly declining, we would not be required to inflict such pain to no avail (R. Union, personal correspondence, Winter 2015).

14. R. Shlomo Zalman Auerbach argues that alleviating pain falls under the obligation to love one's neighbor as oneself (*Minchat Shlomo* 2–3:86). The *Tzitz Eliezer* (13:87) argues that severe pain is considered debilitating and dangerous, and administration of sophisticated pain medications is considered part of a physician's mandate to heal.

15. *Minchat Shlomo* 2–3:86; *Tzitz Eliezer* 13:87; *Nishmat Avraham*, YD 339:1(2ii) (499–500 in 3rd ed.). Some express concerns related to opioids' potential to suppress breathing. However, current medical data suggests that judicious use of opioids does not usually shorten the life of terminally ill patients (R.A. Mularski, K. Puntillo, B. Varkey, B.L. Erstad, M.L. Grap, H.C. Gilbert, D. Li, J. Medina, C. Pasero, and C.N. Sessler, "Pain Management Within the Palliative and End-of-Life Care Experience in the ICU," *CHEST* 135 [2009], 1360–69).

Healthcare professionals can offer patients and families choices for pain control. For example, patients who are alert may choose to receive adequate medication to keep them as comfortable as possible while retaining the ability to communicate. Others may prefer that medication be chosen for maximum comfort, even if it renders the patient less responsive; see J. Loike, M. Gillick, et al., "The Critical Role of Religion," 2.

Others have raised concerns related to patients becoming addicted to narcotics. R. Bleich writes that such concerns are misplaced because the result is worth the price, since "it is preferable to survive as a pain-free addict than to suffer intractable pain or not to survive at all." See Bleich, "Survey of Recent Halakhic

Literature: Palliation of Pain," *Tradition* 36(1) (2002), 109.

16. *Tzitz Eliezer* 13:87; *Teshuvot Ve-Hanhagot* 3:361; *Iggerot Moshe*, CM 2:73; Bleich, "Survey of Recent Halakhic Literature: Palliation of Pain," 89; *Shiurei Torah Le-Rofim*, vol. 3, 396; forthcoming responsum of R. Asher Weiss on "Terminal Sedation."

17. *Nishmat Avraham*, YD 339:1 (4) (499 in 3rd ed.). The principle that one may engage in potentially dangerous medical interventions that are not curative for the sake of relieving pain can also be applied to the case of undergoing a potentially dangerous surgery for the sake of relieving pain (*Iggerot Moshe*, CM 2:73).

18. Although antibiotics must be given even to a DNR patient whenever needed, as in the case of any other patient, they may be discontinued when the patient has responded to the medication and has had the full dose. If the patient does not respond or the lab results demand some other intervention, the antibiotics are changed as medically necessary. If lab results confirm that an antibiotic has been given unnecessarily, then, as in the case of any other patient, it must be stopped (personal communication with Prof. Abraham, Feb. 2015). Additionally, at the end of life, when a patient is suffering, expert medical opinion assumes that there is no chance of a recovery, and life expectancy is estimated to be very short, some rule that supportive medications such as dopamine or very advanced antibiotics need not be renewed once the IV bag has run out (Prof. Avraham Steinberg, in consultation with R. Auerbach and R. Wosner, "Halachic Guidelines for Physicians in Intensive Care Units," *Assia* 4:1 [Feb. 2001], 5–6, reprinted in *Jewish Medical Ethics*, vol. 2 [Jerusalem, 2006], 376–8). This is because antibiotics are only required when they can actually cure an infection. For example, if a dying patient develops an additional illness, such as pneumonia, if it is treatable with antibiotics, we must treat it in order to prolong the patient's life, even though he or she is dying of the underlying illness in any case. However, if the patient develops a very significant secondary illness, such as an overwhelming sepsis, and the regular antibiotics will not resolve it, the sepsis is then considered as part of the dying process. Even though complex fifth generation antibiotic treatment could be attempted to keep the patient alive slightly longer, this illness is now part of the dying process and the advanced antibiotics needed to fight it are not required, unless a specific bacteria that caused the sepsis can be identified and advanced antibiotics can indeed cure it (Prof. Avraham Steinberg, personal communication, Summer 2015). See also *Iggerot Moshe*, CM 2:74(2) and 75(4), who writes that treatable secondary conditions that arise must be treated, even though the patient's primary illness cannot be cured, and *Nishmat Avraham*, YD 339:4(iii) (503 in 3rd ed.). Furthermore, in situations in which placing an intravenous (IV) catheter for antibiotic administration will lead to excessive pain, IV antibiotics may be withheld (personal communication with Prof. Abraham).

19. *Nishmat Avraham*, YD 339:4 (7) (498, 509 in 3rd ed.); *Lev Avraham* 32:10; *Teshuvot Ve-Hanhagot* 6:300; A. Steinberg, "The Halachic Basis of the Dying Patient Law," *Assia* 6(2) (2008), 30–40. Some authorities rule that vasopressor medications ("pressers" for maintaining blood pressure), such as dopamine, may be withheld from a dying patient who is suffering (but not actively withdrawn, especially if it may lead to an immediate drop in blood pressure and death), by simply refraining from restarting the treatment once the infusion pouch has emptied on its own, because this can be considered a medical therapy and not a basic need, such as nutrition or oxygen

(Prof. Avraham Steinberg in the name of R. Auerbach and R. Wosner, *Assia* 63–64 [5729], 18–19; "The Halachic Basis of the Dying Patient Law," *Assia* 6[2] [2008], 30–40, reprinted in *Jewish Medical Ethics*, vol. 3, 419). Similarly, R. Moshe Feinstein has been quoted as ruling that a dying patient who is on a respirator does not need to be given medications to extend his life (R. Aaron Felder, *Rishumei Aharon*, vol. 1, 70). R. Zilberstein, however, includes blood pressure medication as a required basic necessity (*Shiurei Torah Le-Rofim*, vol. 3, 312, 321).

20. R. Zilberstein, *Shiurei Torah Le-Rofim* 189, vol. 3, 312, and ibid., 190, vol. 3, 321; R. Union, *Le-Eit Metzo*, 15. Prof. Abraham clarified in a personal conversation that all major surgical procedures are not considered routine. As a rule of thumb, most procedures for which informed consent is required are not considered routine. Norms for what is considered routine or not routine can change over time as the practice of medicine evolves, and the input of a Rabbinic authority familiar with these details is therefore essential.

21. *Nishmat Avraham, Yoreh De'ah* 339:4 (7) (509 in 3rd ed.); *Lev Avraham* 32:10 (1); *Encyclopedia Hilkhatit Refu'it*, vol. 5, 146. *Shiurei Torah Le-Rofim*, vol. 3, 323–4. Jewish Law does not view the provision of nutrition and hydration as a medical intervention, but rather as simply providing the vehicle for bringing natural nutrition to the body (*Iggerot Moshe*, CM 2:74[3]). Since the food being provided is a basic necessity, it must usually be provided, even artificially, and this does not constitute a medical intervention. A ventilator, in contrast, must be carefully gauged and continuously adjusted; it is thus viewed as a medical intervention and is therefore not always required in every situation. However, oxygen by mask should always be provided, since this is comparable to nutrition and hydration; it provides natural sustenance and is not

a treatment (Prof. Avraham Steinberg, personal communication, Summer 2015).

22. When given the option, some recommend choosing a PEG over an NG tube since a PEG is generally more comfortable and results in fewer complications (Prof. Avraham Steinberg, personal communication, Summer 2015).

23. *Encyclopedia Hilkhatit Refu'it*, vol. 5, 146; *Shiurei Torah Le-Rofim*, vol. 3, 320; *Iggerot Moshe*, CM 2:74 (3); *Minchat Shlomo* 91:24. Nutrition is considered a natural need, not something external that prevents the soul from leaving. Withholding food from an individual, thereby causing him to starve to death, is therefore classified as murder, and nutrition may thus generally not be withheld even from a dying patient. See *Sanhedrin* 77a; Rambam, *Hilkhot Rotzeach* 3:10; Steinberg, "*Retzach Mitoch Rachamim Le-Ohr Ha-Halakhah*," *Assia* 3 (5743), 448. See also discussion in R. Shilat, *Refuah Halakhah Ve-Kavanot Ha-Torah*, 57–59. As precedent, some also quote the ruling of the Ran in *Shavuot* (10a) that if one makes an oath not to eat or drink, their oath is invalid since it is regarded as an oath to commit suicide and thereby transgress the Torah, which is not binding.

R. Shilat (*Refuah Halakhah Ve-Kavanot Ha-Torah*, 51–52) points out an important distinction between the rulings of R. Feinstein and R. Auerbach as they relate to the obligation to provide nutrition, hydration, and oxygen. R. Feinstein requires these interventions because they may reduce pain, even if we cannot perceive that pain. Strengthening the body with nutrition enables a person to better endure pain, such that the reduction of pain is what makes these interventions proper. On the other hand, R. Auerbach seems to require them because they are basic human necessities.

One of the few authorities who allow withdrawal of nutrition/hydration from a terminal patient is R. Zalman Nechemia

Goldberg, who argues that we are obligated to save such a patient only when the patient benefits from being saved. However, there is no obligation to treat a patient who is suffering so much that "death is better than life" or one who has absolutely no cognition or ability to communicate. R. Goldberg claims that withdrawing nourishment would not be considered an indirect cause of death because it is the overall lack of nourishment that the patient dies from, not the action of removing nourishment (*Moriah* 4–5:88–89 [Elul 5738]: 48–56). Some have suggested that if this is done, the IV bag should simply be allowed to run out, instead of actively removing it (see citations in Steinberg, "*Retzach Mitoch Rachamim Le-Ohr Ha-Halakhah*," 448).

Many other authorities have challenged R. Goldberg's position; see, for example, R. Levi Yitzchak Halperin, *Halakhah U-Refuah* (Regensberg Institute, 1981), vol. 2, 146–84, esp. 150–55; R. Bleich, *Bioethical Dilemmas*, vol. 1, 106, fn. 36; R. Zilberstein, *Shiurei Torah Le-Rofim*, vol. 3, 317. R. Halperin argues that withholding nourishment should be viewed as an indirect cause of death and is thus forbidden. He sees no difference between one who disconnects the food supply from the patient and one who acts passively and neglects to replenish it.

In a personal conversation in the summer of 2015, R. Goldberg told this author that his approach was not accepted by most Rabbinic authorities, and that one should therefore follow the rulings of R. Auerbach and R. Feinstein, as outlined in *Nishmat Avraham*. Indeed, in later publications on these issues, R. Goldberg seems to advocate for the views of R. Auerbach and R. Feinstein over his own (see *Assia* 16:3–5 [63–64] 5759, 6–8). However, R. Hershel Schachter told this author that he agrees with R. Goldberg's position, and that one may passively refrain from providing nutrition and hydration for a dying patient, or allow the bags of nutri-

tion to run out, even if it means that the patient will die as a result, if this is what they want because their death is preferable to their life. See also R. Zev Schostak, "Ethical Guidelines for Treatment of the Dying Elderly," *Journal of Halacha and Contemporary Society* 22 (Fall 1991), 84.

24. A. Steinberg and C.L. Sprung, "The Dying Patient: New Israeli Legislation," *Intensive Care Medicine* 32 (2006), 1236. As they note, on a social and emotional level, there is a fundamental difference between provision of food and fluid versus other life-sustaining treatments. Jewish Law views death by starvation or dehydration as a violation of human dignity.

25. *Minchat Shlomo* 91:24; *Iggerot Moshe*, CM 2:74(3); *Encyclopedia Hilkhatit Refu'it*, vol. 5, 146. See also J. Kunin, "Withholding Artificial Feeding from the Severely Demented: Merciful or Immoral? Contrasts Between Secular and Jewish Perspectives," *Journal of Medical Ethics* (2003), 208–12. See, however, the opinion of R. Hershel Schachter quoted above.

26. *Iggerot Moshe*, CM 2:74. Other authorities rule that we should even try to force them (*Minchat Shlomo* 91:24). R. Zilberstein (*Shiurei Torah Le-Rofim* 3:189, p. 314) writes that patients should be encouraged to take medications to prolong their life, but if they refuse because of the suffering they are experiencing, they would be considered "*ones*" (forced/compelled), and thus not sinning.

27. Loike, et al., "The Critical Role of Religion," 3.

28. Ibid.

29. *Encyclopedia Hilkhatit Refu'it*, vol. 5, 147; A. Steinberg, "The Use of Percutaneous Endoscopic Gastrostomy (PEG) in Demented Patients: A Halachic View," *Journal of Jewish Medical Ethics and Halacha* 7 (2009), 41–42; *Encyclopedia Hilkhatit Refu'it*, vol. 5, 112.

30. *Iggerot Moshe*, CM 2:74 (3).

31. R. J.D. Bleich, *Bioethical Dilemmas*, vol. 1, 94.

32. *Lev Avraham* 32:10(2). However, if it has already been initiated, complete withdrawal of nutrition would be forbidden if it will hasten death (*Nishmat Avraham*, YD 339:4 (7) [509 in 3rd ed.]).

33. *Encyclopedia Hilkhatit Refu'it*, vol. 5, 147. This is because a person will normally die much quicker without hydration than they will without food. Thus, even in a situation in which we may not be required to provide nutrition at the end of life, providing hydration is nevertheless encouraged. However, even hydration should be monitored according to the medical situation, not according to philosophical-ethical considerations (Prof. Avraham Steinberg, personal communication, Summer 2015).

34. B. Kinzbrunner, "Medicine and Halakhah: End-of-Life Care," *Be-Ohr Ha-Torah* 24 (2016–2017), 103.

35. A. Steinberg, "The Halachic Basis of the Dying Patient Law," *Assia* 6(2) (2008), 30–40 (*Jewish Medical Ethics*, vol. 3, 419). See also Steinberg, *Encyclopedia of Jewish Medical Ethics*, 1058.

36. See *Encyclopedia Hilkhatit Refu'it*, vol. 5, 443–6, for a list of situations in which it is important to know a person's life expectancy, such as cases of triage, lifesaving, divorce, and inheritance. See also summary of some of the opinions in *Nishmat Avraham*, CM 427:10 (260–1 in 3rd ed.).

37. See N. Christakis, *Death Foretold: Prophecy and Prognosis in Medical Care* (University of Chicago Press, 1999).

38. R. Shlomo Kluger, *Chokhmat Shlomo*, YD 155:1 (quoted by *Darkhei Teshuvah*, YD 155:6), bases this timeframe on the Talmudic definition of a *tereifah* (a person or animal suffering from a fatal anom-

aly). See the discussion of this source in Tatz, *Dangerous Disease and Dangerous Therapy* (2013), 102; Bleich, *Bioethical Dilemmas*, vol. 2, 258–63.; R. A.I. Kook, *Mishpat Kohen* 144:3. Although R. Kook quotes R. Kluger and agrees with his categorization of terminal as one year to live, based on an episode in *Megillat Esther*, he writes that a patient can be considered terminal if they are diagnosed as suffering from a condition that we know will be fatal from the moment of diagnosis, regardless of the patient's particular life expectancy. R. Moshe Feinstein, *Iggerot Moshe*, CM 2:75(2) and YD 3:36, writes that the period of 6 months quoted by the *Achiezer* (2:16[6]) may only have applied in that particular case at hand, but was not intended as a general rule. See also *Nishmat Avraham*, YD 155 (84–85 in 3rd ed.); *Encyclopedia Hilkhatit Refu'it*, vol. 5, 443; R. Zilberstein, *Shiurei Torah Le-Rofim* 2:139.

39. R. Asher Weiss, *Minchat Asher* 1:115(2), based on *Achiezer* 2:16(6). R. Weiss argues that it is impossible to give a precise number, as anyone who is expected to die within a time period that most people consider to be brief can be described as "terminal." However, the general rule of 6 months is the best to establish this status, since a medical prediction that a given patient has 6 months to live is generally somewhat accurate, particularly as opposed to the much more difficult prediction of a year.

40. Prof. Avraham Steinberg, personal communication. The 6-month standard was chosen because some diseases can be more accurately predicted within such a time span, rather than a full year. Furthermore, if there is a mistake in the prognosis and the patient does not die within 6 months, he or she may still die within the 12-month period. However, because R. Elyashiv argued that "terminal" should be defined as having 2 to 3 months to live (see Kunin, "Caring for the Terminally

Ill," *Jewish Medical Ethics*, vol. 3, 318; *Assia* 10:1 [Aug. 2005], 22–28), a provision was made in the law for those who follow his ruling.

41. *Iggerot Moshe*, CM 2:74(1).

42. Tatz, *Dangerous Disease*, 107. It should be noted that according to the *Tzitz Eliezer* (10:25[17]), any patient with an illness that threatens their life even on an intermittent basis can be classified as a *chayei sha'ah*. This would permit high-risk surgery for such patients. In contrast, R. Moshe Feinstein argues that since this patient can theoretically remain in this situation for several years, he is not classified as *chayei sha'ah* and may not risk his life for a chance of a cure (*Iggerot Moshe*, YD 3:36).

43. Prof. Avraham Steinberg, personal communication. However, Prof. Steinberg notes that it is important to take into account the amount of pain and suffering caused to the patient by continued living as a result of the interventions, as well as the pain caused by the treatment itself (see *Minchat Shlomo* 1:91[24] and 2:82[4]).

C. WITHHOLDING VS. WITHDRAWING: Deactivating a Ventilator and Cessation of Dialysis and Cardiac Defibrillators at the End of Life

One of the most common and challenging ethical dilemmas faced in hospitals today concerns the withdrawal of treatment from dying patients. Prof. Avraham Steinberg has reported that when the Dying Patient Law was being debated in the Israeli Parliament (Knesset), one of the ministers protested, "In America they have no problem removing the ventilator from dying patients. I don't understand why we can't allow it as well!" Prof. Steinberg responded, "If that's how you feel, we currently have many patients at Shaare Zedek Medical Center whose lives are being supported artificially. Would you like to volunteer to come and remove the life support from them for us?" The minister responded, "I would never be able to live with myself if I did something like that!" After that exchange, the debate ended . . .

WITHHOLDING VS. WITHDRAWING

As we have seen, Jewish values place great emphasis on the sanctity of human life and the importance of its preservation. This ruling does not distinguish between a patient who is young and vigorous and one who is dying of a terminal malady; Jewish thought attributes sanctity to all human life.[1] Based on this, one might conclude that Jewish Law would require any means necessary to prolong life, and would therefore prohibit withholding any sort of beneficial treatment. Physicians should always be obligated to treat, even in the case of a terminally ill patient.

However, many contemporary authorities in Jewish Law distinguish between patients who may still have a normal lifespan and those who have terminal conditions. These authorities rule that a therapy that only prolongs suffering of a patient with an incurable illness may be withheld if that patient does not want to endure that suffering. In these situations, a physician may passively refrain from acting.[2] For this reason, Jewish Law sometimes permits *withholding* life-prolonging interventions in dying patients. The same, however, cannot be said regarding the *withdrawal* of therapies that have already been initiated. Jewish Law considers stopping therapy to be the performance of an action, whereas withholding therapy is considered passive.[3] In other words, this approach distinguishes between acts of omission (sometimes permitted) and acts of commission (often forbidden), or, as some thinkers have framed it, "allowing" or "letting die" versus "causing death" or "killing."[4]

EXTUBATION AT THE END OF LIFE

Jewish Law regards the provision of oxygen as a basic human necessity.[5] Thus, although it is not always required to intubate (place on a ventilator) a dying patient who is suffering,[6] once the patient has already been intubated, Jewish Law generally prohibits extubation (removing them from the ventilator) if the patient may die shortly thereafter as a result.

The various rulings on this matter are complex and many authorities cannot be neatly categorized. Nevertheless, for the sake of clarity and simpler understanding, we can conceptualize the halakhic opinions into two categories: those who view terminal extubation as murder or hastening death and those who see it as not saving a life. Murder is forbidden and saving a life is obligatory, but the prohibition against murder is much more stringent; saving a life is not obligatory in all situations.

The Accepted View

The majority view is that terminal extubation (sometimes also called "compassionate extubation" or "palliative extubation") is tantamount to killing the patient,[7] and thus it is always prohibited to remove a ventilator that is maintaining life.[8]

This perspective is not necessarily advocating that the life of a suffering dying patient should be prolonged at all costs. Rather, it is based on concerns related to any human intervention in terminating life.

According to some authorities, Jewish Law conceptualizes extubation as killing the patient because of a Talmudic principle that one may not perform any action that directly results (*koach rishon*) in another person's death if the process begins immediately subsequent to the human action (even if that action simply removes an impediment to death).[9] Although some secular ethicists do not view deactivation of a ventilator as being the cause of the patient's death, many authorities in Jewish Law have indeed categorized death soon after extubation as a direct result. Extubation is therefore viewed as *causing* the death of the patient, not merely *allowing* it to happen, in the eyes of Jewish Law.[10] Furthermore, even though when it comes to the laws of Shabbat, some types of indirect causation (*grama*) are sometimes permitted, this is forbidden by the Torah when it comes to the laws of damages and murder.[11]

The Minority Opinion

Although it is generally not followed, there is a more lenient minority opinion based on a certain application of a ruling of the Rema. The Rema writes that it is forbidden to perform an overt act that hastens death, but one may actively remove an external impediment to death of a patient who is already almost certainly in the process of dying imminently and cannot be restored to good health (*gosses*).[12] Based on this principle, some rule that a ventilator can be categorized as an artificial impediment to dying, as it artificially prevents the soul from departing, and it is thus not only permitted to remove it from a dying patient, but it may even be required to do so in certain cases to relieve suffering.[13] These authorities view extubation not as killing the patient, but as simply failing to save them. This can at times be permitted, or even obligatory, in order to minimize suffering.[14]

Those who forbid extubation respond that the Rema's ruling only applies in the case of a patient classified as a *gosses* (one who is actively dying). It is usually difficult to determine with certainty if a given patient can be classified as a *gosses*, and with modern medical technology, few dying patients can be placed in this category.[15] Since this matter is subject to debate, and some argue that deactivating a ventilator falls under the severe prohibition of murder, their conclusion is that it is difficult to be lenient.[16]

When Extubation Is Certainly Permitted

Intubation is always intended to be a temporary measure until a patient stabilizes and can be safely extubated. Thus, if medical experts determine that a patient is stable enough to breathe on their own, it is permitted to extubate them. As long as the patient can survive for some time after being extubated (and assuming an expert in Jewish Law has approved), the patient may be extubated, after which further interventions can be withheld, such that the patient will then not be reintubated should their condition decline at a later time. The amount of time that the patient must be able to survive after extubation in order to adopt this approach is a matter of debate. According to the most lenient view, one must at least be able to survive for a number of hours; according to the most stringent view, the patient must be able to survive for at least a full 48 hours after extubation.[17] Regardless, if the patient's condition deteriorates very soon after extubation and they cannot survive on their own, they must be re-intubated immediately.[18]

Another situation in which many authorities permit extubation is in a case in which the patient shows definite clinical signs of already being deceased and the ventilator is the only thing keeping the patient appearing as if "alive."[19] In such a case, it can be argued that the ventilator is an impediment preventing the soul from leaving the body (although the ventilator should be turned off before physically extubating to avoid the problem of a moving a *gosses*).[20]

OTHER POSSIBLE OPTIONS

It is sometimes not certain that a patient may be safely extubated, but there may be circumstances or methods through which the patient can nevertheless be extubated in order to relieve suffering.[21] For example, if a terminal patient who is suffering greatly has become ventilator dependent, it is sometimes still possible to gradually wean him or her off the ventilator (or certain medications), as long as the patient can tolerate this and it will not cause them to die immediately. This is done by making gradual controlled changes in the settings while monitoring the patient, slowly reducing the rate and oxygen concentration regulated by the ventilator, each time only to a point at which the patient can remain stable. If the patient can indeed be kept stable during this process, one would not be required to increase the settings if, at a later time, the patient should then become unstable, assuming that this is a dying patient whom a Rabbinic authority has ruled does not require further aggressive interventions. This process can be viewed as withholding intervention, instead of withdrawing.[22]

However, this option is not always plausible, as many ventilator dependent patients are unable to safely sustain their own breathing for any period of time and may thus die very soon as a result of this procedure. Furthermore, many Rabbinic authorities do not approve of this option.[23]

Most authorities do not require intubating, or re-intubating, a dying patient who is not currently on a ventilator.[24] There are times, such as in an Emergency Room setting, when it is possible that intubation could be beneficial for a given patient, but if it turns out that it was not beneficial, the patient may become "vent dependent" and it will then be forbidden to extubate them, thus prolonging their suffering and dying processes. To address situations like this and other similar complicated scenarios that sometimes arise, some suggest that hospitals should use ventilators that are regulated by a timer.[25] The timer would cause the machine to operate at regular intervals, briefly switching it off from time to time. When the ventilator is scheduled to be shut off, the patient can be reevaluated; one can then either renew the timer or passively allow it to shut the machine off. If the patient is determined to be dead during the time that the ventilator has switched itself off, it need not be restarted, and the patient may be removed from the machine. Not renewing treatment that has been interrupted can be viewed as withholding treatment, instead of withdrawing it, which is sometimes permitted. Those who permit this option do so only if the patient was connected to such a device from the outset; they may not be transferred to a ventilator with a timer.[26] Others limit its use to triage situations.[27]

However, the specific technology required to implement this system according to Jewish Law is complex and has not yet been approved or implemented with patients in a clinical setting. Moreover, some authorities have ruled that such a system would still be categorized as leading to the killing of the patient, and would thus be prohibited.[28]

In general, physicians advise against leaving patients on a ventilator for too long. When Jewish Law will not permit a patient to be extubated, the next step is to undergo a tracheotomy, in which a hole is made in the patient's neck to open a direct airway through the trachea (the windpipe), with a tube allowing a person to breathe without the use of his or her nose or mouth. Some authorities, realizing that living for years with a tracheostomy in a vegetative-like state in a special vent facility may be suboptimal, instead suggest that the patient be left intubated, despite the risks that entails, allowing the patient to either recover or die of their underlying illness down the line.[29] However, many facilities will not permit this, and keeping a patient on a ventilator entails much potential harm to the patient, including tracheal erosion and new infections (ventilator acquired pneumonia, etc.).

This leads to a dilemma – some physicians or family members do not want a patient to be on a tracheostomy for an indefinite period of time, but if they do not, the patient may die a prolonged and agonizing death related to overwhelming infection. Some of the above strategies can be utilized to navigate this situation, and knowledge of these potential dilemmas should be considered at the outset when a patient or his surrogate is faced with the option to intubate a patient. Palliative care should also be involved in such situations to mitigate the suffering associated with this process.

APPLYING THESE PRINCIPLES TO DIALYSIS

In their discussion of the distinction between withholding and withdrawing, some Rabbinic authorities also distinguish between treatments that are *continuous* (i.e., ventilator or cardiac pacemaker), in which withdrawal of treatment is considered a forbidden act of commission, and treatments that are *cyclical/intermittent* (i.e., dialysis, chemotherapy, or implanted cardiac defibrillators[30]), in which the withholding of the next cycle of treatment may be considered a permissible act of omission.[31] For this reason, although Rabbinic authorities require dialysis treatment when it is medically indicated,[32] some rule that it is permissible to refrain from restarting dialysis between cycles in some circumstances of a dying patient who is suffering.[33]

However, some authorities distinguish between a patient who has already begun receiving dialysis for some time (i.e., chronically), for whom dialysis is considered their regular, and thus required, treatment, and new renal-failure patients who require emergent dialysis for the first time in the face of critical illness. According to these authorities, one is not always required to initiate dialysis; one may instead passively refrain (withhold) from beginning this intervention, as discussed above.[34] Furthermore, if one simply attempted dialysis as a trial, such that it has not become their regular treatment, it may be discontinued between cycles.[35] However, according to this view, a patient who has already begun to receive dialysis routinely for an extended period of time (i.e., not just as a trial) may not discontinue their dialysis treatments, even between cycles, because it is now seen as a normal (not "extraordinary") procedure for them.[36] The dialysis machine is considered as if it has become the patient's kidneys, and it therefore may not be stopped, even though dialysis usually only functions intermittently.[37]

SUMMARY: WHEN MAY A VENTILATOR BE WITHDRAWN IN ACCORDANCE WITH HALAKHAH?

1. The patient is stable enough to breathe on his or her own:
    a. As long as patients can survive for some time after being extubated, if they meet stipulations of Jewish Law to qualify for DNR ("passive inaction"), they need not reintubate either (see previous chapter).
        i.   Most lenient view: The patient must be able to survive at least "a number of hours" to determine if the patient was clinically stable enough for withdrawal.
        ii. Stringent view: The patient must be able to survive a minimum of 48 hours.
2. The patient shows definite clinical signs of already being deceased:
    a. The machine should be turned off before physically extubating to avoid moving a *gosses*.
3. Gradually wean patient from ventilator or lower the settings, as long as this will not cause immediate instability or death, followed by withholding further interventions:
    a. This option is not always medically possible and many *poskim* (authorities in Jewish law) do not accept it
4. If patient is extubated for some reason, may not be obligated to reintubate.
5. Timer:
    a. Only permitted if the patient is initially attached to such a device; he cannot be switched to one
    b. Others permit only in triage situations
    c. Many authorities oppose
6. Remain intubated but allow certain medications, such as "pressers," which are not considered routine basic maintenance, to run out and

then passively avoid refilling IV bag (discussed in previous chapter).
7. Leave patient intubated for extended period of time
   a. Must take into account risks this entails and often against hospital policy
   b. Must ensure pain and discomfort is well managed
8. Tracheotomy

ENDNOTES

1. R. Immanuel Jakobovits, *Jewish Medical Ethics* (Bloch Publishing, 1959), 276; *Nishmat Avraham*, YD 339:1(4) (p. 497 in 3rd ed.); *Iggerot Moshe*, CM 2:74(1). Furthermore, one is obligated to violate Shabbat in order to save a life, even if the person is dying (*Yoma* 85a), and if a physician is able to heal a patient but does not do so, it is considered murder (*Shulchan Arukh*, YD 336:1).

2. *Iggerot Moshe*, CM 2:73, 74(1). R. Feinstein bases his ruling on the story of R. Yehudah Ha-Nasi recorded in *Ketuvot* 104a, as well as the permission of the Rema (YD 339) for a woodcutter in the vicinity of a dying patient to stop chopping wood in order to provide the quiet that will allow the patient to die. *Shevet HaLevi* 6:179 rules similarly based on this source. See also *Teshuvot Minchat Asher* 1:116. See also *Nishmat Avraham*, YD 339:4 (504, 506 in 3rd ed.), where this principle is applied to intubation and initiation of dialysis.

3. Steinberg, *Encyclopedia of Jewish Medical Ethics*, 1059; A. Steinberg, "*Retzach Mitokh Rachamim Le-Ohr Ha-Halakhah*," *Assia* 3(5743), 448 (available: http://98.131.138.124/articles/ASSIA/ASSIA3/R0031424.asp). One of the proofs that Prof. Steinberg cites (n. 94) to support this distinction is the ruling that if one is issued an ultimatum to kill another person or else be killed, one must allow him or herself to be killed and not transgress the prohibition against murdering another person (*Yoma* 82a–b), since murder is one of the three sins that one has to die rather than violate, and fulfilling the ultimatum would constitute an *active* act murder.

On the other hand, if one is in the desert and has only enough water for himself, R. Akiva rules (*Bava Metzia* 62a) that one does not have to give it to the other person that they are with, even though the other person will die as a result, because this is *passive*.

Similarly, one of the classical sources on proper treatment of a dying patient, the *Shiltei Gibborim* (*Moed Katan*, 16b, *Rif*), which is quoted by the Rema (YD 339), rules that "if there is something that is indirectly causing one's soul not to depart, it is permissible to remove that impediment, and this is not problematic at all, because he is not 'placing his finger on the candle,' nor doing an act. But to place something on the dying patient or to move him from place to place so that his soul will depart more quickly is definitely forbidden, because he is 'placing his finger on the candle.'" This ruling implies a distinction between removing an impediment to death (i.e., being an indirect cause), which is sometimes permitted, and doing an action to bring about a direct cause that leads to hastening one's death, which is forbidden. See analysis in Shilat, *Refuah, Halakha, Ve-Kavanot Ha-Torah*, 55–6.

Although some secular ethicists argue that there is actually no true philosophical difference between withholding and withdrawing life-sustaining treatment, many studies have demonstrated that experientially there is in fact a difference, as noted by most practicing clinicians. See S. Glick, "Withholding Versus Withdrawal of Life Support: Is There an Ethical Difference?," *The British Medical Journal (BMJ)* 342 (2011), d728. For this reason, it has been quipped that instead of using the phrase "physician-assisted suicide," the term should be "philosopher assisted suicide" (C. Elliot, "Philosopher Assisted Suicide and Euthanasia," *BMJ* 313 [1996], 1088–89).

4. For example, Dr. Daniel Sulmasy writes that although several contemporary philosophers, clinicians, and U.S. court rulings have suggested that there is no meaningful distinction between *killing* and *allowing to die*, he argues that this distinction has been recognized in common morality, intuition, medicine, and the Hippocratic tradition for many centuries (D. Sulmasy, "Killing and Allowing to Die: Another Look," *Journal of Law, Medicine & Ethics*, 26 (1998), 55–64). In this view, he claims, except in cases of self-defense or rescue, *all killing* is morally wrong, whereas only *some allowing to die* is also morally wrong, but some is not. For further analysis, see also Beauchamp and Childress, *Principles of Biomedical Ethics*, 174.

5. This is based on the ruling of the Rambam (*Hilkhot Rotzeach* 3:1) that walling a person in so that they cannot breathe is a capital offense because it is like strangling them. See *Iggerot Moshe*, CM 2:73a; *Minchat Shlomo* 1:91 (24); A. Steinberg, "The Halakhic Basis of the Dying Patient Law," *Assia* 69–70, 23–58; *Assia* 71–72, 25–39; *Encyclopedia Hilkhatit Refu'it*, vol. 5, 147; R. Moshe Hershler, "*Chiyuv Hatzalah Be-Cholim U-Mesukanim*," in *Halakhah U-Refuah*, vol. 2, 31–34.

6. *Nishmat Avraham*, YD 339:(4) (502–6 in 3rd ed.) quotes R. Shlomo Zalman Auerbach as ruling that in the case of a patient with end-stage disease (but not necessarily a *gosses*) who is suffering and for whom nothing more can be done, major interventions such as intubation that only prolong a life of suffering are not required. R. Shlomo Zalman Auerbach implies that use of a respirator is

not considered "routine" treatment that is always required. See also Shilat, *Refuah Halakhah, Ve-Kavanot Ha-Torah*, 53), and *Encylopedia Hilkhatit Refu'it*, vol. 5, 148.

R. Asher Weiss shared with this author (private correspondence, Winter 2016) that his general rule is that we are only required to intubate a patient if there is a chance that they will eventually recover, be able to be extubated, and return to their level of health prior to being intubated, when the need arose. However, if it is just a stage before the patient's death and there will be little chance of safely extubating the patient, one need not be intubated in the first place. *Teshuvot Ve-Hanhagot* 6:300 provides similar guidelines as to when it is obligatory to connect a dying patient to a ventilator, ruling that if there is no possibility that through intubation the patient will return to living with consciousness, there is no obligation to connect them to a ventilator (although the patient must still receive basic necessities, such as food and oxygen). However, if there is any chance that the patient can return to living with consciousness, even for a very brief time period, they must be intubated. Furthermore, if a patient is able to live fully by being connected to a ventilator, even if they do not have complete consciousness or if they suffer from Alzheimer's disease, they must still be intubated, unless they will suffer from horrible pain. (This is true even if the patient did not state their opinion on the matter, because we can assume that most people would not want a life of suffering to be extended.)

R. Moshe Feinstein has been quoted as ruling that a dying elderly patient who the doctors say cannot be cured from their current illness must only be given fluids and nothing else (R. Aaron Felder, *Rishumei Aharon*, vol. 1, 70). R. Y. Zilberstein has slightly stricter guidelines, ruling that while we are not obligated to extend terminal life if treatment increases or extends suffering, if treatment would mitigate suffering, even if it does not extend life, it would be obligatory and one should be convinced to do so (*Shiurei Torah Le-Rofim* 189, vol. 3, 312). In contrast, R. Hershel Schachter has ruled that one is not required to be intubated "in a situation in which it is normal for people to decline a ventilator or feeding tube" (as reported by R. Mordechai Torczyner; see also *Be-ikvei Ha-Tzon* 34).

7. *Encyclopedia Hilkhatit Refu'it*, vol. 5, 148 (see also *Encyclopedia of Jewish Medical Ethics*, 1058); Loike, et al., "The Critical Role of Religion," 3.

8. *Tzitz Eliezer* 17:72(13); *Iggerot Moshe*, YD 3:132. *Teshuvot Ve-Hanhagot* 1:858 writes that since extubation is categorized as killing, one cannot remove from a ventilator a patient who can only live *chayei sha'ah* for the sake of one who can live *chayei olam*. Furthermore, even once a patient has died (demonstrating no heartbeat or respiration), he may not be extubated for at least another 6 minutes (or more for a trauma victim), out of concern that they are not really dead yet and touching a *gosses* can hasten their death (ibid., 6:300). See also R. Shlomo Zalman Auerbach in Avraham Steinberg, *Assia* 53–54 (5754), 5; R. Yitzchak Isaac Liebes, *Beit Avi* 153; R. Ben Zion Firer, *Techumin* 7 (5746), 219ff.; R. Yitzchak Yedidia Frankel, *Assia* 3 (5743), 463 ff.; R. Yisrael Meir Lau, *Yachel Yisrael* 2:87.

9. *Tzitz Eliezer* 17:72(13), citing *Sanhedrin* 77b; Rambam, *Hilkhot Rotzeach* 3:13; and *Yad Ramah, Sanhedrin* 77b, who explain that simply releasing a stone and allowing it to drop downwards and kill someone, without actively propelling it, nevertheless renders the perpetrator liable to execution because removing an impediment to an object's natural motion is tantamount to actively propelling it. R. Zilberstein discusses this ruling of the *Tzitz Eliezer* and the sources he

quotes, and argues that while extubation is prohibited, if one is simply giving mouth-to-mouth resuscitation or holding their hand on an open wound so that it does not bleed, if one lets go, they are not considered a murderer, because they did not cause the death (especially if one lets go in order to treat another patient, in which case it was an act of saving a life). In contrast, if one extubates a terminal patient, it is not certain if they should be considered a murderer or not. On the one hand, they did not do an action that actually caused the death of the patient; on the other hand, perhaps the ventilator is considered to have become part of the patient's body, and turning it off is like literally taking their life away. R. Zilberstein does not resolve this question (*Shiurei Torah Le-Rofim* 3:161 [69–70, 73, especially n. 3]).

10. *Tzitz Eliezer* 17:72 (13); *Iggerot Moshe*, YD 3:132. Another reason that has been suggested for this prohibition is that the *mishnah* teaches, "Against your will you are born . . . against your will you die" (*Avot* 4:22). Life is not in our hands, but is rather based only on the will of God, so we should not determine when people die (see *Massekhet Avot Oz Vehadar Ha-Mevo'ar*, Metivta, vol. 4, *Aliba De-Hilkhata* 9).

11. R. Auerbach, quoted in *Nishmat Avraham*, CM 425:2 (160 in 3rd ed.) and YD 339 (507 in 3rd ed.), based on Rambam, *Hilkhot Rotzeach* 2:2–3, 3:10, and *Shulchan Arukh*, CM 32:2; R. Levi Yitzchak Halperin, *Halakhah U-Refuah*, vol. 2, 146–84. Furthermore, even in the context of the laws of Shabbat, if one wants to bring about certain results and intends for it to happen, if the action is done via an indirect causation, it is forbidden according to some opinions (Rosh, *Bava Kamma* 60).

12. Rema, YD 339:1. The Rema prohibits removing a pillow or cushion from

under a dying patient, because it is said that the feathers of certain fowl cause a prolongation of dying, but he permits removing salt from the patient's tongue that is preventing their soul from leaving them. Some explain that the removal of the feathers has a mystical power that actually causes the death, which is why it is forbidden (*Levush* 339:1). Others explain that the problem with moving the feathers is that it would involve significant moving of the dying patient (unlike the minor touch involved with removing salt from the tongue), and these movements could lead to the frail patient's death (*Taz*, YD 339:2; *Shakh*, YD 339:7). For an in-depth analysis of this ruling and how it relates to contemporary medical dilemmas, see Prof. Avraham Steinberg, *Assia* 69–70:23–58, and *Assia* 71–72:25–39; David Shabtai, "End-of-Life Therapies," *Journal of Halacha and Contemporary Society* 56 (Fall 2008), 25; Bleich, *Bioethical Dilemmas*, vol. 1, 77, 83.

Beit Yaakov (59) rules that we can violate Shabbat labors to save the life of a *gosses* only when there is an expert medical opinion that there is something that can be done to heal the individual. If the person is certainly dying, we are not permitted to violate Shabbat labors on his behalf. Indeed, even on a weekday, in such a case we would be obligated to allow the soul to depart without causing an impediment. See discussion of this source in R. Goren, *Torat Ha-Refuah*, 73; Bleich, *Bioethical Dilemmas*, 77, 81–83.

13. R. Chaim David HaLevi, *Techumin* 2 (5741), 304; *Aseh Lekha Rav* 5:29–30. R. HaLevi argues that removing a ventilator parallels the Rema's permission to remove salt from a dying patient's tongue. The salt is also put on the tongue with the hope of prolonging life (according to *Beit Lechem Yehudah*), but now that the patient is in the dying process and the salt is only prolonging their suffering, it is an impediment that may be removed to allow the soul to depart (as the experience of the soul trying to leave the body is considered spiritually painful), since there is no prohibition of "do not stand idly by" for a person who is already a *gosses*.

R. Zalman Nechemia Goldberg permits actively removing a therapy, such as a ventilator, from a suffering terminal patient if their death is preferable to life (or for one who has no purpose left in their life because of complete lack of comprehension), but only if it does not directly cause the patient to die right away, in which case removing a ventilator would not be seen simply as removing an impediment, but rather a forbidden act of killing the patient. R. Goldberg bases his opinion on the claim that the person is dying of their own underlying illness and we are not obligated in "do not stand idly by" in the case of a *gosses* unless one benefits more from life than death (which is obviously a value judgment). R. Goldberg argues that a person in excruciating pain may have no will to live on, and he develops an approach that while the prohibition against murder is violated by an "indirect cause" (*grama*), but that simply removing an object that can save a person, such that the patient does not die as a result of one's action but because of his or her own underlying illness, is not considered even an "indirect cause." It is thus not forbidden for a suffering dying patient who would prefer death to life (*Moriah* 4–5:88–9, [Elul 5738], 48–56). For extensive discussion with R. Levi Yitzchak Halperin on this topic, see *Halakhah U-Refuah*, vol. 2, 146–84, especially 146, 151, 154, 159, and 171. R. Halperin argues (160) that regardless of how soon the patient dies, extubation should be viewed as killing him, and thus forbidden. See also *Ma'aseh Choshev* 3:4–5 and R. Bleich, *Bioethical Dilemmas*, vol. 1, 106, n. 36; R. Zilberstein, *Shiurei Torah Le-Rofim*, vol. 3, 317.

In a personal conversation in the summer of 2015, R. Goldberg told this author that his approach was not accepted by most Rabbinic authorities and that one should follow the rulings of R. Auerbach and R. Feinstein, as outlined in *Nishmat Avraham*. Indeed, in more recent guidelines, R. Goldberg has added that not only must death be preferable to life for this patient, but the therapy to be stopped cannot fulfill a natural need of the patient and it cannot be of a routine nature (*Assia* 16:3–5 [63–64] (5759), 6–8).

R. Menashe Klein (*Mishneh Halakhot* 7:287) also rules that removing a ventilator from a dying patient falls under the rubric of removing an impediment and can be permitted in certain situations so as not to prolong death and suffering (although one may not hasten death). R. Klein is careful to point out that one may not move a dying patient and must therefore simply turn the ventilator off, but not actually remove it. For other similar rulings, see R. Baruch Rabinowitz, "Symposium on Establishing the Moment of Death and Organ Donation," *Assia* 1 (5736), 197–8, who rules that a dying patient who is being kept alive by a ventilator but has no natural life of his own left may be extubated, even if he will die right away upon being extubated, because extubation is only "removing an impediment." R. Shlomo Goren (*Me'orot* 2 [5740], 28) argues that this does not violate "do not stand idly by" since it is done for the patient's benefit, but it would not be permitted if it directly causes the patients immediate death. R. Pinchas Toledano (*Barkai* 4 [5747], 53–59) rules that if it is possible to return the patient to breathing on his own, we must still do everything to save him, but if that is not possible and the patient is unable to breathe on his own and thus has no independent life force, we may extubate; this is not killing, but rather removing an impediment. It may even fulfill the mitzvah to "love your neighbor as yourself" to choose for them a peaceful death.

According to this perspective, some have argued that the medical technology that is artificially preventing this individual for whom there is no hope of recovery from actually dying should not be seen as medical *care*, but as medical *interference*. The patient's status is such that the very same medical technology once dedicated to saving life is now only an encumbrance to allowing the soul to leave, and it thus should be removed. See N. Moses, *Really Dead?* (2011), 309, based on R. Mordechai Eliyahu, "*Hashtalat Eivarim al pi Ha-Halakhah*," 30.

14. Many of these rulings were written with regard to triage cases in which the patient who is already intubated is dying and there is another patient who needs the ventilator whose life can be saved indefinitely.

15. R. J.D. Bleich demonstrates that any patient whose life can be prolonged, even by artificial means, cannot be classified as a *gosses*. See "Treatment of the Terminally Ill," in *Bioethical Dilemmas*, 78–79.

16. *Be-Mareh Ha-Bazak* 8:39, n. 35; R. Moshe Hershler, "*Chiyuv Hatzalah Be-Cholim U-Mesukanim*," in *Halakhah U-Refuah*, vol. 2, 33. See also *Nishmat Avraham*, YD 339(2) (552 in 3rd ed.).

17. *Tzitz Eliezer* 17:72 (13) rules that extubation is forbidden only when the death ensues immediately (*meyad*). Prof. Abraham (*Nishmat Avraham*, YD 339:4 (2) [499 in 3rd edition] and OC 328:5(6) [398 in 3rd edition]; *Lev Avraham* 32:9) reports that R. Shlomo Zalman Auerbach ruled that the patient must be able to survive for at least 48 hours, whereas according to Prof. Steinberg (personal communication and *Encyclopedia Hilkhatit Refu'it*, vol. 5, 145), also in the name of R. Auerbach, there is no set time period; even a few hours can be enough to determine if the patient was clinically stable enough for withdrawal. (R. Asher Weiss, in a personal communication, concurred with this second approach.)

18. *Lev Avraham* 32:9.

19. *Iggerot Moshe*, YD 3:132. *Tzitz Eliezer* 14:80–81 does not allow removing a ventilator from a *gosses* who is in the dying process, but only from one who has no independent life force left. He therefore requires that the patient no longer have any independent brain or cardiac function, since he is actually considered irreversibly dead but only shows signs of life because of an external machine. He assumes that this is the type of patient that the Rema was referring to. In contrast, R. Shlomo Zalman Auerbach seems to permit extubation once a patient is brain dead because even though we are no longer certain which patients can be classified as a *gosses*, he assumes that a brain dead patient with no spontaneous respiration can be considered a *gosses* (*Minchat Shlomo, Tinyana* 2–3:86; *Assia* 5754 (53–54), 5–16, #6–8). This ruling is also recorded in *Nishmat Avraham*, YD 339 (550–1 in 3rd ed.), where R. Auerbach adds that this is not permitted for the sake of organ donation until the patient's heart stops and doctors have waited at least 30 seconds (others, however, have reported that he later revised this time period to 5–6 minutes), and that it would be forbidden to run brain death tests at this stage if they include moving the patient, which could hasten death. However, see next note.

20. Even according to some authorities who do not accept brain death as the halakhic definition of death, if the patient is brain dead, the ventilator may be viewed as an impediment that may be removed. R. Ovadia Yosef also ruled that a ventilator may be turned off for a brain dead patient if the family members consent, as long as it can be done without moving the body of the patient (*Shulchan Yosef* 193). See also *Ruach Ya'akov* 1:26. There has been some debate about whether or not R. S.Z. Auerbach would permit the extubation of a brain dead patient. (See in-depth discussion in *Be-Mareh Ha-Bazak* 8:39, n. 35). In *Minchat Shlomo, Tinyana* 2–3:86(5) and 2:83(5) (and quoted and explained in *Shulchan Shlomo, Erkhei Refuah*, vol. 2, 16–18), R. Auerbach argues that since a brain dead patient cannot breathe on their own and this machine was placed on them by the physicians, it can be viewed as prolonging the dying process and may thus be removed. R. Auerbach also writes in this responsum that R. Moshe Feinstein was of the same opinion. See also the discussion of Prof. Steinberg in *Assia* 5754 (53–54), 5–16, #6–8. However, this is not treated as a practical ruling because R. Auerbach ruled that it is forbidden to run such tests on a *gosses*. Even if such tests are done, *Nishmat Avraham* (YD 339[2] [533, 540 in 3rd ed.]) argues that R. Auerbach only entertained the idea that a brain dead patient could be extubated when he was under the impression that in brain death every single cell of the brain is in fact dead. However, when he learned that in most patients, vast areas of the hypothalamus are functional, in addition to other areas of the brain, he completely retracted that ruling. (I thank R. David Shabtai, MD, for pointing this out to me.)

21. Relief of suffering is a valid consideration in such cases, whereas considerations such as saving money, the family's anguish, or preparation of a patient for organ donation are not.

22. R. Avraham Steinberg, in the name of R. Shlomo Zalman Auerbach and R. Shmuel Wosner, in *Assia* 63–64 (1998), 18–19; *Encyclopedia Hilkhatit Refu'it*, vol. 5, 150 (1058 in English ed.); *Jewish Medical Ethics*, vol. 2, 377–8; Loike, et al., "The Critical Role of Religion," 3. Steinberg reports that R. Auerbach issued this ruling regarding an actual case in Jerusalem. R. Mordechai Willig has endorsed this approach (*Beit Yitzchak* 5764, vol. 36, 49).

23. In a private communication, Prof.

Abraham related that he had heard from R. Shlomo Zalman Auerbach that if gradually turning down the amount of oxygen will kill the patient sooner than if we treat him according to his needs, this constitutes *gram retzichah*, and *grama* is a Torah prohibition. In personal conversations, R. Asher Weiss and R. Hershel Schechter both similarly expressed opposition to this course of action, because the ultimate intention is to hasten death and it is known that the patient will die as a result. R. Yitzchak Breitowitz, in a personal conversation, noted that even if one accepts this ruling, one would have to be very careful not to apply it too broadly, but rather only to those dying patients regarding whom there would be no obligation to put on a ventilator in the first place. He further noted that one would have to exercise great caution to ensure that no step in the process of reducing the settings leads to the patient's demise, which would be forbidden.

In response to these concerns, Prof. Steinberg noted in a personal conversation that when this is done, the ventilator is only lowered to a level that makes sense medically at that time, such that the patient can remain stable. If not, it would not be attempted. Furthermore, the intention of weaning a patient off a ventilator is normally that the patient will survive for some time without the ventilator; if they do eventually die, it will only be as a result of an act of omission (i.e., not re-intubating), not a direct act of commission, as in the case of extubation that leads to immediate demise. The primary concern is the process, not the end result (just as it is permissible to use a Shabbat clock to turn on lights, but not to do so by hand). Prof. Steinberg therefore argues that this is a permissible medical process.

24. For example, authorities do not require re-intubating if the machine is momentarily switched off to administer some treatment, such as clearing fluids from the patient's lungs or to maintain the machine. (Although the latter no longer happens in contemporary medical centers, we can learn from the principle.) See *Iggerot Moshe*, YD 3:132; R. Zalman N. Goldberg, *Emek Halakhah, Assia*, 64; *Nishmat Avraham*, YD 339:4 (499 in 3rd ed.).

25. *Tzitz Eliezer* 13:89, 14:81; *Encyclopedia Hilkhatit Refu'it*, vol. 5, 149–50. R. Neuwirth also wrote in support of turning a ventilator off via a timer (*Assia* 81–82, 5768, 103), but he has been quoted elsewhere as not fully understanding the technology and thus not necessarily supporting it (*Nishmat Avraham*, YD 339:4 [509 in 3rd ed.]).

26. *Tzitz Eliezer* 13:89, 14:81.

27. *Teshuvot Ve-Hanhagot* 6:299, 1:858.

28. *Lev Avraham* 32:10; *Nishmat Avraham*, YD 339:4 (507–9 in 3rd ed.). Prof. Abraham writes that utilizing such a timer would be classified as *grama* (indirect cause), which is prohibited in the context of damages. Turning off a ventilator via a timer would thus be classified as indirect murder, which is prohibited. He quotes this ruling in the name of R. Elyashiv and R. Shlomo Zalman Auerbach, who disagreed with the ruling of the *Tzitz Eliezer* on this matter. However, some point out that the *Tzitz Eliezer* only permitted this technology if a patient is initially attached to a ventilator with a timer; he did not allow transferring a patient from a normal ventilator to one with a timer. They argue that R. Elyashiv may have agreed with the *Tzitz Eliezer* in principle and only prohibited use of a timer when the patient is being switched from a conventional ventilator to one with a timer, but R. Elyashiv condemned the technology out of fear that it would not be applied correctly and would be abused. See R. Yaakov Wiener, quoted in *Assia* 10:1 [2005], 22–28; Joshua Kunin, "Caring for the Terminally Ill," *Jewish Medical*

Ethics, vol. 3 [Schlesinger Institute, 2011], 325). Either way, it is clear that R. Elyashiv ruled against the use of timers on ventilators in practice.

Similarly, despite his somewhat permissive ruling about utilizing such a timer in triage situations, R. Moshe Sternbuch expresses reservations about allowing the use of timers on ventilators in practice because it may lead to abusing his limited permission, unless the doctor in the particular situation appreciates the value of life and makes decisions carefully. He also notes some practical challenges in implementing this method (*Teshuvot Ve-Hanhagot* 6:299, 1:858). See also *Shiurei Torah Le-Rofim*, vol. 3, 103–4, for permission to utilize such timers on ventilators in triage cases when there are limited resources. In a personal conversation, R. Zilberstein related that it would be better if a person who is not Jewish connected the patient to the ventilator on a timer. Regarding removing a ventilator in order to give it to another patient in great need, see *Encyclopedia Halkhatit Refu'it*, vol. 5, 150–1.

Another problematic factor with this technology is that the endotracheal tube remains in the patients throat once the timer shuts the ventilator off, and it must be removed, which would not be simply an indirect cause, but rather a direct action. On the other hand, it is possible that even those who oppose the use of timers on ventilators would support them in a situation in which a patient would not be willing to go on a ventilator in the first place unless it was connected to a timer, since in such a situation the timer would in fact be serving to prolong their life, not hasten death.

29. Personal communication with R. Yechezkel Roth, author of the responsa *Emek Ha-Teshuvah*, in which he resorted to the principle of "*shev ve-al ta'aseh adif.*"

30. *Minchat Asher* 2:132–3; Loike, et al.,

"The Critical Role of Religion," 3. On the other hand, R. Zilberstein has written, in the name of R. Elyahsiv, that although a terminal patient is not required to have a cardiac defibrillator implanted, once it is implanted it may not be deactivated, since that would be a direct action. Although it may not be functioning at the moment, once it is implanted, it can be seen as becoming a lifesaving organ or limb of the patient that may not be actively removed (*Shiurei Torah Le-Rofim*, vol. 3, 340; vol. 5, 27–28). However, R. Asher Weiss argues in *Minchat Asher* 2:132–3 that regardless of the fact that an implanted cardiac defibrillator is located inside the patient's body, it should still be regarded as an external mechanical/artificial intervention and not as though it has become part of the patient's body, and it may thus be deactivated in a patient for whom a DNR would be permissible by Halakhah.

31. Loike, et al., "The Critical Role of Religion," 2–3. An example of this approach may be the ruling of R. Moshe Feinstein (from 1976) that even though it would be forbidden to remove a ventilator from a patient who demonstrates no clinical signs of being alive, for fear that the patient may still be alive and this would hasten death, if the oxygen tank needs to be replaced, it need not necessarily be restarted (*Iggerot Moshe*, YD 3:132). (Modern ventilators do not operate with oxygen tanks.)

32. R. Zilberstein, *Shiurei Torah Le-Rofim*, vol. 2, 376.

33. Steinberg, "The Halakhic Basis of the Dying Patient Law," in *Jewish Medical Ethics* (Schlesinger Institute, 2011), vol. 3, 418; Avraham Steinberg, in consultation with R. Auerbach and R. Wosner, "Halakhic Guidelines for Physicians in Intensive Care Units," *Assia* 4(1) (Feb. 2001), 5–6. In a personal conversation (Fall 2015), R. Dovid Feinstein ruled that just like R. Moshe Feinstein ruled that if a ventilator has been stopped for any

reason, such as to change an oxygen tank, it need not be restarted, dialysis may be discontinued between cycles, no matter how long one has been receiving dialysis treatment. R. Yosef Hoffner, rabbinic authority at Ma'ayanei HaYeshua Medical Center in Bnei Brak, Israel, told this author that he follows the same logic and ruling. R. Asher Weiss has also told this author that dialysis may be discontinued in between cycles for a dying patient.

34. *Nishmat Avraham*, YD (86, 504, 506 in 3rd ed.); R. Zilberstein, *Shiurei Torah Le-Rofim*, vol. 3, 384–5. See also ibid., 220–3, where R. Zilberstein rules that patients should be encouraged to pursue dialysis even if they are in great pain (and should focus on pain relief as well). However, if the suffering is too much for them to handle, we are not obligated to prolong their suffering with dialysis (but they should receive nutrition and oxygen). On the question of triage and precedence in receiving dialysis, see ibid., 112–15.

35. Personal conversation with Prof. Steinberg, April 2015.

36. Abraham S. Abraham, "Euthanasia," in *Jewish Medical Ethics*, vol. 2, 371 (also published in *Assia* 1 [1989], 36–39); R. Z.N. Goldberg, "*Ha-Noteh La-Mut*," *Assia* 16(3–4) (Kislev 5759), 7.

37. D. Shabtai, "End-of-Life Therapies," 24–25. These authorities disagree with the ruling of R. Feinstein quoted above that an oxygen tank need not necessarily be replaced when it is removed in order to be changed (personal communication with Prof. Abraham S. Abraham, April 2015).

D.   CASE STUDY:
Deactivating a Total Artificial Heart

A patient suffering from acute heart failure received one of the first total artificial heart procedures that I encountered. Unfortunately, her condition continued to deteriorate. Her respiratory function was very weak, and she had to be put onto a ventilator. Soon afterwards, her kidneys began to fail and she was given continuous dialysis. She was being fed artificiality and receiving numerous aggressive medications to keep her alive. Her body continued to deteriorate to the point that her extremities began to get cold and shrivel up, and the hospital staff felt that they were treating a corpse. However, the family of this patient was willing to pay the millions of dollars needed to keep her body functioning, and since she still had neurological activity, they felt that she was still alive according to Jewish Law and that it would be forbidden to withdraw any of the aggressive interventions that were keeping her alive. As her body continued to deteriorate, sustained almost completely by machines, intense debate broke out throughout the hospital as to the propriety of maintaining this patient's life. This continued until her condition began to deteriorate more rapidly and the medical staff unilaterally decided to deactivate all of their mechanic interventions, leading to the patient's immediate demise.

While Jewish Law is certainly able to address any new circumstance that arise, this requires being intimately aware of those new developments. In this chapter, we will discuss one such innovation and how Jewish Law may relate to it.

An incredible device that could transform cardiac treatment is becoming increasingly refined and popular. This technology, known as a

"Total Artificial Heart," carries with it wonderful potential as well as perplexing ethical dilemmas. The questions that this innovation present are largely unprecedented and have not yet been thoroughly dealt with by Rabbinic authorities.[1] I will therefore provide a medical introduction to this technology, a brief summary of some of the current debate about it in the secular medical ethics literature, suggestions as to how Jewish Law might respond to these questions, and summaries of the initial responsa that I have received from leading Rabbinic authorities on this matter.

The goal of this chapter is to serve as a detailed introduction to the issues presented by this new technology. This chapter should by no means be seen as an attempt at a ruling in Jewish law for any specific situation.

MEDICAL BACKGROUND[2]

For many decades, heart disease has been the leading cause of death in the United States, with many heart failure patients eventually in need of a new heart. Every year, there are over 4,000 patients on the heart transplant waiting list. Unfortunately, only about 2,200 hearts are actually donated annually, and nearly 25% of the people on the list die each year while waiting.[3] Various types of cardiac assistive devices have been developed to serve as a bridge to maintain a patient's cardiac function while one awaits a new heart.

Furthermore, many patients with end stage heart failure, a condition in which the heart cannot pump enough blood to meet the body's needs, are ineligible for a heart transplant. Cardiac assistive devices are thus increasingly being developed as a permanent "destination therapy" to support or completely replace the function of the heart so that many individuals won't even need a transplant. These devices are becoming increasingly sophisticated, and their use has increased six-fold since 2006.[4]

One common technology currently used for such patients is a "ventricular assist device" (VAD), which is essentially a mechanical pump. A VAD is usually connected to a ventricle (chamber of the heart that pumps blood out) on one side and the aorta (the body's main artery) on the other. A VAD assists the function of a failing heart by helping to pump blood from the lower chamber to the body and vital organs, just as a healthy heart would.

In contrast, a "Total Artificial Heart" (TAH) is used for patients whose entire heart is failing. Whereas a VAD is connected to and assists one of the ventricles (usually the left), a TAH completely replaces both of the lower ventricles and serves as a mechanical substitute for the entire heart. The patient's heart is almost completely removed from his or her body, and the TAH, which is typically roughly the size of a heart, is attached to the heart's upper chambers (atria) inside the patient's chest. The TAH has mechanical valves that control the flow of blood in the heart, in addition to pumping the blood.

A TAH thus differs from a VAD in that a TAH requires the removal of most of the patient's heart and is designed to completely take over cardiac function, while a VAD simply attaches to the existing diseased heart and only assists its pump function.

There are situations in which a change or decline in a patient's clinical outlook may cause reevaluation of his or her situation and lead to a decision to deactivate a cardiac device when there is no chance of recovery or a transplant. VAD deactivation usually leads to circulatory arrest within several minutes to hours, whereas TAH deactivation results in immediate circulatory arrest and death.[5] However, continued activation of the device could eventually lead to a patient's entire body decomposing while blood is still being pumped throughout the decaying body. The decision to deactivate a cardiac device therefore involves excruciating ethical dilemmas.

TAH DEACTIVATION AND EUTHANASIA

One of the concerns related to TAH deactivation is determining if it should be considered euthanasia. Some secular ethicists conceptualize artificial life support into two categories:

1. *Supplementing*, such as ventilation, which simply supplements the patient's existing respiratory capacity, but does not replace it.
2. *Replacing*, such as transplantation, after which the patient can rely only upon the new organ to survive.

Based on this, some argue that if a cardiac assist device supplies cardiac function that is essential to maintaining life, and the surgery to implant it includes permanently disabling the patient's own ability to carry out that function, then discontinuing the device would constitute euthanasia, since the patient cannot possibly survive without the artificial support.[6]

While many cardiac assist devices are supplemental (such as pace-makers, defibrillators, and VADs), a TAH replaces cardiac function. Accordingly, many argue that deactivating a TAH would fall under a strict definition of euthanasia.[7] Since a TAH is a perfect substitute for the heart that has become integrated into the patient's body, it might be analogous to a new transplanted heart. Just as removal of a heart would be considered euthanasia, so would deactivation of a TAH.[8] Deactivation does not simply allow death to occur, but assists in its process.[9]

However, many secular ethicists rebut the charge of euthanasia by claiming that euthanasia entails administering a new pathology or drug with the intention of terminating the patient's life. TAH deactivation, on the other hand, simply returns the patient to his preexisting state of cardiac failure.[10] Furthermore, it is claimed, as with all other life-sustaining therapies, American Law has clearly established the right to have artificial medical treatment discontinued. Patients have the autonomous right to informed refusal,[11] which may even include the "right to die."[12]

In Jewish Law, however, the above distinctions are largely irrelevant, as any manner of active euthanasia (hastening of death) is antithetical to Jewish values and strongly prohibited by Jewish Law. As we have previously noted, Judaism limits autonomy and teaches that our lives are not simply utilitarian. Rather, every person is intrinsically sacred, having been created in the image of God, and life thus has value regardless of its relative quality or usefulness.[13] There is therefore a halakhic obligation to attempt to save all life, regardless of how much time a person may have left to live.[14] According to Jewish Law, hastening death is considered murder even if the victim is about to die anyway,[15] and even if the person wants their life taken from them.[16] Causing death indirectly is also a biblical prohibition,[17] and even "passive euthanasia" is prohibited when it involves the omission of therapeutic procedures or withholding necessary medication, since physicians are charged with prolonging life.[18]

Jewish values are certainly sensitive to pain and suffering, but instead of ending life, Jewish Law encourages aggressive use of sophisticated pain relief,[19] even if it involves some risk. However, even if pain and suffering cannot be completely managed, Rabbinic authorities prefer life with suffering over the active cessation of life with concomitant elimination of suffering.[20] The only grey area in Jewish Law when it comes to passive euthanasia is refraining from painful lifesaving therapy or therapy that will prolong great suffering in an imminently dying patient (*gosses*) and under a very specific set of conditions, as will be discussed in the following section.

COMPARISON BETWEEN DEACTIVATING A TAH AND A VENTILATOR

Many ethicists approach TAH deactivation as akin to removing a terminal patient from a ventilator (extubation). They claim that when a TAH is deactivated, the patient can still be considered to have died naturally of the underlying heart disease, because they only required the TAH as a result of the fact that their illness became so all-consuming.[21] Many of these thinkers thus claim that TAH is an artificial intervention and its removal is simply "allowing natural death."[22]

However, since death is immediate when a TAH is deactivated, and because a TAH does not simply assist the heart but completely replaces it, TAH deactivation is unlike withdrawing other artificial interventions, such as a ventilator, dialysis, or artificial feeding.[23] This makes it more difficult to argue that the patient is dying from the underlying organ failure and not the deactivation itself.[24] The fact that death is immediate upon deactivation may also make it experientially seem more like actively killing the patient than simply "ceasing aggressive support."[25] This is why some secular ethicists argue that deactivating a TAH is akin to an execution in which a drug is injected to paralyze the heart muscle or a switch is thrown to cease the function of a patient's heart.[26]

How does Jewish Law guide us in this debate? Jewish Law regards the provision of oxygen as a basic human necessity[27] but often distinguishes between withholding interventions (sometimes permitted) and withdrawing them (often forbidden). Therefore, although it is not always required to intubate (place on a respirator) a terminal patient who is suffering, once the patient has already been intubated, Jewish Law generally prohibits extubation (removal from the respirator) if the patient may die shortly thereafter as a result. The majority view is that terminal extubation (sometimes also called "compassionate extubation" or "palliative extubation") is tantamount to killing the patient, and that it is thus always prohibited to remove a respirator that is maintaining life.[28]

This perspective is not necessarily advocating that the life of a suffering dying patient be prolonged at all costs, but is rather based on concerns related to any human intervention in terminating life. Although some secular ethicists might not view deactivating a respirator as the cause of the patient's death, many authorities in Jewish Law have categorized death after extubation as a "direct result" because of the proximity of the deactivation and the patient's death. In the eyes of Jewish Law, removing a patient from a respirator is therefore as if *causing* the death of the patient, not merely *allowing* it to happen.[29]

Some authorities rely on a certain interpretation of the Rema, who rules that although it is forbidden to perform an *overt act* that hastens death, and although a dying patient is treated as fully alive in all regards, one may *remove an external impediment* to the death of a patient who is already almost certainly in the process of dying imminently (*gosses*) and cannot be restored to good health.[30] Based on this, there is a minority opinion that a respirator can be categorized as an artificial impediment to dying. It is thus not only permitted to remove it from such a dying patient, but it may be required to do so in certain cases to relieve suffering.[31] These authorities view extubation not as killing the patient, but as simply failing to save them, which may be permitted, or even obligatory, under certain circumstances.[32] (For thorough discussion see previous chapter.)

However, those who forbid terminal extubation argue that even if it had not been obligatory to put a patient on a ventilator, doing so fulfilled the Divine commandment to treat the patient, and since the respirator is vital and can be considered attached to the patient in a physiological manner such that it is keeping the patient alive, its removal would be considered actively causing death, not simply removing the impediment to the departure of the soul.[33] By extension, deactivation of a TAH would similarly be considered direct causation of death.

Moreover, some of the most prominent of the Rabbinic authorities who permit extubation as "failure to save" do so only with the explicit caveat that the patient not die immediately as a result.[34] Indeed, many authorities explicitly rule that any action that may lead to the immediate death of a patient is always prohibited.[35] Since TAH deactivation results in immediate death, the "removing an impediment" argument would not work in this case.

Additionally, the Rema's ruling only applies in the case of a patient classified as a *gosses*. It is usually difficult to determine with certainty if a given patient can be classified as a *gosses*, and with modern medical technology few dying patients can be placed into this category.[36]

Therefore, since there is debate on the matter, with some arguing that deactivating a ventilator falls under the severe prohibition of murder, Rabbinic authorities are usually unable to be lenient on the matter.[37]

There is a distinction between a respirator and a TAH that may further limit the applicability of the Rema's ruling in this case. The Rema's permission to remove an impediment to death seems to apply only if that impediment is external to the patient's body. However, it is difficult to regard a TAH as external, since it has replaced internal cardiac function and is located within the body.[38] Indeed, an argument can be made that a TAH not only replaces, but effectively becomes a patient's heart, and deactivating it would thus be tantamount to killing someone by removing their beating heart.[39]

DEFINITION OF DEATH AND PRACTICAL SUGGESTIONS

Some secular ethicists have gone so far as to argue that this issue should force us to revisit the definition of death. Death is currently defined in the United States as the irreversible cessation of *either* brain or heart function. Those who strongly believe that the essence of a living human is related to brain function have argued that changing the definition of death to focus *only* on neurologic criteria would make TAH deactivation less ethically problematic. Stopping a TAH would then conceptually be like removing a ventilator, which does not directly or immediately kill the patient, since although circulation would immediately stop with deactivation, some brain function would continue for a brief time.[40]

One situation in which many Rabbinic authorities permit extubation is in a case in which the patient shows definite clinical signs of already being deceased and the respirator is the only thing keeping their body "alive."[41] In such a case, it can be argued that the respirator is preventing the soul from leaving the body, and it may thus be viewed as an impediment that may be removed.[42] Therefore, those Rabbinic authorities who accept neurological criteria of determining death (brain death) would permit TAH deactivation once a patient is declared brain dead.[43] Even some of the authorities who do not accept brain death as a valid halakhic definition of death may still permit deactivation once the patient is declared brain dead[44] because at the very least such a patient may be considered a *gosses* and the TAH could be viewed as an impediment preventing the soul from leaving (as some rule regarding ventilators).[45] Other authorities might not permit actually deactivating the TAH upon brain death, but would argue that under those circumstances, there is no further obligation to save the patient, and they might therefore allow other medications – such as anti-coagulants or vasopressors that maintain blood pressure[46] – to passively run out and not be refilled.[47] By extension, they might allow the TAH's battery to be used up, without recharging it.[48]

However, the authorities who require cessation of cardiac function to determine death face a dilemma in this situation because the patient will always demonstrate a heartbeat (even though it is not the patient's actual heart) unless the TAH is turned off. Thus, even those who allow a respirator to be shut off when a patient no longer has an independent heartbeat may not permit deactivation of a TAH as long as it continues to pump blood through the patient's body.[49] According to this perspective, the patient is fully alive, despite the fact that it is machines that are artificially sustaining him. A patient may not be declared dead until the patient is incapable of any spontaneous motion whatsoever.

Thus, R. J.D. Bleich rules that a patient whose heart has been removed and replaced with an artificial heart and who is sustained on a ventilator and incapable of spontaneous respiration is considered dead by Halakhah only when incapable of any spontaneous motion whatsoever, including motion of internal organs, such as peristaltic action of the small intestine. Until then, such a patient must be treated, and it would be forbidden to deactivate their TAH.[50] Similarly, R. Yitzchak Zilberstein prohibits deactivation of a TAH until the patient's body begins to decompose, although precisely what this means requires clarification.[51]

Others have suggested that although heartbeat is normally the determinant of life, when it comes to a patient with a TAH, we are compelled to look for other criteria. R. Asher Weiss suggests that as long as a person is alert and able to function, despite not having a natural heart, he or she is obviously still considered alive according to Jewish Law. On the other hand, if a person is completely unresponsive and shows all other signs of death, it seems that it should be permissible to deactivate a TAH.[52] The specific guidelines and criteria for this determination are yet to be worked out.

CONCLUSION

As various types of TAH are utilized for longer periods of time and become more common – perhaps even more common than transplantation – these questions will become all the more challenging and pressing. Most secular writers on this topic contend that TAH deactivation should be permissible in most situations,[53] but as we have seen, it is often problematic according to Jewish Law, even according to those *poskim* who take a more lenient approach to passive euthanasia. The appropriate response demands much fine nuance and case-by-case analysis.

Although medical therapies are often initiated without consideration of eventually ending them, discussion about TAH deactivation should be part of the informed consent process prior to implantation of a TAH, so that patients and families are given the choice and made aware from the outset of the potential moral dilemmas relating to how life could end. This should be part of the conversation when any treatment is begun. Hopefully, some of the perspectives provided in this chapter can assist patients and families in framing those discussions and making difficult decisions.

In addition, understanding of these perspectives should generate respect for those who oppose terminal TAH deactivation for some of the valid religious reasons mentioned above. There should be no social ethical objection, particularly when one is able to raise funds to maintain a patient on a TAH, even if the patient is vegetative, as long as they are not using public resources or competing with the interests of other patients.[54]

This chapter has presented only an initial look at some of the challenging questions and complex resources that can be marshaled to help us approach this technology. It must be emphasized that each Rabbinic ruling quoted in this chapter related to one specific case, and it is frequently impossible to make some of the intricate cross-category comparisons that I have suggested. We must therefore leave it up to the greatest Rabbinic minds of our generation to provide pathways for us to properly navigate these crucial life and death questions. In the meantime, we pray for the time when "I will give you a new heart and put a new spirit within you; I will take the heart of stone out of your flesh and give you a heart of flesh."[55]

ENDNOTES

1. For example, R. Asher Weiss, who is known for having a mastery of all of Rabbinic literature, wrote in an as yet unpublished responsum on this topic (detailed later in this paper), "This is a specific technology that our ancestors have never imagined." He concludes by saying that since the issue of deactivating an artificial heart is such a new question, he will not firmly establish his answer unless another recognized expert authority in Jewish Law agrees with him.

Regarding the permissibility of having an artificial heart implanted in the first place, see *Nishmat Avraham*, YD 155:2(4) (86–87 in 3rd ed.). Although the technology has improved considerably and become much safer in recent years, many other questions (beyond the scope of this paper) have arisen relating to the propriety of putting certain patients on a TAH.

2. I would like to thank Drs. Jaime Moriguchi and Francisco Arabia of the Cedars-Sinai Heart Institute for their input on this section.

3. Katrina A. Bramstedt, "Contemplating Total Artificial Heart Inactivation in Cases of Futility," *Death Studies* 27 (2003), 295.

4. Courtney Bruce, et al., "Challenges in Deactivating a Total Artificial Heart for a Patient with Capacity," *CHEST Journal* 145(3) (2014), 625.

5. Mohamed Y. Rady and Joseph L. Verheijde, "Ethical Considerations in End-of-Life Deactivation of Durable Mechanical Circulatory Support Devices," *Journal of Palliative Medicine* 16(12) (2013), 1498.

6. David Orentlicher, "Deactivating Implanted Cardiac Devices: Euthanasia or the Withdrawal of Treatment?," *William Mitchell Law Review* 39(4) (2013), 1291. Others have framed this distinction as "regulative therapies" vs. "constitutive therapies." Regulative therapies are those that coax the body back towards homeostatic equilibrium, while constitutive therapies take over a function that the body can no longer provide for itself, and for which discontinuation would be more problematic. See Daniel P. Sulmasy, "Within You/Without You: Biotechnology, Ontology, and Ethics," *Journal of General Internal Medicine* 23 (2008), 70, fn. 56.

7. Orentlicher, "Deactivating Implanted Cardiac Devices," 1292.

8. Ibid., 1287. For more on trying to determine which is the better analogy for a TAH, a ventilator or transplanted heart, see Lars Noah, "Turn the Beat Around?: Deactivating Implanted Cardiac-Assist Devices," *William Mitchell Law Review* 39(4) (2013), 1229–30, 1250–52.

9. Rady and Verheijde, "Ethical Considerations," 1500, nn. 16–17. Some emphasize that TAH deactivation is problematic because it is not simply an act of omission, but is an act of commission.

10. Ronald M. Green, "When Is Stopping Killing?" *LAHEY Clinic Journal of Medical Ethics* (Fall 2011), 6, fn. 2; Paula S. Mueller, et al., *Ethical Analysis of the Withdrawal of Pacemaker or Implantable Cardioverter-Defibrillator Support at the End of Life*, 78, Mayo Clinic Proc. 959, 959–962 (2003). Another argument is that although removing a patient's heart would certainly kill them, perhaps a TAH cannot

be considered a perfect replacement for a heart. After all, every intervention involves benefits, burdens, and detriments, and patients have the right to decide which burdens they are willing to endure. As long as risks exist, one has the right to avoid or reduce them, if that is what is better for the patient, without being guilty of euthanasia. See Orentlicher, "Deactivating Implanted Cardiac Devices," 1292–94; Robert M. Veatch, "The Total Artificial Heart: Is Paying for It Immoral and Stopping It Murder?" *LAHEY Clinic Journal of Medical Ethics* (Fall 2011), 2.

11. Bruce, "Challenges in Deactivating a Total Artificial Heart," 626; Rady and Verheijde, "Ethical Considerations," 1500; Timothy E. Quill, "Physician-Assisted Death in the United States: Are the Existing 'Last Resorts' Enough?," *Hastings Center Rep* (Sept.–Oct. 2008), 17, 19.

12. Rady and Verheijde, "Ethical Considerations," 1500, n. 3. Some of these thinkers do not conceptualize a TAH as an actual replacement of the heart, because it does not become physiologically integrated into the body and cannot function without its battery source. See Bruce, "Challenges in Deactivating a Total Artificial Heart," 626, nn. 12–13.

13. *Sanhedrin* 4:2; Rambam, *Hilkhot Rotzeach* 2:6–7; *Shulchan Arukh*, OC 329:4; *Biur Halakhah*, ad loc., s.v. *ela lefi*.

14. See *Nishmat Avraham*, YD 339:4.

15. Rambam, *Hilkhot Rotzeach* 2:7; *Minchat Chinukh*, mitzvah 34; *Gesher Ha-Chaim* 1:2(2), n. 3; *Arukh Ha-Shulchan*, YD 339:1; I. Jakobovits, *Jewish Medical Ethics*, 123–5.

16. This is because of the belief that God owns us and that we thus have very limited autonomy. See *Shulchan Arukh Ha-Rav*, 4; Radbaz, *Sanhedrin* 18:6; *Mor U-Ketzia*, OC 328. Judaism also prohibits most forms of bodily damage, suicide, and assisted suicide. See Rambam, *Hilkhot*

Chovel U-Mazik 5:1 and *Hilkhot Avel* 1:11; *Tur*, YD 345; *Gesher Ha-Chaim* 25. A person who convinces or enables someone to commit suicide violates the biblical rule against placing a stumbling block before the blind (*lifnei iver*). If a person actively ends another's life, he would be guilty of murder. Additionally, there is an obligation to try to rescue another whose life is endangered (*lo ta'amod*). A person who sees another person drowning has an obligation to try to save him, either by swimming in after the person or by hiring somebody else to do so (Rambam, *Hilkhot Rotzeach* 1:14). According to many authorities, this duty to rescue applies even to the saving of someone who is attempting to commit suicide (*Iggerot Moshe*, YD 2:174 (3); *Minchat Yitzchak* 5:8(.

17. R. Goren, *Torat Ha-Refuah*, 77; Steinberg, *Encyclopedia of Jewish Medical Ethics*, 1057, based on Rambam, *Hilkhot Rotzeach* 2:2.

18. Bleich, *Bioethical Dilemmas* (Ktav, 1998), vol. 1, 72.

19. *Minchat Shlomo* 2–3:86; *Teshuvot Ve-Hanhagot* 3:361. See chap. 4B, where we discuss this point.

20. R. Shlomo Zalman Auerbach (*Minchat Shlomo* 1:91:24) writes that one should explain to a patient that Torah philosophy advocates living as long as possible even if one experiences pain. This is indicated by the Talmudic statement (*Sotah* 20a, *Avot* 4:22; see also Rambam, *Hilkhot Sotah* 3:20), "One hour of repentance and good deeds in this world is better than all of the World to Come." One should not infer from this that R. Auerbach encouraged patients to endure pain, but simply that one who must do so is laudable, and that this choice must be selected over actively killing a patient, which is prohibited.

21. Bruce, "Challenges in Deactivating a Total Artificial Heart," 626. Some point

out that the presence of TAH does not necessarily mean that the cardiac disease process has stopped, as even after TAH implantation there can be symptoms of heart disease (e.g., valve calcification and vegetation, hemodynamic instability, etc.). Thus, despite TAH deactivation, they view the cardiac disease process as causing natural death. See Katrina A. Bramstedt, "Replying to Veatch's Concerns: Special Moral Problems with Total Artificial Heart Inactivation," *Death Studies* 27 (2003), 319.

22. Rady and Verheijde, "Ethical Considerations," 1500.

23. Robert M. Veatch, "Inactivating a Total Artificial Heart: Special Moral Problems," *Death Studies* 27 (2003), 309. For example, a person with severe kidney disease can live for several days after stopping dialysis, and legally the AMA considers this person to have died a natural death. However, TAH may be different because the original organ is gone, unlike the case of dialysis, during which the kidney is still there but is bypassed.

24. Bruce, "Challenges in Deactivating a Total Artificial Heart," 626; Bramstedt, "Contemplating Total Artificial Heart Inactivation," 299.

25. Green, "When Is Stopping Killing?," 6, n. 1.

26. Veatch, "Inactivating a Total Artifical Heart," 309; Veatch, "The Total Artificial Heart," 2.

27. See chap. 4B, where we discuss this point.

28. *Tzitz Eliezer* 17:72; *Iggerot Moshe* YD 3:132; *Teshuvot Ve-Hanhagot* 1:858. See *Encyclopedia Hilkhatit Refu'it*, vol. 5, 148, 155 (1058–59 in *Encylclopedia of Jewish Medical Ethics*, English ed.); *Nishmat Avraham*, YD 339:4 (503, 509–10 in 3rd ed.). For extensive treatment of this topic, see previous chapter of this book.

29. *Tzitz Eliezer* 17:72 (13). See previous chapter of this book for further discussion.

30. Rema, *Yoreh Deah* 339:1. The Rema permits a woodcutter in the vicinity of a dying patient to stop chopping wood in order to provide the quiet that will allow a dying patient who is suffering to die. See *Iggerot Moshe*, CM 2:73, 74(1); *Shevet HaLevi* 6:179; *Teshuvot Minchat Asher* 1:116. See chap. 4B, of this book, where we cite sources that discuss how this ruling relates to contemporary medical dilemmas.

31. See chap. 4B, of this book, where we cite authorities who rely on this view.

32. Interestingly, some secular ethicists have suggested that Orthodox Judaism would accept deactivation of a cardiac assistive device based on the Rema's principle. See Green and the response by Rady and Verheijde, "When Is Stopping Killing?", 7.

33. Steinberg, "Halakhic Basis for the Dying Patient Law," *Assia* 69–70, 23–58; *Assia* 71–72, 25–39.

34. R. Z.N. Goldberg (*Moriah* 4–5:88–89) and R. Goren (*Torat Ha-Refuah*, 57, 76). Although R. Goren categorizes extubation as an issue of removing an impediment and failure to save, rather than killing, he compares actively turning off a machine (which may be seen as having become part of the person) that results in a dying patient's immediate demise to snuffing out a flickering flame, which is forbidden (*Shakh*, YD 339:5 based on *Massekhet Semachot*).

35. R. Shlomo Zalman Auerbach and R. Shmuel Wosner, as outlined by Avraham Steinberg in *Assia* 63–64 (5729), 18–19. Even if it is only possible that the action will immediately kill the patient, it is prohibited. If the physicians maintain that the patient's respiration is wholly dependent on a ventilating machine, it is prohibited

to switch it off. R. Zilberstein (*Shiurei Torah Le-Rofim*, vol. 3, 413) writes that even if a patient is a *gosses*, if stopping the ventilator hastens death, it is completely forbidden, as the *Tzitz Eliezer* rules (14:85).

36. R. J.D. Bleich demonstrates that any patient whose life can be prolonged, even by artificial means, cannot be classified as a *gosses* ("Treatment of the Terminally Ill," in *Bioethical Dilemmas*, vol. 1, 78–79).

37. *Be-Mareh Ha-Bazak* 8:39, n. 35.

38. Many commentaries, based on the explanation of the *Shakh* (7) and *Taz* (2), understand the Rema as permitting removing only an *external* factor that holds back the death, as long as one does not also thereby touch the *gosses* and thus hasten death (R. Goren, *Torat Ha-Refuah*, 68, 76).

39. See David Shabtai, "End of Life Therapies," *Journal of Halacha and Contemporary Society* 56 (Fall 2008), 42–43. Shabtai points out that R. S.Z. Auerbach ruled that we may not withdraw basic human needs from a dying patient, and he includes hemodialysis, once initiated, as a basic human need. We can infer from this that the machine essentially becomes the patient's kidneys, just as a respirator becomes a patient's lungs. There is a similar debate regarding deactivating a defibrillator. R. Elyashiv is quoted as ruling that the defibrillator is considered like a limb or organ of the patient's body (just like a ventilator), and may thus not be deactivated (R. Zilberstein, *Shiurei Torah Le-Rofim* 3, 340; see also F. Rosner, *Selected Medical-Halachic Responsa of Rav Yitzchak Zilberstein*, 33). R. Asher Weiss (*Teshuvot Minchat Asher* 2:132–3) disagrees and argues that whereas a natural limb or organ that is transplanted becomes a part of the recipient's body, an artificial/mechanical object does not become a part of the body (although

he notes that perhaps an artificial heart should be considered part of the recipient because it replaces cardiac function).

Support for the contention that a TAH effectively becomes a patient's heart may also possibly be brought from the ruling of the *Binat Adam* (*Sha'ar Issur Ve-Heter* 11) that as long as there is a functional circulatory pump in an animal's body, regardless of whether or not it appears to be "normal," it qualifies as a heart in Halakhah, rendering an animal containing such an organ to be kosher and not a *tereifah*. Furthermore, some have suggested that in cases of surrogate motherhood, the surrogate mother should be considered the mother according to Halakhah, not the biological mother, because once a body part (in that case a fetus) becomes integrated into another body, it is viewed as part of that body (*Be-Mareh Ha-Bazak* 9:46, n. 8, based on *Moreh Nevuchim* 1:72).

40. Veatch, "The Total Artificial Heart," 309–310; Veatch, "Deactivating a Total Artificial Heart," 2.

41. *Iggerot Moshe*, YD 3:132. *Tzitz Eliezer* 14:80–81 requires that the patient no longer have any independent brain or cardiac function, since he is actually considered irreversibly dead and only shows signs of life because of an external machine. He assumes that this is the type of patient that the Rema was referring to, as he does not allow removing a respirator from a *gosses* who is in the dying process, but only one who has no independent life force left.

42. R. Shlomo Zalman Auerbach, quoted by R. Steinberg in *Assia* 53–54 (5754), 5–16, #6–8. In *Minchat Shlomo* (*Tinyana* 2–3:86). R. Waldenberg makes a similar argument in *Tzitz Eliezer* 14:80.

43. Personal correspondence with Prof. Avraham Steinberg (August 2014).

44. Prof. Avraham Steinberg reported to

this author that R. Shmuel Wosner ruled that although he opposed the brain death criteria, in a case of an artificial heart, the combination of brain death with lack of a natural heart could be defined as the moment of death.

45. R. Shlomo Zalman Auerbach rules that if there is certainty that the brain and brainstem are destroyed, thus making the patient a possible *gosses*, one may stop the ventilator, since it is simply holding back the soul (*Shulchan Shlomo Erkhei Refuah*, vol. 2, 18; *Nishmat Avraham*, YD 339 (467 in 3rd edition). Some have challenged this view, arguing that R. Auerbach must have been given misinformation. Since a brain dead patient can survive for longer than three days on a respirator, he cannot be defined as a *gosses* (personal correspondence with R. J.D. Bleich, August 2014). Furthermore, achieving certainty that each and every cell in a patient's brain has died is exceedingly rare even with sensitive modern technology; see David Shabtai, *Defining the Moment* (Shoresh Press, 2012), 339–44. Moreover, determining the death of every cell requires radiographic imaging, which is achieved using intravenous contrast and which involves invasive contact with the body in a way that R. Auerbach himself forbids in the case of a *gosses* (ibid., 335, 344). Indeed, this suggestion of R. Auerbach is not treated as a practical ruling because he ruled that it was forbidden to run such tests on a *gosses*. Even if such tests were done, *Nishmat Avraham*, YD 339(2) (533, 540 in 3rd ed.) argues that R. Auerbach only entertained the idea that a brain dead patient could be extubated when he was under the impression that in brain death every single cell of the brain is in fact dead. However, when he learned that in most patients vast areas of the hypothalamus are functional, in addition to other areas of the brain, and he completely retracted the ruling. (I thank R. Dr. David Shabtai for pointing this out to me.)

46. It should be noted that most patients with a TAH do not need vasopressors unless they have concomitant sepsis or bleeding, because the TAH itself regulates blood pressure. Stopping blood pressure medication in such a patient may drop their pressure slightly, but the patient usually will survive.

47. This is comparable to R. S.Z. Auerbach's ruling regarding a patient who had suffered an extensive, irreversibly damaging heart attack, was comatose and in kidney failure, with extremely low blood pressure and no hope of recovery, and was now defined as a *gosses*. In this case, R. Auerbach ruled that there was no obligation to refill or change the bag of vasopressor medications when the present one ran out, for this would come under the category of "removing the impediment to dying" (*Nishmat Avraham*, YD 339:7 [513 in 3rd ed.]).

48. This may be similar to the permission given by some authorities in certain circumstances in the days when ventilators were connected to an oxygen tank to not replace the tank when one ran out (R. Moshe Hershler, *Halakhah U-Refuah*, vol. 2, 30–49; *Iggerot Moshe*, CM 2:73(1); R. Goren, *Torat Ha-Refuah* 77). When the battery of a TAH is dying, a very loud alarm sounds to warn caregivers of the failing battery. Presumably, it would be permissible to deactivate or muffle such an alarm in this case.

49. This is likely especially true for those *poskim* who define death based on circulation.

50. Personal correspondence with this author, August 2014.

51. Currently unpublished responsum written to this author in September 2014.

52. R. Asher Weiss, in a currently unpublished responsum written to the author, May 2014. R. Weiss notes that there are people who live normal lives with an arti-

ficial heart, and despite not having a natural heart, they are obviously completely
alive. On the other hand, there are people
who are hooked up to a heart bypass
machine during surgery, yet if their heart
does not restart after the surgery, they are
removed from the machine. We do not
consider this to be murder even though
they would still be alive had they not been
hooked up to this machine.

53. Bruce, "Challenges in Deactivating a
Total Artificial Heart," 626, nn. 12–24;
Rady and Verheijde, "Ethical Consider-
ations," 1500, nn. 7, 20–22.

54. Ibid., 314.

55. Ezekiel 36:26.

E. SUPPORTING PATIENTS WHO REQUEST PHYSICIAN-ASSISTED SUICIDE:
Towards a Nuanced Approach

In June 2016, the End of Life Option Act took effect in California, legalizing physician-assisted suicide. As was expected, many patients that I work with began requesting aid in dying. In fact, one patient was so anxious to end his life in this manner that he requested it fifteen days before it became legal; in this way, the mandatory fifteen-day waiting-period after requesting medical-aid in dying would be complete ahead of time, and he would thus be ready to utilize this new right on the very day that it became legal. A few days later, another individual came to meet with me to request Rabbinic support for her desire to engage in medical-aid in dying. She had a diagnosis that would only be terminal if untreated, she was not in pain and had decent quality of life, but she confided in me that she had suffered from depression for her entire life and wanted to take advantage of this new law by exaggerating her symptoms to finally put an end to her misery. Another patient asked me to visit to provide guidance on what are good and what are bad days to have a funeral according to Judaism. After a brief discussion I told this patient that our conversation was purely academic. "After all," I explained, "we can never know when the exact day of our death will occur, and we try to bury very soon after death, so we can't choose the date of our funeral." The patient then shocked me with his response, explaining that he had been prescribed the aid in dying medication and was working on planning his death and subsequent funeral on a date that would be most convenient for his friends and family.

These stories, and countless others like them, have forced us to take this issue very seriously and come up with a sophisticated and principled approach to dealing with it.

As we have seen in previous chapters, any manner of active hastening of death is antithetical to Jewish values and strongly prohibited by Jewish Law. Judaism teaches that we do not own our bodies; we belong to God and do not have the right to destroy that which is not ours.[1] Furthermore, our lives are not simply needed for utilitarian purposes. Each person is sacred, having been created in the image of God, and there is thus a value to life regardless of one's relative quality or usefulness.[2] Not only is human life itself sacred, but every moment of life is valued, and there is thus an obligation to attempt to save all life, regardless of how much time a person has left to live.[3]

Accordingly, in Jewish Law, hastening death is considered murder, even if the victim is about to die anyway.[4] This is true even if a person wants their life taken from them,[5] because of the belief that God owns us and that we thus have very limited autonomy. Judaism also prohibits most forms of bodily damage,[6] suicide,[7] and assisted suicide.[8] Causing death indirectly is also a biblical prohibition.[9]

As we have seen, Jewish Law does not demand that we always pursue "heroic" measures, and there are certainly situations in which Jewish Law permits withholding aggressive life-sustaining treatments. However, there is little room for any nuance when it comes to euthanasia (in which a physician hastens the death of a patient) or physician-assisted suicide[10] (in which the patient performs the final act of taking their own life). Indeed, even "passive euthanasia" is sometimes prohibited when it involves the omission of certain therapeutic procedures or withholding medication, since physicians are charged with prolonging life.[11]

COMPASSION

Physician-assisted suicide is becoming legal in many states, and even where it remains illegal, certain forms of euthanasia and physician-assisted suicide still happen regularly.[12] What is the most appropriate attitude towards people who choose to pursue this forbidden activity, and what approach should we take when asked for guidance from an individual who is considering it?

Although some might think that it is proper for a religious individual to always take a firm stance against physician-assisted suicide, research in the states where it is legal is beginning to point towards a more effective strategy. Paradoxically, it turns out that a non-judgmental, supportive approach from clergy has been more effective in allowing patients to consider alternatives, and to ultimately change their minds, than active opposition to the patient's decision.[13]

A rabbi cannot permit physician-assisted suicide, but it is still possible to have compassion for the suffering of terminally ill individuals who are contemplating such a decision while not endorsing or even condoning it. After all, there are certain cases of suicide, such as that of King Saul recorded in the book of I Samuel (31:3–4), that Jewish Law does not endorse, but for which it offers sympathy and permits traditional burial and mourning practices.[14] Rabbinic authorities generally assume that most cases of suicide are not willful and instead "look for any mitigating circumstances, such as fear or anguish or insanity on the part of the one committing suicide, or if they thought it was a meritorious act to prevent other transgressions."[15] In fact, there are even times when Jewish Law may permit praying for a suffering terminal patient to die,[16] while at the same time obligating us to do everything possible, including violate the laws of Shabbat, to prolong his or her life.[17] Thus, even while prohibiting this behavior in practice, there is room for showing some level of understanding and compassion to the patient.[18]

IDENTIFYING AND ADDRESSING THE ROOT CAUSES

It is crucial to understand why individuals seek physician-assisted suicide so that we can offer the most effective interventions and appropriate alternatives. Studies of patients who opt for physician-assisted suicide in Oregon (where it is legal) consistently show that the primary motivation for making this choice is a desire for control.[19] These patients tend to express a strong desire to control the circumstances of their death (time and manner), to die at home, and to address their worries related to eventual loss of dignity and independence, fear of being a burden on others, quality of life, self-sufficiency, and ability to care for themselves. Interestingly, these concerns are more prevalent than concerns related to depression, poor social support, or uncontrolled pain and physical symptoms, which some had predicted would be the primary motivations to seek physician-assisted suicide.[20]

In light of these findings, the best way to encourage people who are seeking physician-assisted suicide to explore other options would be to focus on interventions that help them maintain a sense of control, independence, and the ability to care for themselves, ideally in a home environment.[21] Instead of trying to convince people that physician-assisted suicide is wrong, it seems that it is most effective for clinicians to focus on eliciting and then addressing the patients' worries and apprehension about their future, with the goal of reducing anxiety about the dying process, educating the patient about how their disease may progress, and offering information about how to manage pain and discomfort while maintaining function and cognition, if that is what they would prefer.[22]

For rabbis, this means working with medical staff to provide information to empower the patient, as well as modeling a non-anxious presence while allowing the patient to work through their fears so they are likely to make a different choice. Many of the patients studied report the feeling of a lack of purpose and meaning in life as a reason for pursuing physician-assisted suicide. This implies that assessing the patient's existential concerns may be crucial in enabling them not to pursue this option.[23]

The assumption that a patient who requests aid in dying is depressed can lead to ineffective and even harmful antidepressant treatments that do not address root causes or lead the patient to change their mind. Similarly, focusing only on addressing physical discomfort ignores the fact that suffering is often existential and cannot be fully treated by pain management alone, and that not all physical pain can always be fully managed, even by expert palliative care.[24]

Nevertheless, symptom management is often a major issue for dying patients, and it should certainly be attended to. Instead of allowing aid in dying, Judaism advocates for improving medical care and comfort at the end of life. The alleviation of pain and suffering is a mitzvah[25] and should not be withheld out of concern for potential adverse effects.[26] It is halakhically permitted for patients to receive narcotic pain medication,[27] even when it may possibly hasten their death, provided that the *intent* is only to alleviate pain, not to shorten the patient's life, and that each dose on its own is not enough to certainly shorten the patient's life.[28] Some Rabbinic authorities have even permitted permanent/continuous sedation[29] for a suffering, terminal patient who so desires.[30]

CONCLUSION

Judaism forbids euthanasia and physician-assisted suicide. Nevertheless, the patients who request it should generally be treated with respect and compassion. It is essential that those who work with patients who are considering or requesting physician-assisted suicide take the time to sincerely listen to their patients and explore the reason(s) for their requests. Studies show that often simply listening to the patients' concerns helps to mitigate many of them.[31] One can then non-judgmentally provide options for an appropriate "substantive intervention" (medical control of pain or other symptoms; referral to a hospice program, a mental health, social work, chaplaincy, or palliative-care consultation; trial of anti-depressant medication when appropriate). This has also been proven effective in enabling patients to change their minds about wanting assisted suicide.[32] In particular, one should seek to address the patient's specific concerns, and determine if there is a way to meet them without opting for physician-assisted suicide.

Hopefully, in this way we can maintain our standards and fealty to Halakhah, while at the same time expressing compassion and finding the most effective method of avoiding physician-assisted suicide or euthanasia.

ENDNOTES

1. *Tzitz Eliezer* 5, *Ramat Rachel* 29(1). See also *Shulchan Arukh Ha-Rav*, CM, 4; *Radbaz, Sanhedrin* 18:6; *Mor U-Ketzia*, OC 328.

2. *Sanhedrin* 4:2; Rambam, *Hilkhot Rotzeach* 2:6–7; *Shulchan Arukh*, OC 329:4; *Bi'ur Halakhah*, s.v. *ela lefi*.

3. See *Nishmat Avraham*, YD 339:4.

4. Rambam, *Hilkhot Rotzeach* 2:7; *Minchat Chinukh*, mitzvah 34; *Gesher Ha-Chaim* 1:2(2), n. 3; *Arukh Ha-Shulchan*, YD 339:1; I. Jakobovits, *Jewish Medical Ethics*, 123–5.

5. *Tzitz Eliezer* 9:47 (5) argues that even if a patient begs not to be saved because their suffering makes them feel that death is preferable to life, everything must nevertheless be done to save and treat them. Similarly, see R. Nathan Friedman, *Netzer Mat'ai* 30.

6. Rambam, *Hilkhot Chovel U-Mazik* 5:1.

7. Rambam, *Hilkhot Avel* 1:11; *Tur*, YD 345. For further discussion, see *Gesher Ha-Chaim* 25. Regarding the prohibition to take one's own life even if one is in severe pain, see *Besamim Rosh* 348 and *Teshuvot Chatam Sofer*, EH 1:69. R. Shilat (*Refuah, Halakhah, V'kavanot Hatorah*, 49), argues (based on Rambam, *Hilkhot Rotzeach*, 1:1, 2:1–3) that suicide violates the prohibition against murder, which not only prohibits killing others, but any murder, even of oneself. *Tzitz Eliezer* 10:25(4) quotes Chatam Sofer on the Torah (beginning of *Parashat Vayeitzei*), who writes that suicide is even worse than murder because death normally atones for one's sins, but one who kills himself, even if he is suffering, forfeits this atonement.

8. The prohibition against active euthanasia is clear from the ruling of the Rambam that one may not kill a healthy person or even a sick person who will die in any case (*Hilkhot Rotzeach* 2:7). *Sefer Chassidim* (315–318, 723) also clearly states that one may not kill another person even if that person is suffering and asks to be killed. The prohibition can also be inferred from the prohibition against suicide. See also *Sefer Refuah Ke-Halakhah*, 446.

A person who convinces or enables someone to commit suicide violates the biblical prohibition of placing a stumbling block before the blind, "*lifnei iver*" (Lev. 19:14). If one person actively ends another's life, they would be guilty of murder. Additionally, there is an obligation to try to rescue someone whose life is endangered, "*lo ta'amod al dam rei'ekha*" (19:16). A person who sees another drowning has an obligation to try to save them, either by personally swimming to help the person or by hiring someone else to do so (Rambam, *Hilkhot Rotzeach* 1:14). According to many authorities, this duty to rescue applies even to the saving of someone who is attempting to commit suicide (*Iggerot Moshe*, YD 2:174 (3); *Minchat Yitzchak* 5:8). However, see the discussion of some Rabbinic authorities regarding the possibility that it is not forbidden for a non-Jewish person to engage in euthanasia when they feel that it is for their benefit (*Teshuvot Ve-Hanhagot* 3:365; *Shiurei Torah Le-Rofim* 4:286, 557, as well as 2:149, 589; *Iggerot Moshe*, CM 2:74[2]).

9. R. Goren, *Torat Ha-Refuah*, 77, and Steinberg, *Encyclopedia of Jewish Medical*

Ethics, 1057, based on Rambam, *Hilkhot Rotzeach* 2:2.

10. It should be noted that those who support physician-assisted suicide object to it being referred to as "suicide" and prefer the term "physician aid in dying" or "medical aid in dying."

11. Bleich, *Bioethical Dilemmas* (Ktav, 1998), vol. 1, 72.

12. E.J. Emanuel, D.L. Fairclough, and L.L. Emanuel, "Attitudes and Desires Related to Euthanasia and Physician-Assisted Suicide Among Terminally Ill Patients and Their Caregivers," *Journal of American Medical Association* 284, 2460–68; A.L. Back, et al, "Physician-Assisted Suicide and Euthanasia in Washington State: Patient Requests and Physician Responses," *Journal of the American Medical Association* 275 (1996), 919–25; D.E. Meier, et al., "A National Survey of Physician-Assisted Suicide and Euthanasia in the United States," *New England Journal of Medicine* 338 (1998), 1193–201; D.E. Meier, C.A. Emmons, A. Litke, S. Wallerstein, R.S. Morrison, "Characteristics of Patients Requesting and Receiving Physician-Assisted Death," *Archives of Internal Medicine* 163 (2003), 1537–42. Furthermore, where it is illegal, physicians report using alternative methods to assist their patients in hastening death; see K. Stone, "When a Patient Chooses Death," *Lancet Nuerology* 8(10) (2009), 882–3.

13. L. Ganzini and S.K. Dobscha, "If It Isn't Depression," *Journal of Palliative Medicine* 6 (2003), 927–30. The authors point out that patients who explore physician-assisted suicide are often very strong-minded, determined, and sensitive to perceived dominance in relationships, and they thus become very resentful of those who try to talk them out of it.

14. See Ramban, *Torat Ha-Adam, Sha'ar Ha-Sof – Inyan Ha-Hesped* 18; Rosh, *Mo'ed Katan* 3:94; *Shulchan Arukh*, YD 345:3; *Tzitz Eliezer 5, Ramat Rachel* 29:2. For a thorough summary and discussion of the approaches to the case of Saul, see A. Steinberg, "*Retzach Mitokh Rachamim Le-Or Ha-Halakhah*," *Assia* 3 (5743), 436–9; R. Zilberstein, *Shiurei Torah Le-Rofim* 3:200, 403–4; *Sefer Refuah Ke-Halachah*, 447–9; R. Z.N. Goldberg, *Moriah* 4–5(5738), 88–89; N. Zohar, "Jewish Deliberations on Suicide," in *Physician-Assisted Suicide* (Routledge Press, 1998), 367; forthcoming responsum of R. Asher Weiss on "Terminal Sedation."

15. *Arukh Ha-Shulchan*, YD 345:5. While this refers to most cases of suicide, physician-assisted suicide is a more complicated question because Jewish Law prohibits burial in a Jewish cemetery for one who intentionally and with a clear mind, knowing the severity of the prohibition, decides to nevertheless take their own life. Since most state laws require very clear informed consent before allowing a patient to do this, most cases of physician-assisted suicide are completely intentional, in which case the prohibition against burial in a Jewish cemetery should apply. However, some authorities have argued that one who takes their own life as a result of severe emotional distress, sorrow, or abject poverty, might not fall into the category of being unintentional (*Besamim Rosh* 345 quoted in *Pitchei Teshuvah* YD 345:2, however, see there for citations of authorities who reject this opinion). Therefore, some would argue that although the act of suicide is still forbidden for such an individual, it is not considered to have been done with a completely clear mind or heretical intention, and may even seem appropriate at the time ("*omer muttar*"), and they may thus be afforded full burial rites (*Maharsham* 6:123). Similarly, in a personal conversation, R. Asher Weiss argued that although suicide is certainly forbidden, after the fact, he would allow for burial based on this line of reasoning, because the emotional suffering

involved is just as significant as physical pain (Spring 2017). Moreover, R. Hershel Schachter notes, as reported to this author by R. Aryeh Lebowitz, that there is an opinion (*Orchot Chaim* 4, *Hilkhot Ahavat Hashem* 1, quoted in *Beit Yosef* YD 157) which permits suicide in order to avoid being tortured, as King Saul did. Although R. Schechter does not rule in accordance with this opinion since it refers specifically to avoiding religious persecution/forced conversion and is a minority view, but since such opinions exists, he argues, we may be able to rely on it after the fact to at least afford this individual proper burial. (See R. Schechter's discussion of this issue in his book *Ginat Egoz* 74, fn.) I also thank R. Nachum Sauer and R. Avrohom Union for pointing out some of these sources to me.

16. Ran, *Ketuvot* 104a; *Arukh Ha-Shulchan*, YD 335:3.

17. *Minchat Shlomo* 1:91(24); *Nishmat Avraham*, YD 339 (500 in 3rd ed.).

18. Many of the points in this paragraph are articulated by R. Mordechai Torczyner, with much more depth and clarity, in his talk available at http://www.yutorah.org/lectures/lecture.cfm/830798/Rabbi_Mordechai_Torczyner/Medical_Ethics:_Physician-Assisted_Suicide

19. L. Ganzini, et al., "Experiences of Oregon Nurses and Social Workers with Hospice Patients who Requested Assistance with Suicide," *New England Journal of Medicine* 347(8) (2002), 584; Ganzini, et al., "Why Oregon Patients Request Assisted Death: Family Members' Views," *Journal of General Internal Medicine* 23(2) (2007),154–7; Ganzini et al., "Oregonians' Reasons for Requesting Physician Aid in Dying," *Archives of Internal Medicine* 169(5) (2009), 489–92. See also Pearlman et al., "Motivations for Physician-Assisted Suicide," *Journal of General Internal Medicine* 20 (2005), 234–9; Monforte-Roy, et al., "What

Lies Behind the Wish to Hasten Death? A Systematic Review and Meta-ethnography from the Perspective of Patients," *PLoS One* 7 (2012):e37117. A paradox of the control issue is that some patients have actually reversed the natural dying process, opting for aggressive measures to keep themselves alive longer (so that they will survive the mandatory waiting period), thereby prolonging their suffering, in order to be able to be in control and end their lives themselves. Some have argued that this desire for control functions as a terror-management strategy by providing an illusion of control (power), choice (options), dignity (meaning), and a "way out" (exit), which make the person's situation seem bearable and manageable, even though the act of bringing about one's own death in reality achieves none of these things, M. Johnstone, "Bioethics and Cultural Differences," *Journal of Medicine and Philosophy* 37 (2012), 193.

20. Ganzini, "Oregonians' Reasons," 489.

21. Ibid., 489, 491.

22. Ganzini, "Why Oregon Patients Request Assisted Death," 156.

23. Carlson, et al., "Oregon Hospice Chaplains' Experiences with Patients Requesting Physician-Assisted Suicide," *Journal of Palliative Medicine* 8(6) (2005), 1165.

24. T.E. Quill, "Doctor, I Want to Die. Will You Help Me?" *JAMA* 270 (1993), 870–3; G.A. Sachs, J.C. Ahtonheim, J.A. Rhymes, L. Volicer, J. Lynn, "Good Care of Dying Patients: The Alternative to Physician-Assisted Suicide and Euthanasia," *Journal of the American Geriatric Society* 43 (1995), 553–62.

25. R. Shlomo Zalman Auerbach argues that the alleviation of pain falls under the obligation to love one's neighbor as oneself (*Minchat Shlomo* 2–3:86). The *Tzitz Eliezer* (13:87) argues that severe pain is considered debilitating and dangerous,

and administration of sophisticated pain medications is thus considered part of a physician's mandate to heal. The classical *poskim* affirmed this mandate even in risky scenarios if the intention is to relieve pain.

26. *Minchat Shlomo* 2–3:86. The concerns are related to opioids' potential to suppress breathing. However, current medical data suggest that judicious use of opioids does not usually shorten the life of terminally ill patients; see R.A. Mularski, et al., "Pain Management Within the Palliative and End-of-Life Care Experience in the ICU," *CHEST* 135 (2009), 1360–9). Healthcare professionals can offer patients and families choices for pain control. For example, patients who are alert may choose to receive adequate medication to keep them as comfortable as possible while retaining the ability to communicate. Others may prefer that medication be chosen for maximum comfort, even if it renders the patient less responsive (Loike, et al., "The Critical Role of Religion," 1–5).

27. *Tzitz Eliezer* 13:87; *Teshuvot Ve-Hanhagot* 3:361; J. D. Bleich, "Survey of Recent Halakhic Literature: Palliation of Pain," *Tradition* 36(1) (2002); *Shiurei Torah Le-Rofim*, vol. 3, 396.

28. *Nishmat Avraham*, YD 339:1 (4) (499 in 3rd ed.).

29. This is also known as "palliative sedation" (or "terminal sedation"), the complete sedation of those who are imminently dying and whose pain and symptoms cannot otherwise be adequately relieved. This always entails making the patient DNR, and sometimes includes the practice of withholding or withdrawing various forms of life-sustaining treatments, including nutrition, hydration, dialysis, and vent support. Removal of these interventions would be prohibited by Jewish Law (see next note). Even many secular ethicists view palliative sedation as a form of euthanasia, particularly when the patient is not imminently dying. See Jonsen, Siegler and Winslade, *Clinical Ethics: A Practical Approach to Ethical Decisions in Clinical Medicine* (McGraw-Hill, 2010), chap. 3. Some secular ethicists argue that while palliative sedation is a last resort when distressing symptoms cannot otherwise be controlled, it is an ethically appropriate approach to end-of-life care. See Blinderman and Billings, "Comfort Care for Patients Dying in the Hospital," *The New England Journal of Medicine* 373(26) (2015), 2559.

30. R. J.D. Bleich and R. Moshe David Tendler have been reported to permit this practice for a dying patient (and even mandated if there is no other effective option), as long as the patient continues to receive all necessary life-sustaining treatments and the intent is not to kill. See R. Dr. Jonah Bardos, "Palliative Sedation: Terminal or Palliation? An Ethical Analysis," *Verapo Yerape* 6 (2015), 24–25. This has also been permitted by R. Dr. Mordechai Halperin; see http://98.131.138.124/db/showQ.asp?ID=6936.

31. D.A. Matthews, A.L. Suchman, W.T. Branch, "Making 'Connexions': Enhancing the Therapeutic Potential of Patient-Clinician Relationships," *Annals of Internal Medicine* 118 (1993), 973–7.

32. Ganzini, et al., "Physicians' Experiences with the Oregon Death with Dignity Act," *New England Journal of Medicine* 342 (2000), 560.

APPENDIX:
Triage: Determining Which Patients to Prioritize in an Emergency According to Jewish Law

Triage, the order of priorities in determining whom to treat, is the subject of much discussion among medical ethicists. The problem is particularly acute when one person is in need of lifesaving treatment and there are insufficient resources to treat all patients. Israeli Rabbinic authorities have written extensively on this topic as a result of the numerous wars and incidents of terror that have unfortunately been faced in that country. In this chapter, we will summarize and prioritize the various values based on the views cited most frequently and prominently, as well as values based on which rules the Talmud has already decided override other rules.[1]

1. **Proximity:** Many Rabbinic authorities have applied the Talmudic principle that one may not pass over an opportunity to perform a commandment (*ein ma'avirin*) to the situation of performing the mitzvah of saving a life.[2] Therefore, *all else being equal,*[3] whichever patient is encountered by the medical team *first* has the priority of being treated first.[4]

2. **Certainty:** However, in Jewish Law, a definite danger takes precedence over a doubtful danger.[5] Therefore, in a situation in which one patient can certainly or likely be saved and the outcome for the other patient is uncertain, priority must be given to the person who can be saved, even if that patient did not arrive first.[6]

3. **Many over the few:** When there are numerous victims in danger, Jewish Law suggests that priority must be given to saving them over efforts to save fewer people, even if the fewer are in closer

178

proximity.[7] For this reason, Rabbinic authorities have approved of the approach to triage that ignores treating those who are very severely or only lightly injured, since treating them will require more time, thereby causing many others to die waiting. Since treating the moderately injured should take less time and fewer resources, thus allowing medics to treat more people, the moderately injured should be the focus of efforts.[8] In some cases, a medic may even abandon a patient who is not certainly salvageable, even if the medic is already working on him or her, in order to save many who are certainly salvageable. This is true even though one may generally not actively withdraw treatment (see note, and #5 below).[9] However, if many people are in danger but the possibility of saving them is uncertain, and there is an individual who can certainly be saved, precedence is given to the individual.[10]

4. **Potential for full life:** When there are two patients and only one can be saved, if one patient has the potential to live a full lifespan after being saved and the other is terminal (see end of Chapter 4B for definition of terminal in Jewish Law), one should prioritize the patient who can live a full lifespan.[11]

5. **If treatment was already initiated:** A patient who is already being treated, even if not certainly salvageable, acquires a certain right to continued treatment, such that one is not permitted to remove treatment from this patient in order to treat another, more salvageable patient.[12] However, some permit moving a patient who is terminal or has less likelihood of being saved out of the emergency room or intensive care unit in order to make room for a patient who can benefit more from that higher level of treatment, provided that nothing is done to actively shorten that patient's life.[13]

ENDNOTES

1. For suggested rankings of priorities, see *Be-Mareh Ha-Bazak* 2:85; *Encyclopedia Hilkhatit Refu'it*, vol. 6, 615–45; *Teshuvot Minchat Asher* 2:126; Tatz, *Dangerous Disease and Dangerous Therapy* (2010), 173–82. The order presented here differs slightly from the order presented in these sources based on recent rulings of R. Yitzchak Zilberstein, who has ruled and written extensively on this topic (*Shiurei Torah Le-Rofim*, vol. 3, 35–120).

2. See the critique of applying this principle to triage medicine in *Teshuvot Minchat Asher* 2:126, who argues that the only relevant factor should be the benefit to the patients and the likelihood of healing them and prolonging their lives, not the order in which they happen to arrive or be found.

3. If one of the patients is in slightly worse condition, this patient should be treated first, depending on the medical determination. Furthermore, if a given medic has much more expertise or experience in saving patients with one type of injury, the medic should attend to that type of patient first, even if a different patient arrived first (*Iggerot Moshe*, CM 2:74(1); *Be-Mareh Ha-Bazak* 2:85).

If all considerations are completely equal, determination may be made based on the ranking of priorities detailed in the *mishnah* in *Horayot* (13a). However, many rule that today it is not customary to follow that *mishnah* (*Iggerot Moshe*, CM 2:75[7]; *Masorat Moshe*, vol. 1, 489; *Minchat Shlomo* 2:82[2]). This is because we do not always know how to properly make these determinations, nor do we know which patient has more merits or

proper lineage (see *Tzitz Eliezer* 18:1 and 69[1]; *Nishmat Avraham*, YD 259:1; *Encyclopedia Hilkhatit Refu'it*, vol. 6, 622–6). However, some authorities argue that we should follow this *mishnah* (*Shevet HaLevi* 10:167).

Another option, when all else is equal, is to conduct a lottery (*Iggerot Moshe*, CM 74:1 and 75[2]. *Be-Mareh Ha-Bazak* (1:89) explains in the name of *Chavot Ya'ir* (61) that if this is done correctly, the results reflect God's providence (see also *Shulchan Arukh*, YD 157; *Pitchei Teshuvah* 13). Moreover, if all else is equal and the medical professional works in a private office and not in a public medical center, priority may be given to a relative (*Shiurei Torah Le-Rofim* 3:158, 50). Others argue that if everything is completely equal, the medic may simply treat whomever he or she prefers (*Shevet Mi-Yehudah*, Sha'ar 1:8).

4. *Iggerot Moshe*, CM 74, 75(2); *Masorat Moshe*, vol. 1, 489. R. Zilberstein argues that this is not dependent upon who actually arrived first to the location of the medic, but is rather based on whom the medic saw first and prepared for. If the medic saw both patients at the exact same time, even though one arrived earlier, they are considered to have equal priority (*Shiurei Torah Le-Rofim* 3:158, p. 51).

5. *Nishmat Avraham*, YD 252 (319 in 3rd ed.), based on *Pri Megadim* 328:47(1); *Tzitz Eliezer* 9:17 (10:5) and 28:3.

6. *Iggerot Moshe*, CM 2:73(2); *Minchat Shlomo* 2:82(2); *Shevet HaLevi* 10:167; *Kovetz Teshuvot* 3:159. R. Zilberstein, *Shiurei Torah Le-Rofim* 3:161, p. 67, bases this on *Mishnah Berurah* 334:68,

who rules that if two people are in a burning house, one healthy and the other in life-threatening danger, and both cannot be saved, one should save the healthy person first, since the other one is not certainly salvageable.

7. R. Zilberstein, *Shiurei Torah Le-Rofim* 3:161, pp. 67–68. One may not remove treatment that causes the individual to die as a result of being abandoned in order to save the many (68–9), but if a medic did so, it would not be classified as murder, but rather as a merciful act of lifesaving (69–70).

8. *Teshuvot Minchat Asher* 1:115, 2:126; *Shiurei Torah Le-Rofim* 3:161, pp. 66–7, 73. R. Zilberstein compares this to the option to save one boat when two are sinking, in which case the boat with more passengers on board should be saved. He ruled this way in answer to a question from first responder medics who are charged with such missions. R. Zilberstein (ibid., and p. 52) also argues that an individual who is needed by the community can be compared to "many" and may thus take precedence over another individual in some cases.

9. R. Zilberstein argues that in this case, abandoning one patient is not an act of murder, but rather an act of saving life. However, this must be a situation in which the medic is simply allowing the patient to die in order to save the many, but not actually performing an action that *causes* the patient's death (*Shiurei Torah Le-Rofim* 3:161, pp. 70–73).

10. R. Zilberstein, in the name of R. Elyashiv, *Shiurei Torah Le-Rofim* 3:163, pp. 83, 91; 3:161, p. 70. This is based on the principle that a doubt never overrides a certainty. However, R. Zilberstein suggests that if there is a good chance of saving many known individuals ("before us"), then perhaps one should try to save the many at the expense of the one, even if it is not absolutely certain that they can be saved (pp. 85, 91).

11. *Iggerot Moshe*, CM 2:73(2) and 75(2). However, R. Feinstein rules that this is only true if the terminal patient is unaware that he or she is being passed over. Otherwise, it could cause acute mental anguish and one must then treat the terminal patient first. See *Tzitz Eliezer* 17:72(15); *Teshuvot Ve-Hanhagot* 1:858, p. 560; *Shiurei Torah Le-Rofim* 3:164, p. 92, based on Chazon Ish and *Mishnah Berurah*. Age should not be a factor. As long as a person is alive and well, they should be treated equally regardless of whether one is very elderly or very young, and one who can live longer than a year takes precedence, regardless of how much longer than a year one can live (*Iggerot Moshe*, CM 2:75[2, 7]). Nor may ability to pay be a factor (*Teshuvot Minchat Asher* 2:126).

If a terminal patient is currently in need of limited medical resources, but there is a strong likelihood that a patient who can still live a full lifespan may arrive in need of this treatment at any time, many leading authorities argue that one who has a chance for a full lifespan still takes priority over the one who is terminal. The hospital thus has the right to designate its devices only for such patients who may arrive, even though the patient who can live a full lifespan is not actually present at the time (*Teshuvot Ve-Hanhagot* 1:858; *Tzitz Eliezer* 17:72; *Minchat Shlomo, Tinyana* 2–3:86:1). On the other hand, some argue that since we currently have no obligation to save anyone else before us, we should give preference to the terminal patient who is present and in immediate need, even if the goal is simply to relieve suffering and not save a life, unless perhaps if the patient with better likelihood of survival is already en route to the hospital (*Shevet HaLevi* 6:242; *Shiurei Torah Le-Rofim* 3:164, pp. 93, 96, 103–4). R. Zilberstein also rules that if one has to choose between a competent patient and one who is mentally incompetent (*shoteh*), one should prioritize saving the competent patient, even though normally one must do everything to save and support the life of one who is mentally incompetent (*Shiurei Torah Le-Rofim* 3:211, p. 511).

12. *Iggerot Moshe*, CM 2:73(2). *Nishmat Avraham*, YD 252 (319), quoting R. Shlomo Zalman Auerbach and R. Asher Weiss (*Teshuvot Minchat Asher* 1:115[4]) argue that this is not because one has been granted a right to the continued treatment, but rather because of the Talmudic ethical principle that we may never sacrifice one life for another, "*ein dochin nefesh mipnei nefesh.*" Similarly, R. Zilberstein (*Shiurei Torah Le-Rofim* 3:161, pp. 67, 102) argues that a medic who is working on one patient cannot leave that patient for the sake of another, because of the principle that one currently involved in performing a mitzvah may not leave it in order to perform another mitzvah, "*osek bemitzvah patur min hamitzvah.*" This remains true even when the second mitzvah opportunity involves a bigger mitzvah (*mitzvah chamurah*) and one is currently engaged only in a smaller mitzvah (*mitzvah kallah*), unless one can do more *mitvzot* (i.e., save many lives) by abandoning the first patient. In the latter case, one patient can be left behind to save the many (ibid., 73). However, as stated above, one may not do anything to cause the patient that is being abandoned to die, unless saving the other is more certain (ibid.). It must be emphasized that this only relates to situations of emergency triage, not simply allowing people to die in normal circumstances. Similarly, in situations in which medics are focused on caring for many moderately wounded patients rather than a few severely injured, if they have already begun working on a

severely injured patient and a moderately wounded one arrives, they may not stop treating the severely injured patient in order to tend to the moderately injured one (*Kovetz Teshuvot* 3:160). However, R. Z.N. Goldberg has ruled that the principle that one currently involved in performing a mitzvah may not leave that mitzvah in order to perform another mitzvah ("*osek bemitzvah patur min hamitzvah*") should not be applied to this case, and that one should indeed abandon the terminal patient in favor of one who arrives later but can potentially live a full lifespan, unless halting interventions for the terminal patient will cause immediate death ("*Hafsakat Tipul BeGosses Leshem Hatzalat Choleh* Acher," Techumin 36, 209–13).

In cases in which triage includes utilizing limited medical resources, such as a respirator, some suggest that the first patient can be put on the respirator with only a limited amount of oxygen or on a timer. The respirator may then be permanently switched off after the timer turns it off (as long as this patient does not notice that he or she is being abandoned, so as not to cause mental anguish). See *Shiurei Torah Le-Rofim* 3:164, pp. 103–4; *Teshuvot Ve-Hanhagot* 6:299, 1:858.

13. *Teshuvot Minchat Asher* 1:115(4). In a personal communication, R. Weiss clarified that this ruling does not permit the active withdrawal of any life-sustaining therapies. In the responsum, R. Weiss points out that the patient being moved out of intensive care must not be told that he or she is being abandoned for the sake of another patient, but must be dealt with in the most sensitive manner possible. See also R. Z.N. Goldberg, "*Hafsakat Tipul BeGosses Leshem Hatzalat Choleh Acher,*" Techumin 36, 209–13.

CHAPTER 5

After Death

A. DEFINITION OF DEATH IN JEWISH LAW

The son of a dying patient once called me to ask me to sit in on a family meeting with him and the doctors caring for his mother in one of our Intensive Care Units. Prior to the meeting, he explained to me that he was well aware of the fact that his mother was in very critical condition and dying, but his focus was on what his role should be. As long as she was alive, he explained to me, he would be by her side, honoring her in whatever way he could as her son; as soon as she was declared dead, he would change his focus to planning the funeral and beginning the grieving process.

The doctors arrived to begin the meeting and explained to the son that his mother had now been declared brain dead. He asked for clarification on what exactly that meant, obviously trying to better understand his mother's status in Jewish Law and his concurrent obligations towards her. One of the fellows, impatient with the son's different way of seeing things, blurted out, "She's dead, that's what it means. Dead!" The son began to cry and the entire discussion had to be reframed to establish better communication.

Shortly thereafter, as we tried to navigate accommodating this patient's religious commitments, which do not accept brain death as a valid definition of death, that particular ICU had become full, and another critically ill patient arrived in the Emergency Room whose life could be saved in that ICU, if only a bed were available. Pressure mounted to withdraw life support from this patient, who had already been declared dead by American Law. However, Jewish Law does not permit sacrificing one life for another life.

185

This complicated story highlights some of the challenges involved in questions of the definition of death that are faced today, which this chapter will attempt to shed light upon.

Death is not simply a medical or biological fact. It is also a religious status that is necessary to determine in numerous contexts, such as the applicability of the laws of inheritance and mourning or the necessity to violate Shabbat. It also indicates the point at which the soul has left the body.[1]

Although the understanding of science and medicine was far less advanced in Talmudic times, Talmudic law presents general case material and principles that can be applied throughout generations. Thus, although the Talmud does not directly address contemporary definitions of death, the Talmud provides the principles that determine the halakhic determination of death.

This question arises in the context of a discussion about a person upon whom a building may have collapsed on Shabbat. It is uncertain if a victim is actually buried there or not, or whether the person is alive or dead. The Talmud permits violating Shabbat in order to determine if a victim is under the rubble, and to continue rescue efforts if the victim is found to be alive.[2] The Talmud then asks until which area of the victim's body one must examine to determine if they are alive or dead. One option is to uncover the victim up until the nose, seemingly indicating that one must look for signs of respiration. The second option is that one must uncover the victim up until the heart, seemingly indicating that one must look for signs of heartbeat.[3] The Talmud concludes that when searching from the head down, it is sufficient to check only until the nose; when searching from the feet up, one opinion states that it is sufficient to check up until the victim's heart, while another nevertheless requires checking up to the nose. The traditional codifiers of Jewish Law all rule that the primary test that must be done is of the nose.[4] The verse that the Talmud quotes to prove this requirement is "All in whose nostrils was the breath of the spirit of life,"[5] which implies that the "breath of the spirit of life" is what defines the status of being alive.

Based on this foundation, widely divergent conclusions have been drawn about the halakhic definition of death, as well as the correlating criteria for its determination. This topic is highly complex, with numerous differing opinions and many fine nuances. For the sake of clarity, we can categorize Rabbinic approaches into those who view this Talmudic passage as defining death as irreversible and compete cessation of all vital bodily motion (including heartbeat), and those who learn from this source that irreversible cessation of spontaneous respiration determines death.

In Talmudic times, cessation of respiration and heartbeat never took place more than a few minutes apart. However, modern technology (such as respirators) makes this issue much more complex and challenging in the modern clinical setting,[6] with very precise definitions of death being difficult to pinpoint but increasingly crucial.[7] Rabbinic interpretation of this source also has ramifications for organ donation, for if a patient cannot be defined as dead until the heart has stopped beating, one often cannot be a donor, as most organs will not be suitable for donation after that point (see Chapter 5C).

The majority of Rabbinic authorities today seem to require complete cessation of bodily motion, including cessation of both cardiac and respiratory function, to define death.[8] A primary basis for their argument is that although the Talmud seems to be concerned with respiration, that is merely the necessary *test*, but not the *criterion* for death. Rashi, a classical Talmudic commentary, explains that the criterion for death is actually the irreversible cessation of heartbeat. However, a heartbeat was often imperceptible through a superficial chest exam, whereas checking for breathing in the nostrils was a more sensitive and accurate determination of continued cardiac activity.[9]

Indeed, many decisors read this Talmudic passage as assuming that there are no other obvious signs of life. In that case, death is determined if both respiration and cardiac function have ceased, assuming that lack of respiration generally indicates lack of cardiac function as well. However, were it not Shabbat, they argue, all efforts would have to be made to discover and support any signs of life, especially cardiac function, regardless of ability for independent respiration.[10] This view understands the Talmudic principle of checking for respiration not as the definition or criterion for death, but merely as one *indication* of death.[11]

On the other hand, many authorities understand the simple reading of the Talmud to be determining death solely based upon respiratory criteria. This claim is especially supported by the conclusion of the Talmud and its proof text, as well as the fact that many textual variants and the version in the Jerusalem Talmud debate checking up until the nose or the abdomen, but do not mention the heart.[12] Based on understanding this text as asserting the principle that irreversible cessation of spontaneous respiration is itself the proper criterion for pronouncing death, and not simply a test to determine other morbidities, some argue that brain death is considered death according to Jewish Law, as one who is brain dead cannot demonstrate spontaneous respiration and breathes only due to the respirator.[13] Indeed, the Israeli Chief Rabbinate accepts neurological criteria for determining death (brain death) based on this Talmudic passage because of the brain's role in controlling spontaneous respiration.[14]

Thus, there are very different ways of reading this seemingly simple Talmudic text. Authorities who understand it as elucidating the proper *criteria* for determining death generally favor the respiratory criterion, and thus brain death. However, reading it as referring to appropriate *tests* precludes that conclusion, since brain dead patients may still have a heartbeat.[15]

There is another potentially relevant Talmudic teaching that is quoted by some authorities that may add a third possibility for defining death according to Jewish Law. This teaching rules that the ritual impurity engendered by a corpse begins once a head is severed, even if the body is still convulsing. Based on this, some have argued that since the loss of neurologically controlled integrated motion in a decapitated person renders one dead, one who is brain dead is in fact dead according to Jewish Law.[16] This has been referred to as "physiological decapitation." Although the brain is still physically attached to the body, if it can be definitely demonstrated that brain functions have ceased, the patient is considered dead by Jewish Law, even if one's heart continues to beat.[17]

Some have argued that both of these Talmudic teachings are based on the same underlying thesis, which is that when the brain no longer integrates or controls the body's function, a person is dead. In Talmudic times, they argue, checking for respiration or cardiac criteria was simply the best way of indicating brainstem dysfunction – brain death – and therefore death.[18]

Determining death is thus predicated on how one understands the above Talmudic principles. Those who require complete cessation of all vital bodily motion, including heartbeat, will require confirmation that the heart has stopped beating and that there is no evidence of any possible signs of life remaining.[19] Those who focus on irreversible cessation of spontaneous respiration will look for proof that independent respiration will never return by showing that either the heart or the brainstem (which controls respiration) have ceased to function.[20] Those who define death as complete absence of the head will require confirmation that the head has been completely separated from the body. This would mean the death of each and every cell of the entire brain,[21] which is much stricter than the legally accepted definition of brain death (and recent research and sensitive diagnostics have shown that this state is exceedingly rare).[22] The approach of Jewish Law towards issues such as declaring patients dead, when to remove them from artificial respiration, and some types of organ donation all hang in the balance of this debate.

Since neurological criteria for determining death (brain death) is recognized in American Law, the withdrawal of medical support and interventions may ensue after this determination. Nevertheless, hospitals are encouraged – and in some places required – to provide reasonable accommodation for a brief period of time to families who do not accept this determination for religious reasons. If this time has passed (usually ranging between 1–3 days) and a family is still at odds with the medical team, hospitals may unilaterally withdraw medical interventions. The only ways to avoid this would either be to transfer the patient to another facility that is willing and able to take them, or to buy more time by petitioning the court for a temporary restraining order if one has a legitimate claim.

GUIDELINES FOR DIAGNOSING BRAIN DEATH IN ACCORDANCE WITH HALAKHAH[23]

Although we have noted that most Rabbinic authorities do not accept determination of death based on neurological criteria (brain death), for those who do, it is essential that the patient is indeed considered brain dead by the strict standard of Jewish Law.[24] Unfortunately, in the United States the rules for judging when a patient is brain dead vary widely from hospital to hospital.[25] Simply because a patient has been declared "brain dead" does not necessarily mean that they satisfy the criteria to be considered dead according to Jewish Law, even according to the standards of the Rabbinic authorities who accept brain death. Observant Jews who accept the definition of death by neurological criteria should thus carefully ensure all of the following to determine the time of death:

DETERMINATION OF RESPIRATORY-BRAIN DEATH

The determination of respiratory-brain death of the patient shall be determined only by two qualified physicians who satisfy all of the following conditions:

(1) They are specialists in one of these medical specialties:
   1. Anesthesiology
   2. General intensive care
   3. Pediatric intensive care
   4. Neurology
   5. Neurosurgery
   6. Emergency medicine
   7. Pediatrics
   8. Internal medicine
   9. Cardiology

and in the case of a patient who is a minor (a person more than 2 months-old and less than 13 years-old), one of them is a specialist in medical specialty 3 or 7.

(2) They are not directly involved in treating the patient.

(3) They are not involved in organ transplantation.

•   *Conditions determining respiratory-brain death:*

The determination of respiratory-brain death must include the following conditions:

(1) The medical cause of the cessation of brain function is known and evident.[26]

(2) There is clear clinical proof of the absolute cessation of spontaneous respiration.

(3) There is clear clinical proof of the complete and irreversible cessation of whole brain function, including brainstem function.[27]

(4) A test by one of these devices has proven the complete and irreversible cessation of brain function, including brainstem function:
   1. Brainstem Auditory Evoked Response (BAER)
   2. Trans-Cranial Doppler (TCD)
   3. Sensory Evoked Potential (SEP)
   4. Computerized Tomography (CT) / Angiography (CT – A)
   5. Magnetic Resonance Imaging (MRI) / Angiography (MRA)

(5) Medical conditions liable to give rise to errors in the findings of the tests aforesaid, have been ruled out.

- *Waiting period:*
(1) If brain death etiology is head injury or hemorrhage in the brain, one must wait at least 6 hours since the event before declaration.
(2) If the etiology is anoxic brain damage, stroke, edema, infection or malignancy, one must wait at least 24 hours from the event.

- *Additionally, the Israeli Chief Rabbinate requires:*
(1) The oversight and verification of all procedures by a qualified rabbi who knows the requirements and serves as an advisor to the family and can consult another expert in cases of doubt.
(2) Whole brain death determined by clinical criteria must be *confirmed* by an ancillary objective test in addition to the initial determination.

Ideal tests and confirmatory test to determine brain death according to Jewish law:
- Ideal test: Apnea test: Must be done properly with pCO_2 (partial pressure of carbon dioxide) measurements up to and above 60 in all cases. (If this cannot be performed on a particular patient, doctors can test to determine if there is no breathing even for a short time and then perform the confirmatory tests below.)
- Confirmation:
    (1) Ideally: TCD (Trans-Cranial Doppler to test blood flow) by an expert who knows how to perform this test properly. *This is the ideal confirmatory test because it is a bedside exam, does not manipulate the body, and is noninvasive.*
    (2) Next best: SPECT (Single-Photon Emission Computed Tomography). One can also do an Intracerebral profusion scan or radionuclide brain death scan or CTA (Computed Tomography Angiography) if SPECT is unavailable.
    (3) If none of these can be done, the next best test is: MRI/MRA to prove no blood flow.
    (4) If none of these, then the least good, but still acceptable is: BAER Brainstem Auditory Evoked Responses (by someone who is an expert in this test).

ENDNOTES

1. R. Menachem Kasher, "*Be'ayat Hashta-lat Lev,*" *Noam* 13 (5730), 20, argues that in Halakhah, death is the actual departure of the soul. See also Moses, *Really Dead* (2011), 115; R. J.D. Bleich, *The Time of Death in Jewish Law* (Z. Berman Pub., 1991), 5, 64–5; R. J.D. Bleich, *Where Halakha and Philosophy Meet* (Brill, 2015), 65. See also *Levush* OC 25.

2. *Yoma* 85a.

3. Bleich, *The Time of Death in Jewish Law*, 10.

4. Rambam, *Hilkhot Shabbat* 2:18–19; *Shulchan Arukh*, OH 329:3–4.

5. Gen. 7:22.

6. Brain death usually involves severe damage to the outer layers of the cerebral hemispheres, the area that controls human consciousness. It also involves severe damage to the brainstem, which controls "vegetative" functions such as respiration, primitive stereotyped reflexes, and the arousal system for the entire brain. However, heartbeat and other vegetative functions may continue since these functions are not completely dependent on the brainstem. With the use of respirators, the brain's inability to control breathing no longer means that an individual will immediately die. Instead, the respirator keeps a patient's blood profused (oxygenated), despite the brain's inability to instruct the lungs to continue functioning. The heart, the function of which is not directly controlled by the brain, has an intrinsic electrical system that can keep it beating as long as it receives oxygenated blood. Thus, the heart may continue to pump even after the brain ceases function-

ing as long as the patient is on a respirator.

7. See chap. 1A for discussion of the distinctions between "definition vs. criterion" and "state vs. status." Even from a secular perspective, the definition of death is not entirely a clinical issue, but a philosophical one as well. In the early 1980s, when the President's Commission developed arguments in favor of brain death, the members of the commission relied on the idea that without the brain integrating the functions of the body, the body would quickly become unsustainable even with maximum life support technologies. However, in recent years, advocates of brain death have focused more on the point that once the brain is not functioning, there is no personhood in the body – arguing that, "This is not human life at this point."

8. *Nishmat Avraham*, YD 339(2) (551–2 in 3rd ed.). See also the letter of R. Neuwirth on pp. 546–7.

9. Rashi, *Yoma* 85a, s.v. *hachi garsinan amar Rav Pappa*. This explanation of Rashi is based on the reading of the Chakham Tzvi, *teshuvah* 77. For further discussion, see David Shabtai, *Defining the Moment* (Shoresh Press, 2012), esp. 76, 151–2. Similarly, the Chatam Sofer (YD 338) seems to deduce his criteria for declaring death from Rashi's comments (Bleich, *The Time of Death in Jewish Law*, 57). He rules that the patient must irreversibly: (1) lay still as an "inanimate stone"; (2) have no discernible pulse; and (3) have no respiration. From the context of the rest of this responsum, the Chatam Sofer seems to rule that the primary factor in determining death is respiration. However, there is much disagreement

regarding how to apply this ruling of the Chatam Sofer to the debate surrounding determining the moment of death (see Shabtai, *Defining the Moment*, 174–82 and *Refuah Ke-Halakhah* 495–6).

Further complicating the matter, some argue that even when Rashi (and the Chakham Tzvi) mentions the heart, he does so in accordance with the medical assumption of his times, which was that the heart was actually an important part of the respiratory system – with air flowing in it, not blood. Read this way, Rashi understood the Talmud to be debating only the best place to examine respiration, with the heart being one possibility. See A. Steinberg, *Respiratory-Brain Death* (Merhavim, 2012), 57, 67–69.

10. *Shevet HaLevi* 7:235, 8:86; *Tzitz Eliezer* 17:66. *Shevet HaLevi* argues that the Talmud in *Yoma* requires complete absence of all signs of life, including cardiac activity, and relies on the validity of the respiration test only in the absence of all of these signs. He goes on to argue, based on the Chakham Tzvi and Chatam Sofer, that despite any medical tests, we have a tradition that the death of brain is only the death of the brain; for a person to be dead, the heart must stop. See also Moses, *Really Dead*, 297.

11. *Teshuvot Maharsham*, YD 6:124; Shabtai, *Defining the Moment*, 347.

12. Shabtai, *Defining the Moment*, 73–75; *Keviat Rega Ha-Mavet* (Schlesinger Institute, 2007), 47.

13. R. Moshe Tendler, "Halakhic Death Means Brain Death," *Jewish Review* (Jan.–Feb. 1990), 7; R. Shaul Yisraeli, "The Principles Underlying the Chief Rabbinate's Decision" [Hebrew], in *Keviat Rega Ha-Mavet*, 299–309.

14. This decision was published in *Techumin* 7, 187–92. It has also been published with additional notes by R. Halperin in *Sefer Assia* 6 (5749), 27–38, and in English translation in *Jewish Medical Ethics*, vol. 1, 392–402.

15. Shabtai, *Defining the Moment*, 95–96.

16. M.D. Tendler, "Halakhic Death Means Brain Death," 7. However, many have questioned if brain dead patients indeed lack all of these capabilities; see Shabtai, *Defining the Moment*, 104 and *Refuah Ke-Halakhah* 497–500.

17. F.J. Veith, J.M. Fein, M.D. Tendler, et al., "Brain Death: A Status Report of Medical and Ethical Considerations," *Journal of the American Medical Association* 238 (1977), 1653. R. Bleich challenges this parallel between missing a brain completely and brain death, because in brain death the brain remains intact and has not completely degenerated, which would be required to actually consider the head to have been severed. See R. J.D. Bleich, "Of Cerebral, Respiratory, and Cardiac Death," in *Contemporary Halakhic Problems* IV (Ktav, 1995), 322–3; R. J.D. Bleich, *The Time of Death in Jewish Law*, 131–43. R. Bleich does find this *mishnah* relevant in determining death by utilizing its unstated assumption that motion is always a sign of life. He thus defines death as the lack of any "vital motion," or clinically observable or perceivable movement that promotes the continued viability or health of an organism ("Of Cerebral, Respiratory, and Cardiac Death," 316–50).

18. Shabtai, *Defining the Moment*, 113.

19. *Tzitz Eliezer* 17:66. R. Waldenberg argues that the Talmud requires both the cessation of respiration and cardiac function to determine death. If there is any evidence of a continued heartbeat, including via EKG recording, he rules that the patient must be considered alive.

20. Avraham Steinberg, "*Keviat Rega Ha-Mavet Ve-Hashtalat Lev*," *Assia* 44 (Nissan 5748), 58, 66. Steinberg notes that actual physical destruction of the brainstem is not needed, only the loss

of function (ibid., 63, 72, and Steinberg, *Respiratory-Brain Death*,14–15). He thus refers to this as "respiratory-brain death," as opposed to "whole brain death." For further analysis, see Moses, *Really Dead*, 238–9; Shabtai, *Defining the Moment*, 259-61; Bleich, *The Time of Death in Jewish Law*, 144–8.

21. Avraham Steinberg, "*Keviat Rega Ha-Mavet – Skirat Amadot*," *Assia* 53–54 (1994); Shabtai, *Defining the Moment*, 108, 336–8.

22. Shabtai, ibid., 262–3, 339–44. This is the position of R. Shlomo Zalman Auerbach, but it would be nearly impossible to implement according to his own positions. Determining the death of every cell in his view would require radiographic imaging, which is achieved using intravenous contrast, and this involves invasive contact with the body in a way that R. Auerbach forbids for a *gosses* (ibid., 335, 344). It is quite likely that R. Auerbach would have required cell death as per halakhic determination, meaning parts of the brain turning to absolute liquid or becoming so dried out that it would fall apart upon contact. This certainly does not exist in any actual situation (personal communication with R. Dr. Shabtai, Nov. 2014). See also Bleich, *The Time of Death in Jewish Law*, 54–55.

23. These guidelines are based on the Israeli "Respiratory-Brain Death Act of 5768 (2008)" and personal conversations with Prof. Avraham Steinberg, who chaired the committee that created that law.

24. R. Shlomo Zalman Auerbach is quoted as ruling that if a patient can in fact be proven to be brain dead beyond a doubt without having to move the patient (which was not possible at the time of his ruling and may still not be possible), then he would be willing to accept brain death (*Encyclopedia Hilkhatit Refu'it*, vol. 6, 886; this is implied in his own writings in *Minchat Shlomo, Tinyana* 2–3:86). Sim-

ilarly, R. Ovadia Yosef writes explicitly that if one can certainly be declared brain dead using each of the criteria in these guidelines for diagnosing brain death in accordance with Jewish Law, then he would accept brain death as a valid determination of death by Jewish Law (*Shulchan Yosef*, 193). See also R. Amar, *Techumin* 31, 23. Indeed, some leading *poskim* in Israel told this author that if a given patient could indeed be declared certainly brain dead, meeting all of these criteria, they would be willing to accept brain death on a case-by-case basis. I did not ask these rabbis for permission to publish this in their names, and because of the controversial nature of the definition of death, I will refrain from doing so.

25. D. Thompson, "Hospitals' Brain Death Policies Vary Dramatically," in *WebMD News from HealthDay*: http://www.webmd.com/brain/news/20151228/hospitals-brain-death-policies-vary-dramatically-study-finds.

26. It is important to rule out a reversible condition that may be mimicking or confounding the diagnosis of brain death, and thus throwing off the exam. This can happen due to drug intoxication, paralytics, metabolic disturbances (such as ammonia), or severe hypothermia. This is why it is crucial to know the cause of the coma and that the cause is irreversible and cannot be treated.

27. Prof. Steinberg explains that from *a pure halakhic perspective*, according to those *poskim* who accept respiratory-brain death, what counts as the definition of the moment of death is the irreversible and absolute cessation of respiration, which can be determined by the absolute cessation of the function of the *respiratory center in the brain stem*. However, from a *practical medical point of view*, in order to verify that indeed this is what has happened, the complete cessation of *the entire brain* must be established.

B.   JEWISH CUSTOMS AT THE END OF LIFE AND AFTER ONE DIES

Halakhah guides the observant Jew in every aspect of life and at every stage, including the process of dying. It is important that family members and medical professionals are aware of what will take place and the halakhically appropriate behavior at this time.[1]

THE ACTIVELY DYING PATIENT

(1) When it seems that the patient may have begun the active dying process, one should consult a rabbi, chaplain, or doctor who is knowledgeable in these matters to determine if the patient may have entered the status of "*gosses*," which refers to a person who is expected to die shortly. If the patient may be in that category, we must treat him or her as delicately as possible so as not to hasten death in any way.

(2) One should not move or touch a patient determined to be a *gosses* unless it is for the patient's own good:

- A physician or anyone else who needs to treat such a patient must do whatever is *medically necessary* until the patient has died, because we do anything to save a life when necessary.

- However, if there is nothing medical that can be done for the patient, we must show extreme caution. This is particularly true in a hospital, where even many *routine* examinations should be avoided. For example, drawing blood for laboratory tests and checking blood pressure, temperature, and even heartbeat should not be done if the results of these examinations will not affect the medical treatment of the patient.

- On the other hand, if the patient is alert and will realize that these routine actions have been stopped, and this knowledge

and its resultant despair and hopelessness may aggravate the
patient's condition, then these treatments should continue, but
with the absolute minimum physical contact needed to put the
patient at ease.

- All nursing care that is necessary for the patient's physical and
  mental comfort, such as washing, cleaning, and changing the
  bed linen, must still be done, even on Shabbat.

- It is permitted to provide supportive contact, such as stroking
  the hand of a *gosses* who is frightened so as to calm him or her.[2]

(3) It is customary to maintain a state of reverence and respect in the
presence of a dying patient. One should not speak about mundane
matters unless the patient wants such conversation.[3] It is also important to avoid loud crying in the presence of a dying patient so
as not to frighten them.[4]

(4) If possible, a person should not be left to die alone.[5]

(5) Anyone in the presence of another person who dies is obligated to
ritually tear a portion of his or her clothing at the moment of death.[6]
However, today this is not always practiced:

- People who are not related to the deceased, such as hospital
  staff, generally do not tear their clothing at this time,[7] because
  we are concerned that no one would want to be at the side of a
  dying person if they were to be obligated to tear their clothing
  at the moment of death.[8] However, anyone in the presence of
  a person who dies should recite the words "*Barukh Dayan
  ha-emet*" (Blessed is the true Judge).[9]

- People who are closely related to the deceased frequently do tear
  their clothing (and recite the full "*Dayan ha-emet*" blessing) at
  the moment of death. However, many are accustomed to wait
  until the funeral to do so because that is considered the time of
  the most intense grief. Furthermore, at the funeral the mourners
  are more focused, the entire family is gathered together, and the
  rabbi can assist them in tearing their clothing properly.[10]

WHEN DEATH OCCURS

(1) When a death occurs, one should make sure that the death certificate
is signed by a physician and that a family member signs a release
form so that a mortuary can pick up the deceased.

- If the death occurs on Shabbat, the release form may not be signed by an observant Jew. However, it may be signed before Shabbat (even though the patient is still alive), or one may give verbal authorization on Shabbat instead of signing.

(2) One should also notify one's rabbi and a Jewish mortuary. If the hospital notifies the mortuary on Shabbat, some may not respond on Shabbat, although they usually have an operator service that will take the message and give instructions. It is often helpful to notify them before Shabbat of an impending death. (In case one is not available in the hospital to sign the release, it is often sufficient to have made pre-arrangements with a mortuary.)

(3) If it has not already been determined, the family will have to decide the place of burial and the timing of the funeral. This should take into consideration both the requirement for prompt burial as well as the importance of properly honoring the deceased by getting the word out and ensuring that loved ones have time to arrive from out of town.

POSITIONING OF THE BODY

(1) After death, a human body is still considered sacred and should be treated with the utmost respect.[11] After death, a nurse generally cleans the body and prepares it to be transferred to the morgue or mortuary. Observant Jews frequently ask that the body be left untouched until the mortuary arrives to handle it in accordance with Jewish custom.

(2) Once death has been established, it is customary not to touch the corpse for about 20 minutes,[12] after which some of the following customs are observed by family members, if possible. (If family members are too overwhelmed to do this themselves, they may wait for the chaplain, rabbi, or mortuary to assist them.)

(3) One should open a window in the room if possible.[13]

(4) The eyes and mouth should be gently closed[14] and the head elevated if possible.

(5) If the mouth remains open, then:
- the chin should be tied with a bandage or towel around the head,[15] or
- one may place a prop, such as a rolled up towel, under the chin, or
- if the mouth still remains open, then it should be covered with a clean cloth.[16]

(6) The body should be lying on its back and straightened out as much as possible.[17] This includes:

- legs straight out
- arms straightened at the side of the body
- hands are to be opened as completely as possible, with the palms facing the ceiling, if possible
- It is important to ensure that none of the limbs of the deceased hang off the side of the bed or stretcher.

(7) If the body must be turned for any reason, it may be turned on either side, but not face down.

(8) The body and head should be completely covered with a sheet (not a warm heavy blanket).

(9) When the body is disrobed, the genital area should remain covered by a cloth at all times.

(10) The room in which the body is located should be kept as cool as possible.[18]

(11) When the body is placed on the appropriate stretcher and transferred to the morgue or mortuary, it should always be transported feet first.

TREATMENT OF THE BODY ON SHABBAT AND FESTIVALS

(1) The book *Shemirat Shabbat Ke-Hilkhatah* states, "On Shabbat and Yom Tov [Festivals], a corpse is *muktzeh* and may not be moved. Consequently, one should not close the eyes of a person who has died, or straighten his limbs. Nevertheless, there are those who are accustomed to be lenient in this respect, and in such a case, one should raise no objection. However, if possible, one should perform these activities with the aid of a non-*muktzeh* object that he holds, so that his hands do not come into direct contact with the dead body."[19]

(2) *Shemirat Shabbat Ke-Hilkhatah* continues that on Shabbat, "One may tie a bandage around the head of the corpse to prevent the jaw from opening wider, but a) one should not tighten the bandage in such a way as to close the already open mouth, and b) one should be careful not to tie a double knot."[20]

(3) If the corpse must be transported to another part of the hospital on Shabbat via an elevator, someone who is not Jewish should trans-

port the body and summon the elevator, but a Jew may accompany the corpse.[21]

(4) When a body is transferred in a car on Shabbat by a driver who is not Jewish to a mortuary where someone designated to watch the body is waiting, it is not necessary to have a Jew watch over the body in the car for this short time (see below).

POST-MORTEM CARE

(1) It is customary to ensure that someone watches over the body from the time of death until the burial[22] as an expression of honor to the deceased and to protect the body.[23]

(2) When the body is in a generally safe place, it is permissible for the person who is watching over it to leave its presence for a short time,[24] such as when the nurses prepare the body to be discharged or one is needed to sign a death certificate or make funeral arrangements.

(3) If it is not possible to watch over the body in the same room, one should stand by the closest door outside of the room in which the deceased is being kept, and remain there.[25]

(4) The body should not be washed by any hospital staff. However, any wound should be contained or covered to prevent flow of blood or any bodily fluids.

(5) Any blood emitted from the body at the time of death is to be buried with the deceased. Consequently, one must ensure that:
- All tubes (e.g., IV lines, gastric tubes, etc.) should be knotted as close to the site as possible, cut above the knot, and taped down in place.
- Urinary catheters may be removed and discarded,[26] but it is best to leave catheters that are inserted into the body for the mortuary to remove.
- No bandages or wound dressings should be removed.
- If any blood is found on the clothing or linen of the deceased, it should be removed, inserted in a plastic bag, and placed in the body bag together with the deceased.
- Amputated limbs are often buried with the person, especially in cases of accidents presenting in the Emergency Department.

(6) Although it is ideal for the mortuary to respectfully handle removal of all tubes, a patient who is intubated may be gently extubated by

the hospital staff before the mortuary arrives in order to prevent disfiguration of the deceased's face.

(7) Dentures should not be removed unless the person made his or her wishes known beforehand to have them discarded. Prosthesis should also not be removed. If dentures or prostheses are not on the deceased at the time of death, they should be placed in a body bag for burial with the deceased. In most instances, they are buried together with the deceased.

ENDNOTES

1. I would like to thank R. Elchonon Zohn, director of the National Association of Chevra Kadisha, who was consulted extensively in the preparation of this section.

2. All of the above is based on *Nishmat Avraham*, YD 339:3, 6; see also pp. 318–19 in the English edition. *Nishmat Avraham* points out that in the emergency room, one may carefully move a *gosses* when that patient's bed, or one of his limbs, is in a position that makes it impossible to move a seriously ill patient to a location in which he or she can receive appropriate treatment (for example, in order to move the seriously ill patient to the intensive care unit or to connect him to a respirator). Because there is a great need to try to save the life of a seriously ill patient, one may move the arm of a *gosses* or his bed, as long as it is done very carefully and there is only a possibility that his death will be hastened by doing so.

3. *Kol Bo al Aveilut*, vol. 1, 22. Some also avoid eating or drinking in the presence of a dying patient.

4. Ibid.

5. Rema, YD 339:4. We believe that it is beneficial to the dying person to sense the presence of his loved ones during the last moments of life (*Kol Bo al Aveilut*, vol. 1, 22, quoting *Ma'avar Yabok* 5:28). For this reason, one may even remain with a dying person if the time for communal prayer will pass (R. Akiva Eiger, YD 339). It is also important for someone to be with the dying patient so that he can ensure that the proper prayers are said and that the body of the deceased is in the proper po-

sition and thus does not become disgraced (*Divrei Sofrim* 329:4 [28]).

6. *Shulchan Arukh*, YD 340:5; *Iggerot Moshe*, CM 2:73 (9).

7. *Nishmat Avraham*, OC 233:2 (6), YD 340:34(2); *Gesher Ha-Chaim* 4:9. Some say that one should nevertheless tear a small amount at the bottom of his or her garment (*Minhagim Ve-Kitzur Piskei Halakhot Ha-Nechutzot Al Kol Tzara She-Lo Tavo*, Chevra Kaddisha Yitav Lev of Satmar, 3; *Divrei Sofrim* 340:29).

8. Ibid. According to this reasoning, those who would want to be with the dying person regardless of the fact that they will have to tear their clothing, such as a close student of the patient, should indeed tear their clothing if they are present at the moment of death.

9. *Be'er Heitev,* OC 223:6.

10. R. Tucazinsky, *Gesher Ha-Chaim* 4:6; R. Gavriel Goldman, *Min Ha-Olam Ve-Ad Ha-Olam*, 5:27. Perhaps even those who do not tear their garment until the funeral should nevertheless make a small tear at the bottom of their garment when they are present at the moment of death; see n. 7 above. Furthermore, perhaps family members who are more distant relatives, and will thus not be tearing their clothing at the funeral, should tear their clothing at the moment of the patient's passing if they are present. One should seek competent rabbinic guidance on these questions.

11. *Gesher Ha-Chaim*, vol. 1, 5:1.

12. Ibid., 3:2 (1), based on Rambam, *Hilkhot Aveilut* 4:5. This is because for a short time the patient may still be clas-

sified as dying, but not yet certainly fully dead, so we do not want to do anything that would hasten their death. According to *Teshuvot Yismach Lev*, YD 9, the custom in Jerusalem is to wait a period of 30 minutes. Some argue, however, that in light of the clinical aids now available to the physician, the considerations that previously necessitated this waiting period are no longer operative. See R. Bleich, *The Time of Death in Jewish Law*, 15–16. The *Tzitz Eliezer* 9:46 (2–3) writes that there is likely not a specific set amount of time that should be waited before touching a corpse, but because the purpose is to ensure that the individual is certainly, irreversibly dead, each case should be judged independently. He thus suggests that if, for example, a person dies a natural death, without numerous medical interventions, such as anesthesia, it is only necessary to wait for a moment, whereas if there is a sudden death or many medications, in which it is more feasible that it is some sort of paralysis, it is proper to wait longer.

13. *Zichron Meir al Aveilut*, 166. There is also a custom when a person dies to pour out all drawn water in the surroundings (*Shulchan Arukh*, YD 339:5), but this is not practiced in a hospital (*Nishmat Avraham*, YD 339:5 [11]).

14. *Shulchan Arukh*, YD 352:4. The *Chokhmat Adam* 157:9 mentions a custom of having the firstborn son of the deceased be the one to close the eyes when possible. See also Rashi, Num. 20:26.

15. *Shulchan Arukh*, ibid.

16. *Yesodei Semachot*, p. 142, 6a.

17. *Gesher Ha-Chaim*, vol. 1, 15:2 (6). See also Rashi, Num. 20:26.

18. R. Goldman, *Min Ha-Olam Ve-Ad Ha-Olam*, 55. This is for the honor of the deceased, so that they do not emit a foul odor. However, one may not violate Shabbat or festivals in order to provide air conditioning for a corpse. It is therefore advisable to use ice when there is no air conditioning available.

19. *Shemirat Shabbat Ke-Hilkhatah* 64:8.

20. Ibid.

21. *Lev Avraham* 13:183; *Nishmat Avraham*, OC 311:1 (6).

22. *Shulchan Arukh*, YD 341:6.

23. *Gesher Ha-Chaim* 5:4 (4).

24. *Iggerot Moshe*, YD 1:225.

25. *Minhagim Ve-Kitzur Piskei Halakhot Ha-Nechutzot Al Kol Tzara She-Lo Tavo*, Chevra Kadisha Yitav Lev of Satmar, 5.

26. *Lev Avraham* 13:179.

C.   ORGAN DONATION

Organ donation is certainly not only an end-of-life issue, but it often arises in discussions about planning for the end of life. This is a very important, complex, and often misunderstood topic. There is a common misconception that Judaism prohibits organ donation. The reality, however, is that while there are indeed some types of donations that are prohibited, many are permitted or even encouraged, and other types fall into a grey area.

The simplest way to understand this topic is to divide it into two categories: (1) transplantation from a living, healthy donor, and (2) transplantation from a deceased donor (cadaveric donation).

LIVING DONORS

In the case of transplantation from a living, healthy donor, there are two primary issues that must be addressed: the obligation to save life, and concerns related to risk-taking. It is clear that Judaism obligates us to attempt to help those in need, particularly when it comes to attempting to save a life.[1] But the degree of risk that one is required (or permitted) to take in order to help others is a matter of debate.[2] The general consensus is that although one is not obligated to put their life at risk in order to save another person, it is praiseworthy to do so, unless there is a significant risk, in which case doing so may be forbidden.[3] Thus, if the potential danger to the organ donor in a given donation is small but present, one may put oneself in such danger to save another person's life. This would be considered a meritorious act, but not obligatory. If the risk of a given procedure is very high, however, such a donation may be prohibited.[4]

This means, for example, that donation of regenerating matter – such as blood – which carries with it negligible risk, could be viewed as obligatory when performed to save a life.[5] As the risk to the donor increases, the obligation becomes less absolute, but donation remains a praiseworthy, highly meritorious act. In the case of a non-regenerating organ donation that carries a more significant threat to the donor's life, the same is true. Thus, for example, kidney donation carries small enough risks to make such donations permissible and meritorious, but significant enough risk to render it non-obligatory. Riskier donations, such as of a liver or lung lobe, are less obligatory, and a donation deemed to be very high risk for a given donor would be forbidden.

As these procedures become safer, they become more meritorious in the eyes of Jewish Law. For this reason, over the last number of years, Rabbinic authorities have tended to become increasingly encouraging of organ donation from living, healthy donors.[6]

Amount of Risk to Life:	*Minimal*	*Significant*	*Very High*
Level of Permissibility:	Encouraged or even obligated	Permissible, pious act, but not obligatory	Forbidden

DEAD DONORS

The organs of a patient who is dead according to Jewish Law may be used for transplantation if there is an identified patient whose life is in danger and who is in need of the organ.[7] Ideally, organs should only be donated after the donor had freely consented while still alive to such donation.[8] Organ transplantation overrides the obligation to bury a body right away, as well as the prohibitions against benefiting from a corpse or desecrating a corpse,[9] particularly when the transplant is performed in order to save a life or possibly even to significantly improve quality of life.[10]

THE GREY AREA

Much of the debate related to the permissibility of organ donation in Jewish Law revolves around the definition of death. Any form of organ donation that hastens death is forbidden. The obligation to save life, as important as it is, does not override the prohibition of murder.[11] Thus, removal of a heart or any other life-sustaining organ that will result in death may be performed according to Jewish Law only once a patient is deceased. American Law similarly permits the removal of life-sustaining organs only from a patient who has been declared dead.

One opportunity for organ donation is from a patient who has been declared brain dead. These patients are still ventilated after brain death is declared. Because the organs still receive oxygen, most vital organs may still be transplanted at this stage. Those who rule that brain death is considered death according to Jewish Law (see Chapter 5A) thus encounter few challenges when it comes to organ transplantation. However, fewer viable organs are available for transplantation from patients after cessation of cardiac function. Viable critical organs, such as liver and lungs, are currently only recovered from brain dead patients. Thus, those who maintain that only irreversible cessation of cardiac function defines death according to Jewish Law are considerably more limited when it comes to organ transplantation. If one considers a beating heart to be a sign of life, then removal of a heart or any other vital organ while the heart is still beating would be considered killing the patient, even if they are brain dead.

A second opportunity for organ donation is a process called "controlled donation after cardiac death" (DCD), sometimes referred to as "non-heart beating donors" (NHBD). In this process, the patient's cardiac arrest is orchestrated in an operating room through the withdrawal of life-sustaining treatment. These patients have usually suffered profound loss of cognitive capacity, but they are not brain dead. If the patient or family has expressed a desire for organ donation, the decision is then made to withdraw life-sustaining interventions from these patients, and they must have a Do-Not-Resuscitate (DNR) order (see Chapter 4B). Instead of the withdrawal of interventions occurring in the ICU, the patient is first moved to the operating room (after much preparation of their body and information given to the family/surrogate decision-makers). Pre-mortem interventions are then initiated to preserve the organs, such as inserting a large catheter into the patient's leg to rapidly supply cooling and preservation fluids, and medication is sometimes introduced to increase blood flow to vital organs. The patient's ventilator support is then withdrawn. Once death is declared, there is a brief waiting period,[12] and the organs are then recovered for transplantation.

This procedure is problematic according to Halakhah for at least three reasons: (1) withdrawing ventilation to hasten death, (2) administering medications to a dying patient without any intention of treating a condition, and (3) initiating organ recovery while the patient may still be considered alive according to Jewish Law, thus prematurely ending their life.[13] Withdrawal of life-support from a patient who is not dead according to Jewish Law (no matter how one defines death) may be prohibited as an act of murder, or at the very least a violation of the commandment, "Do not stand idly by while your neighbor's blood is shed."[14] Even if the removal of the ventilator is itself not forbidden in a given case (see Chapter 4C), removal of organs before the patient is considered to have *irreversibly* died would be categorized as murder, and thus forbidden.[15] Therefore, many rule that organ donation pursuant to the existing DCD protocols is prohibited by Jewish Law.[16] However, if the heart is not stopped through improper and deliberate cessation of life-support, and the lack of heartbeat is irreversible, the donor is a cadaver, and removal of the organs would not be prohibited.[17]

There is another form of DCD, referred to as "uncontrolled donation after cardiac death," which is far less common but not as problematic according to Halakhah, and indeed likely permissible.[18] This procedure pertains to situations in which patients experience cardiac arrest outside of the hospital and undergo full cardiac resuscitative measures. It is only if these measures have been exhausted and the patient is declared to have irreversibly died that organ preserving measures are initiated (such as artificially oxygenating and circulating the blood). The patient is then brought to the hospital, where traditional brain death determinations are undertaken, and organs are then explanted.

Status of Donor	Permissibility
Live Donor	Permissible, depending level of risk
Dying/Brain Dead/DCD	Generally forbidden, differences of opinion on brain death
Cadaveric (Donation from dead body)	Permissible according to most opinions

ORGAN DONOR CARDS AND OTHER RELATED ISSUES

When a person signs and carries an organ donor card, such as on one's driver's license, he or she is essentially beholden to the decisions of hospital staff, without consultation with a rabbi of one's choosing. Doctors may rely on their own criteria for determining death, and may make unilateral decisions even against the will of the patient's family, relying on a donor card, driver's license, or donor registry as legally binding "first-person consent."[19] Therefore, if an observant Jew wishes to be an organ donor after death, it is preferable to have a healthcare proxy listed on a card in one's wallet, instead of simply joining the organ donor registry. Some rabbis permit one to sign and carry an organ donor card provided that it stipulates that organs may not be removed before death has been established as defined by Jewish Law (with either definition of death available to be chosen)[20] and that their rabbi must be notified to ensure that all of the appropriate steps take place.[21]

Another issue relevant for an observant Jewish organ donor is treatment of the body after death. One must ensure that the incision to remove organs is as minimal as possible, that burial takes place as soon as possible after the donation, and that all other organs and tissues remain with the body for burial.[22]

ETHICAL ISSUES IN ACCEPTING ORGANS

Those authorities who accept brain death as halakhic death frequently encourage organ donation from a patient with that diagnosis. Indeed, these authorities maintain that their position has the moral high ground, since it enables more lifesaving potential and allows those who would like to receive organs to give them as well. On the other hand, those authorities who do not accept brain death as halakhic death also make an important ethical claim – namely, that Jewish Law prohibits using one life as a means for saving another. We cannot declare some people dead so that we can save others.[23] The attitude that all human life should be treated with equal dignity, respect, and protection is a core Jewish value, and it may indeed protect against some of the slippery slopes that concern many bioethicists and Rabbinic authorities.[24]

According to those who define death by cardiopulmonary criteria, organ donation from a brain dead patient, whose heart is still pumping, is akin to murdering that patient. An individual who does not accept brain death as death would thus not be permitted by Jewish Law to donate their heart or other vital organs (which require a heartbeat to maintain). However, many Rabbinic authorities nevertheless permit them to *accept* such an organ. Is this morally justifiable?

A.   *Morally permissible only if organ not designated for recipient:*

Some argue that the moral considerations of this issue depend on whether the organ that this individual receives is removed specifically for this recipient or would be removed anyway. According to this view, if the recipient is the only one for whom the organ(s) will be removed, it would indeed be wrong for him or her to request or sanction the removal of the organ from someone else, as that would render the recipient an accessory to murder. However, if the organ would be removed in any event, one may receive it because of the Talmudic principle that "nothing stands in the way of saving a life."[25]

In practice, most vital organs do not come from organ banks, but are rather removed only if there is a designated recipient who agrees to receive that organ prior to the surgery and who is able to receive it. Therefore, according to this view, it would be wrong for a person who does not accept brain death as the definition of death both to donate and to accept a heart donation, since those actions involve the murder of the donor and render the recipient a significant cause in the process of killing that specific donor.[26]

B.   *Always morally permissible:*

However, many Rabbinic authorities permit accepting a vital organ donation from a brain dead patient, even if they forbid making such a donation. Their reasoning is that even if it was forbidden to have removed the organ, once it was removed, it may be accepted to save a life, regardless of how it was obtained or if the recipient him or herself would be willing to donate an organ.[27] According to this view, once the organ is removed, even if it shouldn't have been, there is no prohibition against benefiting from the organ.

Despite the concern that an organ is retrieved only for the sake of a specific recipient, these authorities argue that since there is a long list of individuals in need of these organs, if the organ is not removed for one patient, it will certainly be removed for another patient. Accepting the organ therefore does not constitute "putting a stumbling block before the blind."[28]

C. *Morally permissible to rely on divergent rulings:*

Others who defend this position contend that the definition of death is simply a matter of debate in Jewish Law, with legitimate opinions on both sides. One may thus accept a donation from a patient who is dead according to other Rabbinic authorities, even if the donor is not dead according to the Rabbinic authorities relied upon by the recipient.[29] According to this approach, even though the recipient would not be willing to donate him or herself, there is a certain level of ethical consistency; the person whose life is being saved by receiving a transplant at least acknowledges that there is moral permissibility in retrieving a brain dead patient's vital organ.

However, many authorities who reject determination of death by neurological criteria rule that those who do so are in fact wrong. In the view of these authorities, retrieving organs from a brain dead donor is akin to murder, so that in their view, there is no room for another approach.

D. *Only morally permissible outside of Israel:*

R. Shlomo Zalman Auerbach recognized the problematic nature of receiving organs in cases in which it would be forbidden to donate them (i.e., brain death). In his view, this would make the recipient complicit in the donor's murder and an accomplice to the surgeon's crime of removing the patient's heart. R. Auerbach therefore forbade even putting one's name on a recipient list, since that would constitute being a significant cause of the transplant. However, he distinguished between doing this in Israel, where it is forbidden, and outside of Israel, where he permitted it.[30]

The logic for this distinction is the claim that while Jews are obligated to follow Torah law when it comes to determining death, outside of Israel, a just society may follow its own system of laws. Such legal systems may accept brain death and may not be concerned about moving a dying patient in the way that Jewish Law limits Jews. Therefore, once doctors outside of Israel have performed all of their tests to determine that the donor is in fact dead according to their standards, the recipient is not causing an immoral act of removing vital organs from a patient who is technically still alive.[31]

E.   Morally problematic:

Some have expressed concern that R. Auerbach's policy could be perceived as morally offensive to the family of the organ donor,[32] and that it gives less weight to the life of someone who is not Jewish,[33] although R. Auerbach states explicitly that it is certainly forbidden to kill anybody for an organ, whether or not they are Jewish. Indeed, many thinkers who have trouble with this distinction worry that especially outside of Israel, if Jews will not donate organs but are willing to receive them, it will cause a desecration of God's name and may be potentially very dangerous, perhaps leading to increased anti-Semitism and even bans on Jews receiving organs.[34] For these reasons, in addition to the fact that Judaism prohibits killing one person even to save another person, many Rabbinic authorities forbid a policy of accepting organs that one would be unwilling themselves to donate.[35]

Some have argued that in addition to the fact that it is hypocritical to allow receipt of an organ if one believes that taking it is a prohibited act of killing, if someone really believes that it is wrong to donate or retrieve such organs, they should actively campaign against anyone receiving such organs or even being on a waiting list for them, since this constitutes complicity in an act of killing.[36] It is possible that the reason that Rabbinic leaders have not called for such protests (despite having led significant public demonstrations over the seemingly more benign issue of autopsies) is that no matter what one thinks about the halakhic status of brain death, in the case of organ transplantation, they realize that lives are being saved.[37]

ENDNOTES

1. Lev. 19:16; *Sanhedrin* 73a–74a; Rambam, *Hilkhot Rotzeach* 1:14.

2. The Talmud *Bavli* (*Bava Metzia* 62a), in ruling that one should not put their life in danger in order to save someone else's life, quotes the ruling of R. Akiva that "your own life takes precedence over your fellow's life." The Talmud *Yerushalmi* (*Terumot* 8:4), on the other hand, assumes that one is obligated to undertake a high risk to save another's life, recording a story in which R. Issi was captured and would likely be killed, but R. Shimon ben Lakish risked his life to save him, exclaiming, "I will go and either kill or be killed. . . ." However, the later authorities quote only the ruling of the *Bavli* and not the *Yerushalmi*, implying that the consensus is that one may not put themselves in serious danger to save another (*Arukh Ha-Shulchan*, CM 426:4). There is also a prohibition of self-harm (*chavalah*) for the donor, but this is generally overridden in order to save a life. For an in-depth discussion of risking oneself to help others, see Steinberg, *Encyclopedia Hilkhatit Refu'it*, vol. 5, 736–45, 754–62.

3. Meiri (*Sanhedrin* 73a) understands the obligation to "not stand idly by" when another person's life is in danger as applying only if one can do so without endangering their own life. Similarly, Radvaz (5:218) rules that the obligation to not stand idly by only applies if the danger is not certain (which many understand to mean that the risk is under 50%); if the risk to one's life is more than that, one is not obligated to save the other person. See R. D. Hershler (ed.), *Halacha and Medicine* (Regensburg, 1985), vol. 4, 139–40. In practice, the Radvaz (3:627) rules that if a person risks his life to save another, it is a righteous and praiseworthy act, but if there is a significant risk to one's own life, one would be categorized as a "pious fool" if he or she did so, and it is thus forbidden (see also *Pitchei Teshuvah*, CM 426 and YD 157). The *Mishnah Berurah* (329:19) concludes that one is not obligated to put oneself into even a possible danger in order to save another's life, but one should not be overly cautious about this; the *Arukh Ha-Shulchan* (CM 426:4) rules similarly. See also *Iggerot Moshe*, YD 2:174 (4), and *Nishmat Avraham*, YD 349 (3) and CM 420:31(5:5), (136–7 in 3rd ed.).

R. Asher Weiss rules that it is *obligatory* to put oneself into minimal/remote danger in order to save someone in immediate danger. However, if the danger is considerable (such as greater than a 5–10% chance of risking one's life), then one would not be obligated to endanger themselves, but *may do so* if they wish and it would be considered a pious deed (*middat chassidut*). However, it is *forbidden* to expose oneself to grave danger, similar to the danger that the other person is already in, because there is an obligation to live and one does not possess his own life such that he may risk it in that way. In the context of organ donation, R. Weiss rules that since donating a kidney has become so safe, in a case in which one can save a family member who is in grave danger and has no other option, it would be almost obligatory to do so; a less dangerous donation, such as bone marrow, would be completely obligatory if one is a match (personal conversation;

see also *Teshuvot Minchat Asher* 1:114[1], 2:130 and 3:123). Nevertheless, one may not be *forced or pressured* to donate bone marrow (or other similarly safe tissue donations), especially when there is some physical pain involved, even though it is not very dangerous, but they should be encouraged to donate (*Nishmat Avraham* EH 80:12[1], 315 in 3rd ed. & CM 426:1, 237–8 in 3rd ed.; *Shiurei Torah Le-Rofim* 2:137). However, if the process of preparing the recipient for the bone marrow donation has already begun, the donor may not change his or her mind and can even be forced to continue the donation process, because otherwise the recipient will certainly die as a result (R. Shternbuch, *Assia* 91-92, 9-10). See following notes as well.

4. R. Dr. Akiva Tatz (*Dangerous Disease and Dangerous Therapy* [2010], 52–54) quotes a number of possible thresholds for determining a degree of danger to define "high-risk," from 1 in 6 to 1 in 20, and he suggests a rough rule: If one would undertake a particular risk to save all of one's possessions, one should undertake that same risk in the attempt to save a life. If, however, one would forego all of one's possessions in the face of a particular risk, one may desist from assuming that same level of risk to save a life.

5. R. D. Hershler (ed.), *Halacha and Medicine*, vol. 4, 143; *Iggerot Moshe*, CM 1:103. R. Asher Weiss rules that donating blood or bone marrow to save a life is not only pious, but obligatory (*Teshuvot Minchat Asher* 1:122 and 3:123). Similarly, R. Yaakov Weiner cites a "world renowned elder *posek*" as ruling that one would be required to give blood to save another's life (*Ye Shall Surely Heal* [Jerusalem Center for Research, 1995], 144). Indeed, since Jews are often unable to make certain organ donations, as detailed in this chapter, it may be proper to strongly encourage the donation of those bodily materials that are certainly

permissible to donate to make up for the lack of other types of donations.

6. For example, in 1968, R. Moshe Feinstein ruled that one is not obligated to put oneself into potential danger in order to save another from certain danger, even if they could thereby save that person's life, but that they may do so if they choose (*Iggerot Moshe*, YD 2:174[4]). Around the same time, R. Eliezer Waldenberg ruled that one is not obligated to donate an organ, and if the donation presents a serious danger to the donor, he is in fact forbidden from doing so (as is the surgeon from performing the procedure). When the donation does not present a serious danger, although one is not obligated to donate, it would be an act of piety and permitted (*Tzitz Eliezer* 9:45). However, by 1981, R. Ovadia Yosef ruled that since the vast majority of kidney donors now remain fully healthy, it is certainly a "mitzvah" to donate such organs in order to save someone else from mortal danger (*Yechaveh Da'at* 3:84). In 2015, R. Asher Weiss told this author that he views kidney donation as a "*middat chassidut* [pious act] and a mitzvah beyond doubt." Similarly, concerning dead donors, when heart transplants first became possible, R. Feinstein ruled that it would be forbidden for both the donor and the recipient as murder (*Iggerot Moshe*, YD 2:74[1]). However, by the end of his life, some claimed that R. Feinstein permitted such transplants given the advances in the safety of heart transplantations (*Iggerot Moshe*, YD 4:54). However, he may still have maintained that heart transplantation entails murdering the donor to remove the heart; see *Nishmat Avraham*, YD 339(2) (551 in 3rd ed.). Furthermore, the validity of this responsum has been highly contested. See D. Shabtai, *Defining the Moment* (Shoresh Press, 2012), 249–56.

7. *Nishmat Avraham*, YD 349; *Minchat Shlomo*, *Tinyana* 2–3:86(5). Many authorities permit preservation of some

organs, such as skin, to be put into banks for future use, even if there is currently no identified recipient. See R. Meshash, *Techumin* 7, 193–205; R. Yisraeli, *Techumin* 7, 206–13; R. Steinberg, *Assia* 4 (5743), 249–50; Steinberg, *Encyclopedia of Jewish Medical Ethics*, 1098.

8. Steinberg, *Encyclopedia of Jewish Medical Ethics*, 1097; *Nishmat Avraham* CM 420:31(5:6), 141 in 3rd ed. When the transplantation is being done to save life, some authorities waive the requirement for prior consent (R. Firer, *Noam* 4, 200), although the family of the deceased could give consent (*Iggerot Moshe*, YD 2:174 (3); *Minchat Yitzchak* 5:7). Some rule that a family member may not object if the donation will save a life (R. Yisraeli, *Assia* 59–60, 105ff); others rule that a family member may object if the transplantation is not expected to save a life (R. Arieli, *Torah SheBe'al Peh*, vol. 6, 56; R. Leebes, *Noam* 14, 28).

9. See summary of sources and reasons in *Nishmat Avraham*, YD 349:2, and *Encyclopedia of Jewish Medical Ethics*, 1096–68. As to the concern related to timely burial, if the deceased had expressed a desire to save another's life in this manner, this is permitted. The transplanted body parts themselves can be viewed as coming back to life upon transplantation, thus not requiring burial. This is particularly true if the amount of one's body being donated is less than the size of a *kezayit*, which is not obligated to be buried, and particularly keeping in mind that the obligation to bury is itself only a Rabbinic obligation according to some authorities, and can thus be overridden in order to save or improve another's life.

Regarding the prohibition against deriving benefit from a corpse, many *poskim* have argued that organ and tissue donation from a corpse does not constitute prohibited benefit because: (1) an organ that is transplanted into a living body is considered to have come back

to life, (2) the benefit is obtained in an unusual manner, and (3) in some cases, the amount transplanted is of an insignificant size. Regarding the prohibition against desecrating a corpse, it is argued that this prohibition applies only when it is done for no purpose or a negative purpose, whereas aiding a sick individual is a meritorious act.

Nishmat Avraham (YD 349:2 [583 in 3rd ed.]) also records the views of *poskim* who forbid cadaveric organ donation unless there is currently a patient whose life can be saved who is waiting for that organ, primarily based on the idea that the dead are not obligated in any commandments and thus cannot be used for any purpose (see also *Shiurei Torah Le-Rofim* 2:149, 589).

10. R. Prof. Avraham Steinberg, *Respiratory-Brain Death*, (*Merchavim*, 2012), 122; regarding organ donation for the sake of improving quality of life, see discussions of donating corneas and skin in *Nishmat Avraham*, YD 349:2(2) (581–5 in 3rd ed.); Greenberg and Farber, "Corneal Transplants: Saving a Life or Quality of Life?" in *Halakhic Realities – Collected Essays on Organ Donation*, (Maggid Press, 2017), 419–454.

11. There is a classic Talmudic principle that we can never assume that "one person's blood is redder than another person's blood" (*Pesachim* 25b; *Yoma* 82b; *Sanhedrin* 74a). This principle is reflected in the fundamental rule that we cannot "cast off one life to save another (*ein dochin nefesh mipnei nefesh)*" (*Ohalot* 7:6). Another example of this principle can be found in the ruling that if a group is surrounded and told to hand over one of the people in the group to be killed or they will all be killed, they should allow themselves to be killed rather than turn over another to be killed (*Tosefta, Terumot* 7:20). Similarly, related to the organ donation discussion, the Talmud *Yerushalmi* rules that one may not heal another person through the

murder of another (*Shabbat* 14:4; *Avodah Zarah* 2:2).

12. The waiting period or "observation time" for the determination of death after cardiorespiratory arrest generally ranges from about 2–5 minutes, and is done to confirm that cardiorespiratory arrest is indeed permanent (i.e., circulatory and respiratory functions cannot spontaneously return on their own and will not be restored by medical interventions). See the discussion in D. Gardiner, "International Perspective on the Diagnosis of Death," *British Journal of Anaesthesia* 108 (S1) (2012), i14–i28. Some have critiqued this brief waiting period by arguing that since the loss of circulation in these patients is not yet irreversible, the patient may not be properly pronounced dead yet. Thus, from a biological and conceptual perspective, this may be confusing prognosis (dying) with diagnosis (dead). See J.L. Bernat, R.D. Truog, and F.G. Miller, "Are Donors after Circulatory Death Really Dead, and Does It Matter?" *CHEST* 138(1) (2010), 13–19; J.L. Bernat, "Life or Death for the Dead-Donor Rule?" *New England Journal of Medicine* 369(14) (2013), 1289–91.

Rabbinic authorities have not provided clear guidelines as to how long one must wait after death is declared before organ retrieval begins, other than to make clear that death must be irreversible. R. Shlomo Zalman Auerbach writes that when extubating a patient, they can be declared dead once the medical team has waited at least 30 seconds after the heart stops beating, but they must wait longer than that to retrieve organs (some have reported that he later revised this time period to 5–6 minutes); in his opinion it would be forbidden to run brain death tests at this stage if the tests include moving the patient, which could hasten death of a *gosses* (*Minchat Shlomo, Tinyana* 2–3:86(5); *Assia* 5754 (53–54), 5–16 #6–8; *Nishmat Avraham*, YD 339 [550–51 in 3rd ed.]).

13. R. Dr. David Shabtai, "Donation After

Cardiac Death: Halakhic Perspectives," *Verapo Yerape* 4 (2012), 271.

14. Lev. 19:16. See R. Yitzchok Breitowitz, "What Does Halachah Say About Organ Donation?" *Jewish Action* (Fall 2003), 7; Shabtai, "Donation After Cardiac Death," 272, 289.

15. R. Breitowitz, "What Does Halachah Say About Organ Donation?" For an in-depth discussion of the issue of irreversibility, see Shabtai, "Donation After Cardiac Death," 284–87.

There is an additional potential problem of possibly hastening the death of a dying patient by injecting coolants and anticoagulants into the patient's body while the patient is still on life-support in order to keep the organs "fresh." However, since the risk posed by injection of these medications is minor and it is done to save a life, it may be permissible provided that the donor (or an appointed proxy) had consented to this risk or it can be extrapolated that this is the decision he or she would have made (Shabtai, "Donation After Cardiac Death," 272–79).

16. Shabtai, "Donation After Cardiac Death," 263; Breitowitz, "What Does Halachah Say About Organ Donation? 7.

17. Breitowitz, ibid.

18. Shabtai, "Donation After Cardiac Death," 270–71, 289.

19. Virtual Mentor, "Clinical Case: Family Disagreement over Organ Donation," *Ethics Journal of the American Medical Association* 7(9) (Sept. 2005). Some have also expressed the concern that an organ donor card leaves a patient vulnerable to other experimental procedures being carried out on their body.

20. Steinberg, *Encyclopedia Jewish Medical Ethics*, 1097. For strong encouragement to carry an organ donor card, see the essay by R. Shlomo Aviner in *Me-Olam Ve-Ad Olam*, 281 and R. Yuval Cherlow,

In His Image (Maggid Press, 2016), 109.

21. R. Nachum Rabinovitch, *Siach Nachum* 1:79. R. Rabinovitch expresses concern that in trauma cases, physicians might not always take the proper steps to diagnose and then confirm brain death, and they might not ensure that everything is handled in accordance with Jewish Law. He thus stipulates that an organ donor card must include the stipulation that the patient's rabbi, as chosen by his or her family members, must be involved and in agreement.

22. Ibid.

23. R. Aryeh Klapper, "An Alternative Construction of the Debate," *Halakhic Realities – Organ Donation* (Maggid Press, 2017), 85–103. R. Klapper bases this argument on the principle that we can never assume that "one person's blood is redder than another person's blood" (see chap. 5C, n. 11). R. Klapper further raises the concern of what he calls "The City of Refuge Problem." According to Jewish Law, those who commit accidental homicides are exiled to specially designated cities of refuge until the death of the High Priest. The *mishnah* (*Makkot* 2:6) notes that there is a drawback involved in creating a class of people whose freedom is explicitly prevented by another man's continued life, as the former will certainly pray for the latter's death. The adoption of the brain death criterion leads to a similar concern, as there is a population whose survival depends on the deaths of others, particularly the deaths of young and healthy people by gunshot wounds or auto accidents. See also Shabtai, *Defining the Moment*, 4–5.

24. See, for example, *Shabbat* 151b, which rules that one may violate Shabbat to save a one-day-old living baby, but may not violate Shabbat even for King David if he is dead, because all living people are of equal value until they are deceased.

25. R. Yaakov Love, "The Talmud's Understanding of Life and Death," in *Halakhic Realities: Collected Essays on Brain Death* (Maggid Books, 2015), 162–3. R. Love argues that in such cases, we need not be concerned about *eivah* – causing ill will by using donated organs but not donating them – because the sages did not apply this concern to all cases, and we can assume they would not have done so when saving a life is involved.

26. Ibid., n. 16. See also Eugene Korn's chapter in in *Halakhic Realities: Collected Essays on Organ Donation* for extensive philosophical treatment of this issue. The process of vital organ transplantation was confirmed to the author by the directors of the Cedars-Sinai Heart Institute and the One Legacy organ, eye, and tissue recovery organization.

27. "Halachic Issues in the Determination of Death and in Organ Transplantation," *Rabbinical Council of America Study Guide* (June 2010), 47.

28. R. J.D. Bleich, *Time of Death in Jewish Law* (Z. Berman Publishers, 1991) [Hebrew Section], 89. See also *Nishmat Avraham*, YD 339(2) (541 in 3rd ed.) for R. Elyashiv's similar opinion. Some have further argued that even if it is theoretically hypocritical to accept organs that we would forbid donating, when an actual person is sick and in need of the organ, it is simply uncompassionate to forbid them from receiving the organ; see R. Moshe Hauer, "The Organ Donor Debate and Jewish Medical Ethics," in *The Value of Human Life* (Feldheim, 2010), 61.

29. R. Dr. David Shabtai, "Misplaced Priorities," http://blogs.timesofisrael.com /misplaced-priorities/.

30. R. S.Z. Auerbach, *Minchat Shlomo, Tinyana* 2–3:86(5).

31. See the discussion in Steinberg, *Encyclopedia Hilkhatit Refu'it*, vol. 6, 886. For further insight into R. Auerbach's

view, see also *Nishmat Avraham*, YD
339(2), 535–7, 539–40, 549 (see also
530), where R. Auerbach explains that if
all of the proper tests and follow-up tests
have been done to determine brain death,
the donor is categorized as "maybe dead,"
and "maybe *gosses*" (dying) according to
Jewish Law, but there is a good chance
that they are indeed dead. In this case,
there is an opportunity to save a life, and
in any event, the donor will likely soon
be removed from the respirator. There is
thus more room for leniency outside of
Israel, where Jewish Law is not the law
of the land and where the doctors truly
consider this donor to be dead, so that the
laws of "placing a stumbling block before
the blind" do not apply in the same way.

R. Sternbuch also rules that brain
death may be considered death for non-
Jews since that is the legal definition of
death, despite the fact that he does not
accept that standard of determining death
for Jews (*Teshuvot Ve-Hanhagot* 6:300).
Similarly, R. Moshe Feinstein is quoted
as ruling that it is permissible to retrieve
organs from non-Jewish donors once they
have been declared dead by the laws of
land in which they reside (R. Aaron Felder,
Rishumei Aharon, vol. 1, 70).

32. R. Joseph Telushkin, in *Halakhic
Realities: Collected Essays on Organ
Donation*, 220, argues that to determine
the moral propriety of accepting an organ that the particular recipient would
be unwilling to donate, the donor or the
donor's family should be asked, "Do you
care if your organ is given to a person who
would not make such a donation to save
your life or that of your child?" R. Telushkin assumes that most people who make
such donations would not be pleased to
have their organs given to a person who
opposes helping others in the same way,
and that it would be hard to fault them
on moral grounds if their wish were to
provide organs first to those who would
also want to make their organs available
for others.

33. R. Irving Greenberg, "A Life of Hala-
kha or a Halakha of Life?" in *Halakhic
Realities: Collected Essays on Brain
Death*, 297.

34. *Be-Mareh Ha-Bazak* 7:86(4), 258; R.
Yoel Bin Nun, "Jewish Law and Medical
Science," in *Halakhic Realities: Collected
Essays on Brain Death*, 141. Some also
express concern that even within Israel
this policy could cause enmity toward the
observant and Rabbinic community. See
Eugene Korn's chapter in *Halakhic Realities: Collected Essays on Organ Donation*.

35. *Be-Mareh Ha-Bazak* 7:86(4).

36. Noam Zohar, "Is Our Public Policy
on Brain Death Ethical?" in *Halakhic Realities: Collected Essays on Brain Death*,
396–7.

37. Dr. Naftali Moses, *Really Dead? The
Israeli Brain–Death Controversy 1967–
1986* (2011), 313.

D.   JEWISH GUIDANCE ON THE LOSS
OF A BABY OR FETUS

Facing the loss of a potential human life – whether it is the death of a newborn infant, a stillbirth, a necessary abortion, or a miscarriage – is very challenging and can be a source of tremendous grief. Mourning is normally guided by Jewish Law, which provides detailed rituals that serve as an anchor and whose structure aids in gradually comforting and healing the mourners, providing a theological perspective on the loss. However, when it comes to the death of an unborn fetus or infant who lives less than thirty days after birth, Jewish Law requires no such observance.[1] As a result, the tremendous sense of pain and loss that such a death may entail can be compounded by feelings of disconnection, loneliness, and lack of guidance.[2]

Every person mourns differently, and it is possible that each parent may mourn very differently from the other and have unique needs in response to the death. This chapter will therefore seek to provide a detailed overview of the various options and a checklist to serve as a source of guidance and structure for Jewish parents facing this sort of loss. It also offers several strategies for easing the suffering and confusion that such a death entails.

WHY SOME DO NOT ADVISE OBSERVING
TRADITIONAL MOURNING CUSTOMS

Jewish mourning customs are not necessarily intended to tell us when it is appropriate to be sad in the aftermath of a death. There are times when one must mourn for a close relative even if they are not pained by the death, whereas there are no laws of mourning for a close friend despite the terrible sadness such a loss may entail.[3] The Jewish laws of mourning are not a reflection of the sadness caused to the mourner, but of the loss to the world.[4]

The death of a fetus or newborn is a death of a potential life that never became a "viable" person. From a technical perspective, the world never merited to have this child dwell within it, and the child was thus not "lost" to the world. This may explain why it is customary to observe the Jewish mourning rituals only for a baby who was viable (*bar kayama*), even though the Talmud recognizes the tremendous suffering that the loss of a "non-viable" fetus entails.[5]

Indeed, from a spiritual perspective, the pure soul of a fetus or newborn never completely entered the human realm, and thus never severed its total attachment to God.[6] The soul of the baby thus remained pure and holy; it merits going directly to the World to Come, and eventually to return to life with the resurrection of the dead.[7] There is thus no need to engage in rituals to "elevate" the soul. From this perspective, equating the baby with an adult life only serves to diminish the exalted nature of its unblemished soul.

This is not intended to minimize the terrible pain that the parents often experience. We live in the human realm; despite these spiritual realities, we see things from our perspective and often cannot help but be devastated by such a tragic loss. Parents may thus be very sad and mourn, but they are not required to observe the traditional Jewish mourning customs and rituals.[8] Indeed, included in the Jewish laws of mourning is the requirement not to mourn excessively by observing more mourning rituals than are required.[9]

It may be that our great rabbis did not require mourning observances in such situations because they wanted to help parents suffering from such a loss to return to their normal course of life as quickly as possible so that they might be able to start over and possibly even attempt to have another child (although the time frame is dependent upon a given couple's emotional well-being at the time).[10] Indeed, part of the reason that some Rabbinic authorities oppose engaging in Jewish mourning rituals for a fetus or baby under thirty days old is a result of their perspective that it is emotionally ideal to simply forget about such a loss as quickly as possible.[11] Whatever the reason, it has not been customary to observe Jewish mourning rituals in these circumstances, and some oppose doing so as an attempt to safeguard age-old customs.[12]

WHY SOME RECOMMEND RITUALIZED EXPRESSION OF GRIEF

On the other hand, Jewish Law permits one to voluntarily observe the various mourning customs if they want to, even for those for whom they are not obligated to ritually mourn, as long as they don't violate any prohibitions in so doing (for example, not learning Torah).[13] People often want to express their pain in the traditional Jewish manner and to be guided fully by the laws of mourning.

Miscarriages and early infant death are no longer as common as they were in the distant past, and some have suggested that the sages did not apply the laws of mourning in these cases because they *were* quite common in their time.[14] Since these events are not as common in our day and many people do not have as many children as was once customary, the grief associated with such death is intensified. There is therefore a greater need to deal with that grief through a recognized Jewish set of rituals and through concrete acts that help people fully express and come to terms with their sorrow, should they so desire.[15] Indeed, the argument continues, avoiding talking about the loss intensifies the sense of loneliness and fear of forgetting the life (or potential life) lost. Parents thus need to do something to remember and affirm that life so they can more appropriately grieve and adjust to life without the baby.[16]

Some maintain that it is crucial to allow structured time for grief. It can be therapeutic to take time to feel the pain of the loss, let others know about it, and discuss the hopes and dreams the parents had for their child, whereas denial of these feelings can be more destructive in the long run than recognizing them at the appropriate time.[17] The Jewish mourning customs and rituals in such circumstances may thus play an important role, allowing the emotional and psychological needs of the mourner to be addressed with profound understanding, sensitivity, and compassion. This approach is not suggesting that Jewish Law be changed to accommodate grieving parents' needs, but simply that they may utilize certain approaches that are already found within the framework of Halakhah.[18]

A MIDDLE APPROACH

Some of those who permit engaging in Jewish mourning rituals in these circumstances distinguish between a fetus that was not born alive (i.e., a miscarriage or stillbirth) and a baby who was born alive but died within thirty days of birth. Although there is no obligation to engage in mourning customs in either case, these authorities discourage parents from engaging in these practices if the fetus was not born alive, but they permit[19] or even encourage[20] doing so if the baby was born alive.

Furthermore, some rule that even those who choose to voluntarily take upon themselves the Jewish mourning observances should only observe some of the customs; it is improper to observe all of them.[21] I will therefore detail many of the traditional mourning practices, listing what is customary in such circumstances and what may be done if one chooses. I will also present some suggested ways to maintain the spirit of the traditions without engaging in all of the requirements of full mourning observance.

IN THE HOSPITAL

Upon the death of a fetus or a baby in the hospital, parents are often given a choice. The first option is that they can allow the mortuary to handle everything – from taking the baby to burying him or her – allowing the parents to go home and try to heal. The second option is for the parents to be involved in the various steps in the process, beginning with seeing the baby and holding and talking to him or her, particularly in the case of a stillbirth or a baby that lived a short time after birth. While the first option is more traditional, many advise that the second option is not only permissible, but also preferable.[22] While it may be more difficult in the moment, in the long run, confronting the loss directly facilitates gradual healing, while trying to shut out the loss tends to keep people bound to it.[23] Research has shown that holding the baby after death not only does not make the grief more painful, but actually helps bereaved parents face their loss and relieves later uncertainties about how the baby looked and felt.[24] Of course, we should respect parents who are not comfortable with this option for religious or emotional reasons; they should not be pressured into holding the baby.

Many hospitals will also give the parents the option of taking a picture of the baby. Some Rabbinic thinkers discourage[25] or even prohibit this,[26] while others encourage it.[27] Hospital nursing staff often take these pictures because they find that parents frequently request and cherish them later on. Parents should do what is best for them, ideally after seeking the advice of someone who knows them and understands human psychology and Jewish Law.[28]

Close to the time of losing a baby or fetus,[29] or upon finding out that the fetus has died,[30] it is appropriate to recite the blessing of "*Dayan Ha-Emet*" ("Blessed are You, Lord our God, King of the universe, the True Judge"), which is said whenever one hears tragic news.[31] However, some are accustomed not to say this blessing in these circumstances[32] (and if one is not experiencing suffering and grief they should not say it[33]). One who is unsure can say the blessing without using God's name.[34]

One is not obligated to tear their garment (*keria*) for a fetus or a baby for whom one is not obligated to mourn, and it is not customary to do so.[35] However, parents may do so if they so desire.[36] Parents should seek guidance from their rabbi as to the appropriate time to tear the garment (e.g., in the hospital immediately after the death or at the burial, etc.), since there are different customs and this is a unique case given the differences in the extent of the parents' involvement in the burial (see below).

The body of the baby must be treated with respect and should not be unnecessarily studied or operated on.[37] An autopsy is only permitted if the information gained is likely to prevent the mother from experiencing future miscarriages or infant deaths.[38] One should inquire if the autopsy is indeed absolutely necessary or if the necessary information can be determined by a less invasive biopsy or simply by taking blood or imaging. If an autopsy is deemed necessary, the entire body must be buried afterwards.[39]

PREPARING FOR THE BURIAL: CIRCUMCISION AND NAMING

It is customary to circumcise a baby boy who dies within thirty days of birth[40] and a fetus who dies before birth[41] before burying him.[42] It is also customary to name a baby boy at the time of the circumcision,[43] and to name a girl at the burial[44] (although this can be done later if it was not done at that time, and a *minyan* is not necessary for this[45]). It is customary to give the baby or fetus a name that is somewhat uncommon,[46] but some advise choosing a more usual name.[47] Parents should therefore seek Rabbinic guidance and choose a name that they prefer.[48]

From the time of death until the burial of a fetus or baby who died within thirty days, there is no *aninut* period in which the parents are exempt from any *mitzvot*.[49] However, if they are involved in planning the burial, there is room to be strict, and they may avoid eating meat or drinking wine during this time (but they are not exempt from performing any *mitzvot*).[50]

BURIAL

It is customary to bury babies who were born alive but died within thirty days of birth, even though there is no obligation to mourn for them,[51] and the parents should ensure that this is done.[52] Similarly, from the point that a fetus has the form of a person (from about the end of the third month of pregnancy), it should also be buried.[53] It is best to transfer the fetus to the local Jewish mortuary (Chevrah Kadisha), which will handle it in accordance with local customs.[54]

It is customary to bury fetuses and babies who died within thirty days in a special section of the Jewish cemetery.[55] There is traditionally no individual monument or tombstone placed on the grave in these situations, but if the family would like to place such a marker, they may do so (if the mortuary and cemetery allow it).[56]

FUNERAL

There is no requirement to have full funeral proceedings for a fetus or baby younger than thirty days, and it is not customary to do so.[57] Instead, it is customary for the Jewish mortuary (Chevrah Kadisha) to privately bury the body themselves.[58] However, if the parents want to be present for the burial, they may be.[59] It is not customary to say a eulogy in these situations,[60] but one may say some farewell remarks, as is often done when someone is buried on a day on which formal eulogies are forbidden.[61]

Although many parents follow the custom of allowing the mortuary to handle the burial while they themselves are not present, for those who want to accompany the body to the cemetery, some have suggested the following understated and less ceremonial "funeral" proceedings:[62]

- Graveside service directly before the interment, rather than in a full funeral setting in the chapel.
- Say a few words of consolation and farewell.
- Choose readings from the Psalms and chapters from the Prophets that express your feelings.[63] It is customary not to recite the *Tzidduk*

Ha-Din prayer at the burial of a baby or fetus.[64] If one wants to say *Kaddish* at the cemetery, there must be a *minyan* present and the burial *Kaddish* should be recited.

- Select close friends and relatives may join the parents to demonstrate respect for the deceased child and comfort the family. It is not customary to conclude such a funeral with the mourners passing through rows of friends (*shurot*), as is done at the funeral of an adult.[65]

SHIVAH

After the funeral, if the parents want to be alone, there is no requirement to provide a first meal (*seudat havra'ah*),[66] and their request to remain alone should be honored. However, people should ensure, in an appropriate manner, that the mourners needs are cared for, whether they be personal, emotional, dietary, etc.[67] Although there is technically no requirement to "comfort the mourners," since the Jewish customs of mourning are not obligatory for such mourners, it is important to remember that comforting mourners is part of the more general commandment to "love your neighbor as yourself,"[68] and it is thus still a mitzvah to support the family of the deceased in whatever way is best for them.[69]

Furthermore, as mentioned above, should the parents so desire, they may choose to engage in what some call a "non-halakhic *shivah*." Like one obligated to sit *shivah*, they may voluntarily stay at home, possibly sit on low chairs (although this obviously is not required, and as with all of this, one should keep in mind that the mother has just given birth, and all of the physical and emotional ramifications thereof), and accept close friends and family for visits to provide comfort, whether for just the first day, the first few days, or an entire week.[70] Additionally, the parents may accept upon themselves some of the customs of the *shivah* period, such as not shaving or cutting their hair, not wearing leather shoes, not washing their clothing, and not bathing.[71] It is not customary to light a candle in the house of mourning for a fetus or baby that died within thirty days, but if the parents so desire, they may light a candle in the house, particularly if the baby was born alive but died later.[72]

KADDISH, YEAR OF MOURNING, AND *YAHRTZEIT*

There is no obligation to say *Kaddish* after the passing of a fetus or baby younger than thirty days, and it is not customary to do so.[73] However, if a parent so desires, it is not prohibited,[74] and some argue that it is in fact appropriate to do so.[75] In circumstances in which one is obligated to mourn, it is customary not to say *Kaddish* for more than thirty days for anyone other than parents, and thereafter to say it only on a *yahrtzeit* (day of death) and at *Yizkor* services four times a year, although one may say it more often if they prefer.[76]

During a period of obligatory mourning, one is forbidden to participate in joyous gatherings. One who is not obligated to mourn is obviously permitted to take part in such events and gatherings, but it may not be in the spirit of bereavement. Some have therefore suggested that voluntary mourners should adopt the practice not to participate in these events, at least to some extent.[77] It is certainly permitted, and indeed praiseworthy, to perform good deeds, say prayers, study Torah, and give charity to a worthy cause for the sake of the elevation of the soul of the deceased fetus or baby (even though such a pure soul needs no elevation).[78] It is not customary to assemble to recite prayers in memory of the deceased (*azkara*) or to recite *Yizkor*, but if parents want to, they may memorialize the baby or fetus by, for example, lighting a candle for the soul of the deceased[79] or having a memorial gathering with close friends and family.[80] However, they should keep in mind that they are not thereby taking a vow to observe every *yahrtzeit* for the rest of their lives.[81]

REMEMBERING

For some parents, it is most beneficial to simply try to move on with life after their loss and not to let it depress them. However, many recommend finding ways to remember and affirm the life of their baby or fetus and to help them acknowledge their grief, adjust to life without the baby, and mitigate their sense of loneliness and fears of forgetting the life that was.[82] There are many ways to do this. For example, although it is not customary to light an extra Shabbat candle each week for a fetus or baby who dies within thirty days (although it would not be prohibited to do so), some have suggested taking on the custom of lighting two candles after the departure of Shabbat every week (after completing *Havdalah*) and intending those for the memory of the deceased fetus or baby.[83] Other suggestions include collecting mementos to help remember the baby, which may include writing a letter or poem to the baby or creating artwork.[84] The hospital will often offer a memory box with a picture, foot/hand prints, a lock of hair, and other meaningful items that many people find valuable years later. Some specifically Jewish suggestions, as mentioned above, include studying extra Torah in memory of the deceased, adding a new practice to one's religious observance, and making charitable donations in the baby's memory.[85] Others have suggested using the occasion of the mother's first immersion in the *mikvah* after the loss as a meaningful experience of letting go of the loss and preparing for the future.[86]

CONCLUSION

As detailed in this chapter, Jewish tradition does not require mourning for the loss of a fetus or newborn baby. Parents may choose to follow the traditional approach, but if they feel the need to engage in some level of ritualized mourning, some support can be found for doing so (as detailed above). If parents choose to voluntarily engage in this non-obligatory mourning, they should try to do so in moderation.

No bereaved person should ever be cajoled or imposed upon to observe rituals that our wise sages did not require. We cannot know with certainty what is best for another person. If we are not sure that something is appropriate in a given situation, perhaps we should rely on Jewish Law and custom, which does not require mourning in these situations.[87] Nevertheless, there are many challenging moments and circumstances that arise for a couple after this tragic loss, and there are many decisions that must be made at a time when it is very difficult to think clearly. The grieving parents should be made aware of their range of options, as detailed in this chapter.

Below is a list of some things to be aware of and ways in which people can be helpful during these most intense and traumatic moments:[88]

(1)   *Before Seeing Your Baby*
   a. Consider finding a bereavement doula who may be able to lend support to you and your family during the birth/loss process.
   b. Discuss with the nursing staff the possibility of moving to

a room on another floor away from the maternity ward to mitigate the grief, if you can forgo the specialized care of the maternity floor.

c. Ask the nurse to give you a description of what your baby may look like after he or she is born, so that you can be aware of changes in your baby's skin. Be prepared that if the baby is not born alive, there will be no responsiveness or crying, and the lips may appear red or blue. Your baby's body will become cooler and start to stiffen over a short period of time.

d. If your baby is born alive, ask the nurse to describe what you might see or hear during your baby's dying process (e.g., breathing patterns), so that you will be more prepared and less afraid.

(2)   *Before Departing the Hospital*

a. You can hold, bathe, and dress your baby as much as you would like.

b. Feel free to take your time with your baby. Although many hospitals have a time limit before a body must be picked up or taken to the morgue, staff can sometimes accommodate more time if necessary.

c. You may want to sing, play music, read, or speak to your baby, especially if he or she is born alive, because hearing is often the last of the senses to decline.

d. You may want to have skin-to-skin contact and rock, hold, kiss, and/or cuddle your baby.

e. Consider which family and friends should be with you at the hospital and when you return home. Some of your closest friends and family may unintentionally say things that are hurtful, and you should not feel obligated to speak to or spend time with anyone.

f. You may want to ask hospital staff to make hand/foot prints of your baby and/or to cut a lock of the baby's hair.

g. Consider taking pictures of your baby. Many people cherish these photographs for the rest of their lives and only have this one opportunity to capture these images.

h. Consider speaking with a hospital chaplain or rabbi.

i. You or someone close to you should:
    i.   arrange for completing a death certificate

    ii. arrange for the burial

    iii. arrange for a *bris* if your baby is a boy (a Jewish mortuary will often handle this)

(3)   *In Preparation for the Difficult Days Ahead:*

    a. You have no obligation to behave in any specific manner. Everyone grieves differently, and your grief is your own.

    b. Consider if, when, and how you feel comfortable letting family and friends know what happened.

    c. When the time is right, consider both grief counseling and marital counseling.[89]

    d. Empower one individual to "manage" communications to family members and friends informing them of the news and arranging support, such as delivery of meals when you arrive home. Other needs may include:

        i. Dismantling and removal of baby furniture and other items from the home, car, etc.

        ii. Removal of any wrapped gifts that may be in the house

        iii. Babysitting

        iv. Carpooling

        v. House cleaning

        vi. Payment and administration of hospital bills

        vii. Grief counselors

        viii. Introductions to others who have experienced a similar loss and are available to meet or speak with you

        ix. Obtaining post-delivery care and supplies

        x. Help removing parents' names from mailing lists of companies so you do not receive information about baby products and services

        xi. Planning a memorial service

ENDNOTES

1. A fetus that dies in the womb or is born dead (stillbirth) is called a "*nefel*," and no laws of mourning apply. If the baby is born alive, the rules are more complex. Generally, a baby who lives for less than thirty days is in a category of uncertainty and is categorized as a "*safek nefel*" (even if the baby died from an external cause, such as an accident [*Gesher Ha-Chaim* 19:3(4)]). Since Jewish Law is lenient when it comes to mourning, one is not obligated to observe the laws of mourning for the death of a baby who dies within thirty days of birth (*Semachot* 3:1; *Shabbat* 136a; Rambam, *Hilkhot Avel* 1:6; *Shulchan Arukh*, YD 374:8, all based on *Torat Kohanim, Emor* 1:6.) For discussion, see R. Avraham Stav, *Ke-Chalom Ya'uf*, 23–4; for explanation of the word "*nefel*," see ibid., 33; Steinberg, *Encyclopedia Hilkhatit Refu'it*, vol. 3, 901.

The thirty days conclude at the beginning of the evening of the thirty-first day from the birth. (This is the ruling of *Gesher Ha-Chaim* 19:3(4) and *Yabia Omer* 8:YD 33; see various opinions in *Ke-Chalom Ya'uf*, 94.) However, if it is certain that the baby was born after nine full months of gestation (certainty would require the parents to not have had relations since conceiving nine months prior to the birth), then if the baby is born alive, even if he or she dies that day, the baby is not a "*safek nefel*," but rather a "*ben kayama*" (a "viable" baby, the term normally given to a baby that survives more than thirty days). In this case, one observes all mourning laws and customs (*Shabbat* 136a; *Niddah* 44b; Rambam, *Hilkhot Avel* 1:7; *Shulchan Arukh* YD 374:8), but not the traditional funeral practices. However, in practice, many are not accustomed to observe the mourning customs in this situation unless the baby survives at least a few days after birth (*Ke-Chalom Ya'uf*, 95).

If the baby lived for thirty days in an incubator, see the summary of opinions in *Encyclopedia Hilkhatit Refu'it*, vol. 3, 903–5, 921; *Nishmat Avraham*, YD 374(2); *Yabia Omer* 9:YD 37; and *Ke-Chalom Ya'uf*, 98. See also discussion in *Torat Ha-Yoledet*, 573 (2nd ed.). More recently, R. Moshe Feinstein has been quoted as ruling that if a baby survived longer than a month, but only because of medical interventions such as an incubator, and it is clear that without such interventions the baby would not have survived naturally on its own, the baby is classified as a *nefel* (*Masorat Moshe*, vol. 2, 191). This was also the ruling of R. Wosner (*Shevet HaLevi* 3:143) and R. N. Rabinovitch (*Siach Nachum* 81), but not R. Elyashiv (*Torat Ha-Yoledet*, 57, n. 8, and *Shiurei Torah Le-Rofim*, vol. 2, 630). R. Feinstein is also quoted as ruling that a *pidyon ha-ben* should not be performed for a baby in an incubator (R. Aaron Felder, *Rishumei Aharon*, vol. 1, 69). However, R. Sternbuch disagrees (*Teshuvot Ve-Hanhagot* 3:330).

2. *Ke-Chalom Ya'uf*, 21; R. Yamin Levy, *Confronting the Loss of a Baby* (Ktav Publishing, 1998), xvii, 49, 55. Levy argues that not having specific Jewish laws of mourning in these circumstances makes some parents feel abandoned, as though it is not a significant loss in the eyes of Judaism.

3. *Ke-Chalom Ya'uf*, 21.

4. Ibid., 22.

5. The *mishnah* (*Niddah* 5:3) states, "A one-day-old child who dies . . . is to his parents and family like a full-grown bridegroom." Furthermore, Abba Shaul rules (*Kiddushin* 80b) that certain rules related to *yichud* are waived while one is in mourning, even for a *nefel*, for whom one is not obligated to mourn, since one's evil inclination is broken while mourning. See *Ke-Chalom Ya'uf*, 22. Furthermore, King David's servants were surprised that he did not mourn when his baby died, as some form of weeping and mourning is appropriate even for a week-old baby (Radak, II Samuel 12:20, 22). Indeed, there is disagreement over whether King David mourned for his baby son who died. Ralbag (II Samuel 13:37) maintains that he did indeed mourn for the baby, which Ralbag argues is natural and expected. Abarbanel (II Samuel 13:37), however, demonstrates from the verses that King David did not mourn at all since the baby was always sick and died so young, and because King David knew it was going to happen.

6. *Ke-Chalom Ya'uf*, 23, 110–2. There have been great rabbis who requested specifically to be buried amongst the fetuses in the cemetery because of their exalted purity and holiness.

7. *Iggerot Moshe*, YD 3:138; see also *Ke-Chalom Ya'uf*, 108–10, 141–2; R. Zilberstein, *Torat Ha-Yoledet*, 36, 226.

8. *Ke-Chalom Ya'uf*, 23.

9. *Shulchan Arukh*, YD 394:1, based on *Mo'ed Katan* 27b. This may also apply to mourning too much for a fetus or infant (*Ke-Chalom Ya'uf*, 26). The obligation not to mourn excessively in these circumstances is related to the idea that one who experiences such a loss is called upon to maintain a sense of faith and trust in God, accepting God's will, which in this case was that this baby not be born, for what-ever reason. Engaging in mourning rituals despite this may demonstrate a lack of faith and trust in God (R. Elchonon Zohn, personal communication, Winter 2016).

10. R. Yosef Tzvi Rimon, in *Ke-Chalom Ya'uf*, 23, n. 8; R. Goldman, *Me-Olam Ve-Ad Olam*, 96–7, suggests that for these reasons (favoring life over death, not mourning excessively, and emphasizing continuation and the return to normal life), it has become customary for the mortuary (Chevrah Kadisha) to carry out the burial without the presence of the family.

11. *Ke-Chalom Ya'uf*, 39, fn. 75.

12. Ibid.

13. Rema, YD 374:6. See *Ke-Chalom Ya'uf*, 25; *Encyclopedia Hilkhatit Refu'it*, vol. 3, 923, fn. 447.

14. *Encyclopedia Hilkhatit Refu'it*, vol. 3, 923, fn. 447; Levy, *Confronting the Loss of a Baby*, xviii. Levy also suggests that since families often lived together in one home or in close proximity, they did not need a formal mourning gathering to comfort the parents. In contrast, when a baby dies in our day, the parents may have no community of their own and are left to mourn alone. *Ke-Chalom Ya'uf*, 22, fn. 5, cites studies that show that cultures with high infant mortality tend not to have specific mourning rituals for such losses.

15. *Encyclopedia Hilkhatit Refu'it*, vol. 3, 923, fn. 447; Levy, *Confronting the Loss of a Baby*, xix. Others might argue that the very fact that infant death was so common in the days of our sages but they still chose not to institute the mourning observances shows that they did not feel that it was necessary in this situation. However, the Ramban claims that the reason our sages did not institute the practices of mourning for a baby under thirty days or a fetus is because one does not feel as anguished over such a loss (*Torat Ha-Adam, Sha'ar Ha-Avel, Inyan Ha-Aveilut*, 210–1 in Mosad HaRav Kook, Chavel Edition of

Kitvei Ha-Ramban, vol. 2, based on *Bava Batra* 111b; see also *Badei Ha-Shulchan*, YD 374:8[70]). Now that such losses are much more infrequent, this might not be true for many parents.

16. Levy, *Confronting the Loss of a Baby*, 34.

17. Ibid., 37. Levy writes, "Based on my personal experience and the experience of others, there is no question in my mind but that some sort of religious response is necessary in order to allow the grief process to progress, so that bereaved parents can get on with their lives" (72).

18. Ibid., 52.

19. R. Asher Weiss (personal correspondence, Summer 2015) told this author that it is not customary to have a funeral or observe the laws of mourning for a fetus, and it is not even recommended to know where the fetus is buried, since the *mishnah* says that a fetus is not even a *nefesh* (*Ohalot* 7:6 and Rashi, *Sanhedrin* 72b, s.v. *yatza rosho*). However, R. Weiss suggests that a baby that has been born is in a different category, which is challenging to categorize as easily, and it may be mourned if one so chooses. Indeed, some rule that certain mourning customs (pouring out water) may apply to a baby that has actually been born, but not to one that dies while still in the womb (see *Nishmat Avraham*, YD 339:5(11) (522 in 3rd ed.). Similarly, there is a different status when it comes to the laws of *Yibum* between a woman whose fetus dies, and one which is born alive, even if it dies immediately (*Shulchan Arukh* EH 156:4).

20. R. Rimon, *Ke-Chalom Ya'uf* 39, fn. 75. R. Rimon (personal conversation, Summer 2015) told this author that it is not ideal to observe the laws of mourning for a fetus that was never born, since elevating it to the status of an actual child who died may make the loss more painful for the family. However, a baby that was born alive is different for the family emotionally. If parents want a funeral or *shivah*, it may be recommended to observe these mourning rituals if they developed a connection to the baby in order to help them cope. (This may apply even to saying *Kaddish*, even for an entire year, since this ritual may have a positive influence on the one saying *Kaddish*.)

21. *Pitchei Teshuvah*, YD 374:6, quoted in *Penei Baruch* 9:10, n. 21.

22. Yonit Rothchild in *To Mourn a Child: Jewish Responses to Neonatal and Childhood Death*, Jeffrey Saks, Joel B. Wolowelsky, eds. (OU Press, 2013), 42; *Ke-Chalom Ya'uf*, 47, notes that it is customary not to kiss the corpse, but it is not prohibited.

23. Saks and Woloweslky, eds., *To Mourn a Child*, 43–44.

24. Levy, *Confronting the Loss of a Baby*, 73–74.

25. *Ke-Chalom Ya'uf*, 47, n. 119, quotes R. Yuval Cherlow and R. Avraham Stav as suggesting that this is improper from an emotional/psychological perspective and may constitute an excessive focus on death.

26. *Kol Bo al Aveilut* 1:3(10); *Nitei Gavriel* 42:8; *Ke-Chalom Ya'uf*, 46.

27. Levy, *Confronting the Loss of a Baby*, 59, 73. *Ke-Chalom Ya'uf*, 46, notes that despite the suggestion by some that this is prohibited because it is improper to look at the deceased, it is not technically prohibited.

28. *Ke-Chalom Ya'uf*, 47, n. 119.

29. Ideally, one should make the blessing upon hearing the bad news as close as possible to the time the news is revealed and at least on the same day, but if one did not make the blessing that day it may also be said at the time of the burial. After that point, it should ideally be said without

God's Name (*Ke-Chalom Ya'uf*, 28).

30. Many suggest that the time to make the blessing upon a miscarriage is when one hears the bad news, but others argue that it should be said at the time of the delivery, since that is the most sorrowful moment (*Ke-Chalom Ya'uf*, 28, n. 25).

31. R. Felder, *Mourning and Remembrance: "Yesodei Semachot"* 2 (in the name of R. Moshe Feinstein). However, it is possible that R. Feinstein only referred to saying this blessing for a baby that was born and died, but not necessarily for a fetus. Accordingly, it is possible that one should not recite the blessing for an early stage miscarriage (*Ke-Chalom Ya'uf*, 27, n. 22. See there for other authorities who rule that one should recite this blessing when losing a baby or fetus that one does not mourn for).

32. R. Tucazinsky, *Gesher Ha-Chaim* 4:21. See *Ke-Chalom Ya'uf*, 27, n. 22, who writes that the debate may be related to the root of this blessing. If it is connected to the practice of tearing a garment (*keriah*), then according to those who maintain that one should not tear a garment over a death for which he is not obligated to mourn, one should similarly not recite this blessing in such circumstances.

33. *Ke-Chalom Ya'uf*, 28, based on *Mishnah Berurah* 222:3.

34. *Zichron Meir* 6:1(2); *Ke-Chalom Ya'uf*, 27. Similarly, other relatives of the parents should only say the blessing without God's name (*Ke-Chalom Ya'uf*, 28).

35. *Shulchan Arukh*, YD 340:30.

36. *Ke-Chalom Ya'uf*, 29, fn. 28, based on the Rambam in his commentary on *Mo'ed Katan* 3:7: "Anyone who wants to tear his clothing or remove his shoes should not be prevented from doing so." R. Levy (*Confronting the Loss of a Baby*, 110) further argues that this is not considered wasting a garment (*bal tashchit*), since it

serves a purpose – relieving anguish and frustration to some degree.

37. *Nishmat Avraham*, YD 349:2(4:6) (577 in 3rd ed.).

38. *Minchat Shlomo* 3:103(6). See also *Ke-Chalom Ya'uf*, 48; *Encyclopedia Hilkhatit Refu'it*, vol. 3, 919. *Nishmat Avraham*, YD 349:2(4:6) (577 in 3rd ed.), writes in the name of R. Neuwirth that there is much less of a prohibition to perform an autopsy on a fetus whose limbs have still not developed. See also *Torat Ha-Yoledet* 38:11, end of n. 12 (2nd ed.).

39. *Ke-Chalom Ya'uf*, 48. Making use of the placenta or umbilical cord blood is permissible.

40. *Shulchan Arukh*, YD 263:5. See discussion in *Ke-Chalom Ya'uf*, 39, and R. Immanuel Jakobovits, *Jewish Medical Ethics*, 199–200.

41. *Minchat Shlomo* 2:96(2).

42. The *Shulchan Arukh*, YD 263:5, writes that the circumcision should take place immediately before the burial, although many perform it before that point, such as at the time of the ritual bathing (*taharah*); see *Gesher Ha-Chaim* 1:16:3(2). It is generally done by the mortuary as part of their preparations of the body for burial (*Ke-Chalom Ya'uf*, 41). See *Ke-Chalom Ya'uf*, 40–2, for a detailed description of the reasons for circumcision in this situation and the differences between circumcising these babies and circumcising living babies (for example, no blessing is made on these circumcisions). To underscore the seriousness of this requirement to circumcise a deceased baby, R. J.B. Soloveitchik notes that some authorities require opening the grave in order to perform the circumcision if it was not done before burial. R. Soloveitchik notes, however, that if a baby boy was not circumcised, he may still be buried in a Jewish cemetery (Ziegler, *Halakhic Positions of Rabbi Joseph B. Soloveit-*

chik [Aaronson Inc., 1998], 151). See R.
Akiva Eiger, YD 263, 353. However, if a
fetus was buried uncircumcised with his
mother, their grave should not be opened
to circumcise him (*Pitchei Teshuvah*, YD
263:11).

43. *Shulchan Arukh*, YD 263:5; *Kol
Bo Aveilut* 3:3(6); *Gesher Ha-Chaim*
1:16:3(2); *Ke-Chalom Ya'uf*, 42, n. 93,
points out that at one time in many communities, the custom was to name babies
only if they were born alive, but that is
not the prevailing custom today. The baby
is given a name so that the baby would
merit to be resurrected in the Messianic
era (*Shulchan Arukh*, YD 263:5), and so
the parents would be able to recognize
the child at that time (Rosh, *Mo'ed Katan*
3:88; see *Ke-Chalom Ya'uf*, 42). Many
advise that based on these reasons, a
name can be given to a fetus at any stage
of development, even if it is too early to
discern the gender of the fetus, in which
case it should be given a name that could
fit both a boy and a girl (*Ke-Chalom Ya'uf*,
43, n. 99). In most locales, however, it is
customary to name the fetus only from
the time that it has the form of a person
(from about the end of the third month of
pregnancy), as mentioned below regarding burial (*Ke-Chalom Ya'uf*, 43). Some
permit naming the fetus even earlier –
any time after 40 days from conception
(*Ke-Chalom Ya'uf*, 43, based on Chazon
Ish below). However, others recommend
not doing this so as not to increase the
severity of the pain of the loss (*Ke-Chalom
Ya'uf*, 43, in the name of R. Yosef Tzvi
Rimon).

44. *Sedei Chemed, Aveilut* 202.

45. *Pitchei Teshuvah*, YD 263:1. *Ke-Chalom Ya'uf*, 44. This can be done simply
by reciting *El Malei Rachamim* with the
name inserted.

46. *Minchat Shlomo* 2:96(2); *Nishmat
Avraham*, YD 263:5(14) (365 in 3rd
ed.). R. Auerbach gives the examples of

Metushelach and Rachamim (in those
communities in which this would not be
a common name). See *Ke-Chalom Ya'uf*,
102, for other examples of commonly
used names in these circumstances. R.
Elchonon Zohn told this author that another commonly used name is Yonah, particularly if the gender is indistinguishable,
because there is a *midrash* that states that
the prophet Yonah ben Amitai had been a
child who died and was resurrected.

47. *Ke-Chalom Ya'uf*, 44.

48. Ibid., 43–4. If the parents do not
choose a name, the mortuary (Chevrah
Kadisha) will often choose one.

49. *Gesher Ha-Chaim* 1:18:3(2); see
Ke-Chalom Ya'uf, 24; *Encyclopedia
Hilkhatit Refu'it*, vol. 3, 921.

50. *Ke-Chalom Ya'uf*, 25.

51. *Shulchan Arukh*, OH 526:10, rules
that there is no actual commandment to
bury these fetuses and babies, whereas the
Magen Avraham there (526:20) rules that
there is indeed a commandment to do so.
See *Encyclopedia Hilkhatit Refu'it*, vol. 3,
914; *Ke-Chalom Ya'uf*, 34, n. 50; *Gesher
Ha-Chaim* 16:3(1); and *Kol Bo al Aveilut*
3:3(2) for a summary of the various opinions of contemporary authorities. Even
if it is not a commandment, there is an
obligation to bury these fetuses and babies
due to the following considerations: (1) a
human body is compared to a Torah scroll
that requires burial; (2) the prohibition
against benefiting from the body in any
way; (3) concerns for ritual impurity; (4)
respect for the dead; (5) to enable the
deceased to rise from the grave at the
time of the resurrection of the dead. See
Ke-Chalom Ya'uf, 34–35, for a summary
of these reasons and their sources.

52. Relatives of the deceased are obligated
to ensure proper burial and to prevent the
hospital from delaying burial or treating
the body inappropriately; see *Ke-Chalom
Ya'uf*, 35 and *Torat Ha-Yoledet* 38:11, n.

12 (2nd ed.).

53. The precise point from which the obligation to bury a fetus begins is a matter of some dispute. The majority view is that the main criterion is that the fetus is developed enough to have the form of a person (see *Nitei Gavriel, Niddah* 112:17; *Mei-Olam Ve-Ad Olam* 7:64; *Ke-Chalom Ya'uf*, 35, fn. 57). Some rule that the fetus must be buried only after five months of gestation (*Teshuvot Ve-Hanhagot* 2:602), while others rule that the fetus must be buried after three months of gestation (*Shevet HaLevi* 10:211[3]), and some even require burial after 40 days of gestation (*Chazon Ish, Orchot Rabbeinu*, vol. 4, 109; *Olot Yitzchak* 2:227). See also *Encyclopedia Hilkhatit Refu'it*, vol. 3, 916–7; *Nishmat Avraham*, YD 263:5(11) (362 in 3rd ed.). Within the first 40 days of pregnancy, there is certainly no obligation to bury (*Ke-Chalom Ya'uf*, 35). One may allow the hospital to dispose of the remains of such an early fetus in the usual fashion (Levy, *Confronting the Loss of a Baby*, 88–89), but it is ideal to treat it with respect and even to bury it if possible (*Encyclopedia Hilkhatit Refu'it*, vol. 3, 917). R. Moshe Feinstein is quoted as ruling that it is not certain that a fetus must be buried even up to four months of gestation (although if possible it is best to bury any fetus once it has some flesh and skin). If there is some obligation, it is only in order to prevent a Kohen from coming into contact with it. Thus, if one is unable to have the fetus released from the hospital, R. Feinstein argues that there is no need to put up a fight in order to have it released (*Masorat Moshe*, vol. 1, 376).

54. *Ke-Chalom Ya'uf*, 36. The requirement to have a person dedicated to watching the body and reciting prayers (*shemirah*) does not apply to a fetus or baby that dies within thirty days (*Nitei Gavriel* 135:2–3, based on *Taz*, YD 371:11 and *Shakh* 371:17 in the name of the Bach, who rules that the laws related to honor-

ing the dead do not apply in such a case). However, it should be kept in a protected area (*Gesher Ha-Chaim* 1:12:6(8); see *Ke-Chalom Ya'uf*, 38). There are different customs regarding ritual washing (*taharah*) in such cases (*Gesher Ha-Chaim* 1:12:6(2) says it should be done, whereas *Yesodei Semachot*, 29, and *Zichron Meir* 14:2(1) say not to do it). Therefore, it is customary to simply clean the body, without observing all of the traditional rituals of the washing (*Ke-Chalom Ya'uf*, 38, fn. 70). It is not customary to dress a fetus or baby who dies within thirty days in ritual shrouds (*takhrikhim*), but rather to wrap the body in a white sheet (*Ke-Chalom Ya'uf*, 38; *Gesher Ha-Chaim* 1:12:6[2]).

55. *Ke-Chalom Ya'uf*, 36. If the burial does not take place in a cemetery, the burial place should be properly marked so that Kohanim can avoid it (*Gesher Ha-Chaim* 1:28:1[3]).

56. *Gesher Ha-Chaim* 1:12:6(13).

57. *Shulchan Arukh*, YD 353:4. See also the discussion in R. Zilberstein, *Shiurei Torah Le-Rofim*, vol. 2, 634–7.

58. *Ke-Chalom Ya'uf*, 38.

59. Ibid., 38–9; *Badei Ha-Shulchan* 353:4(7). The extent of the parents' involvement in the burial/funeral is dependent on their ability to handle it (*Ke-Chalom Ya'uf*, 34).

60. *Shulchan Arukh*, YD 344:4, 8. *Arukh Ha-Shulchan*, YD 344:8 writes that it is forbidden to eulogize a fetus or baby who dies before thirty days.

61. *Ke-Chalom Ya'uf*, 30–1, which quotes R. Yosef Tzvi Rimon as suggesting that these remarks be focused on inspiring those listening to repentance, repair, and building, each according to their own way, as a sort of restoration for the one that was lost. It is difficult to eulogize one who lived so briefly, but often the silence and the painful image of the small corpse in

the arms of its parent is the most profound eulogy.

62. R. Maurice Lamm, *The Jewish Way in Death and Mourning* (Jonathan David Publishers, 2000), 221–2.

63. A sample service might include reciting the *El Malei Rachamim* prayer, Psalms 121, 116, 61, 98, 100, and possibly 23, as well as saying the *Birkat Ha-Banim* prayer.

64. *Shulchan Arukh*, YD 376:4. Some have suggested reciting *Tzidduk Ha-Din* privately after the funeral, not as a public prayer (Levy, *Confronting the Loss of a Baby*, 90; see there for a contemporary English rendering of *Tzidduk Ha-Din* that may be recited). See *Zichron Meir* 17:6:1(4) for a special *Tzidduk Ha-Din* prayer that has been composed for children who die within thirty days (quoted in full in *Ke-Chalom Ya'uf*, 29, fn. 30). See also Nina Beth Cardin, *Tears of Sorrow, Seeds of Hope: A Jewish Spiritual Companion for Infertility and Pregnancy Loss* (Jewish Lights Publishing, 1999), 136.

65. *Shulchan Arukh*, YD 353:4.

66. *Gesher Ha-Chaim* 20:2(8).

67. Levy, *Confronting the Loss of a Baby*, 96–97.

68. Rambam, *Hilkhot Avel* 14:1; *Gesher Ha-Chaim* 1:20(5).

69. *Ke-Chalom Ya'uf*, 26.

70. For a description of one parent's experience sitting a "non-halakhic *shivah*" and the therapeutic benefits it afforded, see *To Mourn a Child*, 43.

71. *Ke-Chalom Ya'uf*, 26.

72. Ibid., 31, 122.

73. *Shulchan Arukh*, YD 344:4.

74. *Tzitz Eliezer* 7:49 (*Kuntres Even Yaakov* 6:7) states that "those who recite *Kaddish* for even the youngest baby are

correctly observing the tradition," and he provides kabbalistic reasons for the benefits of doing so. Although "even the youngest baby" could mean one older than thirty days, R. Levy argues that this may very well include babies less than thirty days old (*Confronting the Loss of a Baby*, 93; see detailed discussion there, 92–96). R. Moshe Feinstein is quoted as ruling (*Masorat Moshe*, vol. 2, 190) that one does not even have to recite *Kaddish* for a four-year-old child who dies because a child has no sins and does not need his parents to accrue merits for him. However, if one wants to recite *Kaddish* for the child, he may do so for thirty days as an act of *Tzidduk Ha-Din* (acceptance of the Divine judgement).

75. *Ke-Chalom Ya'uf*, 30; see the detailed discussion of the kabbalistic value of this practice (although they would not take priority in a synagogue over another mourner who has an obligation to lead prayers, etc.).

76. Lamm, *The Jewish Way in Death and Mourning*, 222.

77. Ibid.

78. Ibid.; *Ke-Chalom Ya'uf*, 31, 119. Although the baby is pure and was never contaminated by this world, according to most opinions the baby does have a soul that can be elevated to higher levels of heaven.

79. *Gesher Ha-Chaim* 1:12:6(14); *Ke-Chalom Ya'uf*, 32; Levy, *Confronting the Loss of a Baby*, 119.

80. Levy, ibid.

81. Lamm, *The Jewish Way in Death and Mourning*, 222. R. Shlomo Zalman Auerbach ruled that it is not customary to observe the *yahrtzeit* in these situations (*Ve-Aleihu Lo Yibol*, vol. 2, 136–7).

82. Levy, *Confronting the Loss of a Baby*, 34.

83. *Ke-Chalom Ya'uf*, 122.

84. Levy, *Confronting the Loss of a Baby*, 75, 116.

85. Ibid., 116–7.

86. Miriam Berkowitz, *Taking the Plunge* (Schechter Institute of Jewish Studies, 2009), 156–8; Cardin, 83, 142. Cardin's book includes numerous contemporary prayers and suggested rituals to help parents mourn and heal, such as planting healing plants (like aloe), baking challah, synagogue rituals, *Havdalah* rituals, and various ceremonies.

87. Lamm, *The Jewish Way in Death and Mourning*, 220–2.

88. Based partially on guidelines written up by David and Maytal Shainberg of "Forever my angel," drivymargulies.com, and returntozerohealingcenter.com.

89. For an excellent article on some of the marital challenges faced after the loss of a baby, see the chapter by Miriam Benhaim in *To Mourn a Child*, 137–47.

E.   AUTOPSY AND JEWISH LAW

The permissibility of post-mortem dissections (autopsy and donating bodies to medical/scientific research) has been one of the most contentious issues in contemporary Rabbinic literature.[1] This issue reflects the tension between the obligation to treat the body of the dead with sanctity and respect,[2] including prohibitions against not doing so,[3] and the obligation to attempt to save the lives of those still alive.[4] Respect for the dead and for a human corpse is a crucial Jewish value that emphasizes the dignity of humans, who are created in the image of God, and the belief that a person's body is not owned by the person, their family, or society, but is rather the possession of the Almighty. In general, Rabbinic authorities therefore usually prohibit autopsies. However, saving a life is also a central value, and there are thus some situations in which an autopsy may be permitted.

SITUATIONS IN WHICH AN AUTOPSY MAY BE PERMITTED

Many of the factors related to post-mortem examinations are similar to those that arise with regard to organ donation, with the exception, of course, of the concerns related to risking life. Indeed, there may thus be fewer halakhic challenges to performing certain post-mortem examinations than with donating organs.[5] For example, retrieving an organ from a patient who is not yet dead according to Jewish Law would violate the prohibition against murder, one of the few prohibitions that overrides the obligation to save a life,[6] but there is no such concern with regard to autopsies. In fact, there may be times when post-mortem examinations/autopsies are obligatory if there is a chance that these procedures will save a life.[7]

236

Most Rabbinic authorities require that the person whose life will potentially be saved by information gained from an autopsy be a patient who is clearly identified ("before us") here and now[8] and who is dying of a comparable illness.[9] However, the definition of "before us" can sometimes be expanded to include others suffering from the disease elsewhere in the world who can be helped, in which case the obligation to save lives takes precedence and an autopsy can be permitted (or obligated),[10] since the findings may be helpful immediately.[11] Some have gone so far as to argue that since we live in an era of instantaneous international communication, doctors researching a disease can be viewed as saving the lives of everyone in the world who suffers, or will ever suffer, from that particular illness.[12] For this reason, some argue that any autopsy done in order to learn about a disease is considered potentially lifesaving, since one can learn from that case for other possible similar cases that will eventually arise in the future, and we can thus view many autopsies as cases of a dangerously ill patient "before us."[13]

When there is danger to an entire community, such as during an epidemic, an autopsy is permitted in an attempt to save other people's lives.[14] Similarly, if children in a family have died or suffered from what may be a genetic disease, an autopsy is permitted in order to clarify the cause of death and assist the family with future pregnancies.[15] Likewise, if someone may have died because of an infection and their family members are in need of preventative medication that can be determined by means of an autopsy, it would be permitted. However, in all of these cases, an autopsy is only permitted provided that the same results cannot be determined via imaging technology, such as an MRI.[16]

There are often circumstances in which an entire invasive autopsy is not required, but rather very minor diagnostic testing or examinations can suffice. The general rule is that those minor procedures that would be routinely performed on the living, such as diagnostic procedures, tissue or organ biopsy, or taking blood samples, are not considered a desecration of the dead and may also be done on a corpse if necessary to help others.[17]

In any case in which an autopsy or any sort of post-mortem intervention may be permitted, it must be performed with the express permission of an authority in Jewish Law and in accordance with the guidelines detailed below in order to maintain proper dignity and burial of the deceased.

AUTOPSY TO DETERMINE CAUSE OF DEATH AND FOR LEGAL PURPOSES

It is generally forbidden to perform an autopsy simply to determine the cause of death, as there are now many other ways to reach this conclusion, such as sophisticated imaging, and autopsy frequently does not bring any new relevant information directly to clinicians.[18] However, an autopsy would be permitted if it alone can lead to information that may save another life.[19] One may not cut open a corpse simply to test the DNA except in very rare cases. Instead, a small skin or blood sample should be taken.[20]

Most authorities permit autopsies for legal reasons (forensic medicine), such as to establish guilt or innocence of a murderer.[21] Similarly, if a person dies as a result of medical malpractice, an autopsy may be conducted if needed in a legal case against the doctor, since it can prevent future malpractice.[22] However, autopsies for financial reasons are generally discouraged, such as when heirs want to make a financial claim concerning inheritance.[23] However, if a life insurance claim will not be paid without an autopsy in a case of possible unnatural death, some rule that the heirs need not object to the autopsy (provided it is requested by the insurance company and not by the heirs).[24]

MEDICAL SCHOOL AND DONATING ONE'S BODY TO SCIENCE

Observing or participating in post-mortem dissections is generally part of a medical student's study of human anatomy. Some Rabbinic authorities permit this,[25] especially if the student is simply watching and not actually participating in the cutting or dissection[26] and the deceased had requested that their body be donated to scientific research.[27] However, most Rabbinic authorities prohibit this.[28] Similarly, most authorities prohibit donating one's body to medical/scientific research, since Judaism teaches that we do not own our bodies and may thus not intentionally damage or donate them.[29] However, there are some authorities who permit it if a person requests that their body be donated and the body is buried immediately afterwards.[30]

ROLE OF THE FAMILY OF THE DECEASED

The family of the deceased may not consent to an autopsy that is forbidden by Jewish Law, as no one has ownership rights over a dead body.[31] There is an obligation to obtain family consent for any post-mortem examination, and the family has the right according to Jewish Law to prevent an autopsy, since they are responsible for burial and the prevention of disgrace to the body and to their family.[32] However, when a particular autopsy can potentially save another life, even the family may not object.[33] An autopsy on a deceased individual who has no relatives should be avoided if possible.[34]

The immediate relatives of one who donated their body to science must still observe the laws of mourning, despite the fact that many authorities forbid this donation.[35] The family should begin the *shivah* mourning period once the body is handed over to the place to which it is being donated.[36]

PROPER TREATMENT OF A BODY
DURING AN AUTOPSY[37]

1. In all instances, every effort should be made to expedite the release of the body for burial as quickly as possible.
2. The entire autopsy should be performed in a body pouch.
3. The autopsy procedure should be as minimal as possible, limited only to that which is absolutely necessary to secure pertinent, potentially lifesaving information:[38]
   a. Incisions should be avoided whenever possible.
   b. Samples for pathology should be as small as possible.
4. All parts of the body must be returned for burial. This includes replacing all organs in their proper place; e.g., brain in a suitable small plastic bag in the skull.[39]
5. All instruments should be wiped clean with a cloth and the cloth should be placed in the body pouch.
6. All incisions should be sutured as tightly and leak-proof as possible.
7. All blood or articles of clothing containing blood that are not needed for pathological or evidence purposes should be sent along with the remains to the funeral home. Even those that are needed should be returned for burial once they are no longer needed.

8. The autopsy must be performed with dignity and respect for the deceased. It is therefore forbidden to eat, drink, smoke, or act jokingly in the presence of the body.[40] When possible, the entire body, and especially the genitalia, should be kept covered at all times.

9. A member of the Jewish mortuary (Chevrah Kadisha) or designate thereof, or a rabbi, should be permitted to attend to recite prayers and ensure that proper dignity and decorum are maintained during the autopsy.[41]

ENDNOTES

1. This issue was the subject of heated debate among rabbis and medical professionals throughout modern Jewish history. For example, at a hospital in Denver as early as 1916, and around the same time in Poland, Jewish medical students were told that they would not be permitted to study medicine any longer unless they could provide Jewish corpses for their study of anatomy. This led to heated debates and conflicts (*Encyclopedia Hilkhatit Refu'it*, vol. 5, 570). The problem of the low number of Jewish bodies available for autopsies was often noted by anti-Semites. In 1927, a large group of Polish rabbis came out against autopsies and using bodies for medical research, publishing a strong statement in opposition (see *Teshuvot Ohr Ha-Meir* 74). Nevertheless, Jewish bodies were used for anatomy study in medical schools in Russia and Vilna.

In the modern State of Israel, this was a major concern. Indeed, the Hebrew University Medical School was delayed from opening for over 20 years because of the clashes over this issue. Autopsies eventually became common in Israel without Rabbinic approval and even without approval of the deceased's family, leading to a tremendous uproar and the establishment of organizations dedicated to preventing and protesting autopsies. Eventually, in 1962, the Israeli Ministry of Health created a special committee of physicians and rabbis that restricted autopsies to cases of immediately saving life, organ transplantation, determining if a significant medical error had taken place, or establishing cause of death to avoid danger to the public or family, and also required consultation with the next of kin (see *Encyclopedia Hilkhatit Refu'it*, vol. 5, 573). However, the medical establishment was concerned about these restrictions. At the same time, their attitude led to a diminution of trust in doctors in Israel, particularly on the part of the Rabbinic leadership. Consequently, many Rabbinic authorities became even stricter regarding autopsies, even in cases that would technically be permitted by Jewish Law. All of this acrimony led to much opposition and fighting, protests, violent demonstrations, and parliamentary debates. Some of the fiercest battles in the history of Israel took place over this issue, and eventually a large group of rabbis came out with a strong, uncompromising statement in opposition to autopsies. On this history, see *Encyclopedia Hilkhatit Refu'it*, vol. 5, 569–75. On the Israeli autopsy controversy in particular, see F. Rosner, *Biomedical Ethics and Jewish Law* (Ktav, 2001), 377–84; Glick and Jotkowitz, "Compromise and Dialogue in Bioethical Disputes," *The American Journal of Bioethics* 7(10) (2007), 36–38.

2. A corpse is compared to a Torah scroll, such that even after death a body has intrinsic holiness and must be treated with great respect (see *Berakhot* 18a; *Chatam Sofer* 6:10; *Gesher Ha-Chaim* 1:1[1:1]). Many authorities rule that post-mortem dissection is an affront to this holiness; see R. Arieli, *Torah She-Be'al Peh* 6 (5724), 40; *Noam* 6 (5723), 82. See also *Encyclopedia Hilkhatit Refu'it*, vol. 5, 593, and *Nishmat Avraham*, YD 349:1(4) (571 in 3rd ed.). Based on the concept of the body's intrinsic holiness, there is a prohibition against deriving benefit from the dead, which most authorities rule is a

Torah prohibition; see *Yabia Omer* 3:YD 20–21. Furthermore, some authorities raise concerns related to the idea that even after death, the soul is not completely severed from the body and is pained by bodily disgrace (based on Job 14:22). See *Shabbat* 13b; Rema, YD 363:2; R. Arieli, *Torah Shebe'al Peh* 6 (5724). Some argue that performing an autopsy constitutes denial of belief in this reality (*Torat He-Refuah*, 206; *Sha'arei Shamayim* 2:37). However, others rule that in a case in which autopsy is permitted, it is not denial of this belief (*Mishpatei Uziel* 1:YD 29). Other authorities claim that not only do the deceased not experience any physical or spiritual pain, but knowing that their bodies are being used to save lives would provide them with much comfort and spiritual pleasure (see R. Yudelevich, *Beit Av Hamishai*, 356; R. Isser Yehuda Unterman, *Kol Torah* 7(24) (Nissan-Iyar 5713), 2–4; R. Zilberstein, *Shiurei Torah Le-Rofim*, vol. 2, 614). There is one opinion that permitting an autopsy constitutes denial of the belief in the resurrection of the dead (*Minchat Yitzchak* 5:9), and one authority even claims that as long as some of the body is not buried, the soul is prevented from going to heaven (R. Felder, *Assia* 1, 216) or may be affected on the Judgment Day (*Ohr Ha-Meir* 74; see *Encyclopedia Hilkhatit Refu'it*, vol. 5, 594–5).

3. The Torah obligates burial (although some argue that it is a Rabbinic obligation), and it has been a Jewish practice since time immemorial (*Sanhedrin* 46b). If part of the body remains unburied, there is a continued violation of the precept of burial and the prohibition against leaving a body unburied overnight (see *Encyclopedia Hilkhatit Refu'it*, vol. 5, 601). See the appendix on Burial in a Mausoleum and Jewish Law in this book, where this is discussed at length. Some therefore view autopsy as a nullification of the obligation to bury (see the numerous citations in *Encyclopedia Hilkhatit Refu'it*, vol. 5, 599–600; *Nishmat Avraham*, YD 349:1[2]

[571 in 3rd ed.]).

Most authorities maintain that the prohibition against leaving the dead unburied overnight applies to all deceased people (*Shulchan Arukh*, YD 357:1; see numerous citations in *Encyclopedia Hilkhatit Refu'it*, vol. 5, 602). For the sake of the honor of the deceased, it is permitted to leave them unburied, even for many days, but it must be a true honor, as explicated by our rabbis, and not just a fabricated reason (*Iggerot Moshe*, YD 3:139; see also *Encyclopedia Hilkhatit Refu'it*, vol. 5, 604–5). Some argue that performing an autopsy in order to save a life is the greatest respect for the deceased (*Porat Yosef* 1:17) See also *Teshuvot Maharam Shick*, YD 347–8, who writes that the honor due to the dead pales in comparison with the requirement to save a living person's life. Similarly, some write that it is permitted to prevent burial for the sake of the living, while others disagree (see *Encyclopedia Hilkhatit Refu'it*, vol. 5, 605).

There is an additional biblical prohibition against desecration and disgrace of the body (*nivul ha-met*) (see *Encyclopedia Hilkhatit Refu'it*, vol. 5, 596, nn. 143 and 144 for detailed citations; see also *Nishmat Avraham*, YD 349:1(2) [570 in 3rd ed.]). The law forbidding desecration of the body is derived from the prohibition of leaving the dead unburied overnight (*Encyclopedia Hilkhatit Refu'it*, vol. 5, 596, n. 145), although some say it is derived from the commandment to love one's neighbor as oneself (ibid., n. 146). Some argue that prohibited desecration only occurs when an autopsy is performed disrespectfully and without purpose, but not if there is a definite indication, such as to save life. When the motivation is to gain lifesaving knowledge, it brings the person honor rather than degradation (*Mishpatei Uziel* 1:YD 28–29; *Encyclopedia Hilkhatit Refu'it*, vol. 5, 597, n. 147). For a detailed summary of the prohibitions related to autopsies, see R. Zilberstein, *Shiurei Torah Le-Rofim*, vol. 2, 593–6; and detailed discussion in Greenberg and

Farber, "Autopsies 1: A Survey of the Debate" and "Autopsies II: The National Jewish Hospital for Consumptives" in *Halakhic Realities – Collected Essays on Organ Donation*, 323–417.

4. Some of the authorities who forbid autopsies argue that despite the gravity of the obligation to attempt to save life, once a person is dead, they are not obligated to fulfill any commandments, and their body may thus not be desecrated (*Binyan Tzion* 1:170; *Nachal Eshkol* 2:36[9]).

5. Most authorities permit autopsies when the results can contribute immediately to the saving of a life, because all biblical and Rabbinic precepts are waived to save life, except for the three cardinal sins (*Encyclopedia Hilkhatit Refu'it*, vol. 5, 616–17, n. 264).

6. There are indeed some opinions that the prohibition against theft is not pushed aside even to save a life, and there are those who rule that anatomical dissection falls under that prohibition (*Binyan Tzion* 1:170–1, 3:103; see also the explanations of R. Zilberstein, *Shiurei Torah Le-Rofim*, vol. 2, 432, 445, 603, 604, 613). Others maintain that the prohibition of stealing is pushed aside in order to save a life, just like almost all commandments (*Teshuvot Maharam Shick*, YD 347–8), and it is thus permitted to perform an autopsy in order to save another life (*Encyclopedia Hilkhatit Refu'it*, vol. 5, 610). Others maintain that the prohibition of theft is pushed aside only for the certainty of lifesaving, but not if there is a doubt as to whether the autopsy will save life (R. Zilberstein, *Halakha U-Refuah*, vol. 5, 189). Still other authorities rule that we cannot apply the concept of theft at all to a corpse, because the dead cannot own anything (*Chavalim Be-Ne'imim* 4:YD 64).

7. See sources cited in n. 10 below. See also *Nishmat Avraham*, YD 349:1 (572 in 3rd ed.). R. Zilberstein rules that autopsies are only permitted to save another person's life, but not in order to lengthen the life of a healthy individual (*Shiurei Torah Le-Rofim*, vol. 4, 49).

8. Some authorities disagree with this principle that an autopsy may be performed only for the sake of saving the life of a clearly identified patient "before us." For example, R. Messas argues that if a physician has an opportunity to deepen his or her understanding of a disease and to be prepared in case another patient with the same illness presents, that should be sufficient to consider the situation as possible lifesaving, even if the patient is not currently present before us. Furthermore, he argues that the idea that only lifesaving would allow cutting or destroying the body is not true (based on *Teshuvot Ha-Rashba* 1:369). R. Messas claims that degradation does not happen to the deceased, since they cannot feel anything anymore; the only concern is for the living. R. Messas posits that by increasing medical knowledge through autopsy, the dead are helping future sick people and a mitzvah is being done with their bodies, which are about to decompose anyway. He thus claims that the deceased likely derive some comfort from these factors in the World to Come (*Mayim Chayim* 2:YD 109). Some have noted that Sephardic rabbis have tended to be more lenient regarding permitting autopsies, perhaps because they did not face the scandals related to body snatching and even murder for the sake of anatomical dissection that occurred in European history; see Bar-Ilan, *Jewish Bioethics* (Cambridge University Press, 2014), 117.

9. *Noda Be-Yehuda*, YD 210; *Teshuvot Chatam Sofer*, YD 336; *Teshuvot Maharam Shick*, YD 347–8. These authorities, whose approach has become the standard, allow autopsy only if the patient whose life is to be saved is clearly identified, because allowing any patient to be cut up for any possible future issue that might arise will lead to excessive and unnecessary autopsies (see *Encyclopedia Hilkhatit Refu'it*, vol. 5, 617–18 and notes there

for additional citations). Some authorities rule that if there is no patient in front of us at the moment, autopsy is forbidden even if a patient with a similar condition may arrive later. They argue that we cannot say that the whole world is connected nowadays via modern communications systems, since we see that autopsies in one place do not generally lead to people being saved elsewhere. Furthermore, even if significant new information derived from an autopsy appears in an academic journal, the saving of life based on that information will not take place for quite some time (*Nishmat Avraham*, YD 349:1, 572 and n. 108, quoting R. Arieli; see n. 12 below for an expansion on his ideas).

10. In potentially lifesaving circumstances, some rule that an autopsy is permitted (if the family consents), but not required (*Minchat Yitzchak* 5:9[22–4]). However, other authorities rule that in a lifesaving situation, a rabbi is obligated to persuade the family to grant consent (R. Yakovavitch, *Noam* 6 (5723), 271; see also *Encyclopedia Hilkhatit Refu'it*, vol. 5, 619).

11. Chazon Ish, YD 208(7). According to R. Shlomo Zalman Auerbach, the view of the Chazon Ish is that an autopsy can be permitted even if the patient in need is not currently "before us," but the disease is so common or widespread that a similar patient will certainly be found somewhere in the world and will be helped by this autopsy (*Nishmat Avraham*, YD 349:1 [(572)]). Furthermore, some have suggested that nowadays, since hospitals are filled with patients with a wide variety of diseases, the requirement for "before us" is automatically satisfied (see *Encyclopedia Hilkhatit Refu'it*, vol. 5, 618, and the numerous citations in n. 269). Nevertheless, some permit autopsy only if the patient in need is currently available and there is a strong likelihood that: (1) a life will be saved as result of this autopsy, and (2) the results will be made available

right away. An autopsy performed only to determine the cause of death is considered as if there is no patient available (*Encyclopedia Hilkhatit Refu'it*, vol. 5, 619; R. Yaakov Arieli, *Noam* 6 [5723], 82). According to this approach, autopsy is not permitted solely to clarify the nature of the deceased's illness in order to help future patients, since the results are often unrevealing, there are other clinical methods for obtaining this information, and the results often do not reach the relevant clinicians in a timely manner. Furthermore, R. Zilberstein limits the extent to which the concept of "before us" can be expanded, since it may lead to allowing far too many unnecessary autopsies. For example, he writes that an autopsy to determine if a given drug or therapy is dangerous would be permitted, but only with clear guidelines and only for the number of bodies necessary to determine the potentially lifesaving information. This would not allow one to autopsy dozens of corpses without clear guidelines, which is likely to happen (*Shiurei Torah Le-Rofim*, vol. 2, 602–3).

12. R. Yaakov Yechiel Weinberg, *Techumin* 12, 382–4. R. Weinberg argues that taking a strict approach towards the *Noda Be-Yehuda*'s ruling nowadays can sometimes diminish the importance of saving lives. He also argues that in order for the State of Israel to survive, it requires high quality medical schools and medical care; otherwise, people will both suffer and turn against religion and the rabbis. R. Immanuel Jakobovits further argues that modern medical questions cannot always be properly dealt with by reliance on older responsa, which were responding to a less sophisticated medical reality. This is true because: (1) the increased speed of transportation renders sick people all over the world who are waiting for results of anatomical studies as "before us," (2) the need for autopsies nowadays may be more certain to contribute to lifesaving

than it was in those times, and (3) the benefits of autopsy now go well beyond developing new treatments, extending to testing the efficacy of various drugs and thus protecting people from harm, as well as verifying diagnoses. R. Jakobovits argues that because modern medicine saves lives and one of its tools is autopsy, it must be permitted when necessary in order to value the lives of the living over the bodies of the dead. However, R. Jakobovits expresses sympathy for the opposition to autopsies and highlights the importance of doctors treating the bodies they dissect with respect; see R. Immanuel Jakobovits, *Torah Shebe'al Peh* 6 (1964/5724), 61–66; I. Jakobovits, *Jewish Medical Ethics* (Bloch Publishing, 1959), 282–3. R. Joseph B. Soloveitchik also takes a lenient view regarding autopsies nowadays because of the speed of international communication, as long as the medical discovery can be potentially life-saving (Holzer, *The Rav: Thinking Aloud* (Holzer, 2009), 104).

13. *Mishpatei Uziel* 1:YD 28–29; *Yaskil Avdi* 6:YD 19. See also *Encyclopedia Hilkhatit Refu'it*, vol. 5, 620, and numerous citations in n. 275.

14. *Chazon Ish*, YD 208:7; see also *Encyclopedia Hilkhatit Refu'it*, vol. 5, 621.

15. *Nishmat Avraham*, YD 349:1(5:8) (577 in 3rd ed.) quotes R. Neuwirth and R. Auerbach as allowing an autopsy on a fetus at a very early stage of development (or even up to 30 days post-delivery), or if one has had multiple miscarriages and the autopsy can prevent further miscarriages, or if there is a serious concern regarding a genetic disorder and the autopsy can help to determine the disorder, which will be helpful for future children of that couple, as long as the fetus is buried afterwards. See also *Torat Ha-Yoledet*, 36, n. 7; *Teshuvot Ve-Hanhagot* 2:603; *Encyclopedia Hilkhatit Refu'it*, vol. 5, 621; *Shulchan Yosef*, 195.

16. *Lev Avraham* 38:2. R. Moshe Tendler

extends the permission for autopsy to a case in which a new chemotherapeutic drug is being evaluated for toxicity and efficacy, since the knowledge gained will help determine the treatment to be administered to others (*Responsa of Rav Moshe Feinstein*, 50).

17. *Encyclopedia Hilkhatit Refu'it*, vol. 5, 637–8; *Nishmat Avraham*, YD 349:1(5:8) (577 in 3rd ed.) explains that this is because it can help others and the prohibition against benefiting from a corpse is not violated in this case, since the autopsy is used to learn and gain wisdom in order to help future patients. It may even be done on Shabbat if necessary. Furthermore, even those who prohibit autopsy generally permit taking blood samples from the deceased for testing (*Iggerot Moshe*, YD 2:151 [end]; R. Shlomo Zalman Auerbach, quoted in *Nishmat Avraham*, YD 349:2, n. 121). Examples of post-mortem diagnostic procedures that may be permitted include endoscopy, laparoscopy, cystoscopy, bronchoscopy, and colonoscopy to view internal body parts (R. Moshe Feinstein, *Noam* 8 [5725], 9). However, opening the chest, abdomen, or skull, which is occasionally performed on the living for diagnostic purposes, is not allowed post-mortem except for an immediate lifesaving application, as a large defect remains that would be considered a desecration (*Encyclopedia Hilkhatit Refu'it*, vol. 5, 598–9). Post-mortem cesarean sections to save a baby are also permitted (*Binyan Tziyon* 1:171).

Similarly, some rule that a pacemaker may be removed from a corpse after death (*Nishmat Avraham*, YD 349:1(3) [p. 578–81]. The *Minchat Yizchak* (7:101) disagrees. R. Zilberstein rules that if the pacemaker is very expensive and the hospital wants it back after death, they may remove it, but if it is possible to pay for it in order to avoid having it removed, that is preferable. If the patient owns the pacemaker, it should not be removed unless it is needed to save the life of another patient and no other pacemaker of that quality is available (*Shiurei Torah Le-Rofim*, vol. 2, 617–24). Ideally, when a pacemaker is installed, the patient should sign that he or she is only borrowing it from the hospital during their life, and that upon death it should be removed and returned to the hospital. Since the pacemaker does not actually become part of the patient's body, and even while alive the patient would have consented to such a procedure, this is not considered desecrating the body.

18. *Iggerot Moshe*, YD 4:59; R. Yaakov Arieli, *Noam* 6 (5723), 82 (see n. 10 above); *Nishmat Avraham*, YD 349:1 (572).

19. *Encyclopedia Hilkhatit Refu'it*, vol. 5, 620–1.

20. *Lev Avraham* 38:8. This may sometimes include taking a small sample from muscle or an internal organ, such as the heart or liver.

21. *Tzitz Eliezer* 4:14(9); *Encyclopedia Hilkhatit Refu'it*, vol. 5, 628–9, and numerous citations in n. 299 (although some forbid this, as cited in n. 298). Some permit autopsy only if it will lead to a murderer being executed, but not if it will only lead to imprisonment; others permit autopsy on anyone who did not die a natural death, in which case legal consequences to the deceased or the heirs may be involved (*Encyclopedia Hilkhatit Refu'it*, vol. 5, 629).

22. This is the view of R. Ovadia Yosef, with the stipulation that a family member can be present during the autopsy to ensure that all body parts are returned for burial (*Mei-Olam Ve-Ad Olam*, 62; *Shulchan Yosef*, 195).

23. *Encyclopedia Hilkhatit Refu'it*, vol. 5, 622. An autopsy performed in order to assist the heirs in making financial claims concerning inheritance is forbidden, since they are obligated to honor and bury the

deceased (*Tzitz Eliezer* 4:14; see also *Encyclopedia Hilkhatit Refu'it*, vol. 5, 622, n. 284). Some permit non-heirs to request an autopsy in order to avoid losing money, but most permit only a minor desecration for this purpose (*Iggerot Moshe*, YD 2:151; *Tzitz Eliezer* 14:83 (2); see also *Encyclopedia Hilkhatit Refu'it*, vol. 5, 622, nn. 285–6).

24. Since the heirs are not the ones requesting it, the autopsy is viewed as being performed for the honor and well-being of the deceased, and with the approval of the deceased, since they paid for the life insurance policy for many years and wanted their family to benefit (*Encyclopedia Hilkhatit Refu'it*, vol. 5, 623, and numerous citations in n. 290). However, some rule that it is forbidden for the heirs to agree to this even if they will lose money, since they are obligated to honor the deceased and they cannot cause desecration, even for money, unless it is just an external examination (ibid., n. 291). Furthermore, all of this applies only if the deceased gave permission on their life insurance policy for an autopsy to take place after death. Rabbinic authorities discourage a Jewish life insurance company from including such a clause (*Yechaveh Da'at* 3:85, end of last footnote).

25. *Mishpatei Uziel* 1:YD 28–9; *Yaskil Avdi* 6:YD 19; see also numerous citations in *Encyclopedia Hilkhatit Refu'it*, vol. 5, 613, n. 255. Some of the reasons given for permitting this include:

(1) When the purpose of an autopsy is to save life, it is not considered desecration, and the study of anatomy and pathology is essential for medical training and can lead to saving lives.

(2) Autopsy for a purpose is not considered denial of the resurrection of the dead.

(3) The prohibition against leaving the dead unburied does not apply if it is done for the honor of the dead, including studying medicine.

(4) The Talmudic sages performed post-mortem examinations and had considerable knowledge of anatomy and pathology. Indeed, the rabbis of the Talmud were among the first people in history to operate on corpses in order to learn medical information that had halakhic ramifications. See *Tosefta Niddah* 4:17; *Niddah* 30b; *Bekhorot* 45a. *Chatam Sofer*, YD 336, writes that this was only permitted in the cited case because the corpse was not Jewish (see citations and discussion in *Encyclopedia Hilkhatit Refu'it*, vol. 5, 564).

(5) Some permitted these post-mortem dissections because of concerns about the desecration of God's name and the insult to the Jewish nation as a result of the fact that others are led to believe that Jews do not care about the health needs of the living. *Chavalim Be-Ne'imim* 4:YD 64, explains that preventing a desecration of God's name has the power to override prohibitions, including desecrating the body. *Noda Be-Yehuda*, YD 210, writes the opposite, arguing that if we are more lenient about this than non-Jews, who generally did not allow this in his times either, then non-Jews will come to desecrate everyone. *Encyclopedia Hilkhatit Refu'it*, vol. 5, 614, n. 257, argues that while this was true in the days of the *Noda Be-Yehuda*, today non-Jews generally allow autopsies.

Some also make the argument that the status of medicine in Israel would become very poor if autopsies were not allowed. These authorities maintain that in particular, the State of Israel must permit autopsies (on both Jewish and non-Jewish bodies) because a state cannot exist without proper medical schools, which require these dissections, and we cannot expect to have a Jewish state with only non-Jewish doctors (*Kitvei Rav Yechiel Yaakov Weinberg* 1:22; *Encyclopedia Hilkhatit Refu'it*, vol. 5, 615).

(6) Many rule that learning medicine from a corpse falls under the prohibition of benefit from a corpse, since learning is a benefit (*Teshuvot Chatam Sofer*, YD 336; *Teshuvot Maharam Shick*, YD 347). However, other authorities rule that learning per se is not considered deriving prohibited benefit. Furthermore, the benefit is not obtained in the normal manner, since the benefit is not derived from the body itself, or from the act of cutting – which is prohibited, but from the understanding that derives from viewing the body. Since the learning is a result of "various causes" ("*zeh ve-zeh gorem*"), it is not considered prohibited benefit (*Encyclopedia Hilkhatit Refu'it*, vol. 5, 607–8).

(7) Some authorities maintain that there is no desecration once desecration has already happened ("*ein nivul achar nivul*"), so if it was already begun, it can be continued (ibid., n. 150). However, others disagree (ibid., 598).

R. Messas argues that the Chatam Sofer may have been critical only in the case of donating a body when hundreds of students were involved and dissecting the body into pieces continued for many days. R. Messas suggests that if only 2–3 doctors would examine a body in order to learn, there is no prohibition. Rather, the deceased is performing a mitzvah with their body, even if only a small amount of new medical information is learned (*Mayim Chayim* 2:YD 109).

These dissections must be performed in an honorable manner, with seriousness and care not to belittle the corpse, which must then be buried in its entirety (*Nishmat Avraham*, YD 349:1(5) [572 in 3rd ed.]).

26. *Mishpatei Uziel*, vol. 1:YD 28–9; *Yaskil Avdi* 6:YD 19. See also the numerous citations in *Encyclopedia Hilkhatit Refu'it* 5, p. 613, n. 255; p. 597, n. 148; *Chelkat Yaakov* and *Har Tzvi*, quoted in *Nishmat Avraham*, YD 349:1(5:7) (577 in 3rd ed.). Simply observing does not constitute prohibited benefit from the deceased according to these authorities. There are, however, authorities who prohibit even

simply observing anatomical post-mortem dissection performed by others; see *Teshuvot Maraham Shick*, YD 344; *Kol Bo Aveilut* 1:3(13:3). R. Shlomo Zalman Auerbach (quoted in *Nishmat Avraham*, YD 349:1(5:7) [570, 577 in 3rd ed.]; see also *Encyclopedia Hilkhatit Refu'it*, vol. 5, 608–9) rules that there may be a rabbinically prohibited benefit in observing. Nevertheless, most permit observing when the dissection is performed by someone else (see the numerous citations in *Encyclopedia Hilkhatit Refu'it*, vol. 5, 609, 613, n. 262). Some authorities distinguish between learning by simply looking and not even touching the body, which they permit, and looking, touching, and adding cuts to the body etc., which they prohibit unless done in order to save a life (*Minchat Shlomo* 2:96 (17); see also numerous citations in *Encyclopedia Hilkhatit Refu'it*, vol. 5, 609, n. 236). Some claim that participating in this to learn anatomy is a mitzvah and thus permitted, whereas others argue that there is no obligation to become a doctor and performing an autopsy thus cannot be permitted (see numerous citations ibid., 609–10, nn. 238–9).

27. If a person willed or sold their body to medical science, some authorities permit this, since the individual is forgoing their honor and does not object to the desecration (*Binyan Tzion* 170–1, n. 305). Some even permit a medical student to learn anatomy from the deceased's body if he donated it to science while alive (Rabbis Unterman, Arieli, and Waldenberg; see the numerous citations in *Encyclopedia Hilkhatit Refu'it*, vol. 5, 630, n. 306). However, some stipulate that this is true only if the body will be used to learn about the patient's specific illness and will then be buried right away. If the intention is to learn anatomy in general and the body will be left unburied for some time, it is forbidden regardless of whether the individual consented while alive (*Tzitz Eliezer* 4:14). Furthermore, even those who permit donating one's body in this

way, forbid it if it is done for the sake of financial compensation (*Mishpatei Uziel* 1:YD 28–29). For another important relevant discussion, see *Nishmat Avraham*, YD 349:1 (563–68 in 3rd ed.) and *Encyclopedia Hilkhatit Refu'it*, vol. 5, 633.

28. Most Rabbinic authorities prohibit observing such dissection because of the halakhic problems mentioned above (see n. 26). See also *Encyclopedia Hilkhatit Refu'it*, vol. 5, p. 613, n. 254, p. 631, n. 309, who writes that a person's consent while alive to donate his body to scientific research is invalid. See also end of *Tzitz Eliezer* 9:46.

29. *Teshuvot Chatam Sofer*, YD 336; *Teshuvot Maharam Shick*, YD 347; *Da'at Kohen* 199; *Iggerot Moshe*, YD 3:140. *Yalkut Yosef, Bikkur Cholim Ve-Aveilut* 14:14, rules that the children of a person who asked that the body be dissected after death must not listen to this request, but if it is done anyway, they should sit *shivah* for the person as long as it was not done out of heresy. See *Mei-Olam Ve-Ad Olam*, 63; R. Shlomo Zalman Auerbach, cited in *Nishmat Avraham*, YD 349:1(5:5) (576 in 3rd ed.).

30. *Binyan Tzion* 176; *Tzitz Eliezer* 4:14; *Nishmat Avraham*, YD 349:1(5:5) (576 in 3rd ed.); *Chelkat Yaakov* 4:39 (*Mahadura Batra*, YD 207). Similarly, the Israeli Rabbinate did not oppose anatomical dissection in cases in which people freely willed their bodies to a medical school, as long as all organs and body parts are eventually buried. The reasoning is that the prohibition against donating one's body for research is to prevent disgracing the body, but one may forgo their honor. Although a body must be buried even if someone asks that it not be, since this body will eventually indeed be buried, this prohibition is not transgressed (see *Encyclopedia Hilkhatit Refu'it*, vol. 5, 651, for the details of the agreement). Furthermore, R. Shlomo Zalman Auerbach permitted using a corpse to learn how to intubate

a patient. Since this minor intervention is frequently done for living patients as well, it is not considered desecrating the corpse, unlike cutting up a body (*Nishmat Avraham*, YD 349:1 [578 in 3rd ed.]).

31. *Iggerot Moshe*, YD 3:140, 4:59; *Encyclopedia Hilkhatit Refu'it*, vol. 5, 631–2.

32. *Minchat Yitzchak* 5:9(2); R. Arieli (cited above, n. 11); *Encyclopedia Hilkhatit Refu'it*, vol. 5, 632, n. 314. R. Arieli rules that even non-family members can object to a prohibited autopsy, since it can be viewed as a disgrace to all life and there is a concept of mutual responsibility (*areivut*) (see *Encyclopedia Hilkhatit Refu'it*, vol. 5, 632, n. 315). Furthermore, R. Sternbuch rules that a family is not obligated to prevent their relative's body from being donated if it was donated to science not out of denial of eventual resurrection but in order to help advance medicine, and if the body will eventually be buried. However, if they know that the body will never be buried, they should try to prevent the autopsy. If the deceased made the donation as an act of denial of the Torah, there is no obligation to stop it (*Teshuvot Ve-Hanhagot* 3:368).

33. *Yaskil Avdi* 6:YD 19. When an autopsy is needed, the rabbi should convince the family to allow it, unless it is a case of doubt (R. Joseph Soloveitchik; see *Encyclopedia Hilkhatit Refu'it*, vol. 5, 632, n. 317).

34. *Tzitz Eliezer* 4:14; *Shevet HaLevi* 8:260(7). A deceased individual with no relatives falls in the category of "*met mitzvah*," an abandoned corpse, and it is forbidden to desecrate the body in any way. An autopsy should be especially avoided in this case (*Encyclopedia Hilkhatit Refu'it*, vol. 5, 635).

35. Ibid., 640. Some rule that if not all parts of the deceased are buried, the family cannot begin the seven-day mourning period, even if the post-mortem dissection was done with the consent of relatives. The relatives remain *onenim* until complete burial has occurred. Some rule that if one donates his body because he does not believe in resurrection or the World to Come, one may not mourn for this person at all. However, if one donated his or her body simply thinking it was a good thing to do, then their family does mourn for this person (*Encyclopedia Hilkhatit Refu'it*, vol. 5, 612).

36. Ibid. Although the sources cited in the previous note rule that the *shivah* mourning period can begin only once the body is buried, R. Zalman Nechemia Goldberg (in a private communication) agreed with the opinion that in this case the *shivah* period begins upon donation of the body, not burial, based on the idea that the relatives have given up hope of retrieving the body (based on *Rosh, Berakhot* 3:3). R. Goldberg argues that even if one waits until complete burial to begin *shivah*, family members will not be considered *onenim* for the entire time that they are waiting.

37. Partially based on the guidelines of The National Association of Chevra Kadisha; see http://www.nasck.org/article_00 02.html.

38. Bleich, *Judaism and Healing*, 207. R. Bleich also requires the pathologist to state beforehand in precise clinical terms the exact information being sought, specifying the area to be incised and the organs to be examined in obtaining such information (see ibid., 277, for a sample "Authorization for Limited Autopsy" consent form).

39. *Mishpatei Uziel, Tinyana* 3:YD 2:110; *Encyclopedia Hilkhatit Refu'it*, vol. 5, 637. This is true even if the body parts are guarded in a respectful place; the obligation to bury is not fulfilled until all parts are buried.

40. *Encyclopedia Hilkhatit Refu'it*, vol. 5, 637.

41. Ibid.; R. Zilberstein, *Shiurei Torah Le-Rofim*, vol. 2, 624.

F.   CREMATION AND JEWISH LAW

It is becoming increasingly common for Jews to opt for cremation, for a variety of reasons. However, this is clearly not a practice that is consistent with Jewish Law and tradition. In this chapter, we will examine the status of cremation in Jewish Law, the nature of the prohibition, ramifications of that prohibition, and some practical reflections.

WHY IS CREMATION PROHIBITED?

Throughout the ages, and particularly as cremation has become more popular within the last hundred years, Rabbinic authorities have used very strong language in emphasizing the severity of the prohibition against cremation.[1] In addition to the reality that cremation is simply not the Jewish way, the following are the primary reasons commonly given for prohibiting cremation:

1. Burial in the ground is the time honored Jewish tradition, which is mentioned throughout the Torah (with the Torah even noting that God *buried* Moses).[2] Cremation is prohibited because it is viewed as actively avoiding performing the biblical commandment of burial, "*kavor tikberenu*," as well as violating the prohibition against delaying burial, "*lo talin*."[3]

2. There is a prohibition against defiling a corpse (*nivul ha-met*).[4] Many Rabbinic authorities rule that cremation is a disgrace (*bizayon*) to the deceased and violates the prohibition against defiling a corpse.[5]

3. According to many Rabbinic authorities, burial of the body in the ground is intended to strengthen belief in the eventual resurrection of the dead. They therefore prohibit cremation because it is viewed as a heretical act of denying this belief.[6]

WHAT MAY BE DONE WITH THE ASHES?

If a body has been cremated despite the prohibition, a number of questions arise. For example, should the ashes be buried, and if so, where? Should a funeral be held, and should the family observe the laws and customs of mourning?

Most Rabbinic authorities have prohibited burial of the ashes in a Jewish cemetery.[7] Others distinguish between those who chose to have their body cremated (and may thus not be buried in a Jewish cemetery) and those who were cremated against their will (and may thus be afforded full burial rights in a Jewish cemetery).[8] Some authorities do not allow cremation-ashes to be buried in the midst of a Jewish cemetery, but permit burying them on the outskirts of a Jewish cemetery in a separate section, as a means of communicating that cremation is not accepted but that the ashes should nevertheless be disposed of properly.[9] However, it has remained customary that many Jewish cemeteries run in accordance with Jewish tradition, do not allow the burial of cremation-ashes anywhere within the cemetery, even in a separate section,[10] though exceptions are sometimes made for those cremated against their will or out of ignorance of Jewish tradition.[11]

Most authorities forbid the Chevrah Kadisha (traditional Jewish Mortuary) from having anything to do with a corpse that is going to be or has been cremated.[12] Similarly, many argue that a rabbi should not eulogize someone who is being cremated, nor conduct any sort of a memorial service, since no representative of the Jewish community should show any sort of acceptance of this practice.[13] Furthermore, many authorities forbid engaging in traditional mourning practices for one who chose to be cremated.[14] However, many permit doing so, particularly if the deceased did not actively choose to be cremated or intend to express rebellion against Judaism. There is a difference of opinion as to when the mourning period should begin in such a case.[15]

REFLECTIONS ON CREMATION FROM A CHAPLAIN'S PERSPECTIVE

As a chaplain, my role in the hospital is not to mandate religious doctrine, force individuals into specific choices, or even advocate a particular lifestyle or worldview. Rather, the focus of chaplaincy care tends to be on facilitating the ability of individuals to articulate their own goals and values and helping them uncover, navigate, translate, and resolve some of the issues with which they may be struggling.

People often ask me for guidance when confronted with the choice of cremation, as there is often religious guilt or complicated family tension associated with this decision. While accompanying people through the decision and mourning process, I have begun to notice some patterns that merit serious consideration.

First, it always fascinates me how many similarities there are between the end of life and the beginning of life. Some of the major parallels are the lack of planning, complicated family dynamics, dependence upon other family members, and deeply ingrained emotions associated with the various rituals. For example, a woman once told me that her children were debating whether or not they should circumcise their newborn son. This woman, who was not particularly religiously observant, told me that she would have a difficult time even viewing this child as her grandson if he were not circumcised. The parents opted not to circumcise their baby, and this woman later related to me that she couldn't even bring herself to change the baby's diaper because his lack of circumcision upset her so much. Whether this reaction is right or wrong, logical or not, the fact remains that circumcision is deeply ingrained in the traditional Jewish psyche, much the same way as is burial in the ground. Many Jews cannot articulate why the tradition has preferred subterranean burial of an intact body, but they nevertheless rail against the notion of anything else.

This leads to a second observation. Unfortunately, death and burial often bring about extreme family tension, and many of the decisions made amidst this tension are later regretted. Cremation is permanent, and I have witnessed some excruciating family strife related to regretting such final decisions made in haste. The emotional and financial drain of end-of-life care for many family members sometimes leads to choosing the simplest, fastest, and cheapest way of ending the nightmare that may be experienced at this time. I have encountered people who regret their choice of cremation for a loved one once they have had a chance to collect their thoughts and emotions and realize how final and irreversible cremation is.

Finally, in the process of accompanying grieving family members through this painful decision-making process, I have noticed how cathartic it can be to have a physical grave to visit and care for. At unveiling ceremonies, many families have shared with me how crucial this physical location has been to them during their grieving process. While cremains can also be stored in a specific location, they often are not and it has been my experience that fidelity to tradition and having a set place to experience the presence of a loved one bring a level of comfort and inspiration to the bereaved family that is unparalleled. When possible, I thus try to help families considering cremation to explore other options.

ENDNOTES

1. For example, R. Avraham Yitzchak Kook refers to cremation as "*derekh rishut ve-tumah*," the way of evil and impurity (*Da'at Kohen*, 197). R. Tucazinsky, *Gesher Ha-Chaim* 1:16(9), 155, refers to cremation as an "*issur chamur*," a very severe prohibition. *Kol Bo Al Aveilut*, 54, writes that one is obligated to fight against cremation with full force. Furthermore, many authorities rule that if someone requests to be cremated, the family is not permitted to fulfill these wishes, but must rather bury the deceased (*Gesher Ha-Chaim* 1:16(9), 155; *Kol Bo Al Aveilut*, 53).

2. *Kol Bo Al Aveilut*, 53, notes that burial of the dead is an ancient and widespread Jewish custom dating back to our biblical ancestors, and that there were times in Jewish history when burial was even a sign that someone was Jewish. He also notes that the rabbis of Babylon went to great length to send their bodies to be buried in Israel; they did not simply burn them and spread their ashes in Babylon. He goes on to argue that the Torah goes so far as to permit a Kohen to defile himself in order to bury the dead, instead of allowing him to simply burn the body.

3. Deut. 21:23. See the appendix on Burial in a Mausoleum and Jewish Law in this book, where we discuss these obligations at length. See *Teshuvot Beit Yitzchak*, YD 2:155; *Achiezer* 3:72; *Melamed Le-Ho'il* 2:113–4; *Gesher Ha-Chaim* 1:16(9), 155. See also R. Yosef Eliyahu Henkin, *Kol Kitvei Ha-Rav Henkin*, vol. 2, *Teshuvot Ivra* 65, 89–90, who argues that cremation is a violation of the requirement to bury, but notes that theoretically if a body would

be cremated on the day of death, this might not be a violation, since afterwards even the skeleton does not remain and there is thus no longer a requirement for burial. See also *Badei Ha-Shulchan*, YD 362:1, s.v. *over*, 332, who argues that cremation is certainly in violation of the commandment to bury, since the person is not buried, but may not be a violation of the prohibition against delaying burial, since once the body is cremated it is not there anymore. R. Kook argues (*Da'at Kohen*, 197), in conjunction with many of the leading rabbis of his time, that even if burial in the ground were just a custom and not a biblical command, we would have to follow it closely since ancient customs are extremely binding, and there is no more ancient custom than burial. However, burial is also rooted in the Torah; the word "*kavor*" makes it clear that burial is necessary, and "*tikberenu*" requires burial in the ground. Cremation fulfills neither of these conditions, and is thus forbidden by the Torah.

4. This prohibition is recorded in the Talmud in the name of R. Akiva, who prohibited examining the body of a buried corpse because it would constitute defiling the corpse (*Bava Batra* 154a). This prohibition is one of the reasons that it is forbidden to open a grave, move a corpse to a new grave, or examine a corpse (unless it is being done to save a life). See *Tzitz Eliezer* 4:14, who notes the prohibition against defiling a corpse and the permission to do so for the sake of saving a life. See also *Encyclopedia Hilkhatit Refu'it*, vol. 5, 589. See chap. 5E, where we discuss this prohibition in the context of autopsies.

5. *Da'at Kohen* 197; *Gesher Ha-Chaim* 1:16(9), 155; R. David Zvi Hoffman (*Melamed Le-Ho'il* 2:113–4) writes that the Torah and Talmud view burning a body as a major defilement ("*nivul gadol la-met*"), based on many sources, including Amos 2:1, which records that Moav is punished "because he burned the bones of the King of Edom." Similarly, the Talmud (*Sanhedrin* 82a) views the burning of his corpse as a major punishment for King Yehoyakim. Furthermore, according to Jewish Law, on Shabbat we are permitted to save a body from a fire, and if one has to choose between saving a body and saving holy books, they must first save the body (*Magen Avraham* 334:30). This shows the importance of avoiding burning a body, and that doing so intentionally would constitute a severe disgrace. Moreover, the *Tzitz Eleizer* (4:14) quotes a responsum of the *Ktav Sofer* (YD 174) emphasizing that defiling the body also causes horrible disgrace to the soul. Similarly, the *Gesher Ha-Chaim* (1:16[9], 155) writes, based on the *Zohar*, that one of the reasons that cremation is forbidden is that it causes a major problem ("*takalah gadolah*") for the deceased.

6. *Achiezer* 3:72 (quoting *Teshuvot Beit Yitzchak*, YD 2:155); *Seridei Eish* 2:95; *Kol Bo Al Aveilut*, 54 (who adds, based on the *Sedei Chemed*, that cremation is also prohibited because it has roots in idolatry and non-Jewish practices). *Da'at Kohen*, 197, adds that cremation is not simply denial of resurrection, but is also seen as an act of rebellion against the Torah.

7. *Seridei Eish* 2:95 quotes a view of many leading Rabbinic authorities who forbid the burial of cremation-ashes because those who are cremated should be categorized as those who have "thrown off the yoke of the *mitzvot*," about whom the *Shulchan Arukh* rules (YD 345:5) that it is forbidden to deal with their burial. Those authorities add that burying such ashes also gives the impression that we

are accepting of cremation, an act of "supporting the hands of sinners." They also argue that since these ashes are so small in volume, they do not have the status of a body according to Jewish Law, and thus do not render people ritually impure. Furthermore, they argue, for rabbis to permit burial of such ashes would constitute a *chillul Hashem* (desecration of God's name), because leaders of other religions do not deal with or bury the ashes of those who are cremated, since they see in this a denial of faith in the eternity of the soul. For discussion of these issues, see Adam Ferziger, "Ashes to Outcasts: Cremation, Jewish Law, and Identity in Early Twentieth-Century Germany," *AJS Review* 36:1 (Apr. 2012), 78. See also *Machazeh Avraham* 2:38; *Iggerot Moshe*, YD 3:147.

8. R. Tucazinsky, *Gesher Ha-Chaim* (1:16[9], 153–4) rules that the ashes of one who was cremated against his will should be buried, even though there is no requirement to do so, because one may not benefit from the ashes, and this case is similar to the ashes of sacrifices, which require concealment. However, he writes, the ashes of those who requested to be cremated should not be buried in a Jewish cemetery, since such a person has declared that he does not desire the spiritual benefits of burial and he denies resurrection, and ashes do not require burial (ibid., 155). Similarly, R. D.Z. Hoffman (*Melamed Le-Ho'il* 2:113) rules that even though there is no Torah or Rabbinic requirement to bury cremation-ashes, if someone was cremated against his will, his ashes should be buried, since such burial can serve as atonement, or at least prevent disgrace. However, he rules, there is no obligation to bury one who chooses to be cremated (although it would still be good to conceal the ashes to prevent benefit from them).

9. R. D.Z. Hoffman (*Melamed Le-Ho'il* 2:114) writes that even though it is ideal not to bury cremation-ashes so that it will

be clear that cremation is forbidden, he is concerned that such a policy would cause more damage than good, because people might ignore the prohibition and bury the ashes amongst those who are buried properly. He therefore suggests creating a separate section of the cemetery for burial of ashes in order to distinguish between proper burial that fulfills the commandment to bury and improper burial (of ashes), which does not. In practice, R. Hoffman rules that a Jewish cemetery made up of observant, God-fearing Jews should not include a section for burial of cremation-ashes, but if a request ever arises, such ashes should be buried only on the outskirts of the cemetery. On the other hand, in cemeteries intended for the entire Jewish community, both observant and non-observant Jews, a separate section should be designated for burial of cremation-ashes (both those who requested to be cremated and those who were cremated against their will). R. Mordechai Hirsch (in R. Braun, *Beit Yisrael*, 43b–45b) also rules that cremation-ashes should be buried in a separate section within a Jewish cemetery. This view is also quoted in the name of R. Nathan Adler (in 1888, while he was Chief Rabbi of England), R. Azriel Hildesheimer, and R. Yitzchak Elchanan Spektor (Ehrentreu, "Letter 4," *Or Ha-Emet*, 5, 13).

However, other authorities strongly opposed this ruling and forbade burial of cremation-remains anywhere in a Jewish cemetery, even if they are placed in a separate section. See in particular R. Mayer Lerner, "*Menuchah Nekhonah*," *Ha-Me'asef* 8(3) (1903), 20, 29a–31b. See also the discussion in Ferziger, "Ashes to Outcasts," 75, 89.

In 1957, R. Yosef Eliyahu Henkin recognized that times had changed and argued that although cremation remains strictly forbidden, the fact was that cremation had become increasingly common and was generally not done as an intentional act of rebellion or heresy. Accord-ingly, he ruled that cremation-ashes may be buried in a Jewish cemetery, but only in a separate section and without any sort of prayers or traditional burial shrouds (*takhrikhim*) so as not to strengthen a sinful act (*Kol Kitvei Ha-Rav Henkin*, vol. 2, *Teshuvot Ivra* 65, 89–90).

Other authorities rule that cremation-ashes should be buried in order to prevent people from deriving benefit from them, as it is prohibited to derive benefit from a corpse, but they should not be buried in a Jewish cemetery so that no one will conclude that this is a permitted form of Jewish burial (*Achiezer* 3:72; *Teshuvot Beit Yitzchak*, YD 2:155). R. Kook (*Da'at Kohen*, 197) writes that there is no mitzvah to bury the ashes, but it may be good to do so in order to prevent benefit. R. Y.Y. Weinberg (*Seridei Eish* 2:95) writes that cremation-ashes require burial, but no other rituals, such as a *taharah*, should be performed. R. Ovadia Yosef (*Yabia Omer* 3, YD 22) and R. Tzvi Pesach Frank (*Har Tzvi* YD 275, quoted in *Yishrei Lev* 2:111) also rule that it is proper to bury cremation-ashes.

10. Personal communication with R. Elchanan Zohn, who explained that this is meant to make a clear statement that cremation is wrong according to Judaism and to serve as a disincentive. Furthermore, since the bylaws of many Jewish cemeteries have included the provision that cremation-ashes are not allowed there, to permit such burial would be a form of humiliation to the people buried there who assumed that religious tradition would be upheld in their cemetery.

11. See A. Ferziger "Foreign Ashes in Sovereign Space: Cremation and the Chief Rabbinate of Israel, 1931-1990," *Jewish Studies Quarterly* 23:4 (2016), 290-313, for a discussion of permission granted by the Israeli Chief Rabbinate to bury cremation-ash of Holocaust victims within Israeli cemeteries (301), as well as that of Soviet Jewish immigrants to Israel, who

were not cremated for heretical motivations but due to no option for burial or lack of knowledge of Jewish Law, which can also be seen as "coercion" (306). This leniency, which doesn't require the ashes to be buried in a separate section, is also applied to unaffiliated Jews coming from other countries if they were primarily influenced by the norms of their surroundings (308–9).

12. *Melamed Le-Ho'il* 2:114; *Da'at Kohen*, 197; *Seridei Eish* 2:95.

13. *Melamed Le-Ho'il* 2:114. R. Tzvi Rabinowicz, *A Guide to Life: Jewish Laws and Customs of Mourning*, 19, writes that although a Jewish mortuary may not be involved in any part of the process, a rabbi may conduct memorial services. However, most authorities disagree with this view. Some have suggested that while any acts of mourning for one who was cremated are forbidden, any practices intended to benefit the grieving family may be done. See Joseph Ozarowski, *To Walk in God's Ways* (Rowman & Littlefield, 1995), 100.

14. *Kol Bo Al Aveilut*, 54.

15. According to *Gesher Ha-Chaim* (1:16[9], 155), unlike typical mourning, which begins only upon completion of the burial, in the case of cremation, one should begin mourning from the time of the cremation, not the time of the burial of the ashes, even if it is on a different day. Similarly, R. Hershel Schachter told this author that in his opinion one may mourn for one who has been cremated, since we assume that it was not done out of denial of the concept of resurrection, and the *shivah* should begin at the time of the cremation, since there is nothing that must be buried after that. However, the *Melamed Le-Ho'il* (2:114) rules that the mourning should begin at the time that the ashes are buried.

R. Elchanan Zohn told this author that since the family should not be involved in any part of the process of the cremation, they can begin the mourning practices immediately upon death and need not wait for the cremation to take place (unless they would like to wait for other family members who are not going to begin sitting *shivah* until after the cremation, since there might be a benefit to waiting so that the family can participate in *shivah* together).

APPENDIX:
Ethical Issues in the Sale of Organs

The ability to transplant organs is a modern medical miracle with the potential to save and enhance countless lives. But many people are unwilling to altruistically donate their organs to needy strangers, resulting in an extremely long waiting list for suitable organs. This lack of available organs is a health crisis, often leading to desperation and the growth of dangerous, unregulated black markets. In order to protect both donors and recipients, and to save the maximum number of lives, some believe that we must find a way to permit compensation for organs within strict guidelines and carefully constructed public policy. This appendix will seek to understand Jewish views on the sale of organs and policy suggestions to avoid black market sales.

THE CASE FOR

Many arguments have been advanced in the general literature in favor of legalizing organ sales. Legalization of organ sales would help meet the demand and save lives, while at the same time ensuring that donors and recipients receive high quality medical care.[1] If we view this as an additional opportunity to save lives, selling organs can be seen as increasing respect for the human body.[2] Many other human products, such as blood, sperm, and eggs, are commonly sold with minimal ethical debate.[3] Additionally, selling organs can provide an option for individuals in the developing world, who might not otherwise have many opportunities to earn a decent living, to enhance their economic prospects.[4]

CASE AGAINST

However, there has been much opposition to commercialization of organs, which is why such sales are illegal in almost every country in the world. Much of this opposition stems from the concern that desperately impoverished and vulnerable individuals with few options sometimes make decisions that are not fully informed or in their best interest, and might be the result of coercion or flawed consent.[5] Exacerbating this issue is the fact that agents in black markets frequently exploit the donors and keep much of the profit for themselves,[6] and that there is often inadequate medical care (screening, surgical technique, follow up care, etc. for donors, and sometimes for the recipients).[7] Additional concerns include the possibility that the sale of organs can lead to viewing the human body as an object and a commodity that can be exploited, thus decreasing human dignity[8] and overriding altruistic motivations for donation.[9]

JEWISH VIEWS

As a general rule, Jewish Law does not permit an action if it is forbidden by the local government. For this reason, Jewish Law forbids the sale of organs in countries in which it is against the law.[10] However, separate from that concern, what would Jewish Law say about selling one's organs?

The general consensus amongst the leading Rabbinic decisors is that selling organs is permitted.[11] The reasoning is that although Jewish Law forbids damaging oneself[12] and affirms that we do not own our bodies, and are thus unable to sell any portion of them[13] or even give them as a gift,[14] saving a life takes precedence and overrides these prohibitions. This is true even if one's motivations are not altruistic, but simply to make money.[15] As long as the action does indeed contribute to saving a life or increasing its quality, it is considered pious (though not obligatory) to donate an organ and one may receive payment for it.[16] However, it would not be permitted to sell an organ for research or in any other case in which it is not directly saving a life or contributing to its quality.[17]

Nevertheless, not everything is permitted for the sake of saving a life. Some halakhic authorities have ruled that obtaining an organ by fraud or deception is forbidden, even if the goal is to save a life and even if it is a broker who is deceiving the donor and not the recipient.[18] A patient who is purchasing an organ would thus be obligated to ensure that the donor is fully informed and not coerced.[19] Many authorities make note of the emphasis that Jewish Law puts on protecting the poor from exploitation,[20] and they would therefore require the involvement of an advisory board in each case to determine the level of need for the recipient, as well as the capacity and informed consent of the donor.[21]

Similarly, Rabbinic authorities recognize that even with legalization of organ sales, Jewish Law would discourage[22] or prohibit[23] selling organs at exorbitant prices and would forbid organ sales if they were to involve taking advantage of desperate individuals.[24] Rabbinic authorities have thus suggested halakhically acceptable public policy guidelines to protect society in order to be able to permit the sale of organs.

These guidelines include preventing unnecessary pressure on the donor by separating him or her from the potential recipient and maintaining confidentiality, as well as psychological screening for potential donors to ensure that they are fully willing and informed. Additionally, the system should not actually include the sale of organs, but rather a structured method of compensation for donors. These payments can be partially covered by imposing a small national tax, which would also serve to engage the entire society in the issue of organ donation. The rate of compensation should be reasonable, taking into account the importance and danger of the action, while not serving as an excessive temptation. In addition to financial compensation, there can be other benefits, such as tax breaks, tuition assistance, and being moved to the top of the recipient list should such a need ever arise for the donor. Furthermore, the implementation of such a system should include the government's strict enforcement, with very severe penalties for those who fail to uphold the law.[25] Along these lines, Israeli legislators have developed a protocol whereby there would be a single waiting list for all patients, in which the donor cannot choose the recipient, and all expenses would be covered by the National Transplant Center.[26]

CONCLUSION

The arguments against the sale of organs are compelling and important. However, when we prioritize the value and sanctity of human life, the arguments in favor of compensation for organ donation are very strong as well. Permitting compensation for organs, when done responsibly,[27] could allow us to respect individual liberty and save human lives. Conceptualizing the transaction not as payment for an organ, but as compensation for time and risk, could mitigate some of the potential for exploitation. Some Rabbinic authorities nevertheless find organ sales ethically repugnant,[28] despite the argument that keeping them illegal may remove the only hope for both the destitute and the dying and miss opportunities to save lives.[29] If they are approved, organ markets must be regulated and adequate pre-donation information for the donors and the availability of counseling and follow-up must be ensured.[30]

ENDNOTES

1. See A.J. Matas, "Should We Pay Donors to Increase the Supply of Organs for Transplantation? Yes," *BMJ* 14:336 (June 2008), 1343.

2. See Henry Hansmann, "The Economics and Ethics of Markets for Human Organs," *Organ Transplantation Policy: Issues and Prospects* (Duke University Press, 1989).

3. A.M. Capron, "Whose Child Is This?" *Hastings Center Report* 21 (1991), 37–38. Some argue that introduction of financial incentives actually expands individual choice and thus leads to higher benefits, just as when we add the possibility of selling blood to a voluntary blood donor system, we expand the range of alternatives. Furthermore, if one derives satisfaction from giving, nothing is done to impair that right; see Kenneth Arrow, "Gifts and Exchanges," *Philosophy and Public Affairs* 1 (1972), 350. On the other hand, unlike organs such as kidneys, many of these body parts are regenerative and are not essential, and their removal does not involve highly invasive, dangerous surgery.

4. M. Kuczewski, "The Gift of Life and Starfish on the Beach: The Ethics of Organ Procurement," *The American Journal of Bioethics* 2(3) (2002), 54.

5. See Project of the ABIM Foundation, ACP–ASIM Foundation, and European Federation of Internal Medicine, "Medical Professionalism in the New Millennium: A Physician Charter," *Annals of Internal Medicine* 136 (2002), 243–6.

6. L. Turner, "Let's Wave Goodbye to 'Transplant Tourism,'" *BMJ* 336 (June

2008), 1377.

7. Dr. Alan Jotkowitz, "A Jewish Perspective on Compensation for Kidney Donation," *Jewish Medical Ethics and Halacha* 7(2) (Mar. 2010), 14.

8. F.L. Delmonico and N. Scheper-Hughes, "Why We Should Not Pay for Human Organs," *Zygon* 38 (2003), 689–98. Others conceptualize selling a body part as almost equivalent to selling one's self, and thus a form of self-enslavement; see Charles Fried, *Right and Wrong* (Cambridge, 1978), 142.

9. S. Wilkinson, "Commodification Arguments for the Legal Prohibition of Organ Sale," *Health Care Analysis* 8(2) (2000), 189-201.

10. Fred Rosner and Edward Reichman, "Payment for Organ Donation in Jewish Law," in Aaron Levine (ed.), *Judaism and Economics* (Oxford University Press, 2010), 337–8.

11. A. Steinberg, "Compensation for Kidney Donation: A Price Worth Paying," *Israeli Medical Association Journal* 4(12) (Dec. 2002), 1139–40; *Nishmat Avraham* CM 420:31(5:6), 37–9 in 3rd ed. For a more detailed summary of the opinions of the leading Rabbinic authorities, see A. Steinberg, "Ethical and Halakhic Perspectives in Organ Donation" [Hebrew], in S. Raz (ed.), *Kovetz Ha-Tziyonut Ha-Datit* (*Histaderut Ha-Mizrachi*, 2001), 438–9.

12. *Bava Kamma* 90b.

13. See S.Y. Zevin, "The Case of Shylock," in *Le-Ohr Ha-Halakhah* (Beit Hillel, 1988), 318–28; Moshe Hershler (ed.), *Halakhah U-Refuah* (Regensburg Insti-

tute, 1980), vol. 2, 93–100. In addition to arguing that one cannot sell something owned by God, this argument affirms that since God created our bodies and owns them, one may only use his or her body in accordance with the conditions and limitations established by the Creator, as articulated by Jewish Law. However, R. Shaul Yisraeli maintains that a person does have certain rights over his or her body, in partnership with God, and may therefore receive compensation (Yisraeli, *Ha-Torah Ve-Ha-Medinah* 5–6 (1953–54), 106–10 and *Amud Ha-Yemini* 16, 16ff). If we accept that people have no autonomous rights over their bodies, one could argue that the donor is not paid for the organ, but rather for the benefit he or she confers to the other and the money lost/damages as a result of undergoing the procedure. See Steinberg, "Ethical and Halakhic Perspectives in Organ Donation," 437.

14. Y. Zilberstein, *Shiurei Torah Le-Rofim*, vol. 2, 506.

15. *Nishmat Avraham,* CM 420:1 (English ed., vol. 3, 271), in the name of R. Shlomo Zalman Auerbach.

16. Self-wounding is only permitted in a case of great need. Although there is consensus that earning a profit is not considered a great need, relieving significant pain, improving quality of life, and certainly saving a life do constitute sufficient need. See M. Halperin, "Selling Tissues and Organs," *Be-Ohr Ha-Torah* 8 (1993), 48–49; Zilberstein, *Shiurei Torah Le-Rofim,* vol. 2, 506, based on *Pnei Yehoshua* on Tosafot, *Bava Kamma* 91b, and *Pitchei Teshuvah,* YD 157:15.

R. Zilberstein notes, based on *Biur Halacha* 38, s.v. *heim,* that although it is generally forbidden to be paid to do a mitzvah, one who sells *tefillin* and *mezuzot* to help the community may nevertheless be paid for this and is considered to be engaged in a mitzvah. R. Zilberstein points out that just as one may put himself

into danger in order to earn a livelihood, one may similarly receive payment for this mitzvah (*Shiurei Torah Le-Rofim,* vol. 2, 480). See also Steinberg, "Ethical and Halakhic Perspectives in Organ Donation," 432–6, on the precedent for putting oneself into danger in order to earn a living. Many authorities permit one to receive compensation for one's time or to be paid to do a mitzvah activity that is not obligatory, such as donating organs (Steinberg, ibid., 436–7). For a critique of this ruling, see Y. Bar-Ilan, *Jewish Bioethics* (Cambridge University Press, 2014), 105.

17. Zilberstein, *Shiurei Torah Le-Rofim,* vol. 2, 506; M. Halperin, "On Selling Tissues and Organs," 8, 49, based on *Shulchan Arukh,* CM 420:31.

18. *Be-Mareh Ha-Bazak* 7:87. It should be noted that some religious authorities permit a broker to receive payment for the time and effort put into connecting the recipient to the donor (R. Shlomo Zalman Auerbach, cited in *Nishmat Avraham,* CM 420:1), whereas others do not permit payment for such a role (R. Yisraeli, *"Terumat Eivarim Mei-Adam Chai,"* Assia 57–58 [15, 1–2] [Kislev 5757], 8). R. Yisraeli argues that serving as an agent in such a fashion is obligatory as an act of saving a life and one may therefore not be paid for it, and he argues that this should be mandated by law. R. Yisraeli does, however, permit compensation to the agent for the time spent in which he could have been earning his livelihood.

19. Jewish Law does not require consent for an operation that saves a life or prolongs it (see M. Halperin, "Consent to Surgery – Signing on Shabbat," *Assia* 44 (11, 4), 31–33). However, removing an organ for the sake of another person does require consent, and lack of consent would make it forbidden. For this reason, the surgical team must devote time to explaining the procedure to the donor and obtaining their total willingness, even if

he or she is being paid. Since it is possible that the desire for payment will excessively influence the donor, it is possible that this problem always makes payment for organs prohibited by Jewish Law unless each case is reviewed by a committee (consisting of both Rabbinic and medical experts), similar to those convened for surrogacy deliberations to determine proper consent (M. Halperin, "On Selling Tissues and Organs," 8, 52; R. Rabinovitz, *Assia* 61–62 (vol. 17, 1–2) (Nissan 5758).

20. M. Halperin, "On Selling Tissues and Organs," 51–2, and *Assia* 46 (12, 1–2) (Tevet 5749), notes the law that one may not remarry his divorced wife if she married another man in the meantime, out of fear that the poor might be taken advantage of by wealthy men who would attempt to temporarily take their wives (Deut. 24:4, based on commentary of Ramban, Malbim, and R. Yehuda Ha-Chasid), indicating that we must be concerned about this issue. This concern does not preclude commercialization of organ donation, as we do not invent new *takanot*, but it teaches us a value that must be taken into consideration. Some have made a similar point based on the Talmudic rule that all Jews, whether rich or poor, must be buried in the simplest garments and coffins in order not to embarrass the poor; see F. Rosner and E. Reichman, "Payment for Organ Donation in Jewish Law," 33, n. 68. Similarly, the *Pitchei Teshuvah* rules that "there is certainly no injustice greater than taxing the rich and the poor the same amount," for which reason he recommends uprooting the custom of doing so in order to protect the poor (*Pitchei Teshuvah*, CM 163:3).

21. See n. 19 above.

22. R. Alfred Cohen, "Sale or Donation of Human Organs," *Journal of Halacha and Contemporary Society* 52 (Fall 2006), 64.

23. One scholar suggests using the paradigm of the rule that emerges in the context of ransoming of captives, *pidyon shevuyim* (*Gittin* 4:6), that one cannot comply with a ransom demand that is in excess of the person's worth. This rule was enacted to maintain social order (*tikkun olam*), either to avoid communal impoverishment or to discourage our enemies from making exorbitant demands for similar acts in the future (*Gittin* 45a). While some authorities argue that physical danger would be enough of a reason to redeem a captive at any price (Tosafot, *Gittin* 58a, s.v. *kol mammon*), others rule that the enactment applies even in the case of mortal danger (*Chiddushei Ha-Ramban, Gittin* 45a, s.v. *mishum*; *Teshuvot Maharam Lublin*, 15). Based on this, R. Y. Warburg suggests that if in the case of redeeming captives, which is a mitzvah and saves lives, our rabbis proscribed a ceiling for such expenditures, then kidney commerce, which is not obligated, should be prohibited or strictly limited. See Y. Warburg, "Renal Transplantation: Living Donors and Markets for Body Parts – *Halakha* in Concert with Halakhic Policy or Public Policy?" *Tradition* 40:2 (2007), 31–33.

24. R. Cohen, "Sale or Donation of Human Organs," 64. This would fall under the prohibition of placing a stumbling block before the blind (Lev. 19:14).

25. All of these suggestions are made by A. Steinberg, "Ethical and Halakhic Perspectives in Organ Donation," 439–41.

26. M.M Friedlander, "A Protocol for Paid Kidney Donation in Israel," *Israeli Medical Association Journal* 9(61) (Sept. 2003), 1–4. Similarly, in 2008, the Israeli parliament passed a law providing limited benefits to those who donate a kidney for altruistic reasons, but which prohibits sales in Israel or abroad. See *Journal of Medicine and Law* 38 (June 2008), 180–91.

27. For example, some have cautioned that "a legislated policy permitting organ

sale would not obviate the need for an individual to obtain a rabbinic approval, making certain that the need was sufficiently great; that the goal was achievable in order to justify the prohibition against injuring oneself, and that the person was physically fit so there would be no concern about any health consequences" (J.D. Kunin, "The Search for Organs: Halachic Perspectives on Altruistic Giving and the Selling of Organs," *Jewish Medical Ethics* 31 (2005), 272). Indeed, that article quotes a ruling of R. Elyashiv that to permit organ sales, the need must be great and the sale must accomplish the financial goal; otherwise it cannot be considered of sufficient value to override the prohibition of injuring oneself. Moreover, others have written that "the ultimate permissibility of selling organs is inextricably connected to solving a series of pragmatic problems, such as creating a system that ensures that potential vendors and donors are properly informed and not exploited . . .[and] regulation of payments so they reasonably reflect compensation for pain and suffering" (R.V. Grazi and J.B. Wolowelsky, "Non-Altruistic Kidney Donations in Contemporary Jewish Law and Ethics," *Transplantation* 75 (2003), 250–52).

28. In a personal conversation, R. Asher Weiss told this author that he agrees with the approach of modern law that prohibits selling organs. He argued that not only

shouldn't one engage in organ sales, but one should not even turn a blind eye to them, because the practice of selling organs takes advantage of desperately poor people who do not have sound judgment and makes organs less available for those who really need them, since they will only be obtained by those who can afford them. Similarly, R. Yoel Bin Nun argues ("Jewish Law and Medical Science," in *Halakhic Realities: Collected Essays on Brain Death*, 140) that participating in organ sales even passively is a grievous Torah violation. He has written, "It is a terrible sin to take or purchase organs from certain countries (mainly China), since there is a real concern that opponents of the government are being murdered and their organs sold." Interestingly, the Chafetz Chaim, writing well before such technology was even imaginable, wrote about the immorality of selling any part of one's body, including even blood, in exchange for money (*Zakhor Le-Miryam*, 19).

29. J. Radcliffe-Richards, "The Case for Allowing Kidney Sales," *International Forum for Transplant Ethics*, Lancet 351 (9120) (June 1998), 1950–52.

30. See also B. Hippen and A. Matas, "Incentives for Organ Donation in the United States: Feasible Alternative for Forthcoming Apocalypse? *Curr Opin Organ Transplant* 14 (2009), 140–6.

APPENDIX:
Burial in a Mausoleum and Jewish Law

While traditional Jewish burial has generally been underground, various contemporary concerns, such as finances and lack of space, have led to a number of alternative methods of burial. As a result of general reticence to discuss end-of-life matters, as well as due to the complex issues involved, this topic is generally not seriously addressed in a thorough manner in Jewish publications, leaving many individuals to make swift decisions without properly understanding the issues involved.

The question of whether mausoleum burial meets the demands of Jewish Law, and under what conditions, is a challenging contemporary halakhic issue.[1] In this appendix, we will explore the traditional requirements of Jewish burial, elucidate the reasons behind these requirements, review the opinions of the great *poskim* on these matters, and analyze if mausoleums are acceptable in either the letter or spirit of the tradition.

THE OBLIGATION TO BURY

In describing what is done after a criminal is put to death by the court, the Torah commands, "A body shall not remain overnight. . . . You shall surely bury him."[2] Most authorities conclude that this verse teaches a Torah obligation to bury the dead, as well as a prohibition to leave a body unburied.[3]

It is insufficient to simply place the body into a coffin; the corpse must actually be buried in the ground,[4] in order to comply with the verse, "To dust shall you return."[5] Although a body placed in a coffin and then buried under the earth is still considered to have been buried in the ground, the ideal manner of burial is for the body to actually be in contact with the ground,[6] as the verse says, "The dust returns to the ground, as it was."[7]

I.   MAUSOLEUM: THE PERMISSIVE APPROACH

A.   *The Reasons for Burial and Their Implications*

The Talmud provides two reasons for the requirement of burial.[8] The first reason is that if a body is allowed to decompose in public view, it is a disgrace (*bizayon*) to the deceased,[9] their family,[10] and all humanity.[11] The second reason is that burial achieves atonement for the deceased. The Talmud raises this point in discussing the case of one who declares that they do not wish to be buried. Since disgrace is suffered by other people in addition to the deceased, if the reason for burial is to avoid disgrace, one is not permitted to refuse burial. However, according to the reason that burial is intended to gain atonement, one may state that they do not desire atonement, and thus forgo burial. The Talmud does not resolve the question of which of these two reasons is the essential rationale for the institution of burial. Since this is a doubt about a Torah prohibition, the Halakhah takes both reasons into account, so that even if someone makes it known that they would not like to be buried, they are buried nevertheless.[12]

Leaving a body unburied is a disgrace because everyone can see the human remains decompose in public.[13] Indeed, the Torah considers this to be a particularly horrendous form of humiliation, which it describes as a curse for breach of the covenant: "Your carcass will be food for every bird of the sky and animal of the earth."[14] The prophets often repeat this threat as well. For example, Jeremiah prophesies, "With the burial of a donkey will he be buried – dragged and thrown beyond the gates of Jerusalem."[15]

Although the *Shulchan Arukh* rules that simply placing a body into a casket without burying it in the ground is insufficient,[16] once a corpse is placed in a casket and shielded from public view, one could argue that there is no longer a concern of disgrace. As the *Arukh Ha-Shulchan* writes, to avoid disgrace and to fulfill the verse "You shall surely bury," all one would technically have to do is place the body in a casket and put it into a basement.[17] Indeed, the idea that simply removing a body from public view by placing it into a casket, even without burial, is some level of fulfillment of the mitzvah can be seen in the ruling of the *Shulchan Arukh* that if people are in a city that is under siege and they are unable to bury a body in the ground, they may begin the official mourning process once the body is placed into a casket. The *Shulchan Arukh* states that "closing the coffin is like burial."[18] The *Shakh* explains this to mean that although we would normally require burial to take place in the ground, in difficult circumstances, simply placing a body into a casket and putting it into another house would constitute perfectly acceptable burial, *kevurah ma'aliyuta*.[19]

However, sources indicate that the obligation to bury is not only about concealing the body. According to Rashi, burial in the ground effects atonement because a person is being lowered down into the depths.[20] Similarly, the Ran writes that this lowering down helps to grant a person atonement because it is tremendously humbling for a human being, who had been accustomed to rule over all other living beings of the earth, to be lowered beneath them.[21]

The Ran adds another intriguing comment about the reason for burial in earth – that one does not fulfill the obligation of burial unless there is soil involved in the burial.[22] This is based on the verse "to dust shall you return," which teaches us that "soil is healing" (*she-ha'afar refuato*).[23] It is also based on this verse that the *Arukh Ha-Shulchan* concludes that burial in a casket that is simply placed in a basement would not be sufficient. Based on this idea, one might argue that this verse could be fulfilled not only through being buried "in the depths" underground, as Rashi and the Ran argued, but also, to at least some degree, by simply placing soil into the casket and on the corpse. This idea may in fact be referred to by the Ran himself when he writes that burial in the ground is better (*yoter tov*) than being left on the surface of the earth,[24] but not that it is necessarily obligatory. This leaves room for the suggestion that while subterranean burial is ideal, there may be ways to inter a corpse above-ground that have at least some degree of validity.

In fact, as noted above, the *Shakh* rules that even though burial is supposed to take place in direct contact with the earth, a corpse may nevertheless be buried in a coffin because the earthen material that we place on the face of the deceased takes the place of the burial in the soil mentioned in the earlier sources.[25] The *Be'er Heitev* adds that the custom was to place a linen sack of soil under the head of the deceased, which is enough to be considered like burial in the earth.[26]

We thus see that while placing a body into a coffin without burying it in the ground does not completely fulfill the mitzvah of burial,[27] it does seem to address the concern of disgrace. Burial above-ground (but still in contact with some soil) may not grant complete atonement, but the Ran, followed by the *Shakh* and others, implies that there is still some atonement value. Furthermore, as we have seen, the Talmud rules that a person may choose to forgo this atonement altogether.[28]

Support for this approach can be found in the rulings of R. Ovadia Yosef, who quotes a responsum of R. Yitzchak Yehudah Shmelkis, published in 1875, suggesting that based on the Ran's comment, it may be sufficient to bury a body in a building above the ground.[29] R. Yosef argues that everyone would agree that this is permitted if the building is made out of soil, as was done in the days of the Talmud. If the building is made of cement, R. Yosef argues that it would be better to at least add some dirt to the floor of the building, as well as soil between each casket. However, R. Yosef argues that while allowing the body to touch the soil is of great benefit to the deceased, it is not absolutely required to fulfill the basic mitzvah of burial.[30]

B.   History

In biblical and Talmudic times, burial was generally not performed in the type of grave that we are accustomed to today, but rather often took place in a cave tomb, usually a natural cave or in a chamber cut into soft rock. The most prominent biblical example of this practice is the burial cave that Abraham purchased in which to bury his wife Sarah[31] and in which Jacob later requested to be buried.[32] Similarly, the prophet Isaiah, in referring to digging a grave, instructs to "carve out an abode in the rock."[33] Biblical references indicate that bodies would be laid on rock shelves on three sides of a chamber or on the floor. Since generations of the same family used the tomb,[34] skeletons and grave goods might be heaped up along the sides or put into a side chamber to make room for new burials.[35]

The Talmud also suggests that burial often took place in caves, hewn tombs, and catacombs. The *mishnah* describes the custom of burial in recesses carved into the walls of chambers beneath the ground.[36] These catacombs were often family burial places that consisted of multiple chambers with numerous recessed niches (*kuchin*), which served as the graves.[37] The *mishnah* explains that the catacombs were built depending on the nature of the rock into which they were dug and the consistency of the soil in which they were constructed.[38] Additionally, reference is also made in the Talmud to a structure called a *kever binyan*, which may also have been considered burial in the ground.[39] According to many Rishonim, these structures were above-ground burial tombs.[40]

Although rock vault burial may be the most ancient custom, when Jewish life moved to Babylon, where the soil was not suited for cave interment, ground burial became the norm.[41] Another change that has developed over time is that outside of Israel, burial is no longer necessarily done in direct contact with the soil, but rather usually in a coffin.[42]

This issue became especially pertinent in the nineteenth century. R. Yitzchak Elchanan Spector (1817–1896) was asked about the permissibility of temporarily interning bodies in a "house" (a mausoleum-like structure on the ground) that was surrounded by stones and sealed with a locked iron door, into which corpses could be placed in multiple niches. This was needed as a temporary emergency measure to protect the bodies, possibly against autopsies and medical research.[43] R. Spector quotes the Rambam, who rules that the process of burial in a cave is that once the corpse is placed into it, "we then place the earth and the stones back in place above it."[44] The soil was only placed on the corpse after it had been placed in the hollows of the cave. However, R. Spector cites the Tur's comment that every locality buried according to its own custom, generally based on the climate and composition of the local soil, and the Tur explicitly states that in some places, no soil was put onto the corpse.[45]

Since historically there were places that did not put soil on the corpse, R. Spector concludes that burial in a cave underneath the ground is sufficient to be considered burial in the earth. Furthermore, placing soil and earthen material onto the mouth and eyes of the corpse would fulfill the need to return the corpse to the earth. R. Spector argues that even though the proposed temporary tomb was not beneath the earth, its construction of bricks and stones would still be considered earth in Jewish Law,[46] so that this could nevertheless be considered burial with soil. Indeed, although most mausoleum structures are built out of cement, and not actual soil, most *poskim* rule that substances such as brick, cement,[47] and marble[48] are considered soil with regard to burial. R. Spector thus permitted *temporarily* placing bodies into this mausoleum-like structure, with soil placed on the bodies, followed by moving them into a subterranean grave when possible.[49]

C.   Contemporary Applications

This question has become particularly relevant today because many cemeteries are filled to capacity, and it is not always practical to build new cemeteries far away from established communities.[50] Based on the above sources, R. Ovadia Yosef allowed the Chevrah Kadisha of Argentina to bury in niches in a wall built above the ground. In fact, he reports that he himself advised the building of a wall in which to inter bodies in Alexandria when the cemetery there ran out of space.[51] Other than requiring at least six *tefachim* of soil between each grave, R. Yosef does not make clear the specifications and design of this "wall."

The issue of lack of space is particularly acute in Israel, where the Chief Rabbinate came up with the idea of building layered burial chambers. These were to be constructed in such a way that although above-ground, they would be contained within an artificial earthen mound, each grave concealed within soil on all sides, with concrete walls surrounding them.[52] Although a number of the rabbis had differing opinions on the matter, the Israeli Chief Rabbinate ultimately permitted the construction of these structures as long as they maintained very specific criteria.[53]

In 1987, R. Shalom Masas, chief Sephardic rabbi of Jerusalem and Head of the Jerusalem Rabbinical Court, issued his permissive ruling based on the argument that while it would not be permitted to bury a corpse completely above-ground without it being in the soil, it is permitted to construct a hill in such a way that the graves are surrounded by earth on all sides. R. Masas based his ruling on the discussion in the Talmud that prohibits deriving benefit from an object that has been used for the burial of a body, unless it is *mechubar le-karka* (attached to the earth). His discussion concludes that one may not derive benefit from a *kever binyan* (burial structure), because it is separate from the ground.[54] However, R. Masas argues that since the Talmud refers to the digging of a *kever binyan*, it must refer to the construction of walls and a floor to strengthen the grave after it has been dug in the ground, creating a vault wherein a corpse can be placed, separate from the ground. He further argues that as long as the structure is connected to the ground and the corpses are surrounded on all sides by soil in a structure constructed from concrete, this would be a permitted form of burial in a case of great need (such as lack of space).[55]

Similarly, R. David Chaim Shloush, who was Chief Rabbi of Netanya at the time of the Israeli Rabbinate's ruling, basing his ruling on a number of novel interpretations of the above sources,[56] permitted the construction of concrete burial plots in the side of artificial mounds of soil in such a manner that each grave would be surrounded by earth and would include soil in the bottom of each casket.[57]

We thus see that some *poskim* do deem mausoleum-like burial structures, *when properly constructed beneath earth to emulate caves*, as acceptable burial in the ground. Furthermore, many *poskim* are of the opinion that the reasons for burial are satisfied by these structures, and that it can thus be permitted under extenuating circumstances. However, many leading authorities have expressed a great deal of opposition to these opinions, as will be discussed below.

II.   MAUSOLEUM: THE CASE AGAINST

Despite the possible reasons for permissibility listed above, the vast majority of contemporary *poskim* have been strongly opposed to burial in mausoleums.[58] One of the primary arguments against this sort of burial is that it does not properly fulfill the commandment to be buried or the simple understanding of the mitzvah of burial in the ground,[59] and one who is buried in such a structure is thus in violation of the command, "A body shall not remain overnight. . . ."[60]

A.   History

Many *poskim* further argue that burial in a mausoleum is simply not in accordance with the age-old Jewish custom of using plots in the earth,[61] but is rather an imitation of non-Jewish practices, and thus in violation of the prohibition "You shall not walk in their statutes."[62] Today, mausoleums are often a cheaper form of burial than subterranean interment, but because they used to be much more expensive, many *poskim* felt that those mausoleums also contradicted the ancient Jewish burial philosophy of equalizing everyone, rich and poor alike, by displaying arrogance above the simple coffins in the ground.[63]

R. Shaul Yisraeli, as a member of the Israeli Rabbinate's high court, challenged a number of the sources that his colleagues in the Rabbinate marshaled in their approval of mausoleum-like structures in artificial above-ground mounds (as cited above). He pointed out, based on a *midrash* recounting the burial of Aaron that is quoted by Rashi,[64] that while it is true that ancient burial took place in caves, the bodies were in the sides of mountains and completely enclosed within earth, and thus technically underground.[65] A similar point was made by R. Nissan

Yablonsky, the Rosh Yeshiva of Beit Midrash L'Torah in Chicago in the 1920s. R. Yablonsky ruled that burial in a mausoleum would not satisfy the requirements of burial because proper interment requires complete enclosing and encasing of the body. A mausoleum does not fulfill this requirement if a body can be easily accessed and removed.[66] R. Yablonsky concludes that while mausoleums existed in the world in the days of the Talmud, the Jews did not make use of them, which implies that they rejected them.[67]

B.   *Disgrace*

Moving on to the issue of avoidance of disgrace as a reason for the mitzvah of burial, some explain that burial in the ground was intended to preclude the likelihood that people could easily open the casket. Since simply placing a body in a casket and leaving it above-ground does not address this issue, it does not fulfill the mitzvah.[68] Similarly, many *poskim* rule that burial in a building above-ground raises the concern that because it lacks permanence, it may one day fall or be destroyed.[69] Indeed, R. Y.Y. Greenwald noted that it was specifically the corpses of Jews interred in mausoleums in Germany that were the first to be removed from their graves by the Nazis and thrown to the dogs, precisely a concern that burial in the ground was intended to prevent.[70]

C.   *Atonement*

In reference to the goal of burial to bring about atonement, some have pointed to the comment of Rashi in *Sanhedrin*, where he explains that the fact that the body is specifically "lowered down into the depths" serves as atonement for the soul of the deceased, and if a body is left above-ground, this atonement is not achieved.[71] Furthermore, many also argue that burial helps to induce the decomposition of the body, and as long as a body is not able to decompose it is unable to be granted atonement.[72] It is argued that delaying the body's decomposition by withholding burial in the ground serves to extend the period of judgment, delaying and slowing the process of atonement, and causing increased anguish to the soul of the deceased.[73]

Although some have conceded that burial in a mausoleum does address the concern of disgrace by enclosing the body away from sight, as noted above, the Rif, Rambam, and Rosh do not conclude whether the primary purpose of burial is to avoid disgrace or to bring about atonement. Instead, all of them seem to try to satisfy both concerns, in which case they would apparently all oppose burial in a mausoleum.[74]

D.   "Kever Binyan"

R. Greenwald argues that the "kever binyan" was a structure used in the times of the Talmud only in order to allow the bodies to decompose, after which their bones were properly buried in the ground.[75] In fact, the Talmud never clearly states that these buildings were an acceptable form of Jewish burial.[76] R. Yablonsky argues that since most authorities require burial in the ground, and since a kever binyan or mausoleum is to be considered above and separate from the ground, it does not fulfill the requirements of burial. Additionally, if there is no soil in the mausoleum, it would certainly not fulfill the verse "to dust shall you return," which is ideally fulfilled through contact with the earth. Although this verse can be fulfilled even through burial in a sealed casket that is beneath the ground, it is not fulfilled in an above-ground structure.[77] Although the Beit Yitzchak permitted such burial if there is earth placed on the body in the casket, R. Yitzchak Yaakov Weiss argues that this would still not be considered burial in the ground, which is why this ruling seems to have been retracted by the Beit Yitzchak in his next responsum.[78]

Another approach was taken by a number of authorities who explained that the kever binyan mentioned in Sanhedrin is not a building that was on top of the ground, but rather, as the Ramban[79] and Yad Ramah write,[80] refers to large holes or vaults in the ground, in which niches were cut out for the placement of bodies.[81] According to this approach, despite the construction of these structures, the actual burial still took place beneath the ground. R. Yisraeli argued, based on a reading of the Talmud in Sanhedrin, that the concept of a kever binyan would only be a permissible form of burial if the structure was attached to the ground. Indeed, while others quote Rashi's statement that this structure was built above-ground as proof that it can be compared to today's mausoleums, R. Yisraeli notes that Rashi only mentions that the building was above-ground, implying (based on another statement of Rashi)[82] that perhaps the corpse was in fact buried below the ground; the kever binyan simply served as a monument for the deceased, built above the grave.[83]

E. Coffins

In response to the point made above that Jewish burial has shifted from direct contact with the soil to burial within coffins, numerous Rabbinic sources make it clear that coffins have, in fact, been used throughout Jewish history and are thus an ancient Jewish practice.[84] Some have pointed out that this was simply a matter of location. In the Land of Israel, burial took place in cave tombs, whereas in Babylonia burial took place in coffins, with soil placed on the body of the corpse.[85] The authorities note that it has indeed always been perfectly permissible (*le-khatchila*) for one to be buried in a coffin; it is simply better to be buried directly in the ground when possible.[86] The Rambam writes explicitly that "we may bury in a wooden coffin," and the Radbaz goes so far as to claim that a wooden casket can in fact be considered soil because everything comes from the earth and will return to the earth.[87] Similarly, some sources consider wooden coffins to be permissible because they eventually decompose and allow contact with the earth, something that is not true of a mausoleum.[88] In fact, the *Avnei Nezer* writes that being buried in a wooden coffin in the ground is "*chashiv ke-ara samichta*," as if one is connected to the ground.[89]

While many *Rishonim* permit the use of a coffin,[90] the *Yad Ramah* actually suggests that there is a mitzvah to use one. The Ravan explains that this is based on a *midrash* in which R. Levi interprets the biblical phrase that Adam and Eve hid themselves in the wood (forest) of the garden to mean that their descendants would be placed within coffins of wood.[91]

IV. CONCLUSION

This topic is complex and, as always, in any practical case one should consult a competent Rabbinic authority for guidance. From the above sources and discussion, it is clear that Jewish burial is ideally fulfilled through burial in the ground and that internment in a mausoleum is problematic from the standpoint of Jewish Law. However, we have also seen that the concept "burial in the ground" has many nuances. It is also important to understand that Halakhah recognizes gradations of preference; some acts are better than others, while other options are worse than others. Today, various concerns lead many away from traditional Jewish burial and Jewish cemeteries. To our sorrow, they often opt for cremation instead, which is certainly worse than interment in a mausoleum from the perspective of Halakhah.

It should thus be kept in mind that to the extent that mausoleum burial can constitute some form of burial in the ground if done correctly, and to the extent that it can address some of the reasons for burial, it may be possible to justify certain types of mausoleum-like burials if they are built and utilized appropriately. This would clearly only be true in cases of great need when traditional underground burial is for some reason not an option, and in consultation with a competent rabbi, as a choice that is not as good as burial in the ground, but may be better than many other "alternative" forms of burial.

Many contemporary mausoleums are not constructed or utilized in a manner that conforms to the above requirements. Furthermore, despite any sources or historical precedent that can be marshaled, we must remain cognizant of the fact that the traditional Jewish psyche often expects underground burial and can be highly uncomfortable with the notion of any sort of internment above the ground or in a wall.

ENDNOTES

1. Originally referring to the ancient tomb of King Mausolus of Caria, built in 350 BCE, and known as one of the Seven Wonders of the World, the term "mausoleum" refers to a structure built for multiple above-ground interments. These above-ground structures, also known as "crypts" or "wall spaces" are generally pre-fabricated and can accommodate a single family or as many as a few thousand corpses in a relatively small area. Although the use of a mausoleum was once seen as a sign of status, today they are often erected simply because of limited ground space for side by side burial.

2. Deut. 21:23.

3. *Sanhedrin* 46b; Rambam, *Hilkhot Avel* 12:1; *Sefer Ha-Mitzvot, mitzvat ase*h 231; *Sefer Ha-Chinuch*, mitzvah 537. According to most Rishonim, this verse not only applies to those who are killed by the court, but also to anyone who has died, and the vast majority of Acharonim accept this view. There is a minority opinion that burial for anyone other than an executed criminal is a Rabbinic obligation; see R. Sa'adya Gaon, *Sefer Ha-Mitzvot*, pos. precept 19; Rabbeinu Chananel, *Sanhedrin* 46b, s.v. *amar lei*; *Chavot Yair* 139. (See *Chazon Ovadia, Aveilut*, vol. 1, 369, for a summary of the opinions.) The *She'iltot* 133 bases the obligation to bury on the verse detailing Miriam's death and burial (Num. 20:1).

4. *Tur* and *Shulchan Arukh*, YD 362:1; *Arukh Ha-Shulchan*, YD 362:1–2.

5. Gen. 3:19.

6. *Tur* and *Shulchan Arukh*, YD 362:1; *Arukh Ha-Shulchan*, YD 362:1–2. The Talmud *Yerushalmi* (*Kelayim* 9:3) records the last will of R. Yehudah Ha-Nasi, in which he requested not to be buried with too many shrouds and that his casket be perforated. The Ramban (*Torat Ha-Adam*, 117) and *Tur* (YD 362:1) explain that Rebbi wanted the bottom board removed from his casket so that his body would actually be in contact with the ground. This form of burial is still commonly practiced in Israel, where the verse "and His land will atone for His people" (Deut. 32:43) is applied. Although the verse "to dust shall you return" applies everywhere, in accordance with the local custom (*Tur*, YD 362:1), "His land will atone" implies even greater attributes of atonement to the soil of the Land of Israel.

7. Eccl. 12:7.

8. *Sanhedrin* 46b. Additional reasons that have been suggested for the mitzvah of burial include the prohibition of deriving benefit from a corpse, and the idea that the body belongs to the earth and returning it to its rightful owner is akin to returning a stolen object (*Kli Chemdah*). Furthermore, *Kol Bo al Aveilut*, vol. 1, 173, points out that a corpse is owed respect in gratitude for its service to us and to demonstrate faith in its ultimate resurrection.

9. Rashi, *Sanhedrin* 46b, s.v. *mishum bizyona*; *Chiddushei Ha-Ran, Sanhedrin* 46b, s.v. *le-mai nafkah mina*.

10. Rashi, ibid., s.v. *lav kol ke-minei*; *Chiddushei Ha-Ran*, ibid.

11. *Tur*, YD 348; *Chiddushei Ha-Ramban, Sanhedrin* 46b, s.v. *iba'i lahu. Divrei Chaim*, YD 1:64, argues that the disgrace

of a human corpse being left out to decay is to humanity as a whole because all humans are created in the image of God.

12. Rambam, *Hilkhot Avel* 12:1; *Tur* and *Shulchan Arukh*, YD 348:3 and *Shakh* 6. Tosafot (*Sanhedrin* 46b, s.v. *kevurah mishum bizyona*) notes that although the Talmud does not directly answer which of these reasons is the main purpose (*ikar*) of burial, it is clear from *Sanhedrin* 47b that whichever is the primary purpose, gaining atonement is indeed part of the purpose of burial. According to Rabbeinu Chananel (*Sanhedrin* 47a, s.v. *iba'i lehu*), the conclusion of this discussion in the Talmud implies that atonement is in fact the essential reason.

13. Rashi, *Sanhedrin* 46b, s.v. *mishum bizyona*. The *Arukh Ha-Shulchan*, YD 262:1, argues that the purpose of burial is to ensure that the body does not remain out in the open, which he considers "an obvious, logical idea."

14. Deut. 28:26.

15. Jer. 22:19.

16. *Shulchan Arukh*, YD 362:1.

17. *Arukh Ha-Shulchan*, YD 362:1.

18. *Shulchan Arukh*, YD 375:4.

19. *Shakh*, YD 375:5; *Teshuvot Ve-Hanhagot* 3 YD 370.

20. Rashi, *Sanhedrin* 46b, s.v. *oh*.

21. *Chiddushei Ha-Ran, Sanhedrin* 46b, s.v. *lemai nafkah mina*.

22. Interestingly, the Ran does not say that there must be "*kevurah be-karka*" (burial *in* the ground), but rather "*kevurat karka*" (burial *with* ground).

23. *Chiddushei Ha-Ran, Sanhedrin* 46b, s.v. *remez le-kevurah*.

24. Ibid., s.v. *le-mai nafkah mina*.

25. *Shakh*, YD 362:1.

26. *Be'er Heitev,* YD 362:1. The *Be'er Heitev* adds that using dirt from the Land of Israel is even better. If one is unable to obtain soil from Israel, lime should be used because it assists in the speedy decomposition of the body (Rema, YD 363:2).

27. This is assuming, as most sources do, that burial in the ground is the Torah obligation. However, according to those who conclude that burial in the ground is a Rabbinic obligation, placing a body in a coffin may in fact fulfill the primary obligation to bury. See also *Teshuvot Ve-Hanhagot* 3:YD 370.

28. R. Sternbuch was asked if a woman who lived in Israel may choose to be buried outside of Israel, even though the ground of Israel atones ("*ve-kaper admato amo*"). He writes that one has the right to forgo atonement if she so chooses, as one cannot be forced into atonement: "*Ein kaparah ba'al korkha*." Furthermore, if a person does not desire this atonement, according to Rashi (*Sanhedrin* 46b, s.v. *ha-amar*), the ground would not atone for them (*Teshuvot Ve-Hanhagot* 3:YD 370).

29. *Beit Yitzchak*, YD 2:161. Nevertheless, the *Beit Yitzchak* quotes other sources that imply that this would not be permitted, and he concludes that it is best to follow the ruling of Rebbi that the body be buried in direct contact with the ground.

30. *Chazon Ovadia, Aveilut*, vol. 1, 431–3.

31. Gen. 23:9, 19.

32. Ibid., 49:29–32; 50:13.

33. Isaiah 22:16.

34. This practice of family burial is one source of the expressions "to sleep with one's fathers" (I Kings 11:23) or "to be gathered to one's kin" (Gen. 25:8, 49:29) in reference to death.

35. Delbert Hillers and Reuben Kashani, "Burial," in *Encyclopedia Judaica*, ed. Mi-

chael Berenbaum and Fred Skolnik (Macmillan Reference, 2007), vol. 4, 291–4.

36. *Bava Batra* 100b; *Mo'ed Katan* 8b.

37. Rashbam, *Bava Batra* 100b.

38. *Bava Batra* 101a.

39. *Mo'ed Katan* 8b; *Sanhedrin* 47b.

40. Rashi, *Sanhedrin* 47b, s.v. *be-kever binyan*, explains that this was a structure built above and separate from the ground. The *Nimukei Yosef* also writes that these were above-ground burial chambers, and *Talmid Rav Yechiel Mi-Paris* adds that these were constructed of hewn stone covered with lime. The Rambam refers to "building" a grave in *Hilkhot Yom Tov* 7:15, which the *Hagahot Maimoniyot* 20 writes refers to a *kever binyan*, and in his commentary on the Mishnah (*Mo'ed Katan* 1:6), the Rambam defines "*kevarot*" as structures for graves built above-ground. The Rosh (*Mo'ed Katan* 3:9) also writes that a *kever binyan* is on top of and separate from the ground. See also *Or Zarua*, *Hilkhot Avel* 423.

41. *Tur*, YD 362:1; *Encyclopedia Judaica*, vol. 4, 291–4.

42. *Tur*, ibid.

43. In the 19th century, bodies were often sold for profit by grave robbers, who exhumed bodies from their graves and sold them to medical schools and researchers at very high prices. Jewish graves were especially desirable because the requirement for speedy burial rendered most Jewish cadavers fresher. See R. Dr. Edward Reichman, "The Anatomy of Halacha," in *Berakhah Le-Avraham: A Collection of Articles in Honor of Rabbi Professor Avraham Steinberg's Sixtieth Birthday* (Jerusalem, 2008), 87–90. See also Ruth Richardson, *Death, Dissection, and the Destitute* (Univ. of Chicago Press, 2001), 15; M.P. Hutchens, "Grave Robbing and Ethics in the 19th Century," *JAMA* 278(13) (Oct. 1997), 1115; Immanuel

Jakobovits, *Jewish Medical Ethics* (Bloch Publishing, 1975), 144.

44. *Hilkhot Avel* 4:4.

45. *Tur*, YD 362. See also the explanation of the Bach.

46. *Chullin* 88b, codified by the *Shulchan Arukh*, YD 28:23, regarding which substances may be used to fulfill the mitzvah of covering the blood of a slaughtered animal with earth.

47. *Chavalim Be-Ne'imim* 3:63; *Iggerot Moshe*, YD 3:144.

48. *Beit Yitzchak*, YD 2:153.

49. *Ein Yitzchak*, YD 2:33.

50. In addition to the solution of mausoleums, R. Shlomo Amar, the Chief Sephardic Rabbi of Israel, permitted the Jewish community of Istanbul to address this concern by bringing in additional soil to their cemetery to cover up the existing graves and bury a new layer of bodies above the current ones (*Techumin* 27, 429–35).

51. *Chazon Ovadia, Aveilut*, vol. 1, 431–3.

52. In R. Shaul Yisraeli's ruling on the matter (discussed below), he specified that there should be at least an *amah* of soil surrounding and above the structure, and it should be firm enough not to erode as a result of rain and wind, in order for it to be considered cave burial (*Be-Mareh Ha-Bazak* 4:181). R. David Chaim Shloush added that the appearance of the artificial mounds should resemble a hill and should not just look like a building with some soil on top of it (ibid., 184).

53. The specifications were that the local Chevrah Kadisha, rabbi, and family agree, and the Chief Rabbinate would have the opportunity to inspect the construction of each structure before it was utilized (see *Be-Mareh Ha-Bazak* 4:176).

54. Rashi explains that a *kever binyan*

"is built above, and separate from, the ground."

55. *Be-Netivei Chessed Ve-Emet*, Annual Journal of the Tel Aviv-Yafo Chevrah Kadisha (1988), 102–5.

56. Based on a close reading of the Talmud and Rishonim, R. Shloush argued that even if we rule that burial is a Torah obligation, burial in the ground is not a Torah obligation and is only possibly a Rabbinic obligation (ibid., 95). He goes on to note that even though the Ramban clearly states that burial directly in the ground is part of the mitzvah (basing himself on the will of Rebbi), which is the source of the ruling in the Tur and *Shulchan Arukh*, even the Ramban does not require direct contact with the earth, but simply favors it (ibid., 97). He argues that the Rambam, Rif, and the Rosh do not quote this obligation, which R. Shloush feels is not implied by the Talmud either (ibid., 95, 97). Furthermore, he argues that a close reading of the Ramban indicates that the dead do not need to be buried underground, but simply that they must be in contact with soil on top of them (ibid., 96). He goes on to make the claim that even when Rashi states that the atonement of burial is achieved by being lowered down into the depths, he does not mean that one must be buried beneath the earth to effect this atonement. His reasoning is that Rashi further explains the concept of atonement through burial as being related to the "pain of the grave," not of being lowered down (Rashi, *Sanhedrin* 47b, s.v. *Rav Ashi amar*). He thus explains Rashi in terms of the atonement effected by the "pain of the grave" after the body has been sealed away, not that the atonement is a result of the body being lowered. He points out that this explanation fits with Rashi's understanding that a person may be buried in a *kever binyan*, which is above-ground. (R. Shloush argues in *Be-Netivei Chessed Ve-Emet*, 98, that the *gemara* permits burial in a *kever*

binyan.) According to R. Shloush, these graves in the side of a mound address the concern of disgrace because the body is shielded from public view, and they also effect atonement, which he views as being primarily accomplished by the decomposition of the flesh, a process which he claims is aided by soil but not dependent upon it. He bases this on the explanation of the Rambam that one's sins are not atoned for until their flesh decomposes (Commentary on the Mishnah, *Sanhedrin*, end of chap. 6). He thus explains statements such as those of Rebbi and the Ran that soil brings about atonement as indicating that the soil is simply a means to an end, not that the soil is an end in and of itself. R. Shloush concludes that since all of this is generally conjecture about the ways of God and hard to understand, "The secret things are left to the Lord our God."

57. *Be-Netivei Chessed Ve-Emet*, 89–101.

58. For example, R. Moshe Feinstein refers to burial in a mausoleum as an "*issur gadol*," a major prohibition (*Iggerot Moshe*, YD 3:143). R. Avraham Aharon Yudelovitz, the head Rabbinical authority of the Aggudat Ha-Kehillot of New York, strongly prohibited the practice of burial in a mausoleum in his book *Av Be-Chochmah* (1927). He wrote that this prohibition must be publicized because "nearly all of the rabbis are unaware of this prohibition and rule mistakenly in the matter." R. Nissan Yablonsky, the Rosh Yeshiva of Beit Midrash L'Torah in Chicago in the 1920s, ruled that burial in a mausoleum is "certainly forbidden" (*Nitzanei Nissan*, 166–171).

59. R. Yitzchak Yaakov Weiss, head of the Rabbinical court of the Eidah Ha-Chareidit in Jerusalem, wrote in 1985 that the mitzvah is burial in the actual ground (*eretz mamash*), not just having earth placed on the body (*Minchat Yitzchak* 10:122). R. Moshe Feinstein does not maintain that burial in a mausoleum vio-

lates "A body shall not remain overnight . . .," but rather does constitute some form of burial since the mausoleum building is made of cement, bricks, and stones that are connected to the ground, and is thus "like ground," but he argues that it is improper and that one certainly has not fulfilled the mitzvah of burial in this manner (*Iggerot Moshe*, YD 3:143).

60. *Sefer Av Be-Chokhmah*, 124–125; *Kol Bo al Aveilut*, vol. 2, 48; *Minchat Yitzchak* 10:122; R. Shaul Yisraeli in *Chavot Binyamin* 1:24.

61. *Iggerot Moshe*, YD 3:144.

62. Lev. 18:3. See *Nitzanei Nissan*, 166–171; *Sefer Av Be-Chokhmah*, 124–125; *Kol Bo al Aveilut*, vol. 2, 48.

63. *Nitzanei Nissan*, 166–171; *Kol Bo al Aveilut*, vol. 2, 48; *Iggerot Moshe*, YD 3:144.

64. Num. 20:26.

65. *Chavot Binyamin* 1:24; *Nitzanei Nissan*, 166–171, makes a similar point.

66. *Nitzanei Nissan*, ibid.

67. Ibid.

68. R. Aharon Dovid Goldberg, *Sefer Avodat Dovid*, Sanhedrin 46b.

69. *Sefer Av Be-Chokhmah*, 124–125; *Iggerot Moshe*, YD 3:143.

70. *Kol Bo al Aveilut*, vol. 2, 48.

71. *Sefer Av Be-Chokhmah*, 124–125; *Nitzanei Nissan*, 166–171; R. Shaul Yisraeli, quoted in *Be-Netivei Chessed Ve-Emet*, 96.

72. *Kol Bo al Aveilut*, vol. 2, 48; *Iggerot Moshe*, YD 3:143. R. Feinstein bases this on the Rema (YD 363:2), who writes that one would be permitted to place lime onto a corpse in order to speed up decomposition. The Taz (3) explains that this is based on the verse in Job 14:22, "His flesh will be pained over itself," which means that

as long as one's flesh remains intact, one cannot rest from judgment.

73. R. Feinstein bases this on the ruling in the *Shulchan Aruh* (YD 363:1) that one should not re-inter someone who has already been buried. According to the *Shakh* (1), this prohibition is rooted in the concept that the confusion would strike fear in the dead, and we are prohibited from causing them increased pain.

74. *Nitzanei Nissan*, 166–171.

75. *Kol Bo al Aveilut*, vol. 2, 48.

76. A similar point can be made in response to the claim that archeological finds have shown mausoleum-like graves in ancient Israel. There is no indication that these were sanctioned Jewish graves. Some are Samaritan, and the vast majority of archeological finds have been beneath-ground graves.

77. *Nitzanei Nissan*, 166–171.

78. *Minchat Yitzchak* 10:122.

79. *Torat Ha-Adam*.

80. *Yad Ramah*, Sanhedrin 47b.

81. *Sefer Av Be-Chokhmah*, 124–125; *Beit Yitzchak*, YD 2:161. This can be seen from the fact that the Talmud in Sanhedrin refers to it as being "dug out," the implication being that the *kever binyan* was a structure within the soil, not above it.

82. Rashi, *Sanhedrin* 48a, s.v. *nefesh*. Rashi states that a *nefesh* was a tomb-structure that was ornamentally erected over a burial plot. R. Yisraeli's point is that this *nefesh* is also called a "*kever binyan*."

83. *Chavot Binyamin* 1:24. R. Yisraeli makes the same point on the Yad Ramah's explanation of "*kever binyan*," implying that he also believes that the structure was simply built in the earth and that the corpse was placed into this underground structure.

84. Some examples of Talmudic reference to their use of coffins include *Berakhot* 19b; *Shabbat* 151a; *Sanhedrin* 46a; *Sanhedrin* 98a–b; Talmud *Yerushalmi, Kilayim* 9:3, 32b.

85. *Hilkhot Rabbeinu Yitzchak Ibn Geyut* (Bamburger ed.), 2:30.

86. *Divrei Soferim,* YD 362:3. The *Levush,* YD 362:1, is one exception. Although he also notes that one may be buried in a coffin, he writes that burial directly in the ground is the true intention of the mitzvah ("*stam kavur be-aretz mamash mashma*"), and is thus the ideal form of burial.

87. *Hilkhot Avel* 4:4.

88. Rashi, *Nazir* 51a, s.v. *eizehu meit.* See Talmud *Yerushalmi, Pesachim* 8:8, and *Korban Ha-Eidah* ad loc., which refers to burial in a wooden coffin as "*ke-kavur,*" like being buried.

89. *Avnei Nezer,* YD 472.

90. See, for example, *Chiddushei Ha-Ran, Sanhedrin* 46b, *remez le-kevurah.*

91. *Bereishit Rabbah* 19:8.

CHAPTER 6

Reproductive Questions

A.   GENETIC TESTING, DISCLOSURE OF RESULTS, AND PGD

I strongly encourage all couples whose marriages I perform to undergo genetic testing before getting married (ideally, even before getting engaged). One time, upon receiving their results, the bride shared with me that she discovered that she is a carrier for a number of genetic diseases and that she was afraid of the ramifications of telling her fiancé. I told her that if she is going to be married to him, she needs to be able to have these conversations and should be open about sharing this reality. Once she shared her results with him, they found out that they were both carriers for a very serious illness; if they were to get married, there would be a 25% likelihood each time she got pregnant, their child would have this very serious illness. By this point, they were very much in love and had to decide if they should proceed with their planned marriage or separate.

This is a fairly common, and excruciating, dilemma, I will discuss some of the relevant factors in this chapter.

IS GENETIC TESTING REQUIRED?

Until relatively recently, hereditary diseases were investigated based on family history. Today, however, genetic disorders can be diagnosed by specific genetic testing, which studies the DNA in one's cells to identify an abnormal gene. This method is also used to determine if one is a carrier of a genetic disease. Genetic testing is generally performed on a sample of blood, hair, skin, amniotic fluid, or mouthwash swished in the mouth to collect the cells. This testing can determine the presence of genetic diseases, vulnerabilities to inherited diseases, or mutant forms of genes associated with increased risk of developing or passing on genetic disorders. Several hundred genetic tests are currently in use, and more are being developed.[1]

There are different forms of genetic testing, generally categorized as "diagnostic" (#1–2 below) or "predictive" (#2–4 below). The perspective of Jewish Law on genetic testing differs depending on the purpose of the testing:

1. Genetic tests performed to *confirm the diagnosis* of a person already exhibiting specific symptoms to ensure proper treatment (or rule out other possibilities) are easily justified according to Jewish Law, as such a test is a component of healing the patient and is potentially even lifesaving.[2]

    a. However, genetic screening for a disease for which no effective treatment yet exists is sometimes not sanctioned by Jewish Law, because of the significant emotional burden such knowledge may present.[3]

2. *Prenatal genetic testing* is also encouraged, but one should seek the advice of experienced genetic counselors and rabbis[4] to determine which of the many conditions are worth testing for.[5] These tests can either be for the purpose of screening or diagnosis. To evaluate their permissibility in Jewish Law, one must determine what will be done with the information gained by these tests.

    a. If the goal is to improve the treatment of the fetus or child once it is born, it is certainly laudatory.[6]

    b. However, if the results of the testing may lead to aborting an imperfect fetus, careful halakhic guidance is essential.

    c. Furthermore, diagnosing genetic diseases in a fetus often requires invasive procedures (such as in chorionic villi sampling [CVS] or amniocentesis), which slightly increase the risk of miscarriage. This therefore becomes a serious halakhic question of balancing the risk with potential benefits.[7]

3. *Preconception Testing* is performed to determine if an already married couple will be at risk of genetic diseases when they conceive a child. If it is determined that a couple has a likelihood of conceiving a child with a genetic disease, they may be encouraged to pursue PGD (see below) in order to conceive a healthy child. If PGD is not an option for some reason, guidance will need to be sought regarding whether they are obligated to risk having a diseased child or if they should not attempt at all.[8]

4. *Premarital Genetic Testing* is critically important in terms of Jewish

Law because the information gleaned can encourage a couple not to get married in the first place, thereby avoiding all of the problems mentioned above.[9] Exactly when in a relationship such testing should be done and what to do if a couple wishes to get married despite learning of their genetic incompatibility are issues that require expert Rabbinic guidance and the input of a genetic counselor.[10] However, performing such testing may in fact be required by Jewish Law.[11]

In general, although engaging in genetic testing and screening has the potential to cause much fear, worry, guilt,[12] and sometimes discrimination/stigmatization,[13] it can also improve and even save lives,[14] as well as alleviate a tremendous amount of unnecessary physical pain and mental anguish.[15] Consequently, based on the obligation to guard one's health,[16] before one gets married or when there is reason to suspect that an illness or carrier status is present in an individual, Jewish Law may in fact *require* genetic testing (assuming it is an affordable test with a high success rate and that there is something that can be done about the results).[17]

REVELATION OF CARRIER STATUS

A common question that arises is what one should do if she learns that she is a carrier of the BRCA mutation, and thus has an increased likelihood of breast or ovarian cancer, but she does not currently have cancer. Once one learns this information, she may be able to take certain medications to prevent cancer, and she should certainly increase surveillance, which can help detect breast cancer (although ovarian cancer generally is not detected by screening). But is a woman who is found to be a carrier of the BRCA gene permitted to perform more significant preventative procedures? Ovarian cancer can be prevented through complicated prophylactic surgery to remove the woman's ovaries (oophorectomy), rendering her infertile and causing early menopause. Similarly, breast cancer can be prevented by engaging in a bilateral mastectomy (surgical removal of the breasts). However, these procedures have psychological ramifications and entail a halakhic issue of causing damage to oneself.

According to Jewish Law, a woman is not required to engage in a prophylactic bilateral mastectomy in order to prevent breast cancer from developing, but it is permissible to do so.[18] Oophorectomy, removing one's ovaries when no ovarian cancer is present, is a much more complicated question in Jewish Law because of the prohibition against preventing the physical ability to procreate (*sirus*). However, as medical data has become more conclusive, some contemporary Rabbinic authorities have begun to permit this as well in certain cases.[19]

One may also consider freezing her eggs before such a procedure in order to be able to have children later. One is also encouraged to share their results with members of their family, so that they can be tested as well, but since it is not certain that they will also be carriers, many rabbinic authorities do not *require* one to share their results with other family members.[20]

CONFIDENTIALITY

Now that such personal and otherwise generally hidden information can be discovered, many wonder if they must share this information about themselves with others – such as a potential spouse – or if a third party would be obligated to reveal this information to protect others. On the one hand, many Jewish values discourage slander and "talebearing,"[21] protecting confidentiality and sometimes even advocating concealing certain minor details.[22] On the other hand, values such as "do not stand idly by,"[23] "do not place a stumbling block before the blind,"[24] and the prohibition against causing others to suffer (*ona'ah*),[25] as well as the obligation to testify,[26] often limit the scope of confidentiality.

When it comes to revealing genetic information to prospective marriage partners, Rabbinic guidance should be sought on a case-by-case basis, since there is much grey area. The basic principle is that *if someone has a condition that is serious enough that a spouse would not have entered into a relationship had they known about it, it must be disclosed.*[27] For example, if one is found to be a carrier of a very serious illness that will likely cause a severely negative impact on one's offspring, this *must* be disclosed to family members or a prospective marriage partner – even by a third party[28] – or else the marriage could potentially be annulled.[29] However, before revealing any such information, one must:

- be as certain as possible
- may not exaggerate the severity or likelihood of illness

- must take numerous other factors into account regarding why and how the information is being expressed (see note).[30]

If the illness is less severe, does not cause objective harm, and some people in our society would not be concerned about it while others would, a third party may only be obligated to tell if they are asked,[31] or may not be obligated to disclose at all.[32] However, the carrier of the disease should be encouraged to disclose the information him or herself to parties who may be affected, especially to a potential spouse.[33] Regarding conditions that have minimal to no impact on others, or those that can be easily treated, there may be no obligation for an individual to reveal carrier status.[34]

PRE-IMPLANTATION GENETIC DIAGNOSIS (PGD OR PIGD)

Development of the IVF process has enabled the creation of embryos outside of the uterus for subsequent implantation. At the same time, enhanced scientific understanding of human genome and developments in gene mapping have improved medicine's ability to test for various genetic indications and diseases. PGD is an adjunct to assisted reproductive technology, as it combines genetic screening/profiling and IVF, allowing for testing of genetic abnormalities or the presence of genetic material linked to disease development even before the embryo is implanted in the womb. This process can thus serve as an early alternative to prenatal diagnosis by screening for specific traits, abnormalities, or even mutations whose onset is later in life, such as Alzheimer's disease, or those that simply present a possible risk factor, such as for breast cancer. One then has the option to select and implant a preferred embryo.

While this form of procreation may be less than ideal, such methods provide options in circumstances in which the ideal method is not possible. These new technologies are generally not categorically permitted or forbidden by Jewish Law, but rather analyzed case-by-case based on various factors. Although it is debated if producing children in this manner fulfills the commandment to be fruitful and multiply,[35] Rabbinic tradition recognizes the tremendous value in enabling people to satisfy their desire to have children.[36] Most authorities thus permit the use of PGD, when justified, just as they permit IVF (when the concerns mentioned in Chapter 6B are properly dealt with).[37] However, while assisted reproduction is often allowed but not obligatory, there are situations in which PGD can be viewed as an actual medical treatment, which may thus be required to prevent serious illness.[38]

Contemporary thinkers have debated various ethical issues associated with PGD,[39] and Jewish Law directly addresses a number of concerns related to use of this technology.[40] Although some ethicists have expressed the concern that such interventions are "playing God," Jewish thought views humans as the caretakers of the world.[41] Judaism therefore encourages humanity to develop technology (including genetic engineering), innovate new medicines, and influence the world, as long as it is all done in the best interests of humanity.[42] However, not all genetic manipulation that is possible is encouraged. There is a Talmudic principle that there are circumstances in which we should not interfere with the ways of heaven (*kavshei de-Rachmana*).[43] The most challenging questions thus concern which circumstances would justify engaging in PGD, especially because it generally involves discarding the pre-embryos that are not implanted.[44]

There are situations in which PGD would be welcomed as a medical therapy in order to enable a couple to have healthy children (such as to prevent having a child with Tay-Sachs disease),[45] and thus possibly fulfill *peru u-revu*, and there are situations in which it would be discouraged (such as PGD simply to choose specific traits or create "designer babies"). But there is a very large grey area in between. Rabbinic authorities take various issues into account on a case-by-case basis to permit or forbid PGD. While most Rabbinic authorities permit PGD when it is done for a serious medical/genetic concern,[46] they differ on which conditions rise to the level of necessitating PGD.[47] For example, some permit PGD to screen for BRCA, while others forbid it in this situation.[48]

One of the most debated questions with regards to PGD relates to the appropriateness of using this technology to choose the gender of the child.[49] Rabbinic authorities generally only permit this if there is a medically indicated reason to choose a given gender[50] or other strong mitigating circumstances, but not if it is simply for the sake of the parents' preference.[51]

Another challenging dilemma relates to utilizing PGD primarily in order to give birth to a child who will be a genetic match for an ill individual who needs an organ or bone marrow donor. While some have expressed concerns that this is an inappropriate reason to create a child, Judaism regards such donations as commendable[52] and the creation of more children as a blessed activity, which would render creating such a child as a doubly positive act.[53] On the other hand, intentionally producing a child with some sort of illness, birth defect, or abnormality would be problematic in the eyes of Jewish Law.[54]

SUMMARY

- Genetic testing to confirm a diagnosis is permissible.
- Surgery to prevent development of a genetically predicted cancer is usually permissible.
- Prenatal genetic testing is encouraged, although what to do about the results requires Rabbinic guidance.
- Premarital genetic testing is crucial and may even be a requirement. (One must seek expert guidance about what to do about the results.)
  - □ Whether or not results must be shared with potential marriage partners is decided case-by-case:
    - ◇ **Must disclose:** If the condition is serious enough that a spouse would not have entered into a relationship had they known about it, *even a third party is required to inform the potential spouse* (but care must be taken in how the information is shared, and it is ideal for the couple to share it with each other, rather than through a third party).
    - ◇ **Encouraged to disclose:** If it is a less severe illness (or one that does not cause objective harm), the carrier should disclose the information him or herself to parties who may be effected, but a third party must only tell if asked, and may not be required to tell at all.
    - ◇ **No obligation to reveal:** If the condition has minimal to no impact on others, or can be easily treated, there is no obligation to reveal it.
- Most Rabbinic authorities permit PGD when it is done for a serious medical/genetic concern (but there is much debate regarding which medical issues rise to that level).

ENDNOTES

1. For more info, see: http://www.myje wishgenetichealth.com/ and www.Gene TestNow.com.

2. Dr. Deena Zimmerman, *Genetics and Genetic Diseases: Jewish Legal and Ethical Perspectives* (Ktav, 2013), 31.

3. Dr. Fred Rosner, *Biomedical Ethics and Jewish Law* (Ktav, 2001), 213.

4. Some companies engage in "direct to consumer" genetic testing, in which cases the consumers do not get the opportunity to properly understand their results with the guidance of an expert genetic counselor. This is very problematic given the complication of understanding genetic results and their ramifications, not to mention the problems related to the safety and accuracy of such testing (Zimmerman, *Genetics and Genetic Diseases*, 51). On the other hand, genetic counselors may often encourage couples not to have children in a situation in which rabbis would encourage or even require a couple to have children. Therefore, an observant Jewish couple should seek Rabbinic guidance as well.

5. Zimmerman, *Genetics and Genetic Diseases*, 33. It should be kept in mind that when engaging in predictive genetic testing, the results could mean that a person will certainly develop the disease or that he or she are simply at increased likelihood of developing it.

6. Ibid., 38.

7. Ibid., 39. This is particularly problematic if one is testing for a condition for which an abortion will be forbidden even if the fetus is diagnosed. Neverthe-less, some authorities permit this kind of testing even if they will not permit an abortion in such cases.

8. R. Asher Weiss told this author that if such a couple already has children, they are *not obligated* to risk having more, but they *may do so*; if they do not yet have any children, they *should* risk doing so. See Zimmerman, *Genetics and Genetic Diseases*, 40–1, which lists other authorities who require a couple at risk for producing children with genetic diseases to nevertheless attempt to have children based on a story recorded in *Berakhot* 10a, in which King Chizkiyahu is told that he would die for not having children even though he had not done so only because he foresaw that his child would do great evil. However, other authorities have suggested that the commandment to procreate may not apply when a family is known to be effected with a severe genetic condition for which there is no other choice (*Nishmat Avraham*, EH 1:1[1]).

9. See, for example, Bleich, *Bioethical Dilemmas*, vol. 2, 107; R. Zilberstein (*Torat Ha-Yoledet* 64:10 (2nd ed.) and *Shiurei Torah Le-Rofim*, vol. 4, 117–27) rules that a couple that is not genetically compatible should not get married; if they are already married when they find out, he rules that they should ideally get divorced, but if they do not want to, they may attempt to have children if they do not have any yet. R. Hershel Schachter told this author (Summer 2016) that the ideal option for such a couple is to break off their engagement; as difficult as that may be, that pain is less than the many challenges the couple will likely face down the road

and throughout their marriage. (For this reason, R. Schachter encourages genetic testing very early in a relationship.) If they do get married, R. Schachter argues that they should conceive children only through PGD; they should not take their chances and abort a fetus should testing determine that it is diseased.

R. Aryeh Katz of the Puah Institute has written that although in the case of a recessive gene only 25% of a couple's children would have the disorder, this is a danger that most people would consider severe and attempt to avoid. He thus writes that a married couple who are deemed to be carriers of such a gene would be obligated to engage in PGD to avoid having a child with a genetic disorder because one must avoid causing pain to another ("love your neighbor as yourself"), which outweighs any discomfort of these fertility treatments (*Techumin* 36, 217).

R. Avraham Stav has written a responsum (along with his father, R. David Stav) that will be published in his forthcoming book on family law regarding whether or not an engaged couple who finds out that they are genetically incompatible may nevertheless get married. The couple's options are to separate, practice birth control and only become pregnant via PGD, or to risk getting pregnant and check each pregnancy early on via CVS or AFT testing to determine if the fetus is diseased, and if so, to abort. From the perspective of Jewish Law, he argues, the least problematic option is to separate, but many couples are unwilling to do so. R. Stav makes the halakhic argument that such a couple would not be *obligated* to separate. The second best option, in his opinion, would be to utilize PGD, but from an emotional, physical, and even financial perspective, this could be very burdensome. The question thus becomes whether one can ever take a chance of becoming pregnant naturally and rely on the option to abort in these cases (although this also carries emotional and physical risks, not to men-

tion halakhic concerns). At this point in time, the tests administered to determine if the fetus carries a genetic disease cannot be performed before 40 days of gestation, which would be the least problematic time to abort according to Jewish Law. However, they are done within 3 months of gestation, during which time the *Chavot Yair* (31), R. Ovadia Yosef (*Yabia Omer* 4:EH 1), and others sometimes permit an abortion (see also A. Stav, *Techumin* 31 [5771], 53–62). Although it may be more problematic for the couple to allow themselves to get into the situation in which they may have to rely on an abortion, R. Stav makes the case that this can nevertheless be permitted. R. Stav thus concludes that although the couple may opt for PGD, they are not obligated to do so, and may instead engage in normal marital relations, testing the fetus as early in the pregnancy as possible and performing an abortion if necessary.

However, many authorities who do not take as lenient a view of abortion would certainly recommend that the couple should ideally opt for having children via PGD if they indeed choose to get married. R. Katz (cited above) writes that one should not rely on the lenient opinions permitting abortion in these cases because they only permit abortion in order to relieve great suffering. Since there is now another way to avoid that suffering altogether, without violating any transgressions (i.e., PGD), a couple may not intentionally put themselves into a situation that may cause them to choose abortion. Furthermore, the many strong opinions that abortion is not permitted even in these situations must be taken into account, and there is thus no room to allow a couple to intentionally put themselves in a situation that may result in requiring an abortion (*Techumin* 36, 218–9).

Although it seems that the *Tzitz Eliezer* might have encouraged one to attempt pregnancy and have an abortion if necessary rather than utilize PGD, as he permitted abortions in these cases and forbids IVF, R. Katz argues (ibid.) that today even the *Tzitz Eliezer* would have encouraged PGD over possible abortion, since PGD has become so accepted and safe.

It goes without saying that each couple should engage in genetic testing in order to be aware of these issues ahead of time and to plan accordingly.

10. Zimmerman, *Genetics and Genetic Diseases*, 41–3. See also R. Daniel Feldman, *False Facts and True Rumors*, 108–110, 116, 259. The general principle is that such testing should be performed early enough in a relationship that a couple has not created too close of an emotional bond, but late enough in the relationship that the genetic issue can be evaluated in the context of the whole person. There are different approaches to this among the Rabbinic authorities, but they generally assume that very early disclosure can unnecessarily end a potentially good relationship, while disclosure too late in the courtship, when engagement is being discussed or has taken place, may cause undue stress. Either way, one cannot remain ignorant of these significant genetic facts. If a genetic incompatibility is found, most Rabbinic authorities strongly suggest that such couples not get married, though today the definitiveness of such a decision may be mitigated by the possibility of a couple having healthy children by engaging in PGD (see previous note). However, the ramifications of such a difficult choice should be carefully taken into consideration. Zimmerman also discusses the pros and cons of open versus closed testing.

11. Zimmerman, *Genetics and Genetic Diseases*, 43.

12. This mental anguish and emotional distress can be exacerbated by the fact that although some of the diseases can be treated, others are difficult to screen for and treat. For example, if BRCA is discovered, mammography is not fully reliable and the preemptive measures are not completely effective. Some have even ruled that the mental anguish of finding out that one carries BRCA is so severe that one is not obligated to test. See Dr. Ari Mozenkis, "Genetic Screening for Breast Cancer Susceptibility: A Torah Perspective," *Journal of Halacha and Contemporary Society* 34 (Fall 1997), 17.

13. If determination of carrier status for a genetic disease becomes known, some fear that it will be more difficult for them to find a mate, employers, or insurance. In fact, in the early days of this testing, the Rabbinic community discouraged it out of fear of producing anxiety and stigmatization (see Dr. Fred Rosner, "Tay-Sachs Disease: To Screen or Not to Screen," *Tradition* 15[4] [1976], 101–112). R. Moshe Feinstein challenged this precedent in 1973, when he advocated screening, but he wrote that the results should remain confidential in order to mitigate these concerns.

It should be pointed out that "recessive" mutations (such as those that cause Tay-Sachs) are different than those that are "dominant" (such as BRCA). One who carries a recessive mutation can simply make sure not to marry another carrier, and thus avoid passing it on; the carrier will remain completely unaffected. On the other hand, when the mutation is dominant, the carrier will likely develop the disease him or herself, and there is not always a guaranteed method of treatment.

14. For example, knowledge of carrier status may enable a person to exercise more careful surveillance. If the person indeed contracts the disease, this knowledge can help the physician decide between aggressive or conservative treatment. Furthermore, one can take measures to prevent passing on a gene to one's offspring (i.e., by selecting a spouse who is not a carrier). Another reason to encourage testing is

thus for the sake of informing one's spouse, or potential spouse, of this reality. The *Shulchan Arukh* (EH 2:7) rules, "One may not marry a woman from a family of lepers or epileptics, if it is established that this has occurred to their family members three times." Some argue that this prohibition (or suggestion) is restricted only to the epileptics and lepers mentioned by the *Shulchan Arukh*, while others maintain that anyone predisposed to any hereditary disease is included (see Dr. A. Mozenkis, "Genetic Screening for Breast Cancer Susceptibility," 24). R. Y. Zilberstein (*Chashukei Chemed* to *Yoma* 82a) rules that this teaches us that one should counsel a healthy person not to marry someone who carries these genetic mutations. This status must therefore be revealed to a potential mate.

15. Studies have shown that those with a history of breast cancer, or any person fearful of developing a disease, often prefer knowing (and possibly planning treatment, early detection, or prevention) over the lingering anxiety that results from uncertainty. See F.J. Couch, M.L. De-Shano, M.A. Blackwood, et al., "BRCA1 Mutations in Women Attending Clinics that Evaluate the Risk of Breast Cancer," *New Engl J Med* 336 (1997), 1409–15, cited by Dr. A. Mozenkis, "Genetic Screening for Breast Cancer Susceptibility, 8–9.

16. Deut. 4:15: "*Ve-nishmartem me'od le-nafshoteikhem*," "And you shall be exceedingly watchful of your lives."

17. R. J. David Bleich, "Genetic Screening," *Tradition* 34(1) (2000), 74, 77. R. Bleich concludes, "Genetic testing, including testing for BRCA1 and BRCA2, should be regarded as halakhically mandated in circumstances in which medical science believes that the results are likely to affect treatment in a manner that will enhance longevity anticipation or well-being. Certainly, a person identified as being at risk for a specific disease is obligated to

pursue all available measures in order to ward off the disease or to diagnose its presence while the disease is yet in an incipient stage and still amenable to cure." Similarly, R. Dr. Eddie Reichman ("The Mandate of Genetic Testing," Yeshiva University, *A To-Go Series* (Cheshvan 5773), 79–81), advises, "Just as a rabbi is charged with educating his congregation about the halachic permissibility of violating Shabbat in the face of *pikuach nefesh*, so he is now equally obligated to inform his congregation of the availability of genetic testing, which can prevent disease in children and unimaginable anguish for parents. . . . The genetic landscape is admittedly complex and evolving, and questions raised by genetic testing are manifold: whom to test, how to test, what to test, and when to test, but not, IF to test – as test we must. . . . The ever-expanding mandate of *ve-rapo yerapei* (you shall surely heal) surely includes genetic testing in its purview."

R. Moshe Feinstein argues that genetic screening does not violate the biblical command to be "perfect" with God (Deut. 18:13), because it is so simple and reliable that it is similar to simply opening one's eyes to that which is visible (*Iggerot Moshe*, EH 4:10). Furthermore, it may even be obligatory to screen when there is a concern; the verse "The Lord protects the simple" (Ps. 116:6), which sometimes allows us to leave our fate in the hands of God, does not apply when a danger is easy to detect (see *Halakhah U-Refuah* 5 (1987), 255–56, based on *Sanhedrin* 110; *Niddah* 31a; *Avodah Zarah* 30b; *Yevamot* 72a; *Shabbat* 129b; *Tosefta Niddah* 2:4).

18. *Nishmat Avraham*, CM 427:8 (245–6).

19. Prof. Steinberg reported to this author that R. Z.N. Goldberg and R. Asher Weiss both ruled that based on the new data related to the likelihood of disease developing and the effectiveness of surgery, it is permissible for a BRCA carrier to perform prophylactic oophorectomy, because ac-

cording to most Rabbinic authorities *sirus* of a woman is only a Rabbinic prohibition (except for the Vilna Gaon, who argued that it is a Torah prohibition for women as well). Although at the moment it is performed such a procedure is not life-saving, R. Goldberg and R. Weiss contend that the *rodef* (the pursuer), i.e., the gene with high probability to develop cancer, is already present, and the Rabbinic prohibition of *sirus* therefore can be overridden (though ideally one should try to establish a family first). On use of the concept of *rodef* in circumstances such as this, see *Shemirat Shabbat Ke-Hilkhatah*, 32, fn. 2, and *Nishmat Avraham*, OC 328(20). Regarding removal of a testicle to prevent the spread of prostate cancer in a man, see *Nishmat Avraham*, EH 5:7 (99–102 in 3rd ed.).

20. *Nishmat Avraham*, CM 427:8 (245 in 3rd ed.).

21. Violation of confidentiality falls under the prohibition of *rechilut* (talebearing), prohibited by Lev. 19:16 and Rambam, *Hilkhot De'ot* 7:1–2 (see also Prov. 25:9 and *Sanhedrin* 44b). Although many in our society tend to assume that they may share information that they have heard unless they are specifically asked not to, the Torah instructs the opposite – we may only share private information if we were given clear permission to do so (*Yoma* 4b). The *Tzitz Eliezer* (13:104) writes that in addition to the prohibition against revealing secrets when no potential damage will result from keeping the secret, physicians may have taken an oath to protect confidentiality that forbids them from revealing anything.

22. R. Yaakov Kanievsky (the Steipler Gaon) rules that a person may withhold minor information from a prospective spouse if revealing it might result in unwarranted discrimination (*Kehillat Yaakov, Yevamot*, 44). This ruling is based on the Talmud's statement (*Yevamot* 45a)

that in cases in which someone was halakhically Jewish, if his mother was Jewish but his father was not, there were people who would not marry him. The Talmud records that R. Yehudah advised someone whose father wasn't Jewish to move to a place where no one would know his lineage, so that this ancestry would not prevent anyone from marrying him. See *Teshuvot Ve-Hanhagot* 6:297(17) for a critique of this ruling.

23. Lev. 19:16. (Interestingly, this is the continuation of the verse quoted above regarding talebearing.) See *Sanhedrin* 73a, which states that this verse obligates one who sees another person drowning or being attacked by wild beats or bandits to try to save the victim.

24. Lev. 19:14. The *Sifra* (*Kedoshim* 2) extends this verse to prohibit deception and giving bad advice.

25. Lev. 25:17 prohibits causing another person to suffer verbally or intellectually (including suffering caused by lack of knowledge), which is another reason one should be obligated to share certain information (*Bava Metzia* 58b). See *Berakhah Le-Avraham*, 308–309, for R. Yitzchak Zilberstein's explanation of how this issue is primarily a concern of violating the prohibition against *ona'ah*. See also *Nishmat Avraham*, EH 2:7(1:5) (61 in 3rd ed.).

26. The obligation to provide testimony is based on Lev. 5:1. See *Bava Kamma* 56a; *Shulchan Arukh*, CM 28:1 (see also *Shakh* 1). The *Sefer Ha-Chinukh* (mitzvah 122) distinguishes between monetary cases (in which one must only testify if asked) and capital cases (in which one must share whatever he knows). *Minchat Chinukh* 237:7 claims that failure to provide necessary testimony transgresses the prohibition of "do not stand idly by." Furthermore, since there is a mitzvah to testify, an oath taken by a doctor to protect confidentiality might not always be binding (see *mishnah* in *Shevuot* 29a).

27. *Sefer Chassidim* 507; Chafetz Chaim, *Hilkhot Rekhilut* 9 (3:4). For a similar but slightly different approach in the name of R. Moshe Feinstein, see *Masorat Moshe*, vol, 1, 383. See also *Nishmat Avraham*, EH 2:7(1:6) (61–7 in 3rd ed.) and *Minchat Asher* 1:68.

28. Chafetz Chaim, *Hilkhot Rekhilut* 9:1 and 3(4, 6). See notes in the *Be'er Mayim Chayim*, sect. 8, where the Chafetz Chaim points out that the harm that could be caused by withholding information must be significant, i.e., not simply a minor weakness. For example, R. Yitzchak Zilberstein rules that if one is known to carry a very serious illness, such as Huntington's disease, he must reveal this to a potential marriage partner, and if he does not, the doctor or whoever knows the information must share it (*Berakhah Le-Avraham*, 312–13). See also *Tzitz Eliezer* 16:4, who argues that major deficiencies must be revealed by a third party, but that a physician may be required to first assemble a *beit din* to be *matir neder* (release avow), as he or she may have obligated themselves to an oath to maintain confidentiality. Similarly, many authorities rule that if one has a hidden illness that will render it dangerous for him or her to drive, a third party, such as a doctor, is obligated to alert the Department of Motor Vehicles in order to prevent potential dangerous accidents (*Yechaveh Da'at* 4:60; *Siach Nachum* 1:117). For a related discussion on a doctor's obligation to reveal suspected infidelity, see *Nishmat Avraham*, EH 115:1 (319–21 in 3rd ed.).

29. R. J. David Bleich, "Genetic Screening," *Tradition* 34(1) (2000), 79. The example that R. Bleich gives is if one is a carrier for Huntington's disease, which is so severe and lethal that R. Bleich argues it is obvious that disclosure is obligatory, and if one does not disclose this information, annulment of marriage is likely. R. Yitzchak Zilberstein expands on this point in *Berakhah Le-Avraham*, 309–10.

(See previous note).

30. *Chafetz Chaim, Hilkhot Rekhilut* 9:1, stipulates that before revealing any information, the one doing so must (1) give the matter much thought to determine that the partnership will likely be detrimental, (2) not exaggerate the extent to which the partnership can prove damaging, (3) be motivated solely by the desire to aid the person who is to be warned and not by any considerations of dislike for the other person, (4) determine if it is possible to prevent the intended partnership without mentioning anything derogatory about the other person, and (5) ensure that the warning must not cause any other injury to the person being warned besides the prevention of the partnership. On these conditions, see R. Feldman, *False Facts and True Rumors*, 97–103.

31. Out of concern for the prohibition of *geneivat da'at*, R. Shlomo Zalman Auerbach ruled, "If the father of the bride or the bride asks one about his parents (even if she does not suspect that they are not Jewish), one must tell the truth. But if they do not ask, this implies that they do not care so much, and it is thus not deceptive not to tell them" (*Nishmat Avraham*, EH 5:8). On this issue, see R. Feldman, *False Facts and True Rumors*, 113.

32. For example, R. Bleich argues ("Genetic Screening," 80) that since not all carriers of BRCA develop breast or ovarian cancer, and since both cancers can be treated to some degree, it is doubtful that any Rabbinic authority would require, or even permit, a third party to disclose the BRCA carrier state. Nevertheless, he feels that since marriage is based on trust and openness, for an individual to conceal such information from a potential spouse would be very unwise, even if it is permitted. See also R. Feldman, *False Facts and True Rumors*, 261.

33. Most *poskim* encourage one to share such information with a potential spouse,

even in these more minor situations in which a third party would not be obligated to disclose (*Nishmat Avraham*, EH 115). See also *Tzitz Eliezer* 16:4, who argues that even when a third party is obligated to reveal such information, they should gently inform the individual about whom they will be speaking that they are required to share this information and it would be best if they would share it themselves.

34. See, for example, the ruling of R. Yitzchak Zilberstein that if one is a carrier for a minor illness that can be treated, such as hemophilia, this would not have to be revealed by anyone, although it is still proper to do so (*Berakhah Le-Avraham*, 313).

35. The question of whether the commandment to be fruitful and multiply is fulfilled in this manner is relevant for two reasons. First, such fulfillment would mitigate concerns related to wasting seed (Y. Shilat, *Refuah, Halakhah, Ve-Kavanat Ha-Torah*, 182). Second, it affects the question of whether someone who cannot otherwise have children would be obligated to go through assisted reproduction in order to fulfill the commandment ideally, i.e., by having both a girl and a boy. The Talmud (*Chagigah* 15a) describes a situation in which a woman becomes pregnant in a bathhouse, concluding that the person whose sperm impregnated the woman is considered the father. Furthermore, *Rabbeinu Peretz* (cited in *Bach*, YD 195) rules that a woman should not sit on the sheets of another man, since she can become impregnated and the child may marry a sibling, implying that the sperm contributor is considered the father by Jewish Law. Based on this, *Beit Shmuel* (EH 1:10) writes that artificially impregnating a woman would fulfill the mitzvah to be fruitful and multiply. The *Taz* (EH 1:8) disagrees, since we might only be concerned about paternity in this case to be careful (*le-chumrah*), but not to the extent

that it fulfills the commandment. Others argue that this case cannot be compared to artificial insemination, because the impregnation was not intentional. When the sperm is given intentionally to impregnate (as in the case of various forms of artificial insemination), then it does fulfill the mitzvah (*Teshuvot Emek Halakhah* 1:68; *Minchat Yitzchak* 1:50; see *Tzitz Eliezer* 3:27:3 and *Teshuvot Ve-Hanhagot* 2:689, who disagree).

See also Rambam, *Hilkhot Ishut* 15:2; *Iggerot Moshe*, EH 2:18; and R. J.D. Bleich, "Pre-Implantation Genetic Diagnosis and Jewish Law," in *The Value of Human Life* (Feldheim, 2010), 130, who write that the primary obligation is to *attempt* to have children, not to give birth to children. Once one has engaged in normal intercourse, one is not obligated to engage in "heroic measures" to have children. Along similar lines, R. Shlomo Zalman Auerbach writes that even if this technology fulfills the mitzvah, one is not obligated to take extraordinary steps (*tachbulot*) in order to perform this mitzvah (*Minchat Shlomo, Tinyana* 124). R. Asher Weiss similarly rules that there is no obligation to enter a pregnancy when there is a high risk of having children with genetic illness. Since he rules that there is no obligation to have children in unnatural ways, one is not obligated to pursue PGD in order to have children. Nevertheless, one should be encouraged to do so and it would fulfill the mitzvah (*Teshuvot Minchat Asher* 1:69).

Others write that now that the possibility of PGD exists, it is obligatory to have children via PGD if necessary (R. Aryeh Katz, *Techumin* 36, 216, 219). Some rule that this does, in fact, fulfill the mitzvah to be fruitful and multiply, while others argue that even if it does not fulfill this mitzvah, it fulfills the verse "*la-shevet yitzarah*" ("He fashioned it to be inhabited," [Isaiah 45:18]). However, other prominent contemporary authorities rule that having children in this manner fulfills no mitzvah whatsoever (see *Encyclope-dia Hilkhatit Refu'it*, vol. 2, 851). For an in-depth discussion of this issue, see R. Joshua Flug, "A Boy or a Girl? The Ethics of Preconception Gender Selection," *Journal of Halacha and Contemporary Society* 48 (2004), 5–27. R. Flug concludes that undergoing IVF/PGD simply to fulfill the commandment to procreate would be tantamount to doing it for non-medical, non-mitzvah purposes. Therefore, one would not be *obligated* to pursue these reproductive techniques only in order to fulfill this commandment (although doing so may exempt one from the mitzvah once done).

36. As R. Zilberstein writes in a responsum about PGD: "If their primary intention is to satisfy the natural desire to have children, it is difficult to withhold this from them" (*Assia* 51–52 [Iyar 5752], 54–58). Similarly, *Teshuvot Be-Mareh Ha-Bazak* 9:46 points out that there is a natural desire for a couple to have children, as we learn from such biblical examples as Isaac and Rebecca's heartfelt prayer for children (Gen. 25:21) and Rachel's statement that without children it is as if she is dead (30:1). Furthermore, although women are not obligated to reproduce, this could be partially a result of the fact that women have a natural desire for children and thus do not need to be commanded. (Some maintain that women are commanded in the commandment of "*la-shevet yitzrah*;" see *Be-Mareh Ha-Bazak* 9:46, n. 3.) For this reason, it is a great accomplishment (*mitzvah rabbah*) to support one with assisted reproduction and contribute to advances in this technology. Moreover, some have even classified assisting a couple with conceiving a child as almost akin to the category of *pikuach nefesh* – saving a life (*Teshuvot Ve-Hanhagot* 3:407).

37. To briefly summarize here: Although some authorities rule that IVF violates the prohibition against wasting seed (see *Mishpetei Uziel*, EH 1:19; *Divrei Malkiel*

4:107; and *Tzitz Eliezer* 15:45, who write that IUI is acceptable but IVF is not), most Rabbinic authorities permit IVF, arguing that since the intention is producing a child, it is not considered wasting seed (when it is done to overcome infertility, and not simply to try to choose the gender of a child). See, for example, R. Ovadia Yosef, quoted in *Nishmat Avraham*, EH 1:5(3), and *Yabia Omer*, EH 2:1; R. Avigdor Nevenzahl, *Assia* 5, 92–93. The *poskim* also permit artificial insemination (AI) for a childless couple if the woman cannot be impregnated normally, as long as the doctors establish that it will be effective and there is Rabbinic oversight of the process to ensure that the sperm is not switched. See *Iggerot Moshe*, EH 1:71; 2:11, 18; 4:32(5) (although R. Feinstein in 2:18 does not permit discarding unused embryos); R. Shlomo Zalman Auerbach, *Noam*, vol. 1, 145–66 and *Minchat Shlomo*, *Tinyana* 124; *Minchat Yitzchak* 1:40; *Yabia Omer* 2, EH 1; *Seridei Eish* 3:5; R. Rabinovitch, *Techumin* 2, 510–11. Most authorities also rule that IVF and AI fulfill the commandment to be fruitful and multiply (see especially *Yabia Omer*, cited above). Although each situation requires a case-by-case analysis, R. Elyashiv and R. Neuwirth have been quoted as permitting PGD in certain situations (*Nishmat Avraham*, EH 2:7(1:5) (60 in 3rd ed.) and CM 427:8 (244 in 3rd ed.). For a summary, see *Be-Mareh Ha-Bazak* 5:104.

38. Assisted reproduction is not mandatory in Jewish law, but PGD can be seen not as a fertility treatment, but rather as treatment for the child's underlying illness (assuming PGD can certainly resolve a given condition). Jewish Law sees both treating and avoiding illness as mandatory. Just like one must take a vaccine to immunize from certain problems, PGD can be viewed as an inoculation against disease in certain cases. (This is not true regarding using PGD to enhance physical attributes, but rather only to prevent ill-

ness.) However, the high cost may prevent PGD from actually being obligatory. See Michael Broyde, "Pre-Implantation Genetic Diagnosis, Stem Cells, and Jewish Law," *Tradition* 38(1) (2004), 66.

In addition to PGD, fertility treatment today often includes PGS, (pre-implantation genetic screening), which is where one or more cells are removed from an IVF embryo to test for chromosomal normalcy. Though there has not been much rabbinic writing on this topic yet, Prof. Steinberg told this author (Spring 2017) that in his opinion:

(a) From a medical point of view there is still great controversy whether it is beneficial enough and/or safe enough.

(b) Assuming new techniques will produce better results, it seems that according to Jewish Law it should not be different from PGD: Although in PGD one is looking for a specific and known genetic abnormality and in PGS one is screening for chromosomal abnormality without any hint of such a problem in the family, nevertheless since the basis of the permission in Jewish Law to perform PGD is because the fertilized egg is outside of the womb and before 40 days of gestation it has no human status, and the act is done to avoid the birth of a seriously defective child, the same should hold true for screening for chromosomal abnormalities.

(c) Nonetheless a slippery slope should be avoided by allowing the screening in PGS only for serious chromosomal abnormalities (which has also been true for PGD).

39. Nina Robinson, "Is Non-Selection of Disabled and Diseased Embryos Using PGD Ethically Acceptable, Legally Permissible, and Halachic?," *Jewish Medical Ethics and Halacha* 7(1) (June 2009), 8–9, notes a number of ethical issues. When used to screen for a specific genetic disease, PGD avoids selective pregnancy termination, as it makes it highly likely that the fetus will be free of the disease

under consideration. PGD is thus ethically/legally preferable than the alternative, which is abortion. Abortion due to fetal abnormalities is often done after 24 week's gestation, whereas PGD takes place at a much earlier stage of development (under 3 days old, and before the embryo has even been implanted). On the other hand, PGD highlights the issue of consumerism versus viewing children as gifts to love unconditionally. (This can be framed as whether one sees the person *as* their disability or a person *with* a disability.) Using PGD can be viewed as a consumerist choice, on the one hand, or as reflective of a desire to prevent pain and suffering for potential offspring. Regarding resource allocation, the financial costs of PGD/IVF can be justified by the alternative expenses of continued support throughout a disabled child's life. Similarly, PGD can also be viewed as a kindness towards parents who need help reproducing healthy children and enabling embryos to develop with the ability to reach their maximum halakhic potential, i.e., full healthy functionality. See also R. Dr. Mordechai Halperin, "In-Vitro Fertilization, Insemination, and Egg-Donation," *Jewish Medical Ethics*, vol. 2 (Schlesinger Institute, 2006), 165.

Some have critiqued PGD on the grounds that it only benefits the wealthy and creates inequality in access. However, preventing the use of PGD on this basis would be like disallowing use of insulin when it was initially only available for the wealthy. Instead, we are encouraged to support the advancement of medicine/technology and hope it will become accessible to all (see Broyde, "Pre-Implantation Genetic Diagnosis," 62). Some would prohibit PGD out of fear that irresponsible people will abuse the technology and create individuals that are not human to be utilized for organs, forced labor, etc. However, others argue that this would not be a reason to prohibit PGD, but rather to temporarily restrict/limit this intrinsically permitted technology (ibid., 63). Others have pointed out that PGD for gender selection has the potential to offset percentages of males/females in the world, resulting in many not having anyone to marry (see Flug, "A Boy or a Girl?," 24–25). There are also concerns related to choosing specific features, which could lead people to forgo natural means of reproduction, opting instead for designer babies (ibid., 25–26).

40. In addition to the concerns related to wasting seed and discarding pre-embryos, there is also the issue of the risk to the mother and the fetuses engendered by multiple pregnancies. Furthermore, PGD is still a relatively new procedure and there is insufficient data to determine its long-term safety (see R. Bleich, "Pre-Implantation Genetic Diagnosis and Jewish Law," 134). These risks should not be deterrents for those unable to conceive, but should be factored in when considering elective procedures. Self-endangerment is only prohibited when it is a risk that the general population would avoid, but one may nevertheless not engage in even acceptable risks unless there is a need to do so (such as for the sake of one's health or to fulfill a mitzvah). It is therefore forbidden to assume risks for entirely elective purposes. See *Shabbat* 129b; *Yevamot* 72a; *Yabia Omer*, YD 3:7(3); Flug, "A Boy or a Girl?," 20–23. On the general permissibility of utilizing PGD, see *Nishmat Avraham*, EH 5(1).

41. Gen. 1:28. *Midrash Kohelet* 7:28 explains that although the world was created for humanity to enjoy, we must be extra careful to safeguard it.

42. See the introduction to this book, n. 2.

43. *Berakhot* 10a. See also the explanation of R. Moshe Feinstein of this story in *Dibberot Moshe, Shabbat* 42.

44. Although PGD can be viewed as simply a variation of the process of IVF that allows for a greater degree of analysis of the embryo prior to implantation, in the IVF process, unused embryos are often frozen and saved for future pregnancies, whereas in PGD the unused embryos are more frequently discarded. Destroying pre-embryos is morally problematic in Jewish Law because they have the status of potential life. See Ramban, *Torat Ha-Adam, Sha'ar Ha-Sakanah*, who rules in accordance with the Behag that one may go so far as to violate Shabbat or Yom Kippur in order to save a fetus even within forty days of conception because it has the potential to live. Destroying embryos may also fall under the prohibition of wasting seed; see R. Unterman, *Noam* 6; R. J.D. Bleich, "Survey of Recent Halachic Periodic Literature: Stem Cell Research," *Tradition* 36 (2002), 72. However, there are a number of arguments to permit the destruction of embryos if necessary (i.e., valid medical need):

(1) Before 40 days, an embryo has no human value, and it is thus not considered killing if it is destroyed (R. Chaim David Halevi, "*Al Dilul Ubarim*," *Assia* 47–48 (12, 3–4) (Kislev 5750), 15.

(2) The prohibition against abortion only applies when the fetus is inside the womb (*ha-adam ba-adam*), whereas outside of the womb – where the fetus would not be able to naturally develop on its own – such embryos do not have the status of life (*nefesh*), and not actively implanting these pre-embryos would therefore not be considered killing (R. M. Sternbuch, *Be-Shevilei Ha-Refuah* 8, 29; R. Zilberstein, *Assia* 51–52 [13, 3–4] [Iyar 5762], 54–58). For a critique of this view, see R. Bleich, "Pre-Implantation Genetic Diagnosis and Jewish Law," 136–7.

For these reasons, destroying pre-embryos is likely not considered murder, nor does it fall under most of the concerns about abortion noted in chap. 6C. The concern about wounding the mother (Maharit) does not apply in this case, as the embryo is not inside the mother's body, nor can it be viewed as wounding the fetus (*Seridei Eish*), since it does not yet have limbs or the status of a full life. Regarding wasting seed, it can be argued that this sperm was not emitted in vain, but rather with the intent of producing life. Since a defective embryo is not viable for that purpose, it is thus not considered wasting. See Y. Breitowitz, "Halakhic Approaches to the Resolution of Disputes Concerning the Disposition of Pre-Embryos" *Tradition* 27(4), 59–89 (also published in *Jewish Law and the New Reproductive Technologies* [Ktav, 1997], 155). Jewish Law thus does not require that all pre-embryos be implanted.

45. R. Zilberstein points out in his responsum on the topic (*Assia* 51–52 [13, 3–4] [Iyar 5752], 54–58) that PGD has tremendous value because it can allay the serious mental anguish that can result from producing a profoundly ill child: "One can't block the way for people suffering terrible anguish when their children are suffering from debilitating diseases, and sometimes causing the woman to lose her mind. Therefore, in the case of severe genetic diseases that affect the couple, it is hard to prohibit artificial insemination and new technology to fertilize eggs that aren't susceptible to the disease."

Furthermore, it can prevent situations in which one might have otherwise considered having an abortion.

46. *Nishmat Avraham*, EH 2:5a (60 in 3rd edition). See also Zimmerman, *Genetics and Genetic Diseases*, 75.

47. In addition to concerns related to risk and destroying pre-embryos, mentioned above, there is also an issue of sperm procurement. While wasting seed is not an issue according to many authorities when the goal is to produce children, this may not be as easily permitted when a couple could produce children naturally but is simply using this technology in order to choose a gender, or even to eliminate congenital defects. See Bleich, "Pre-Implantation Genetic Diagnosis and Jewish Law," 134–5.

48. R. Asher Weiss told this author that PGD would not be obligatory for a carrier of BRCA, but that she may use it if she so chooses. It is reported that R. Yitzchak Zilberstein and R. Mordechia Willig have ruled that one who is a carrier for BRCA should not procreate via IVF and PGD, whereas R. Bakshi Doron ruled that she must (unpublished responsum of R. Mordechai Willig, dated 8th of Tishrei 5774). R. Willig goes on to rule that if one has a fertility problem for which they must use IVF anyway in order to procreate, then they may utilize PGD as well in order to ensure that the child won't be a carrier for BRCA.

49. See Zimmerman, *Genetics and Genetic Diseases*, 82–7 for discussion of ethical issues in gender selection.

50. *Nishmat Avraham*, EH 1:5, quotes R. Shlomo Zalman Auerbach as ruling that it is not desirable to permit sperm separation for gender selection, because besides intentionally destroying some seed, this violates the Talmud's injunction: "Why do you wish to interfere in the ways of Heaven?" On the other hand, R. Auerbach rules that for medical reasons, such as if the wife is known to be a carrier of a gene that will affect their male children (as in hemophilia), such a procedure would be permitted so that their children would only be girls (if this is their wish). R. Zilberstein and others agree with this, adding concerns about interrupting normal marital relations without good reason (*Noam* 8, 47–48). Non-medical (and thus prohibited) reasons to engage in gender selection may include cultural, religious, or convenience purposes, all of which could result in detrimental societal changes if fully allowed unchecked. Indeed, many *poskim* forbid PGD for gender selection alone; see Zimmerman,

Genetics and Genetic Diseases, 86.

51. For example, R. Amar has written that there may be room to permit sex selection in PGD for medical reasons, to fulfill the commandment to be fruitful and multiply, or even for the sake of peace in the home. There may also be those who would choose a female child in order to prevent embarrassment to the child of a Kohen, who himself would not be considered a Kohen or engage in rituals as such, and some may prefer a male if a donor sperm is used and the father is concerned about laws of seclusion with members of the opposite gender who are not immediate relatives. Rabbinic guidance would need to be sought on these cases, as some feel that these advantages would not be sufficient to justify sex selection on their own, unless PGD was already being done for a legitimate medical reason (M. Broyde, "Pre-Implantation Genetic Diagnosis, Stem Cells, and Jewish Law," 66).

Be-Mareh Ha-Bazak 5:104 quotes differing opinions amongst Rabbinic authorities regarding a case in which a family already has many children from one gender and they want a child from the other gender. R. Shlomo Zalman Auerbach and R. Nachum Rabinovitch do not feel that this is sufficient reason to engage in the minor risks involved in the procedure, whereas R. Mordechai Eliyahu permits it in a case of a couple who already has 5 children of one gender or if the woman is 42 years old and strongly desires a child of the opposite gender. Similarly, R. Ovadia Yosef is reported to have permitted PGD for a couple with 6 children of one gender and who were not willing to have more children unless they could be assured that the seventh would be of the opposite gender. See J. Wolowelsky and R. Grazi, "Sex Selection and Halachic Ethics: A Contemporary Discussion," *Tradition* 40 (2007), 45–52. See also Prof. Steinberg's "*Bechirat Min Ha-Ubar*," *Sefer Assia*, vol. 13, 293–306.

52. Jewish Law views the donation of bone marrow as commendable or even obligatory, such that it could be compelled even from a child, as this does not entail harmful or excessively painful procedures and enables fulfillment of the mitzvah of "do not stand idly by," similar to jumping into river to save drowning person (R. J.D. Bleich, "Compelling Tissue Donations," *Tradition* 27[4] [1993], 59–89). See discussions of this issue in chaps. 2C and 5C.

53. Judaism accepts the idea of having children for reasons other than fulfilling the commandment to be fruitful and multiply, even with the motivation of having children so that they will eventually take care of a person in his old age (*Yevamot* 64a; *Shulchan Arukh*, EH 154:6–7; *Arukh Ha-Shulchan*, EH 154:52–53). Having such a child thus does two good deeds, having a child and saving the other, which renders this a morally appropriate birth. In the words of R. Dr. Akiva Tatz, "In secular values, justification is necessary to conceive and bear a child; in Judaism, justification is necessary to desist from that activity" (*Dangerous Disease and Dangerous Therapy*, 87, n. 18). See also M. Broyde, "Pre-Implantation Genetic Diagnosis," 64: "Having a child is a wonderful, blessed activity; having a child to save the life of another child is an even more blessed activity. Such conduct should be encouraged rather than discouraged. Motives for genetic engineering ought not to be seen as so important."

54. Adults have the right to make decisions that are in the best interest of children, such as producing a child without a specific illness, but if PGD is used in a way that could harm a child, even if the parents believe it is not harmful, it would violate Jewish Law and should be prevented. See M. Broyde, "Pre-Implantation Genetic Diagnosis," 65, and "Child Custody and Jewish Law: A Review," *Journal of Halacha and Contemporary Society* 36 (1999), 21–46.

B. ASSISTED REPRODUCTIVE TECHNOLOGY:
Fertility Issues, Artificial Insemination, IVF

FERTILITY TESTING

Fertility treatment can be a stressful, awkward, and exhausting experience, and it can be very uncomfortable to put additional burdens on the couple and the medical staff. The guidelines in this chapter should thus be sensitively weighed with the needs of each and every couple and the particular fertility specialists they are working with, to carefully gauge which of the standards outlined below can be followed, and where there may be a need for some flexibility in Rabbinic guidance (see end notes to this chapter). In all cases, it is essential to provide support and show compassion to the couple bearing this difficult emotional (and financial) burden.

When a couple experiences difficulty getting pregnant, there are a number of halakhic issues that affect the methods and types of fertility testing that they may engage in. Ordinarily, evaluation of the husband and wife is simultaneous (or the husband is tested first to check the quality of his sperm). However, although fertility issues are often indeed the result of male factors,[1] the prohibition against wasting seed[2] may sometimes influence the order of fertility testing for observant Jewish couples, such that they may choose to first thoroughly evaluate the wife and ensure that other factors, such as proper intercourse education and the possibility of "halakhic infertility,"[3] have been addressed prior to testing the male sperm.[4]

When male factors are investigated, precedence is given to evaluating issues that do not require ejaculation in order to be examined, such as a varicocele.[5] Nevertheless, it is often necessary to evaluate sperm. Although masturbation, coitus interruptus (withdrawal), and ejaculating only for the sake of testing may be problematic according to Jewish Law, when the ultimate goal is procreation, they can be justified.[6] The following general list presents the order of preference, from least problematic to most problematic, according to Jewish Law:[7]

1. "PCT" (post coital test): Semen collection from the vagina following normal intercourse[8]
2. "SCD" (seminal collection device): Use of a special condom during intercourse. This is a medical grade condom that is not coated with spermicide. It is worn during intercourse to collect ejaculated semen. According to some this may be the most preferred method according to Jewish Law,[9] particularly if a tiny hole is made in the condom to mitigate concerns related to wasting seed.[10]
3. Coitus interruptus: During intercourse, the man withdraws and ejaculates into a utensil.[11]
4. A collecting receptacle placed intravaginally
5. Masturbation[12]
6. Removal directly from testicles[13]

Other halakhic considerations, such as those relating to Shabbat, may arise during fertility therapy. A couple should notify their doctor that prior to beginning ovulation induction, the timing of the therapy should be arranged to best assure that insemination, egg retrieval, and/or embryo transfer do not occur on Shabbat or festivals, if possible.[14] Furthermore, the laws of family purity govern when a couple may have sexual relations. Some standard treatments can lead to the *niddah* status, which frustrates the couple's ability to conceive. The couple's rabbi should be in contact with the doctor about this.[15] Many of these issues also arise with questions related to sperm banking.[16]

ARTIFICIAL INSEMINATION FROM THE HUSBAND (AIH)

Once a couple has been unable to have children naturally for some time[17] and a doctor has established with certainty that they will not be able to get pregnant naturally, they can begin attempting artificial insemination, presuming that expert opinion asserts that there is a strong likelihood that artificial insemination will be effective for this couple (i.e., there is no abnormality in the woman's reproductive capacity).[18] Artificial insemination of the husband's sperm (AIH) into his wife is usually recommended in situations in which his sperm count is too low to father a child through normal intercourse, or when he is impotent or experiences retrograde ejaculation, or if there is a reason that the woman cannot accept her husband's sperm, such as cervical or uterine abnormalities, scarring, tumors, or other anatomical disparities between the husband and wife. In such cases, AIH is necessary for a successful pregnancy to occur.

In AIH, a fine catheter (tube) is inserted through the cervix (the natural opening of the uterus) into the uterus (the womb) to deposit a sperm sample from the woman's husband directly into the uterus. Although some halakhic authorities forbade this procedure because they viewed it as wasting seed,[19] the majority view is that it is permissible because there is no wasting of seed when it is taken from the husband with the intention of impregnating his wife.[20] Since the goal is to have children, it does not matter if conception happens in the usual manner or not. Some argue that AIH fulfills the commandment to procreate,[21] and it is thus obligatory if there is no other option.[22]

Some authorities suggest that when utilizing AIH, it is preferable to procure a large quantity of sperm from the husband at one time. The sperm can then be stored and utilized multiple times until there is a successful pregnancy. This minimizes the number of procedures and consequent emissions of seed. However, it must be stipulated that the sperm bank will not use any of the man's sperm to impregnate another woman.[23]

IN VITRO FERTILIZATION (IVF)

IVF is the process of fertilization by manually combining an egg and sperm outside of the woman's body, in a laboratory dish. ("Vitro" means glass, referring to the petri dish in which the egg and sperm are combined.) The fertilized embryo(s) is then implanted in the uterus. IVF was originally intended to circumvent damaged or absent fallopian tubes (which connect ovaries to the uterus), but is now utilized in response to many fertility problems. Usually, multiple eggs are fertilized in order to increase the chances of a successful pregnancy. After a couple of days, once they develop to the stage of 2–8 cells, some of them are transferred to the uterus.

Although this technology is more advanced than AIH, most authorities argue that the halakhic issues concerning IVF are the same as those for AIH. Some additional concerns regarding IVF include determining parental identity, potential need for fetal reduction, and what to do with defective or excess embryos.[24] Many of the authorities who permit AIH for an infertile couple also permit IVF when used to combine a husband's sperm and his wife's egg.

When the technology was newer, many halakhic authorities forbade IVF.[25] However, with time it has become increasingly accepted.[26] Most authorities now permit IVF if a couple cannot conceive in any other way,[27] as long as care is taken to ensure that donor sperm is not mixed with that of the husband (see section on "Supervision" below).[28] According to these authorities, the husband (who supplied the sperm) is considered the father of the child for halakhic purposes,[29] and the woman is considered the mother.[30] According to most Rabbinic authorities, IVF fulfills the commandment to procreate.[31]

Many authorities also permit IVF for a husband and wife whenever a severe genetic disease is suspected, so that the fertilized egg can be tested to ensure that only "healthy" fertilized eggs are implanted (see Chapter 6A on PGD).[32]

One challenge related to IVF is the risk of multiple births due to the implantation of multiple fertilized embryos. For discussion of issues related to destruction of a fertilized egg before it has been implanted in the uterus, see the discussion of stem cell research in Chapter 6C. Regarding issues related to aborting some of the developed fetuses when they present a danger to the other fetuses, see the section on "Multifetal Pregnancy Reduction" in that chapter.

One way to minimize the risk of multiple births while maintaining patients' overall chances of becoming pregnant is by transferring only one embryo to IVF patients who have the highest chance of fertilization success, and are therefore are at the highest risk of conceiving twins. This is known as elective single embryo transfer (eSET), and it has been encouraged by some authorities in Jewish Law in order to minimize the need to discard fertilized embryos or abort a fetus at a later date.[33]

ARTIFICIAL INSEMINATION FROM A DONOR (AID) OTHER THAN THE HUSBAND

Artificial insemination of sperm from a donor (AID) is very similar to AIH, but the sperm comes from a man other than the woman's husband. AID is a matter of much more concern and debate in the eyes of Jewish Law than AIH.[34] Some authorities classify AID as violating the Torah prohibition of adultery.[35] Even those who do not rule that AID is adultery still forbid it because it can lead to a child inadvertently marrying a half-sibling (which is forbidden), and because they view it as improper, a corruption of the family structure, and leading to spiritual confusion and a desecration of God's name. There are also other halakhic concerns, such as issues related to levirate marriage and inheritance.[36] Therefore, according to virtually all opinions, AID from a Jewish donor is forbidden.[37]

However, since the concern about accidentally marrying a sibling is unlikely to arise if the donor is not Jewish,[38] some permit AID in a case of great need (such as emotional anguish) if a non-Jewish donor is utilized.[39] Outside of Israel, this would include utilizing an anonymous sperm bank.[40] Many authorities nevertheless forbid AID even from a donor who is not Jewish, for the other reasons mentioned above.[41] Many authorities also strongly discourage AID for a single woman for additional sociological reasons.[42] For further discussion of issues related to IVF using donor eggs, see Chapter 6D.[43]

SUPERVISION (HASHGACHAH)

Some Rabbinic authorities only permit artificial insemination/IVF if there is supervision and oversight of the process to ensure that the sperm is not mixed with another man's sperm.[44] Although governmental health agencies provide general oversight and regulate the credentials of practitioners, human error is always possible. The consequences of such mistakes in terms of Jewish Law would be of great significance for an observant couple (e.g., lineage, forbidden relationships, etc.), and additional supervision is therefore beneficial.[45] These authorities require Rabbinic oversight for the entire process, from the moment the sperm is submitted until the procedure is completely finished.[46] This oversight is commonly available in places with large observant communities, and it is generally provided by a representative of a rabbi who is reliable, God-fearing, and able to maintain strict confidentiality and work well with the lab staff.[47] For reasons of modesty, this representative is usually a woman.[48]

ENDNOTES

1. It is estimated that in 40% of cases, infertility is wholly or partially due to male factors. See Yoel Jakobovits, "A General Overview of Male Infertility," in R. Grazi, *Overcoming Infertility* (Toby Press, 2004), 227.

2. The prohibition of wasting seed is codified in *Shulchan Arukh*, EH 23:1.

3. "Halakhic infertility" refers to the situation that can result when a woman ovulates before it becomes permissible for her to immerse in a *mikveh* and thus have relations with her husband. See D. Zimmerman, *A Lifetime Companion to the Laws of Jewish Family Life* (Urim, 2011), 157–9.

4. *Nishmat Avraham*, EH 23:2 (239 in 3rd ed.); Zimmerman, *A Lifetime Companion to the Laws of Jewish Family Life*, 160. However, R. Nachum Rabinovitch told this author that since the ultimate goal is procreation, it is not considered "wasting seed" and a man may thus be tested at the same time as his wife. Of course, before evaluating a man's sperm, other factors should be ruled out first by performing a physical examination and taking a thorough medical history.

5. Varicocele is an abnormal dilation of veins within the spermatic cord, which has a deleterious effect on sperm production and can be corrected surgically and even by some non-surgical procedures. However, such interventions are usually insufficient, and there are often multiple factors in fertility problems.

6. Some Rabbinic authorities forbade emission of semen even for the purpose of testing it, including *Divrei Malkiel* 1:70, 3:91,

4:107, 5:157; *Maharsham* 3:268; *Dovev Meisharim* 1:20; *Maharash Engel* 6:75. However, much of their concern related to the uncertainty in their times whether such tests would be medically beneficial, whereas today we now know that they are. See R. Baniel, *Refuah Ke-Halakhah* (Ma'aneh Simcha Inst., under guidance of R. Moshe Schlesinger, 2014), 58. See also R. Dichovsky, *Techumin* 18, 161–9, and *Be-Mareh Ha-Bazak* 9:46, n. 13. Most contemporary authorities permit seminal procurement for analysis, since it is intended to facilitate procreation and thus not wasteful. See *Achiezer* 3:24(4); *Tzitz Eliezer* 7:48:1(7), 9:51:1; *Yabia Omer* 2:EH 1:7; *Iggerot Moshe*, EH 3:1:70, 2:16, EH 5:3:14, and EH 7:4:27; *Minchat Shlomo* 3:103(16); *Kovetz Teshuvot* of R. Elyashiv 2:78, 3:189; *Minchat Yitzchak* 3:108; *Shevet HaLevi* 7:205. Regarding the permissibility of an unmarried man who suspects potential fertility problems having his sperm tested before becoming engaged, see *Nishmat Avraham*, EH 23:2 (240–1 in 3rd ed.). For an overview of the issues involved and the various opinions related to testing sperm, see *Nishmat Avraham*, EH 23:2 (236–40 in 3rd ed.). R. Shlomo Zalman Auerbach rules that even when a man already has a male and female child (the halakhic minimum to fulfill the commandment to procreate), he is permitted to obtain sperm in order to fulfill the imperative of *"la-shevet yitzarah"* ("He fashioned it to be inhabited" [Isaiah 45:18], which some rule women are also obligated in; see Tosafot, *Bava Batra* 13a, s.v. *she-ne'emar*, and *Gittin* 41b, s.v. *lo tohu*), or when his wife is in significant psychological distress resulting from a desire for more children (*Nishmat Avraham*, EH 23:2 [238, 242 in 3rd ed.]; *Encyclopedia Hilkhatit Refu'it*, vol. 5, 375). See also *Refuah Ke-Halakhah*, 64–76, and R. J.D. Bleich, *Bioethical Dilemmas* (Ktav, 1998), 221–4, for analysis of the sources and reasons for the permissibility of ejaculating for this purpose.

7. *Tzitz Eliezer* 9:51(1); *Nishmat Avraham*, EH 23:2 (240 in 3rd ed.); R. Zilberstein, *Shiurei Torah Le-Rofim*, vol. 4, 298; *Be-Mareh Ha-Bazak* 9:46, n. 14; Zimmerman, *A Lifetime Companion to the Laws of Jewish Family Life*, 161. See also 161–2 for discussion of issues relating to evaluation of female factors.

8. R. Shlomo Zalman Auerbach recommends that the sperm retrieval then be done by a female medical professional (*Nishmat Avraham*, EH 23:2 [p. 112]). Many obstetricians report that this method is often ineffective because the sperm is difficult to retrieve and becomes weaker, and is thus of both inferior quality and quantity. On the preference for this method, see also the Satmar Rav in *Ha-Me'or*, 5724; *Kitvei Rav Henkin* 2; *Teshuvot Ivra* 73.

9. See *Achiezer* 3:24 (4); *Minchat Yitzchak* 3:108(6); *Zaken Aharon* 2:97; *Iggerot Moshe*, EH 1:70–1. Although some authorities in the past recommended coitus interuptus over use of a condom, today many authorities note that use of the condom is preferable. See *Refuah Ke-Halakhah*, 85, based on R. Feinstein, and *Shiurei Torah Le-Rofim*, vol. 4, 298. See also *Nishmat Avraham*, EH 23:2 [240 in 3rd ed.], *She'elat Ya'avetz* 1:43, *Mishpatei Uziel*, EH 42.

10. Many authorities recommend that when a condom is used, a small perforation should be made so that some sperm can enter the reproductive tract, and thus the act is not considered wasteful. See R. Neuwirth and R. Auerbach, cited in *Nishmat Avraham*, EH 1:6(2) (14 in

3rd ed.) and EH 23:2 (239 in 3rd ed.); *Shevet HaLevi* 5:109; R. Elyashiv, quoted in *Birkat Banim* 5:5. Indeed, use of such a condom has become the most common method of collecting sperm today (*Refuah Ke-Halakhah*, 82), and it is often the ideal option according to Jewish Law, particularly when sperm is collected for a treatment such as IUI, IVF, or cryopreservation.

11. R. Feinstein prefers this method to masturbation (*Iggerot Moshe*, EH 1:70–1 and EH 4:34(5). See also *Zaken Aharon* 1:67, 2:97, who writes that this is the preferred method. However, R. Feinstein is concerned that this method, as well as the first one, would be immodest if the intercourse must take place in the doctor's office (EH 1:70–1). Other authorities, however, permit intercourse in the doctor's office for this purpose as long as a special room is set aside and modesty is preserved (A. Friedlander, "Rabbinical Supervision During Fertility Therapy," *Overcoming Infertility*, 393).

12. Although it is the worst option halakhically, masturbation by hand is defended when its purpose is for procreation and there is no other option; see *Achiezer* 3:24(4); *Zaken Aharon* 2:97; *Minchat Shlomo* 3:103(16). The *poskim* encourage utilizing some kind of mechanical stimulation instead of masturbating by hand, unless nothing else works. See *Iggerot Moshe*, EH 1:71 and EH 2:18 for a detailed discussion of this issue. R. Feinstein prefers other methods of sperm retrieval because he rules that masturbation violates two prohibitions, that of wasting seed and "*lo tinaf*" ("do not commit adultery"). R. Elyashiv rules similarly in his *Kovetz Teshuvot* 2:74, 3:189.

13. A testicular biopsy is sometimes necessary. This is not considered a problem related to sterilization (*sirus*) because it does not result in infertility and it heals completely. Since sperm removed in this

process is undeveloped, it is not subject to restrictions on sperm emission (*Nishmat Avraham*, EH 23:2 [243–9 in 3rd ed.]; *Minchat Yitzchak* 3:108:7, *Iggerot Moshe*, EH 2 3:2).

14. Friedlander, "Rabbinical Supervision," 402–3; *Nishmat Avraham*, OH 330:7 (564 in 3rd ed.). R. Asher Weiss rules that Rabbinic prohibitions can be violated on Shabbat for the purposes of IVF (personal conversation, Summer 2015). For an in-depth discussion of fertility treatment on Shabbat and festivals, see *Refuah Ke-Halakhah*, 95–125 and R. Weitzman, "Fertility Treatment on the Sabbath and Festivals" in Grazi, *Overcoming Infertility* (Toby Press, 2004), 369-89.

15. For a thorough discussion of issues related to early ovulation, see *Encyclopedia Hilkhatit Refu'it*, vol. 2, 561. R. Feinstein (*Iggerot Moshe*, EH 2:18) writes that if the concern is that the woman will ovulate before going to the *mikveh*, it is permissible to inseminate beforehand, since the prohibition is only against intercourse before going to the *mikveh*, not the injection of sperm. (This is based on the ruling that a woman can sit on her husband's sheets while she is in a state of *niddah* and we are not concerned that she will get pregnant.) The woman should not go to the *mikveh* before the procedure – even after waiting the biblically mandated seven-day period – because this could lead to mistakes; the couple might have intercourse afterwards, which would certainly be forbidden.

16. For example, in cases in which a patient will receive radiation to the testes or chemotherapy for conditions such as Hodgkin's disease or non-Hodgkin's lymphoma, which may result in sterility, many permit (but do not obligate) men to have their semen frozen and stored in sperm banks beforehand, depending on how the sperm is collected (*Binyan Av* 2:60; see Bleich, *Bioethical Dilemmas*, vol. 1, 227–31, for an interesting explanation).

However, if the man is not married, some prohibit this procedure because it cannot fulfill the commandment to procreate (*Binyan Av* 2:60). See also *Nishmat Avraham*, EH 23:2 (241 in 3rd ed.), who quotes R. Auerbach as arguing that there is no distinction between married and unmarried men in fulfilling this obligation, although neither is obligated to freeze sperm, but he discourages unmarried men from doing so. See also Bleich, *Bioethical Dilemmas*, vol. 1, 231–2, and *Encyclopedia of Jewish Medical Ethics*, 556–7 and 574–6, for issues related to lineage when seed is taken from a deceased donor.

17. Some rule that a couple can do this only after at least 10 years of infertility and if they will otherwise get divorced (*Teshuvot Marasham* 3:268; *Bnei Banim* 1:32; *Minchat Yitzchak* 1:50; *Yabia Omer* 2:EH 1). Others rule that five years is sufficient (*Iggerot Moshe*, EH 2:16). However, R. Feinstein has also been quoted as ruling that a man may have his sperm tested, even if he already has a son, once four infertile years have passed; see R. Aaron Felder, *Rishumei Aharon*, vol. 1, 74. Others require only two years of trying (*Chazon Ish*, quoted in *Nishmat Avraham*, EH 23[2]). Others rule that each case must be judged individually. Although couples should not rush to a fertility doctor right away, according to this opinion, if they have reason to believe that there is a medical problem or expert medical opinion has determined that they cannot get pregnant via natural intercourse, they may utilize this procedure right away and there is no need to wait (*Tzitz Eliezer* 9:51[1]; *Shevet HaLevi* 3:186, 8:251[10]. See also *Tzitz Eliezer* 15:45 and *Refuah Ke-Halakhah*, 48.)

18. Some rule that if it is certain that a couple cannot get pregnant, they may begin attempting fertility treatment before waiting 10 years (*Shevet HaLevi* 8:251(10); *Encyclopedia Hilkhatit Refu'it*, vol. 2, 558). This is true assuming

that medical experts have confirmed that artificial insemination may be effective, because the issue is not the woman's physiology, and the husband's semen can therefore effectively impregnate her in this manner (see previous note).

19. *Divrei Malkiel* 4:107–8; *Mishpatei Uziel* 2:EH 19; *Yaskil Avdi* 5:EH 10; *Chazon Ish*, quoted in *Tzitz Eliezer* 9:51(4:6); the Steipler Gaon, quoted by R. Chaim Kanievsky in *Ratz KaTzvi* on EH, 12; *Chelkat Yaakov* 1:24; *Encylcolpedia of Jewish Medical Ethics*, vol. 2, 533. These authorities argue that emitting seed in this way is wasteful, even though it may be used at a later time to impregnate the man's wife, because it may not impregnate her or there might be a mistake and the doctor will have to ask for another sample, and certainly some of the seed will not be utilized even if she does become pregnant. Furthermore, these authorities view the prohibition of wasting seed as independent of one's intentions. They are also concerned about the possibility of error, such as the mixing of the husband's sperm with that of another man. Similarly, those who maintain that only the birth of a child as a result of natural intercourse serves to fulfill the commandment to procreate are less likely to permit a procedure whereby sperm is ejaculated when it is not in order to fulfill a mitzvah (see Bleich, *Bioethical Dilemmas*, vol. 1, 250). Some also forbid this because they rule that the child will not be related to his father in this case (*Teshuvot Ve-Hanhagot* 2:670. See also 3:407, where he writes that the Brisker Rav did not prohibit AIH, but also would not say that it is permitted, so that people would not take the matter lightly.).

20. *Maharsham* 3:268; *Har Tzvi*, quoted in *Otzar Ha-Poskim* 23:1(1:17); *Zaken Aharon* 2:97; *She'elat Ya'avetz* 1:43; *Minchat Yitzchak* 1:50; *Yabia Omer* 2:EH 1; R. Auerbach in *Minchat Shlomo* 3:98, and *Noam* 1 (5718), 154, and *Nishmat Avraham*, EH 1:6 (13 in 3rd ed.). R.

Auerbach concludes that AIH may also be done while the wife is a *niddah*; since there are no relations taking place, see *Nishmat Avraham*, EH 1:6 (20 in 3rd ed.) as well as the opinions of other *poskim* (pp. 14–17, though in *Ma'adanei Shlomo* [326], R. Auerbach is quoted as saying that if possible it is better not to impregnate the woman during her *niddah* period). See also *Iggerot Moshe*, EH 1:70–71, 2:11, 18, 4:35(5); *Seridei Eish* 3:5; *Nishmat Avraham*, EH 1:6(2) (11–14 in 3rd ed.); *Encyclopedia of Jewish Medical Ethics*, 554–5; Bleich, *Bioethical Dilemmas*, vol. 1, 220. According to some, this is true even if the couple has already fulfilled the commandment to procreate (*Nishmat Avraham*, EH 23:2), but others question this (*Binyan Av* 2:60 [11], and some forbid the procedure once a couple has already had a boy and a girl (*Shevet HaLevi* 8:251[11]). See the discussion in *Nishmat Avraham*, EH 1:6 (1114).

21. *Tzitz Eliezer* (15:45) rules that AIH fulfills the commandment to "be fruitful and multiply," but IVF does not. However, R. A. Nevenzahl argues that since IVF has become so common, it has become a natural method of conception, and even the *Tzitz Eliezer* would agree that it fulfills the commandment to procreate (*Assia* 34 [5743]; *Nishmat Avraham*, EH 1:6 [28–9 in 3rd ed.]; see *Ratz KaTzvi* on EH, 35). R. Yaakov Ariel also writes that both forms of artificial insemination fulfill the commandment to "be fruitful and multiply" (*Be-Ohalah Shel Torah* 1:69). Similarly, *Har Tzvi*, EH 4, rules that because the father begins this process with the intention of having children, it fulfills the commandment to procreate and is thus not considered "wasting seed." *Shevet HaLevi* 8:251 only permits AIH when it is being done to fulfill this commandment, but not if the couple already have children and simply want more. See *Ratz KaTzvi* on EH, 25–32; R.Shilat, *Refuah, Halakhah, Ve-Kavanot Ha-Torah*, 182–6, for analysis

of the commandment to "be fruitful and multiply" and if artificial insemination can fulfill it, based on the questions of if the commandment is fulfilled via intercourse or simply by having a child, and the ramifications of a woman being impregnated from sperm floating in a bath and not directly from a man.

22. Although some ruled that a couple is not required to utilize AIH in order to become pregnant if they do not want to or cannot afford the procedure (R. Auerbach, *Noam* 1, 148; *Ratz KaTzvi* on EH, 36–37), many now rule that a couple is indeed obligated to attempt to become pregnant in this manner if they cannot in any other way (*Teshuvot Ve-hanhagot* 6:241; *Ratz KaTzvi* on EH, 35–38).

23. R. Drori, *Techumin* 1, 288; Rabinovitch, *Techumin* 2, 511.

24. R. J.D. Bleich, "Mitochondrial DNA Replacement: How Many Mothers?" *Tradition* 48:4 (Winter 2015): 66.

25. *Tzitz Eleizer* 15:45 (and *Assia 5*, 84–92). The *Tzitz Eliezer*'s arguments in opposition (written in 1981, when IVF was still very new) included the concern that artificial insemination would break down the traditional family structure and cohesion, leading to immorality and wantonly mixing seed (thus possibly allowing siblings to accidentally marry each other). Furthermore, he argued that AIH is better than IVF because the husband's sperm is introduced directly into his wife's uterus, so that the process occurs naturally and failure to fertilize the egg does not mean sperm was wasted or that anything different from normal relations occurred. In contrast, in the case of IVF, the fertilization takes place in a laboratory, making the entire process artificial, and if it does not work, then the seed was emitted in vain. He further argued that AIH is often used due to male infertility problems, so that he must produce sperm in a different manner, whereas IVF is often used due

to female infertility, giving the husband less permission to produce sperm outside of normal relations. Moreover, because IVF is so artificial, it might not fulfill the mitzvah of procreation (as the artificial environment destroys the relationship between the woman and her egg). Additionally, while strict supervision is possible in AIH, since IVF takes much longer, it is very difficult to supervise properly. For these reasons, the *Tzitz Eliezer* does not view IVF as fulfillment of the commandment to procreate. He writes that neither of the parents is considered to be the child's parent according to Jewish Law, and he therefore forbids IVF.

R. J.D. Bleich, *Bioethical Dilemmas*, vol. 1, 211-13, noted in 1998 that research was not yet conclusive regarding whether IVF is completely safe or whether it may pose some danger to the child born via this procedure at some point in the future. R. Bleich rules that until we can prove its long-term safety, IVF would be forbidden. (On the health effects of children born via IVF, see *Nishmat Avraham*, EH 1:6 [42–43 in 3rd ed.].) R. Bleich (209–11) also raises the issue that in IVF, a number of ova are fertilized and many are not re-implanted into the mother, so their disposal could present a problem. He argues, however, that during the first 40 days after conception the prohibition is much less severe, especially since the embryo is so small as to be unrecognizable, and it therefore may be destroyed.

Other authorities prohibit IVF for moral and ethical reasons, although they admit that it is not strictly forbidden by Jewish Law; see R. Amsel, *Ha-Ma'or* 30(5) (Sivan-Tammuz, 5738/1978): 44-45; R. Isaacson, *Ha-Ma'or* 30(6) (Av-Elul, 5738/1978): 16. For a philosophical discussion of the ethical considerations related to IVF, such as tampering with God's creation, family harmony, etc., see *Encyclopedia of Jewish Medical Ethics*, 575–6.

26. *Ratz KaTzvi* on EH, 14; personal communication with R. Asher Weiss. R. Aryeh Katz of the Puah Institute argues that today the *Tzitz Eliezer* would permit IVF, since his concerns were primarily related to switching or making mistakes with sperm, and those issues have been largely resolved with careful supervision (R. Katz, *Techumin* 36, 218, n. 18).

The move towards acceptance of IVF over time can be seen in the rulings of R. Sternbuch. In 1991, he wrote that it is totally prohibited because of wasting seed and breakdown of the holiness and purity of lineage (*Teshuvot Ve-Hanhagot* 2:689, 3:406-7). In 1997, he slightly reduced his opposition, but still avoiding permitting it (ibid., 3:406-7), and in 2002 he softened his prohibition further (ibid., 4:285), and then more so in 2009 (ibid. 5:317). By 2014, he wrote that he had changed his mind and IVF is now not only not forbidden, but *obligatory* and fulfills the commandment to procreate. He writes that the Steipler Goan, who forbade IVF, would likely permit it given the situation today (ibid., 6:241). See discussion of this and quote of R. Mendel Shafran in *Ratz KaTzvi* on EH, 21, who explains that the rulings changed in this matter, and other similar areas, because it is important for authorities in Jewish Law to cautiously see how new technology works and what it leads to before permitting it.

27. Steinberg, *Encyclopedia of Jewish Medical Ethics*, 581. For a summary, see *Be-Mareh Ha-Bazak* 5:104.

28. R. Auerbach, quoted in *Nishmat Avraham*, EH 1:6(2) (13, 29 in 3rd ed.) and *Shulchan Shlomo, Erkhei Refuah*, vol. 3, 82. *Nishmat Avraham*, EH 1:6(5) (29 in 3rd ed.) quotes R. Elyashiv as permitting IVF for a married couple as long as there is complete supervision. R. Nevenzahl also permits IVF (*Nishmat Avraham*, EH 1:6 (28–29 in 3rd ed.), arguing that if IVF is forbidden, then the man certainly will not fulfill the obligation to procreate

and may either become depressed or end their marriage, which would be a much worse outcome. He feels that we should not prohibit these young couples from fulfilling their strong desire to have children. Furthermore, he argues that a goal of marriage is to create children to serve God, and IVF represents an attempt to do that, so it should not be viewed as wasting seed. He goes on to argue that even though this is not the traditional manner of becoming pregnant, it is basically still producing children in the natural way, since the entire fetal development takes place in utero. The process simply starts in a different place, and it should thus still fulfill the commandment to procreate (see also R. Nevenzahl, *Assia* 5 [5746/1986], 92–93). R. Ovadia Yosef also permitted IVF (*Yabia Omer* 8:EH 21:4), arguing that the children are considered the children of their parents according to Jewish Law, the parents fulfill the commandment to procreate, and that IVF may even be done when the woman is a *niddah*. R. Yosef also rules that there are no concerns related to illegitimacy, particularly if the couple's infertility results from early ovulation, because there is no forbidden intercourse taking place. Moreover, he argues, retrieving semen in this manner does not constitute wasting seed, because it is used to impregnate. Even though some of the sperm is wasted, this also happens during natural intercourse. R. Asher Weiss told this author that IVF is permitted, but not obligatory.

29. See the summary of rulings in *Nishmat Avraham*, EH 1:6 (18–19 in 3rd ed.).

30. Most authorities conclude that the sperm donor is considered the father, as well as the determiner of status (i.e., *kohen, levi*, etc.), and with regard to the laws of mourning, which relatives he or she is forbidden to marry, and inheritance (see *Yabia Omer* 2:EH 1, 8; 8:EH 21; *Minchat Yitzchak* 1:50). See also some other opinions in Bleich, *Bioethical Dilemmas*, vol. 1, 226-7.

31. R. Baniel, *Refuah Ke-Halakhah*, 40, argues that the majority of Rabbinic authorities maintain that artificial insemination and IVF fulfill the commandment to procreate. See the summary and analysis in *Be-Mareh Ha-Bazak* 5:104, 9:46, fn. 13. See R. Nevenzahl, *Assia* 5 (5746/1986): 92-93; *Shevet HaLevi* 9:209; *Minchat Yitzchak* 1:50; letter signed by R. Elyashiv and R. Ovadia Yosef, quoted in *Ratz KaTzvi on Even HaEzer*, 21; *Teshuvot Ve-Hanhagot* 6:241. For analysis of why IVF fulfills the command to procreate, see R. Shilat, *Refuah, Halakhah, Ve-Kavanot Ha-Torah,* 217-19.

Others rule that use of IVF does not fulfill the commandment to procreate, but does fulfill the verse *"la-shevet"* (R. Girshuni, *Or Ha-Mizrach* 92 [Tishrei 5839/1979], 15-21). However, the *Tzitz Eliezer* (15:45) rules that it fulfills neither. R. Zilberstein rules that artificial insemination does not fulfill the commandment to procreate (*Shiurei Torah Le-Rofim*, vol. 4, 278-81; see 327 and 339 for R. Zilberstein's general opposition to artificial insemination in most, but not all, situations). See also Bleich, *Bioethical Dilemmas*, vol. 1, 207, for a discussion related to the view that IVF does not fulfill the commandment to procreate and is thus not a mitzvah, but may still be done. See 241, n. 10, where he points out that the requirement to procreate only requires one to engage in sexual activity within the context of a marital relationship, but assisted procreation is not obligated. Although Jewish Law sometimes demands extraordinary heroic measures to prolong life, to generate life it requires only that which is ordinary, natural, and normal, and its fulfillment requires undertaking no risks (243).

R. Shlomo Zalman Auerbach also ruled that while IVF is permissible, a couple who is unable to have children is not obligated to pursue IVF in order to fulfill the commandment to procreate, since the Torah only obligates one to attempt naturally and not necessarily through such means. However, there is also an obligation for one to make his wife happy, and assuming that having a child would make her very happy, one should attempt as much as possible to do so (*Shulchan Shlomo, Erkhei Refuah*, vol. 3, 99, n. 7). More recently, Israeli Sephardic Chief Rabbi Yitzchak Yosef has ruled that IVF is now part of the natural effort one must engage in to fulfill the commandment to procreate (quoted by R. Aryeh Katz, *Techumin* 36, 215, n. 6).

32. R. Zilberstein, *Assia* 51-52 (Iyar 5772/1992): 92-93. R. Zilberstein also permits discarding the "sick" fertilized eggs.

33. R. Bleich, *Judaism and Healing*, 95.

34. Secular ethicists also raise more concerns about AID than AIH. For example, when the ethics committee of the American Fertility Society approved procedures involving donor gametes, it recorded a dissent on the involvement of third-party donors because this: (1) severs procreation from the marital bond; (2) brings into the world a child with no bond of origin; (3) encourages adultery because it makes accepting the sperm of another man acceptable; (4) marks a move towards eugenics; (5) makes sterility a disvalue and childbearing a value, thus threatening the value of marriage and family (*Overcoming Infertility*, 417).

35. This is based on Lev. 18:20 and the commentary of Nachmanides on that verse. Many authorities note that although all other sexual prohibitions in the Torah forbid penetration rather than ejaculation, this verse formulates the prohibition as depositing semen into another woman. This is because a primary concern about adultery is uncertain paternal identity, involving not only the act of intercourse, but also the deposit of semen into the genital tract of a married woman by someone other than her husband. See in particular

Tzitz Eliezer 9:51(4); *Divrei Yoel* 107–110, *Otzar Ha-Poskim*, EH 1:1:42; *Shevet HaLevi* 3:175. See also *Yabia Omer* 2:EH 1(9). See also Bleich, *Bioethical Dilemmas*, 208, where he articulates concerns related to violation of marital bonds, and 244–7, related to AID and adultery; See also *Nishmat Avraham* 1:6 (20–21 in 3rd ed.); *Encyclopedia Hilkhatit Refu'it*, vol. 2, 567, n. 88.

36. *Encyclopedia Hilkhatit Refu'it*, vol. 2, 567, 569, 572, as well as other problems listed there. *Nishmat Avraham*, EH 1:6 (22–23 in 3rd ed.) quotes opinions ruling that AID is strongly prohibited, even though it is not adultery and the child is not illegitimate or is only possibly illegitimate. The Satmar Rav raises the concern that permitting AID encourages sperm donation, which he prohibits (*Ha-Ma'or* [Av–Elul 5724], quoted in *Otzar Ha-Poskim*, vol. 9, 127).

The *Tzitz Eleizer* lists the following concerns regarding AID: (1) It is immoral, profanes the purity of the Jewish family, and introduces the seed of a person with potentially poor traits, and if the donor is not Jewish, it cuts off the chain of connection from child to father. (2) The wife may be forbidden to her husband as a result of AID. (3) If this is done without the husband's knowledge, the husband may force his wife to accept a divorce even if the AID was unsuccessful, and he should be advised to do so (and she will lose her *ketubah*; see also *Shevet HaLevi* 3:175). (4) The child born from AID may be considered illegitimate and thus cannot marry a born Jew. (5) There is concern that one may unknowingly come to marry his sister. (6) It entails forbidden emission of seed.

37. *Encyclopedia Hilkhatit Refu'it*, vol. 2, 566.

38. According to Jewish Law, a child's religious status is conferred via his or her mother. If the father is not Jewish, Jewish Law recognizes no official connection between the child and the non-Jewish father. The child is thus not related to his or her biological father's other children, and is therefore not forbidden from marrying them. This is true even in the case of natural impregnation, and certainly so here (*Encyclopedia Hilkhatit Refu'it*, vol. 2, 580). Everyone agrees that a baby born from a Jewish mother and non-Jewish sperm is Jewish and that there is thus no need for conversion, and such a female baby can marry a Kohen (ibid., 582). However, there is debate regarding whether the wife is required to separate from her husband for three months to be sure that it is not her husband's child (ibid., 582, nn. 155, 156).

39. *Iggerot Moshe*, EH 1:71, 2:11, 18. In EH 1:10, 71, R. Feinstein explains that the child would not be illegitimate because that status can only be conferred via forbidden intercourse, and he argues that adultery is only committed via penetration. (This is based on the ruling of the *Smak*, quoted by *Taz*, YD 195:7, that a woman may sit on her husband's bed sheets while she is a *niddah* and we are not concerned that she will become impregnated with his sperm since there is no forbidden intercourse; the child is completely legitimate. However, the *Smak* points out that we are concerned about the sperm of another man because the child may eventually marry his sister.) R. Feinstein also notes (EH 1:71) that the Torah extols raising an orphan, and no one is concerned that the adopted orphan will mistakenly be considered the child of the new parent and marry a sibling. Furthermore, although some (R. Breisch, *Chelkat Yaakov* 3) argue that artificial insemination is problematic because it confuses genealogy, and it thus requires a couple to abstain from intercourse for 90 days prior to conception in order to have clarity about the fatherhood of the child, R. Feinstein argues that this is not

necessary if the husband is infertile (2:71). It should be noted that in some of his later writings on the topic (EH 70, 71), R. Feinstein writes that separating is not necessary because neither the man nor the woman is fulfilling the commandment to procreate, and such separation could cause jealousy and marital strife, and is thus not a good thing. See also the discussion in *Encyclopedia Hilkhatit Refu'it*, vol. 2, 581, n. 153; *Nishmat Avraham*, EH 1:6 (26–27 in 3rd ed.); *Shulchan Shlomo, Hilkhot Niddah Ve-Tevillah*, 181.

40. R. Feinstein (*Iggerot Moshe* EH 1:10) rules that if the sperm comes from an anonymous sperm bank, then outside of Israel we can assume the donor was not Jewish. (However, if the sperm of the husband is mixed with that of a donor, we assume it is the sperm of the donor that impregnates, and it is thus an act of forbidden wasting of seed by the husband; see Steinberg, *Encyclopedia of Jewish Medical Ethics*, 584–5).

41. See *Yabia Omer* 8:EH 21(5); *Nishmat Avraham*, EH 1:6 (26–27 in 3rd ed.); *Encyclopedia Hilkhatit Refu'it*, vol. 2, 581. On the debate over the permissibility of AID, see R. Shilat, *Refuah, Halakhah Ve-kavanot Ha-Torah*, 189–205, 213.

42. Although the fact that the woman is single avoids many of the issues with AID, such as adultery and illegitimacy concerns, the procedure is still prohibited by many authorities because it undermines family norms, out of concern for the best interest of the child, fear that the child may accidentally marry a sibling from his or her unknown father, and because people may think the woman behaved inappropriately, in addition to other concerns (*Tzitz Eliezer* 15:4; *Nishmat Avraham*, EH 1:13(10) [51–52 in 3rd ed.]; *Ratz KaTzvi on Even HaEzer*, 103–13; *Encyclopedia Hilkhatit Refu'it*, vol. 2, 585; see there for solutions). Nevertheless, if a woman does this, the child is considered

legitimate by Jewish Law and should be embraced by the community (letter from R. Ralbag, published in *Ratz KaTzvi on Even HaEzer*, 112–3). See also analysis of this issue in R. Shilat, *Refuah, Halakhah Ve-Kananot Ha-Torah*, 209–12, 214. See also the extensive writings on this topic by R. Yuval Cherlow, who (under specific circumstances) permits a 37-year-old single woman who has tried very hard to get married but has been unsuccessful to receive artificial insemination: https://www.ypt.co.il/beit-hamidrash/view.asp?id=4442 and https://www.ypt.co.il/beit-ha midrash/view.asp?id=4452. See also http://www.responsafortoday.com/vol3/7.pdf and extensive discussion in D. Lichtenstein, *Headlines 2*, (OU Press, 2017), chp. 10.

43. See also *Enyclopedia of Jewish Medical Ethics*, 577.

44. R. Auerbach, *Nishmat Avraham*, EH 1:6(2) (13 in 3rd ed.); *Encyclopedia Hilkhatit Refu'it*, vol. 2, 559, n. 4; *Yabia Omer* 2:EH 1(13); R. Elyashiv, quoted in *Nishmat Avraham*, EH 1:6 (29 in 3rd ed.). *Nishmat Avraham*, EH 1:6(2) (14 in 3rd ed.) writes that the most essential thing is to choose reliable, God-fearing doctors to carry out the procedure. The Lubavitcher Rebbe also permitted artificial insemination and required supervision (*Assia* 61–62 [5758]; *Ratz KaTzvi on Even HaEzer*, 418). *Tzitz Eliezer* 9:51(4:6), 19:57, also rules that if the doctor becomes aware that seed was mixed, he or she is obligated to inform the couple. Many rule that supervision is not a stringency, but a requirement (R. B. Dovid, *Beit Hillel* 31, 76; *Ratz KaTzvi on Even HaEzer*, 419). Others have argued that supervision is a preferable stringency, but that it is not obligatory today. R. Ariel, *Ohalah Shel Torah* 1:71, argues that R. Auerbach also felt it is preferable but not obligatory, because for modesty reasons the supervision cannot oversee every moment of the process, and we indeed rely on the father's

testimony that the sperm is his; see *Ratz KaTzvi on Even HaEzer*, 432–6.

Others have argued (see ibid., 436–7) that the Rabbinic authorities who required supervision wrote most of their rulings in the 1950s, when this technology was still new, mistakes were more common, and there was less oversight then there is today. Furthermore, today it is possible to do DNA genetic testing to determine accuracy. Therefore, R. Asher Weiss rules that today supervision is technically not required. However, since this is such an important matter, it is a very good thing to do (published in *Ratz KaTzvi on Even HaEzer*, 428–9). Indeed, even today many Rabbinic authorities do require supervision (ibid., 439–441), and the emotional sensitivities and tragedy of making a mistake make additional supervision especially valuable (ibid., 440–1). For discussion of how IVF clinics in Israel initially collaborated with Rabbinic supervision, see Martha Kahn, *Reproducing Jews* (Duke Univ. Press, 2000).

45. Some feel that DNA testing is sufficient to ensure that gamete switching does not occur and that the lab workers will be meticulous. They also point to the authority of the law to prosecute. However, since the consequences of these issues are very severe, they require the strictest supervision possible to ensure certainty (Friedlander, "Rabbinical Supervision," 397).

46. See Friedlander, "Rabbinical Supervision," 391. This includes all lab procedures (including ensuring that specimens are double sealed and stored in a special locked location and that all lab materials are inspected), semen analysis, sperm washing, sperm freezing for the purpose of using in the near or distant future, egg retrieval for IVF, in vitro insemination of the oocyte, intracytoplasmic sperm injection, embryo transfer, cryopreservation of sperm or embryos, and washing of sperm in preparation for intrauterine insemination. See also the outline in *Ratz KaTzvi on Even HaEzer*, 416.

47. Friedlander, "Rabbinical Supervision," 397–8.

48. Regarding the validity of using a woman to serve as a supervisor for this task, see *Teshuvot Minchat Asher* 2:135; *Teshuvot Ve-Hanhagot* 6:242; *Ratz KaTzvi on Even HaEzer*, 421–31.

C. ABORTION, PREGNANCY REDUCTION, AND STEM CELL RESEARCH

INTRODUCTION AND BACKGROUND

Although there are certain specific situations in which Jewish Law permits or even requires abortion, abortion is generally forbidden. Like most cases in Jewish Law, there are various multifaceted factors that must be assessed in reaching a Jewish legal determination in regard to abortion. Thus, Rabbinic consultation must be sought on a case-by-case basis, particularly because this issue may include the taking of a life (or at the very least a potential life), a serious moral offense that must be treated with utmost reverence and caution.[1]

I will therefore provide an overview of the background sources that form the basis for the halakhic discussion related to abortion, as well as some of the cases and factors that play a role in specific cases in which the question may arise most acutely, but I will limit my discussion to general principles rather than concrete directives, which are best provided by a competent Rabbinic authority on a case-by-case basis.

PRIMARY SOURCES

Jewish tradition emphasizes the sanctity of life and does not grant us complete autonomy over our bodies, particularly not that of an unborn child. Jewish sources do not allow wanton destruction of a fetus. Indeed, many sources stress the importance and potential of a fetus, and thus require great care in order to avoid harming it in any way.[2] At the same time, Jewish Law does not view a fetus as equal in value to a living, born person.[3]

One of the primary sources frequently quoted on this topic is a *mishnah* that states that if a woman is suffering from dangerous labor and her life is threatened, "The fetus must be cut up in her womb and brought out piecemeal, for her life takes precedence over its life." The *mishnah* concludes, however, that once the fetus's head or majority of its body have exited the womb, "it must not be touched, for the claim of one life cannot supersede that of another life."[4] This teaching assumes that aborting a fetus is prohibited unless the abortion is performed in order to save the mother's life.

Two primary, and perhaps contradictory, reasons are given for this. One suggestion is that the fetus may be aborted in certain cases because it is classified as one who is pursuing another. Thus, one must kill the fetus in self-defense to save the life of the mother, who is being pursued.[5] This approach assumes that abortion is actually murder and abortion is not sanctioned, but it is considered justified murder in certain very limited lifesaving cases, specifically when the mother's life is directly threatened as a result of the pregnancy.[6] Once the child is born, however, we do not know who is chasing whom – that is, if the mother's life is threatening that of the baby or vice versa – and we must therefore treat both lives equally.[7] The mother's life has priority over the fetus's life until it is born, when they become equally persons under the law.

A different reason suggested for the permission to kill the fetus in this case is that until the fetus is born, it is not classified as a human being.[8] According to this reason, abortion is not considered murder, and it can thus be permitted in certain cases of tremendous need or danger, not only to save the mother's life.[9]

Another classical source, potentially much more restricting, is the Talmudic interpretation of the verse, "Whoever sheds the blood of man within another man, his blood shall be shed" (Gen. 9:6). The Talmud suggests that a "man within another man" refers to an embryo in its mother's womb.[10] Although this commandment was given before the formation of the Jewish People, and thus specifically directed to people who are not Jewish, there is a halakhic principle that no action forbidden to a non-Jew can be permitted to a Jew, as the Torah requires a less specific moral standard of non-Jews.[11] This source thus serves as a source for the prohibition against abortion for Jews as well,[12] leading to the conclusion of most decisors that abortion is biblically prohibited.[13]

CATEGORIZATION OF THE PROHIBITION

Although some rule that abortion is rabbinically prohibited, most authorities rule that abortion is a biblical prohibition.[14] Which biblical prohibition it falls under makes a significant difference. There are a number of suggestions as to the precise nature of the prohibition against abortion. These range from:

- murder[15]
- ancillary to homicide (*abizrayhu de-retzicha*)[16]
- tort/damage (the prohibition of injuring or wounding human beings, including oneself)[17]
- the obligation to preserve potential life and the corollary prohibition of negligence[18]

The ruling related to the permissibility of abortion in various situations often hinges upon how the prohibition is categorized. If it is concluded that abortion constitutes murder, then in most circumstances, one would be obligated to avoid transgressing it at all costs. However, if the prohibition is based primarily on one of the other concerns, there are potentially more situations of great need in which abortion could possibly be justified.[19]

STAGES OF PREGNANCY

There is a Talmudic notion that prior to forty days of gestation, an embryo is viewed as mere liquid because it is not fully formed before that point.[20] Aborting a fetus during this stage of pregnancy is thus sometimes treated with more leniency in cases of great need,[21] and sometimes even further into the pregnancy than that.[22] However, while this stage of pregnancy may be relevant to those who consider abortion homicide or damaging, for example, it may be irrelevant to those who classify it as ancillary homicide or protection of potential life, which may apply to the pre-forty-day embryo as well.[23] There are therefore decisors who reject the distinction between early stages of pregnancy in most cases, viewing abortion as equally forbidden at any stage of pregnancy.[24]

THERAPEUTIC ABORTION AND MULTIFETAL PREGNANCY REDUCTION

Jewish Law does not sanction abortion as post facto birth control or for social, financial, or other such reasons.[25] Since some authorities categorize abortion as a Torah prohibition of murder, they conclude that it can only be permitted if there is near certainty that the mother will lose her life if the fetus is not aborted.[26] Others – particularly those who view the prohibition as Rabbinic,[27] categorize abortion not as murder but as improper emission of seed (referred to as "ancillary to homicide" above),[28] or maintain that it violates the prohibition against wounding[29] – are more lenient in cases of grave necessity, even if the mother's life is not in danger.[30] Many of the questions dealt with by Rabbinic authorities relate to maternal health, including emotional well-being[31] and various complex scenarios.[32]

Most abortion questions that arise today do not relate to a need to abort a fetus in order to save the mother. Rather, it is more common to encounter concerns that result from being informed by advanced testing that a fetus may have some sort of illness or disability, such as a genetic mutation.[33] There are circumstances – such as diagnosis of anencephaly, hydrocephaly, or Tay-Sachs in the fetus – when fetal indications may warrant performing an abortion,[34] although some authorities do not permit abortions even under these circumstances.[35] The new technology of pre-implantation genetic diagnosis (PGD) can help couples avoid conceiving a child with a genetic defect and having to abort (see Chapter 6A).

Sometimes, a woman pregnant with multiple fetuses may require a procedure called "fetal reduction," in which some of the fetuses will be aborted, either to protect her life or to enable some of the other fetuses to survive.[36] This is sometimes permitted, depending on the situation and amount of danger involved.[37]

Rabbinic authorities further raise concerns related to who should perform an abortion,[38] the manner of carrying it out,[39] and the tremendous degree of certainty required to permit it.[40]

STEM CELL RESEARCH

It is becoming increasingly common to utilize induced pluripotent adult stem cells for research, instead of embryonic stem cells. There is no moral dilemma associated with procuring stem cells from the placenta or adult cells as there is with the use of embryonic stem cells. Nevertheless, although embryonic stem cells are presently used less often than they were when controversy first arose about them, since they can be very useful to scientists for research purposes and represent tremendous lifesaving and life-improving potential,[41] it is helpful to analyze a Jewish approach to their utilization.

Procuring embryonic stem cells involves preventing the continued development of an early-stage embryo (usually about four-five days post-fertilization). As noted above, Talmudic sources designate an embryo within forty days of gestation as "mere liquid," and many authorities are thus often permissive of abortions during this period for certain significant reasons. This would seem to imply that embryonic stem cell research may be justified. On the other hand, one must violate the laws of Shabbat in order to save the life of a fetus, even within this early period,[42] because it has the potential to live.[43] This implies that such an embryo has human-like moral status.

The major contemporary Rabbinic desicors rule that we are only concerned with an entity that has the potential for life if it is indeed likely to develop into a human in its current state. Since the embryos in question are in a petri dish and cannot develop into a fetus and then a human on their own in their current state, they do not represent the same degree of potential, and one may thus not violate Shabbat to save such a fetus (implying that its status is such that it may be utilized for stem cell research).[44]

Jewish Law can thus permit embryonic stem cell research. Most authorities caution, however, that these stem cells should only be taken from existing embryos, such as those created for IVF purposes that remain after the procedure, which would otherwise be disposed of (assuming there has been informed consent).[45] Creating an embryo intentionally for the sake of conducting this form of research is generally not permitted.[46]

CONCLUSION

Jewish sources take a nuanced approach to abortion, calling upon us to show sensitivity to those suffering in various challenging situations, while taking very seriously the possibility that abortion may transgress biblical commands and prohibitions. Furthermore, there are often alternate means of dealing with the dilemmas that lead to abortion, such as through the assistance of organizations that provide counseling and financial assistance. While we tend to be stringent and err on the side of caution when it comes to abortion, our approach must always value kindness and mercy, to both the mother and the potential child.

ENDNOTES

1. R. Aharon Lichtenstein compared a rabbi rendering a halakhic decision in the area of abortion to a physician conducting a liver transplant. "Just as an ordinary physician should not perform a liver transplant, so too an ordinary rabbi should not render a decision regarding an abortion. Only a Rav of eminent stature may render a decision regarding abortion." See R. Howard Jachter, "Embryonic Stem Cell Research," http://www.koltorah.org/ravj /Embryonic%20Stem%20Cell%20Rese arch.htm). On the severity of the prohibition against abortion and the need for caution in Rabbinic rulings, see *Nishmat Avraham*, CM 425:1(34) (184 in 3rd ed.); *Shiurei Torah Le-Rofim*, vol. 4, 493–4; Y. Shilat, *Refuah, Halakhah, VeKavanot Ha-Torah* (Jerusalem, 5774), 141.

2. For example, the Talmud (*Niddah* 31a; *Yevamot* 42a) restricts a couple's marital relations while the mother is pregnant because we are obligated to avoid any act that might lead to aborting a fetus (see the explanation of *Torat Chessed* 42:29 and *Pnei Levi*).

3. Abortion is only referred to directly once in the Torah in the context of the case of one who strikes a pregnant woman in her abdomen (note that this is not intentional or induced abortion). The perpetrator is liable to the death penalty if the woman is killed, but only financial remuneration if only the fetus is killed (Exod. 21:22–23; *Bava Kamma* 42a). Similarly, the Talmud in *Arakhin* 7a rules that a pregnant woman who is convicted of a capital crime is not only killed along with the fetus (unless she is already in the birthing process), but that the rabbis would induce an abortion prior to the execution in order to protect her dignity. While this source implies a lenient attitude towards abortion, standard commentaries point out that abortion is ordinarily forbidden and this case is unique because the fetus will die in any event when the mother is killed (*Chavot Yair* 31), or because we consider it to be already sentenced to die along with the mother, so that killing the fetus does not violate any prohibition (*Iggerot Moshe*, CM 69:3).

4. *Ohalot* 7:6. The *Shulchan Aruckh* (YD 194:10) codifies this piece of the *mishnah* and rules that once the majority of the baby's forehead has emerged, it is considered to have been born and takes upon the status of a full human life. In a case in which both the mother and the baby would die during childbirth, the commentaries say that we may prioritize the life of the mother (see *Tiferet Yisrael* and R. Akiva Eiger on this *mishnah*, as well as *Shoel U-Meishiv* 1:22). Now that open-fetal surgery is possible, an interesting halakhic question relates to the status of a fetus that has emerged from the womb but has then been returned to the womb to complete its gestational period prior to birth.

5. Rambam, *Hilkhot Rotzeach* 1:9. The law of pursuit (*rodef*) requires the bystander to disable the aggressor, fatally if necessary, in order to prevent the pursuer's intent to kill (ibid., 1:6).

6. This follows the explanation of the *Noda Be-Yehuda* (CM 59) and others, who therefore do not permit abortion even if the mother's life is endangered as a result of complications of an already

present medical condition, because in that case the fetus cannot be viewed as the direct aggressor.

7. This explanation is based on the Talmud *Yerushalmi*, as explained by R. Moshe Feinstein, *Iggerot Moshe*, CM 2:69(2).

8. Rashi, *Sanhedrin* 72b.

9. The *Beit Shlomo* (CM 120) expounds the view that since a fetus is not a life, there is more leeway to declare that abortion is not murder, and is thus like any other action that may be sanctioned in order to save – or possibly save – a life. (However, he concludes that in cases of only *possible* danger to the mother's life, an abortion should generally not be carried out.)

10. *Sanhedrin* 57b.

11. *Sanhedrin* 59a; *Chullin* 33a.

12. Tosafot, *Sanhedrin* 59a. (According to Tosafot, although abortion is prohibited to Jews as well, it is not a capital offense). See also *Meshekh Chokhmah*, Exod. 35:2, and R. Eliyahu Mizrachi, Exod. 21:12.

13. See the summary of contemporary opinions in *Nishmat Avraham*, CM 425:2 (148 in 3rd ed.). See also *Achiezer* 3:65; *Iggerot Moshe*, CM 2:69; *Tzitz Eliezer* 8:36, 9:51(3); *Yabia Omer* 4, EH 1(5); and *Torat Hayoledet* 66:1 (2nd ed.). For a discussion of the minority position that the prohibition against abortion is Rabbinic, see *Yabia Omer* 4, EH 1:5; *Tzitz Eliezer* 7:48, 8:36, 9:51 (3), 13:102, 20:2, 21:29. There is also a view that medicinally induced abortion is only rabbinically prohibited, whereas direct removal of the fetus is a biblical prohibition (*Beit Yehuda*, EH 14; see *Nishmat Avraham* CM 425[5], (162 in 3rd ed.).

14. *Nishmat Avraham*, CM 425:2 (148–60 in 3rd ed.) and R. Zilberstein write that the majority of Rabbinic authorities hold that abortion is a Torah prohibition and only a minority of authorities hold that it is a Rabbinic prohibition (*Shiurei Torah Le-Rofim*, vol. 4, 261).

15. *Iggerot Moshe*, CM 2:69. Those who argue that abortion is akin to actual homicide conclude that although a Jew who kills a fetus is not punished by the judicial system as a murderer, he has nonetheless violated the prohibition of murder. This is similar to the case of one who kills a *tereifah* (an individual with a fatal wound or defect), for which one is not liable for capital punishment, but nevertheless violates the prohibition on murder and is liable for divine retribution. See R. Lichtenstein, "*Hapalot Melachutiot*," *Techumin*, vol. 21, 93.

16. R. Isser Yehuda Unterman, "*B'inyan pikuach nefesh shel ubar*," *Noam*, vol. 6, 1–11. The school of thought that abortion is ancillary to homicide ("*senif retzichah*" or "*abizrayhu de-shefichat damim*") places it in a category not of murder, but as being similar to "improper emission of seed," which is viewed by the Talmud (*Niddah* 13a) as tantamount to "the shedding of blood." See *Chavot Yair* 31).

17. *Teshuvot Maharit* 1:97. Unlawful wounding is forbidden in Deut. 25:3.

18. This view sees abortion as being prohibited as a result of the commandment to save life, either based on the command "You shall not stand idly by while your brother's blood is shed," on the obligation to return lost property (which includes restoration of the body), or the concept of "You shall live by them." Even if the prohibition of murder applies solely to a person who has already been born, the positive obligation to preserve life (and the prohibition against shortening it) may be extended to a fetus, since it represents potentially viable existence. Even before the fortieth day, a fetus is therefore viewed as a future human being who will one day have the opportunity to live and do *mitzvot*. See the elaboration on this theme by R. Unterman, *Noam*, vol. 6, and *She-*

vet HaLevi 7:208. R. Unterman suggests, based on the ruling that we violate Shabbat to save a fetus and *Teshuvot Maharit* 1:99, that the Ramban permitted abortion for a non-Jew because non-Jews may not be prohibited from wasting seed or are not obligated to preserve life that is under forty days of gestation. Non-Jews may thus be permitted to abort a fetus during this time period (see also n. 24 below).

19. R. Hershel Schachter told this author that the majority view amongst Rabbinic authorities is that abortion falls under the prohibition against wounding oneself, which is a prohibition that can sometimes be justified for a need. However, R. Yitzchak Shilat writes that the primary position of Rabbinic authorities is that abortion falls under the prohibition of murder (Shilat, *Refuah, Halakhah Ve-Kavanot Ha-Torah*, 142).

20. This ruling arises in various situations in the Talmud. For instance, the birth of a stillborn child ordinarily precludes the next child from the status of firstborn, unless the miscarriage occurred prior to the fortieth day of gestation, in which case it is disregarded and the next male offspring is considered the first of the womb (*Berakhot* 47a). Similarly, a woman who miscarries before the fortieth day from conception need not be concerned with ritual impurity that normally ensues, because the embryo is not considered a child until forty days (*Niddah* 30a; Rashi, ad loc., s.v. *eina chosheshet*). See *Yevamot* 69b for another example.

It is important to note that when physicians discuss the age of a fetus, they generally count from the beginning of the woman's last period. In Jewish Law, however, the age of the fetus is determined based on when the woman last immersed herself in the *mikveh* (or from the date of the first relations after that). Thus, the age of the fetus in Jewish Law is about two weeks less than the medical age (in a woman with a twenty-eight day cycle,

since ovulation occurs fourteen days before the next period). Thus, a fetus that according to the doctor is forty days old is halakhically only about twenty-six days old. See *Nishmat Avraham* (English ed., vol. 3, 280).

The concept that a fetus younger than forty days is "mere water" raises some difficulty, since at forty days (that is, eight weeks of pregnancy counting from the date of the last period) the fetus is clearly visible via sonograph as a formed being. On the other hand, the Rambam writes that the form and features of the fetus are not complete until forty days after conception. This is borne out by a description taken from a standard textbook of gynecology: "Organogenesis occurs from developmental days 28 to 56. It is characterized by the formation of organs . . . The face forms . . . The heart tube folds, and its chambers and outflow tracts are formed . . . The fetal period begins after eight weeks of life and continues until birth." Thus, since the fetus's form and features are incomplete before forty days, the sages considered it to be "mere water."

Moreover, some 30% of spontaneous miscarriages take place before the woman is even aware that she is pregnant. The Talmudic description that before forty days the fetus is considered to be "mere water" could therefore also be interpreted to refer to its risky state of viability consequent upon its not yet being completely formed (*Nishmat Avraham*, CM 425:1[4] [161 in 3rd ed.]). For views of contemporary American ethicists who also only grant moral status to a fetus around this stage, see Bauchamp and Childress, *Principles of Bioethics*, 7th ed. (Oxford Univ. Press, 2013), 74.

21. *Nishmat Avraham*, CM 425:1(4) (162 in 3rd ed.), in the name of R. Shlomo Zalman Auerbach; *Beit Shlomo*, CM 132; *Torat Chessed*, EH 42:33; *Seridei Eish* 3:127; *Achiezer* 3:65; *Teshuvot Bnei Banim* 3:38–39. See *Encyclopedia Hilkha-*

tit Refu'it, vol. 2, 786, n. 328, for a list of *poskim* who are lenient within the first 40 days if there is a great need (n. 329 lists Rabbinic authorities who forbid abortion even within 40 days). See R. Avraham Stav, *Ke-Chalom Ya'uf*, 81–83, for questions related to the timing of an abortion within 40 days, such as on or near Shabbat/holidays or if waiting until after Shabbat will cause the 40 days to pass. See also responsum of R. Yitzchak Zilberstein (*Torat Hayoledet*, 438 in 2nd ed.), on the question of whether one should hurry to perform an abortion within 40 days of gestation, in a case that is *possibly* dangerous to the mother, or wait until there is more certainty, even though that might necessitate an abortion after 40 days. He suggests that it may be best to perform the abortion within 40 days.

22. Some extend this leniency to the first three months of pregnancy (unless fetal movement has been perceived); see *Tzitz Eliezer* 9:51 (3:9). Some permit in certain situation before the third month of gestation because pregnancy is not recognized before then (*Yabia Omer* 4:EH 1 and 9:EH 1:10), but others reject this leniency (*Chavot Ya'ir* 31). *Tzitz Eliezer* agrees that there is much more room for leniency within the first 40 days (9:51:3), but in certain situations even permits as late as seven months into the pregnancy (13:102). *Iggerot Moshe*, CM 2:69 challenges this point. *Yaavetz* (1:43) discusses the possibility of permitting up until actual labor begins. On abortion at different stages of pregnancy, see A. Stav, *Techumin* 31 (5771), 53–62.

23. For example, R. Lichtenstein argues that according to the view that abortion constitutes homicide, after the fortieth day, it would clearly be prohibited. Prior to that point, however, he argues that it is still an open question, as those who are of this view have only ruled that saving such a fetus does not justify violating various prohibitions. However, they did

not suggest that there is no obligation to preserve the fetus when attempting to save life does not collide with Torah prohibitions. If, however, we conclude that abortion is prohibited destruction of seed, the prohibition becomes relevant from the first moment of conception. Nevertheless, if we assume that destruction of seed only applies to the person who ejaculates the semen, this may not be relevant. If the prohibition is related to the prohibition of injuring and wounding other human beings and we apply this due to the fetus's status as a living organism, then the most reasonable cut-off mark is again the fortieth day of gestation. Prior to that, this prohibition would certainly not apply, and the later stages are not sufficiently clear-cut to be used as standards. If the concern about abortion is the physical injury to the mother, the fetus is no less significant than any other limb of the mother, which may not be dismembered unnecessarily. The fate of the fetus itself is subservient to its status as part and parcel of the mother, and the forty-day mark may therefore be irrelevant. However, one might suggest that prior to the forty-day mark, removal of the fetus (categorized as "mere liquid") does not constitute injury to the mother, while removal after forty days does involve injury. This is because the fetus, having become a significant halakhic entity, renders the abortion a significant injury to the mother. If the prohibition against abortion is categorized as the obligation to preserve potential life, the justification of "violate one Shabbat for him in order that he may observe many Shabbatot in the future" (*Yoma* 85b) would apply, as the obligation to save life applies to the pre-forty-day embryo as well (although not all agree with this point).

24. See *Iggerot Moshe*, CM 2:69 (based on R. Unterman, *Noam*, vol. 6), who writes that from the fact that we are allowed to violate Shabbat in order to save the life of a fetus under forty days old, we

see that even before forty days, we judge the fetus based on its potential and not its current state, and thus may not abort it. This would not apply to non-Jews, whose prohibition only begins after day 40. For this reason, R. Y.H. Henkin suggests that before day 40 of gestation, it is preferable to have a doctor who is not Jewish perform the abortion. This is not the case at any later stage of the pregnancy, during which time it may be preferable that a Jew perform the abortion (*Bnei Banim* 3:38–39; R. A. Stav, *Ke-Chalom Ya'uf*, 80).

25. Abortion is never permitted for such reasons (*Nishmat Avraham*, CM 425:1[16] [170 in 3rd ed.]; *Tzitz Eliezer* 7:48).

26. Categorizing abortion as "murder" is the opinion of R. Moshe Feinstein (*Iggerot Moshe*, CM 2:69). R. Feinstein's ruling is based on the fact that one may only save a life by killing a pursuer when it is virtually certain that the pursuer is intending to kill. The prohibition of homicide can only be waived in cases of actual threat to life. R. Feinstein thus does not permit abortion even if it is known that the child will be very sick (from Tay-Sachs, for example), because there is no direct physical danger to the mother as a result. He thus counseled against performing prenatal examinations to determine if the fetus has any such diseases when it is born, since it would not be permitted to abort in any case and would just cause pain to the parents. Many other Rabbinic authorities also only permit abortion in the face of a definite threat of death to the mother; see, for example, *Levushei Mordechai*, CM 36; *Beit Shlomo*, CM 132. For others who rule that abortion is prohibited as murder, see *Encyclopedia Hilkhatit Refu'it*, vol. 2, 756, n. 200.

However, some have argued that R. Feinstein was overly strict on this matter, possibly in response to the overly permissive culture of abortion-on-demand at that time in the United States and due to his fears of a slippery slope; see R. Moshe Hauer, "The Organ Donor Debate and Jewish Medical Ethics," in *The Value of Human Life* (Feldheim, 2010), 63. Others have argued that R. Feinstein was so strict in response to Nazi medical crimes; see R. Shabtai Rappaport, quoted in Y. Bar-Ilan, *Jewish Bioethics* (Cambridge University Press, 2014), 169. A problem with these claims, however, is that R. Feinstein writes in YD 2:60(2) (left column of p. 84) that he formulated his arguments on the matter even before he came to the United States (in 1936), preceding both of these events.

The question of how much danger the mother must be in to justify an abortion is a sensitive one because medical professionals may assume a standard of danger that is much less severe than a rabbi would require. It is therefore essential to consult with a qualified rabbi in each case (as early in the pregnancy as possible), and to allow the rabbi to be in touch with the doctor as well (R. A. Stav, *Ke-Chalom Ya'uf*, 77). R. Zilberstein rules that if there is a difference of opinion amongst the doctors as to the amount of danger a pregnant woman is in as a result of her pregnancy, then if one doctor says there is danger to her life but another doctor disagrees, since it is danger to life, in a case of doubt the fetus should be aborted (unless the women nevertheless wishes to continue with the pregnancy). However, he rules, if more doctors are of the opinion that the woman's life is not in danger, she should not abort (*Torat Ha-Yoledet* 66:9, 2nd ed.). See also *Nishmat Avraham*, CM 425:1 (167 in 3rd ed.).

27. According to those who maintain that abortion is only prohibited rabbinically (such as *Tzitz Eliezer* 13:102), there is some room to expand the range of factors that are likely to tilt the equation towards leniency in cases of "great need" in exceptional cases, but not as a general policy. It should be noted that this lenient position

is a minority view and that the concept of "great need" is so flexible and lacking in clear content that it is difficult to apply practically. See also *Achiezer* 3:65(14) and various *poskim* quoted in *Be-Mareh Ha-Bazak* 8:38, n. 2.

28. *Chavot Ya'ir* 31. See also R. Yaakov Emden, *She'elat Ya'avetz* 1:43, and *Encyclopedia Hilkhatit Refu'it*, vol. 2, 755. When the prohibition is categorized as improper emission of seed, saving a life is not the only sanction for permitting an abortion. Since this prohibition is waived to facilitate normal family relations (for example, during times when a woman cannot become pregnant, the emission is not considered "wasteful"), it follows that other humane factors may also be taken into account. R. M. Feinstein (*Iggerot Moshe*, CM 2:69) took strong exception to the Yaavetz's view, arguing that the Yaavetz had only suggested it knowing that it was better not to rely on it.

29. *Teshuvot Maharit* 1:99. If the prohibition is injuring the mother, there is room for leniency when the abortion is performed for her benefit, analogous to surgery. Hence, if the health of the mother requires an abortion, even though there is no real danger to her life, or if she will be devastated by bringing to term a child who is seriously crippled, then there may be room to rule leniently out of concern for social and familial stigma or impediments to the child's marriageability. On the other hand, if the problem is categorized as damage and injury to the fetus itself, leniency is less likely, but still much more likely than if we categorize abortion as murder, as there are situations in which wounding can be justified even to save a third party. See R. J.D. Bleich, "May Tissue Donations Be Compelled?," *Contemporary Halakhic Problems* IV (Ktav, 1995), 302–8. Most authorities seem to assume that the concern here is wounding the mother and not the fetus, but there is some disagreement on the matter (*Ency-*

clopedia Hilkhatit Refu'it, vol. 2, 755).

30. *Ko'ach Shor* 20; *Achiezer* 3:72(3); and *Beit Shlomo*, CM 132, all permit abortion in certain cases, even if there is no danger at the moment but there is a possibility of danger to the mother from continued pregnancy (particularly within the first 40 days of gestation). *Shevet HaLevi* 5:193 permits in certain cases even for remote danger. However, others require certainty of danger to the mother in order to permit. See *Torat Ha-Yoledet* 60:4 and *Nishmat Avraham*, CM 425:1(9) (165–7 in 3rd ed.) for more on this topic.

Even if the danger to the mother stems from an illness that preceded the pregnancy, such as advanced heart or kidney disease, *Yabia Omer* 4:EH 1, and *Tzitz Elizer* 9:51(3) permit abortions in certain situations. *Tzitz Eliezer* 7:48 (1:5); 8:36; 9:51(3) permits in certain cases to protect the mother's fragile health or to stop severe pain, even if there is no danger to life. Some authorities (including some who rule that abortion is a Torah prohibition) permit abortion if pregnancy poses danger to a limb, such as vision or hearing. See *Minchat Yitzchak, Lekutei Teshuvot* 138, who permits in a case of blindness, and *Mishpatei Uziel*, CM 3:46, regarding a woman with approaching deafness if her pregnancy were to run its normal course. Others argue that these permissive rulings can only be considered within the first 40 days of gestation (*Teshuvot Ve-Hanhagot* 3:359 and R. Moshe Zweig, *Noam* 7, 48), and others prohibit if the danger is only to a limb (*Torat Ha-Yoledet*, 60, n. 3). See also *Yabia Omer* 4:EH 1 and 9:1(8), and *Nishmat Avraham*, CM 425:1[10] [167 in 3rd ed.]. The need for a cesarean section would not be sufficient to permit abortion (*Nishmat Avraham*, CM 425:1[7] [163 in 3rd ed.]).

31. *Tzitz Eliezer* (13:102) rules that the abortion can be permitted to prevent great pain to the mother. He writes that emotional pain is much worse than phys-

ical pain, and abortions can therefore be permitted on psychiatric grounds. (This statement was made in reference to the emotional suffering related to having a child with Tay-Sachs.) Prof. Avraham Steinberg reported to this author that when R. Shlomo Zalman Auerbach was asked questions related to performing an abortion to protect the mother's psychological health, he would first meet with the woman to determine firsthand her ability to cope. On abortion in situations of mental illness, see also *Minchat Yitzchak* 1:115; *Iggerot Moshe*, EH 1:65; *Torat Ha-Yoledet*, 60, n. 4; *Nishmat Avraham*, CM 425:1 (168 in 3rd ed.).

Levushei Mordechai, CM 39, and others argue that mental illness can be considered a form of danger to life that could make abortion permissible in certain cases, whereas *Ko'ach Shor* 20 prohibits abortion even when the pregnancy produces mental illness in the woman. R. Zilberstein, "*Emek Halakhah*," *Assia* 1 (1986), 205–9, permits abortion in a case in which the woman would otherwise commit suicide. *Nishmat Avraham*, CM 425:1(12) (168 in 3rd ed.) notes that depression during and after pregnancy is common and treatable and it is preferable to help the mother get psychiatric support rather than abort.

If a single woman accidentally becomes pregnant and wants to abort the fetus, most decisors encourage finding other solutions and do not permit abortion (*Encyclopedia Hilkhatit Refu'it*, vol. 2, 770). *Rav Po'alim* 1:EH 4, permits abortion in certain circumstances to prevent shame to a family, but this is not the majority view. However, if a woman is raped and thus wants to abort, most decisors rule that it may be done right after conception (i.e., within 72 hours) because some see this not as abortion, but inhibiting/delaying ovulation or preventing implantation (*Nishmat Avraham*, CM 425:1 [27] [180 in 3rd ed.]. However, see also *Shiurei Torah Le-Rofim* 4:242, 230). For a thorough discussion

of psychological factors in abortion, see Moshe Halevi Spero, *Handbook of Psychotherapy and Jewish Ethics* (Feldheim, 1986), chap. 4.

32. For example, if a woman develops cancer during pregnancy and treatment would harm the fetus (and provide limited assistance to the mother), R. Elyashiv permits an abortion to extend the mother's life, even if for a short time (*Torat Ha-Yoledet* 60:2). Others prohibit the use of the therapy or abortion since the fetus cannot be viewed as a pursuer in this case; the cancer is causing the harm (*Torat Ha-Yoledet* in the name of R. Chaim Pinchas Scheinberg; see also range of opinions in *Nishmat Avraham*, CM 425:1 [15] [165, 169–70 in 3rd ed.]).

Another challenging scenario concerns a woman who nearly died in childbirth and became pregnant again, who asked if she could terminate the pregnancy out of fear that complications may arise once again. The Ben Ish Chai ruled that she should not abort in such a case, although there may be room for leniency within the first 40 days of gestation (*Rav Po'alim* 4:YD 14).

33. On the possibility of aborting a fetus in cases such as this, see R. Shilat, *Refuah, Halakhah Ve-Kavanot Ha-Torah*, 142.

34. See *Encyclopedia Hilkhatit Refu'it*, vol. 2, 776; *Nishmat Avraham*, CM 425:1(22–3) (176 in 3rd ed.). A fetus with anencephaly (missing the upper part of brain) may be aborted if the diagnosis is certain and there is a concern about the mother becoming depressed, because such a fetus does not have the status of a potential person (R. Zilberstein, *Shiurei Torah Le-Rofim* 4:239, 198; *Torat Ha-Yoledet*, p. 579 [2nd ed.]). However, once such a child is born, its death may not be hastened in any way (*Nishmat Avraham*, CM 425:1[23] [176 in 3rd ed.]). In a case of hydrocephalus (skull filled with water), some decisors prohibit abortion because

the fetus cannot be classified as a pursuer. R. Zilberstein writes (*Torat Ha-Yoledet* 61:7, 576–9 [2nd ed.]; *Shiurei Torah Le-Rofim* 4:240, 205) that it is preferable to deliver this baby, who will die anyway, via cesarean section, rather than to kill it in the womb during natural delivery.

35. For example, if a pregnant woman contracted German measles or her fetus became deformed or in danger of deafness or blindness as a result of drug or radiation exposure, many rule that the fetus may not be terminated (R. Unterman, *Noam* 6; R. Zweig, *Noam* 7, 36–56; *Iggerot Moshe*, CM 2:69; *Nishmat Avraham*, CM 425:1[19] [174 in 3rd ed.]). In contrast, R. Waldenberg (*Tzitz Eliezer* 13:102) permits abortion in some situations like this, as well as in the case of strong evidence that the baby will have Tay-Sachs disease, as long as the abortion would not endanger the mother and is done before the seventh month, at which point the fetus is viable. (Prof. Avraham Steinberg also reports that the *Tzitz Eliezer* told him that his reasoning may also permit abortions in other cases, such as Down syndrome, cystic fibrosis, neurofibromatosis, etc.).

R. Feinstein and R. Auerbach do not permit abortions in such cases and therefore do not permit amniocentesis testing, since there will be no practical benefit to its results (*Nishmat Avraham*, CM 425:1[18] [173–4 in 3rd ed.]). If there is evidence that a fetus will have Down syndrome, many prohibit aborting the fetus (R. S. Goren and R. Y.Y. Frankel, *Me'orot*, vol. 2 (1980), 26–27, 55fn). The *Tzitz Eliezer* (14:101–102, 15:43[4]) only permits abortion in the case of Down syndrome based on mental health of parents and up until the seventh month of gestation. He encourages people not to have amniocentesis done to test for this unless there is a high likelihood based on age of the mother or previous children, and the parents are extremely worried. See also *Shiurei Torah Le-Rofim* 4:231.

Another possible option today, instead of amniocentesis, is NIPT (non-invasive pre-natal testing), which can be done earlier in the pregnancy (thus minimizing the abortion issue), which is accurate, not dangerous, and does not present a risk of miscarriage (unlike amniocentesis). However, NIPT is not as accurate as amniocentesis and it can result in finding hundreds of genetic mutations, which may lead to many frivolous abortions for no good reason. However, NIPT is a good option for high-risk pregnancies or situations in which someone would do an amniocentesis anyways. It is essential to have good genetic counseling in order to understand the limits of the test and to have fully informed consent. It is therefore best not to use NIPT in all cases (personal communication with Prof. Avraham Steinberg, Summer 2015).

36. "Fetal reduction" is an attempt to reduce the risks of multiple pregnancy by reducing the number of fetuses in utero by selective abortion. Fetuses are usually selected for destruction by doctors based on size, position, and viability.

Multiple gestations have a higher incidence of adverse impacts on the health of the children born. Such pregnancies greatly increase the risk of prenatal death. Multiple pregnancies are also more likely to lead to premature birth, and prematurity is associated with many health problems, including serious infection, respiratory distress syndrome, and heart defects. One in ten children born following high-order pregnancies dies before one year of age. Children born following a multiple pregnancy are at greater risk for such disabilities as blindness, respiratory dysfunction, and brain damage. Moreover, infants born following such a pregnancy tend to have an extremely low birth weight, which is itself associated with a number of health problems, including some that manifest themselves only later in life, such as hypertension, cardiac disease, stroke, and osteoporosis in middle age.

Although fetal reduction aims to reduce the problems associated with multiple pregnancy, it is itself potentially associated with a number of adverse effects on the children who remain following the procedure. One study shows that following transabdominal multifetal reduction, there is a miscarriage rate of 16.2%, and 16.5% of the remaining pregnancies end in premature birth. The alternative method, transvaginal multifetal reduction, carries a higher risk of infection and has been associated with a higher risk of infant mortality than its counterpart. It has been observed that children born following fetal reduction (by either method) tend to be premature, thus exposing them to the complications described above. One study has suggested that children born following fetal reduction are more vulnerable to periventricular leukomalacia, which is characterized by brain dysfunction and developmental difficulties.

37. See discussion in *Nishmat Avraham*, EH 1:6(6) (30–31 in 3rd ed.). See also the opinion of R. Shlomo Zalman Auerbach and others in *Nishmat Avraham*, CM 425:1(30) (181–2 in 3rd ed.). For further discussion, see R. Zilberstein, *Torat Ha-Yoledet* 66:15–6 (2nd ed.), and *Assia* 45–46 (Tevet 1989), 62–68, who writes that abortion of some or all of the fetuses may be permitted if multiple fetuses constitute a danger to the mother (and one may even choose which gender they would prefer to keep). See also *Teshuvot Ve-Hanhagot* 3:358, who writes that it is permissible to abort some or all of the fetuses even if the danger is not to the mother, but to the other fetuses. This is always preferably done before 40 days of gestation; see R. M. Eliyahu, *Techumim* 11 (1990), 272. R. J.D. Bleich permits fetal reduction when failure to intervene will certainly result in the loss of the other fe-

tuses (*Bioethical Dilemmas*, 270). See also R. Avraham Stav, *Ke-Chalom Ya'uf*, 77–8, who cites numerous authorities and notes that in cases of quadruplets or more, most authorities permit fetal reduction, but one must first consult with a qualified rabbi. For an in-depth analysis of this topic, see R. Shilat, *Refuah, Halakhah Ve-Kavanot Ha-Torah*, 217–19. For a discussion of how one chooses which fetuses to abort and which to keep alive, see *Nishmat Avraham*, CM 425:1(30) (181–2 in 3rd ed.] and Bleich, *Judaism and Healing*, 118–119, and *Bioethical Dilemmas*, 275–8.

38. *Tzitz Eliezer* stipulates that consent of the husband must be obtained (9:51:3), and that the physician should ideally be an observant Jew, or at least someone who relates to the laws of the Torah with honor and concern when determining the medical necessity of an abortion (9:51[3] and 12:190). In a lifesaving scenario, *Nishmat Avraham* (English ed., vol. 3, 282–3) notes that obviously any physician can do it. He also suggests that the abortion be done by a woman, since she is not obligated to "be fruitful and multiply" and the prohibition of wasting seed does not apply to her (CM 425:1[31] [182 in 3rd ed.]; *Tzitz Eliezer* 9:51[3:3],13:102). See also R. A. Stav, *Ke-Chalom Ya'uf*, 81.

39. *Tzitz Eliezer* (9:51:3); *Yabia Omer* 4:EH 1. *Bnei Banim* 3:38–39 suggests that it is preferable to perform an abortion through ingesting medication than by performing an operation and aborting "by hand." However, R. S.Z. Auerbach rejects the need for this distinction (*Nishmat Avraham*, CM 425:1[2] [160 in 3rd ed.]; see also R. Stav, *Ke-Chalom Ya'uf*, 78-9).

40. Many authorities require two medical opinions (*Yabia Omer* 4:EH 1), each of whom are unaware of the other's opinion (*Binyan David* 60). *Shevet HaLevi* 5:193 argues that all of the physicians must unanimously agree, and we must verify

that there is indeed unexaggerated danger to the mother. R. M. Feinstein (*Iggerot Moshe*, CM 2:69) writes that the doctors must be virtually certain. *Tzitz Eliezer* 13:102 also requires that there be no significant danger to the mother in the procedure.

Another question relates to removing a fetus that has already lost its pulse. Rabbinic authorities recommend that before doing so, it should be verified via a confirmatory exam by an expert second opinion that the fetus has indeed died (Stav, *Ke-Chalom Ya'uf*, 76). This is recommended when the D&C (dilation [or dilatation] and curettage) procedure is performed for an abortion or miscarriage, because doing so necessarily kills the fetus, and in many cases Rabbinic authorities would require first ensuring that the fetus is already indeed dead.

41. In addition to the question of procuring embryonic stem cells, there are serious moral debates related to embryo research that this discussion may be relevant for. For overview of the issue, see http://www.npr.org/sections/health-shots/2016/05/04/476539552/advance-in-human-embryo-research-rekindles-ethical-debate.

42. *Tur*, OC 617; *Tzitz Eliezer* 11:43; *Shemirat Shabbat Ke-Hilkhatah* 36:2. This ruling is based on the position of the *Bahag*, which is accepted by the Ramban (*Torat Ha-Adam, Sha'ar Ha-Meichush, Inyan Ha-Sakanah*), Rashba (*Shabbat* 151b), and Ritva (*Niddah* 44b, s.v. *dichtiv*).

43. The Ramban (*Torat Ha-Adam, Sha'ar Ha-Meichush, Inyan Ha-Sakanah*) explains this ruling to violate Shabbat in order to save a fetus – despite the fact that Judaism allows abortion to save the mother's life and the Torah does not proscribe capital punishment for accidentally killing a fetus (implying that a fetus has a lower status than a person who has been born). This is based on the concept that sometimes we may violate one Shabbat so that many Shabbatot will eventually be observed (thus granting potentially human moral status to the fetus).

44. R. Shmuel Wosner (*Shevet HaLevi* 5:47); R. Moshe Sternbuch (*Shevilei Ha-Refuah* 5 [5746] and no. 8 [5747]). Some suggest that the verse quoted above, "Whoever sheds the blood of man within another man, his blood shall be shed," which the Talmud interprets as forbidding abortion, does not apply to an embryo that is not within the womb. It is possible that even those who oppose abortion within the first 40 days of gestation and see it as murder would be more lenient in this situation for these reasons. See the discussion in *Nishmat Avraham*, EH 1:6(6) (29–30 in 3rd ed.).

45. *Nishmat Avraham*, CM 425:1 (203–10 in 3rd ed.). This permissive ruling would also apply to stem cells removed from a fetus after miscarriage or abortion, and likely apply to embryos fertilized in vitro that are discarded by fertility clinics because they manifest abnormalities that render it highly unlikely that they would survive if transferred to a women's uterus.

46. Ibid. This is because of the transgression of emitting sperm not for the purpose of procreation.

D. SURROGACY AND EGG DONATION

A researcher was receiving an egg donation in order to get pregnant, and she shared with me her reluctance to do so. She was convinced, based on science, that the true biological mother of this child would be the egg donor and not her. However, after giving birth to this child, she told me that she had changed her perspective; she truly felt that this was her child, just as though the baby had been conceived naturally by her. "Medically and biologically," she said, "this baby descends from someone else. But emotionally and socially, this is my child! Although I am a scientist," she concluded, "I'm beginning to have a lot more sympathy for the emotional perspective now!"

This woman's conflict articulates some of the dilemmas surrounding surrogacy and egg donation that we will explore in this chapter.

We have already discussed various forms of artificial insemination typically utilized when a couple is unable to become pregnant through normal intercourse. We now turn our attention to:

- Surrogacy: an arrangement for a third-party to carry a pregnancy when pregnancy is risky, not possible, or otherwise undesirable for a woman.
- Egg donation: a woman who does not have functioning eggs becomes pregnant by having another woman's egg implanted in her uterus.

In both of these arrangements, the gestational carrier (also known as the "surrogate mother," or simply as the mother in the case of egg donation) carries a pregnancy that was created from the sperm and egg of two other individuals via an IVF-like procedure in which the fertilized egg is transferred from the laboratory to the gestational carrier. These procedures raise a number of difficult halakhic questions.

IS SURROGACY PERMITTED BY JEWISH LAW?

While there are a number of ethical considerations that must be taken into account,[1] since surrogacy entails inseminating a woman with the semen of a man who is not her husband (even if that semen has already impregnated another woman's ovum), the question of its permissibility is similar to that regarding AID (with concerns of adultery, illegitimacy, semen procurement, paternity, etc.). Many authorities forbid or discourage utilizing surrogacy,[2] while others permit it when there are no other viable options remaining for a given couple to have children,[3] as long as everything is done to ensure there are no lab mistakes in the process of inseminating the eggs and transferring them to the surrogate.[4] It is also necessary to ensure detailed documentation of the identity of the surrogate in order to prevent the child from ever marrying another child of either the egg donor or the surrogate.[5]

WHO IS CONSIDERED THE MOTHER ACCORDING TO JEWISH LAW?

Determining the maternity of a child born through surrogacy is essential in the contexts of religious status, inheritance, laws of honoring parents, who one can and cannot marry, etc. Determining the appropriate precedent in Jewish Law for this issue is extremely complex,[6] as are the medical[7] and social factors,[8] and there are therefore a range of opinions amongst contemporary authorities regarding who is the mother for purposes of Jewish Law. The primary opinions are:

(1) The donor of the ovum (egg), who is often referred to as the genetic mother.[9]

(2) The woman in whom the fetus is gestated and birthed (gestational carrier).[10]

While various approaches are taken by different authorities, there is much nuance, and not all authorities simply choose one of these options.[11]

It appears that the majority view amongst Rabbinic decisors in the past was that the gestational carrier (i.e., the host/surrogate mother who carries and then gives birth to the baby) was considered the mother for purposes of Jewish Law.[12] However, in recent years, many authorities have begun to view the genetic mother (i.e., the egg donor) as the mother according to Jewish Law.[13] Nevertheless, some rule that both the genetic mother and the surrogate mother should be considered the mothers of the child.[14] Since there is so much doubt about the matter, most rule that we should take into account the possibility that either the egg donor or the gestational carrier could indeed be the mother.[15] For this reason, if one utilizes a non-Jewish surrogate or egg donor,[16] the baby will have to be converted out of doubt,[17] and if it is a girl, she will not be permitted to marry a Kohen.[18] Similarly, it would be forbidden for the child to marry a relative of either the genetic mother (i.e., the egg donor) or the gestational carrier.[19]

MITOCHONDRIAL REPLACEMENT THERAPY

A similar question arises when utilizing MRT (mitochondria replacement therapy), also known as mitochondria donation or three-parent IVF. In this procedure, an egg is removed from the mother (a woman with mitochondria disease) and fertilized with her partner's sperm, thus creating an embryo. After this, the nucleus containing the embryo's DNA is removed and placed in a de-nucleated donor-egg that has healthy mitochondria. Then, the embryo is implanted in the mother's uterus to establish pregnancy. Thus, the three-parent embryo is 99% identical to its mother and father, and carries less than 0.0005% of egg-donor mitochondrial DNA.[20]

Although not as many Rabbinic authorities have ruled on this issue yet, it seems to involve many similar issues as surrogacy. R. Asher Weiss has ruled that this procedure would be permissible when needed to avoid serious disease, and that the child may be considered the complete child of the two parents, disregarding the mitochondria donor. Nevertheless, it would be best to convert the child if the donor is not Jewish to avoid any doubt.[21] However, R. J.D. Bleich disagrees with R. Weiss's ruling and prohibits utilizing mitochondrial DNA replacement.[22] He argues that if it is done, the question of the identity of the halakhic mother or if the child will be considered to have multiple mothers is a matter of significant unresolved dispute.[23]

WHO SHOULD SERVE AS A SURROGATE?

When choosing a surrogate, most authorities advise choosing an unmarried[24] Jewish woman,[25] but some also permit a married[26] or non-Jewish surrogate if necessary.[27] Similar principles would apply in the case of a woman who relies on an egg donor to become pregnant, although such an arrangement is slightly more problematic according to Jewish Law.[28]

Contemporary Israeli Law, based on Rabbinic input, has developed a number of safeguards to protect the gestational carrier in this arrangement,[29] in an attempt to ensure that she is acting out of her own free will and that both her physical and emotional health are as protected as possible (see notes for details).[30]

CONCLUSION

As should be clear from the various differences of opinion amongst Rabbinic authorities, surrogacy and egg donation are significant, multifaceted, and very complex matters. Nevertheless, according to many authorities one may still choose to pursue their strong desire to have children in this manner if all other practical options have been exhausted, but they should do so responsibly, well-informed of the various halakhic and ethical issues involved, and with careful, expert Rabbinic guidance.

ENDNOTES

1. One ethical dilemma related to surrogacy is if the identity of the gestational carrier can be concealed. R. Moshe Feinstein, *Iggerot Moshe*, EH 1:7, forbids suppression of this information, because siblings may unknowingly marry each other. Furthermore, although people often sign contracts with a surrogate lest she have a change of heart, R. Bleich points out that surrogate contracts are not enforceable, because they are made before the woman is even inseminated, because children are not property, and because custody is an obligation, not a right, that is determined on a case-by-case basis based on the best interest of the child; it is thus not something that may be sold or written up in a contract. See Bleich, *Bioethical Dilemmas* (Ktav, 1998), 256–8, and *Judaism and Healing* (Ktav, 2002), 102–4. On the halakhic issues of sperm or egg donors revoking their donation, see also the discussion in Z. Ryzman, *Ratz KaTzvi* on *Even HaEzer*, 343–51. Some have also reported that challenges finding a gestational carrier have led to the creation of "baby farms" in developing countries, which many feel is ethically very problematic; see R. Gideon Weitzman, "Egg Donation and Gestational Carriers – A View from the Field," *Be-Ohr Ha-Torah* 24 (2016–2017), 75. There are also concerns related to the potential exploitation of gestational carriers; see *Be-Mareh Ha-Bazak* 9:46 and the last section of this chapter.

2. Those authorities who do not permit AID generally forbid surrogacy as well (R. Elyashiv, R. Auerbach, R. Wosner, quoted in *Nishmat Avraham*, EH 1 [34–37 in 3rd ed.] and EH 5 [160–2 in 3rd ed.]). Those who forbid IVF entirely, even if it involves the sperm and ovum of the married couple themselves, oppose surrogacy (*Tzitz Eliezer* 15:45, 19:40; *Teshuvot Ve-Hanhagot* 2:689, 4:285; *Shevet HaLevi* 9:264.

According to *Encyclopedia Hilkhatit Refu'it*, vol. 2, 855, and *Ratz KaTzvi* on *Even HaEzer*, 53, the majority of authorities rule that surrogacy is forbidden. In addition to the sources quoted there, R. Moshe Feinstein is quoted as ruling that surrogacy is forbidden (R. Aaron Felder, *Rishumei Aharon*, vol. 1, 71).

In addition to the halakhic problems that overlap with those that relate to AID, surrogacy raises other potential problems as well. R. Bleich points out that if the surrogate is not Jewish, as is often the case, the child must be converted and the father does not fulfill the commandment to procreate, which may render his emission of semen for this purpose as forbidden (*Bioethical Dilemmas*, 251). Some forbid surrogacy because they rule that the genetic mother/egg donor is considered the mother by Jewish Law, which may lead to many halakhic problems, such as a child accidentally marrying a sibling (see the opinion of R. Meir Brondsdorfer, *Teshuvot Kana Be-Sheim* 4:95(1), quoted in *Ratz KaTzvi*, 45). Furthermore, because of the doubt as to who is considered the mother according to Jewish Law and the lack of solid sources in the Talmud upon which to base such a ruling, some authorities rule that the situation is best avoided altogether (*Teshuvot Ve-Hanhagot* 5:318). See also *Nishmat Avraham*, EH 1:6(11). Because of these positions in opposition to utilizing surrogacy, R. Zilberstein suggests that a woman who is unable to get pregnant any other way should instead adopt children (*Shiurei Torah Le-Rofim*, vol. 4, 340).

3. Those authorities who permit AID tend to permit surrogacy (R. Shlomo Goren, *Torat Ha-Refuah*, 173; R. Zalman Nechemia Goldberg, *Assia* 65–66, 45; R. Ovadia Yosef, as quoted by R. Amar, cited in *Be-Mareh Ha-Bazak* 9:46, n. 5 and *Ratz KaTzvi*, 51; R. Mordechai Eliyahu, cited in *Ratz KaTzvi*, 45). *Be-Mareh Ha-Bazak* 9:46, n. 4 rules that a couple who are unable to have children naturally are permitted to utilize surrogacy.

Those who permit surrogacy generally do not obligate it (see *Nishmat Avraham*, EH 1:1), because according to most authorities, one is required to attempt to have children, but not obligated to go beyond attempting. Thus, while people may want to go to these lengths, they are not obligated to do so. Furthermore, one is never required to assume risks associated with surgery or other dangerous procedures in order to fulfill a mitzvah (see Bleich, "Surrogate Motherhood," in *Bioethical Dilemmas*, vol. 1, 241). Thus, for example R. Feinstein (*Iggerot Moshe*, EH 3:12) rules that a woman for whom it is risky to bear children may use contraceptives and is not obligated to undergo a procedure to remove ova or therapy to produce multiple ova. For discussion of issues related specifically to egg donation, see R. Shilat, *Refuah, Halakhah, Ve-Kavanot Ha-Torah*, 239.

See *Be-Mareh Ha-Bazak* 9:46, n. 11 for a discussion of the various thresholds that different authorities provide in order for a couple to be permitted to engage in surrogacy, ranging from 10 years without the ability to have children naturally, to 5 years, 2 years, or once expert physicians have determined that there is a medical reason for infertility and that this is the only option.

4. *Yabia Omer* 8:EH:21; *Minchat Shlomo* 2:124; see also *Tzitz Eliezer* 15:45. See the discussion of this issue in the chapter on artificial insemination in this book.

5. R. Zalman Nechamia Goldberg (*Techumin* 19, 273–81). Knowing the identity (or at least some basic identifying information) of the gestational carrier is necessary to ensure that the child does not accidentally marry a relative in the future. This concern is particularly pressing according to those who rule that the surrogate is the mother. See also *Be-Mareh Ha-Bazak* 9:46, n. 17 for a discussion of this, and permission for an individual to marry even if he or she was unable to verify the identity of their surrogate mother or egg donor.

6. *Nishmat Avraham*, EH 1 (37 in 3rd ed.) quotes R. Shlomo Zalman Auerbach as arguing that there is no clear proof in the entire Rabbinic corpus to be able to issue a ruling as to who is considered the mother when a surrogate mother is utilized. See also the *teshuvot* of R. Asher Weiss available at http://www.medicalhalacha.org/ and cited in *Ratz KaTzvi*, 55, 93–96; *BeMareh Ha-Bazak* 9:46, n. 7, and *Teshuvot Ve-Hanhagot* 5:318, explain that there is no clear precedent in the Rabbinic source material for this issue and we are thus forced to rely on logic (*sevarah*) in order to determine an approach.

7. From a medical/scientific perspective, the egg donor should be considered the mother, since she is the one who provides the primary genetic material and DNA from which the child is fashioned, and the child may thus resemble this woman in appearance and character. On the other hand, it is the gestational carrier whose body transforms an egg into a human being and nurtures it. Furthermore, we are now aware of "epigenetics," whereby an external environment can alter one's genes. This certainly takes place to some extent when a fetus is developing inside a womb, and that environment may thus influence the epigenetic information of the

fetus. Additionally, more is being learned about maternal-fetal cell exchange (also called microchimerism), the process by which cells from the woman who gestates a fetus migrate across the placenta and become embedded into the body of the fetus; see J. Loike, "New Biotechnological Ways to Begin Life," *Be-Ohr Ha-Torah* 24 (2016–2017), 35–46. Nevertheless, the egg has tremendously more genetic impact on the fetus than these influences may have. Furthermore, this is a question of Jewish Law, which must be decided based on precedent in Jewish sources, not scientific evidence; see Weitzman, "Egg Donation and Gestational Carriers," 73–74.

8. Many women experiencing fertility challenges opt to receive an egg donation, usually using eggs that come from women who are not Jewish. When these women become pregnant, those who see her assume that this is an ordinary pregnancy and that the child is her own baby. Since parents also frequently do not want others to know about the procedure, they do not convert the child and raise him or her as any other born Jew. While the ramifications in Jewish Law are potentially severe, most people remain completely unaware of the issue.

9. Authorities who rule that the egg donor/ genetic-biological mother is the halakhic mother in all regards include: R. Goren (*Torat Ha-Refuah*, 173–83), R. Amar, and R. Ovadia Yosef (*Assia* 22[3] [5770], 101; *Nishmat Avraham*, EH 5 [162 in 3rd ed.]; *Ratz KaTzvi*, 51); R. Moshe Feinstein (as quoted in *Masorat Moshe*, vol. 2, 320). Many of these authorities therefore rule that as long as the egg donor is Jewish, then even if the surrogate is not Jewish, no conversion will be necessary, and even if the child does convert, she can marry a Kohen (*Nishmat Avraham*, EH 5 [162–3 in 3rd ed.]; R. Yaakov Ariel, *Ohalah Shel Torah* 1 EH 70; R. Nevenzahl, *Yeshurun* 21, 585; *Ratz KaTzvi*, 48; *Chemdah*

Genuzah 3:27). Although most argue that R. Shlomo Zalman Auerbach ruled that both the genetic and the gestational mother must be considered the mothers out of doubt, Prof. Ze'ev Lev and R. Avigdor Nevenzahl claim that R. Auerbach told them that the genetic mother/egg donor is considered the halakhic mother (*Be-Mareh Ha-Bazak* 9:46, n. 7).

Some of the sources that these authorities quote include the fact that the Torah (Exod. 21:22) refers to a damaged fetus as the mother's "child," even though the pregnant woman has not yet given birth; the statement of the Talmud (*Sanhedrin* 91b) that one's soul enters their body at conception, not birth, so that the essence of a person is determined at the earliest stage, that of fertilization; the ruling that if a Kohen marries a pregnant divorcee, her child is legitimate because he was not conceived in sin, although she is profaned (*chalalah*) when she gives birth (*Kiddushin* 77a; Rambam, *Hilkhot Bi'ot Assurot* 19:7), implying that conception, and not pregnancy or birth, is the determining factor.

Other authorities base this ruling not on precedent, but on logic (*sevarah*), arguing that it is the genetic mother who provides the genetic material; gestation, which can technically be done by an incubator and simply brings the potential into reality, does not confer identity.

Another logical argument made in favor of determining that it is the egg donor/genetic mother who should legally be regarded as the mother is that the sperm determines paternity according to many *poskim*, and *sevarah* indicates that it should be the same with regard to the mother's ovum. However, the sperm is all that the men contribute, while women also gestate and give birth to the baby, which are very significant processes. Furthermore, Chazal refer to sperm, but not to ovaries. See *Be-Mareh Ha-Bazak* 9:46. See the responsum of R. Asher Weiss on this topic, where he claims that it seems most logical that the genetic mother should be considered the mother in the eyes of Jewish Law, just as a sperm donor is considered the father (available at http://www.medicalhalacha.org and *Ratz KaTzvi*, 55, 93–96). In another responsum on the same website (about three-parent IVF), R. Asher Weiss rules that even when it seems that the biological mother is regarded as the mother by Jewish Law, it is always best to convert the child just to be strict, but the child should be converted privately and can still marry a Kohen should she so desire (though he only said this regarding Mitochondrial DNA Replacement Therapy, not standard surrogacy/egg donation). For more reasons based on logic, not source material, that the genetic mother should be considered the halakhic mother, see *Be-Mareh Ha-Bazak* 9:46, n. 7.

R. Zalman Nechemia Goldberg (*Techumin 5*) challenges the view based on logic, arguing that identity is not determined by *sevarah*; as the *Maggid Mishnah* notes regarding prohibited relationships (*arayot*), it is based on scriptural verses (*gezerot ha-katuv*) and not logical reasoning. Furthermore, we know that the gestational environment does have an influence on the fetus.

Ruling that the genetic mother/egg donor is the mother could ease difficulties in the face of future questions that may arise from new technologies. For example, if a baby is born through "ectogenesis" (wherein the entire growth process takes place outside of the body in an artificial environment), this ruling would still enable the egg donor to be considered the mother by Jewish Law; adopting the view that only the gestational/birth mother is the mother would render such a child motherless. Similarly, if it ever becomes possible for a uterus to be implanted in an animal and to gestate a baby inside of it, this ruling would still allow the egg donor to be considered the mother and not require us to view the animal host as the

mother. However, it is unlikely that either of these technologies will be desirable or possible in the near future.

10. Authorities who rule that the gestational mother is the halakhic mother in all regards include: R. Waldenberg (*Tzitz Eliezer* 20:49, 19:40; *Nishmat Avraham*, EH 1 [36 in 3rd ed.]); R. M. Soloveitchik (*Ohr Ha-Mizrach* 100 [5741]: 122); R. Ezra Bick (*Techumin* 7, 266–70); R. Ralbag (*Techumin* 20, 317). R. Mordechai Eliyahu rules similarly and accordingly does not require conversion if the egg donor was not Jewish, as long as the gestational mother is Jewish (quoted in *Ratz KaTzvi*, 45, and Weitzman, "Egg Donation and Gestational Carriers," 70). R. Nachum Rabinowitz (*Siach Nachum* 101) and R. Zalman Nechemia Goldberg (*Techumin* 5, 248–59) rule that the one who gives birth to the baby is considered the mother. *Nishmat Avraham*, EH 1 (37 in 3rd ed.) quotes R. Shlomo Zalman Auerbach as arguing that based on logic, it seems that the surrogate should be considered the mother. R. J.D. Bleich (*New Reproductive Technologies*, 69–70) also considers the surrogate to be the mother. In the same volume, R. Ezra Bick challenges R. Bleich's methodology, but similarly concludes that the gestational mother ("host") is the mother according to Jewish Law. A similar view is suggested by R. Yisraeli, who claims that the place of "formation of the fetus" (rabbinically considered to be after the first 40 days) determines motherhood (*Chavot Binyamin* 2:68 and 3:108).

One of the commonly cited precedents quoted in support of the view that the gestational mother is considered the mother in Jewish Law is the case of a non-Jewish woman who is pregnant with twins and converts during pregnancy. The Talmud (*Yevamot* 97b; see also *Yevamot* 78a) rules that the twins still have a maternal relationship (even though that is normally severed upon conversion), implying that the maternal relationship is established throughout the pregnancy and until the actual birth (not simply at conception). Another commonly cited support for this view is a *midrash* that quotes Targum Yonatan ben Uziel on Gen. 29:22, in the context of the birth of Dina. Targum Yonatan states that originally Dina was conceived in Rachel's womb, but God transferred her after conception to Leah's womb so that Rachel could give birth to Joseph. Nevertheless, the Bible unquestionably refers to Leah as Dina's mother, and to Rachel as Joseph's mother. This *midrash* appears to state authoritatively that the woman who gives birth to the child is the mother. However, some reject this source because from the Talmudic account (*Berakhot* 60a) it appears that the fetus was only changed from male to female in the womb, not switched. Others reject the applicability of this source because we do not learn Halakhah from a *midrash*.

Some argue that just as when one grafts a branch form a young tree (under 3 years old) onto an old tree, the branch becomes incorporated and its fruits are permissible (*Sotah* 43b), if one implants an egg from one woman into another, it should "belong" to the new mother. For a number of other suggested proofs for this view, see *Be-Mareh Ha-Bazak* 9:46, n. 7. For analysis of all of the suggested proofs for both sides, see R. Shilat, *Refuah, Halakhah, Ve-Kavanot Ha-Torah*, 222–32.

11. For example, R. Kalev (*Techumin* 5, 260–7) argues that the eggs determine Jewish status and the birth determines motherhood. *Tzitz Eliezer* (15:45; see also *Assia* 5 [5746], 84–92), *Teshuvot Ve-Hanhagot* (4:284), and *Ma'aseh Choshev* (3:1) argue that a child born through IVF or surrogacy has no mother or father (even if the biological and gestational mother are the same), because: (1) Fertilization occurs in an unnatural manner via a third power, outside the parents; (2) Conception occurs in a way that has no relationship to genealogy; and (3) The ovum is not attached to the body, but is instead severed, thus destroying the relationship to the mother. This approach has not gained traction and is firmly rejected by R. Bleich (*Reproductive Technologies*, 48) and R. Asher Weiss (http://www.medicalhalacha.org and *Ratz KaTzvi*, 55, 93–6), who argue that the baby was indeed created naturally and something must have created it, so it must have a mother. The Talmud similarly rules that a man who impregnates a woman by means of semen left in the waters of a bathhouse is still considered the father, even though there was no act of intercourse.

12. R. Bleich (*New Reproductive Technologies*, 69–70, a reprint of an article originally published in 1991) concludes his article on this topic by claiming that the majority of Rabbinic evidence seems to support the birth mother as the determiner of Jewish status, rendering the gestational carrier as the mother according to Jewish Law, although he argues that the egg donor should also be viewed as possibly the mother. See also *Tzitz Eliezer* 19:40, 20:49 (summarized in *Nishmat Avraham* EH 5 [160–2 in 3rd ed.]). Similarly, Prof. Steinberg writes in the 2006 edition of his *Encyclopedia Hilkhatit Refu'it*, vol. 2, 860, that the majority of *poskim* who deal with this issue rule that the gestational carrier is considered the halakhic mother in all regards.

13. In a private communication with Prof. Steinberg in the summer of 2015, he acknowledged that there has been a shift towards recognizing the genetic mother as the halakhic mother. *Nishmat Avraham*, EH 1, records in the 2014 3rd edition (34–35) that when he had originally asked R. Elyashiv about this question twenty years earlier, R. Elyashiv ruled that there is no clear ruling about the maternity of such a baby, but that it seemed that the gestational carrier should be considered the mother, and if she is not Jewish, the baby would have to be converted.

However, when R. Elyashiv's view was recorded later, he had come to see the egg donor as the true mother (see also *Assia* 87–88, 100; *Yeshurun* 21, 535–45; *Ratz KaTzvi*, 48). R. Elyashiv's final position was that the egg donor is the mother, but since this is only a *sevarah* (based on logic with no supporting sources) and it could be that the opposite is true, he required a conversion (*giyur le-chumra*) in both cases (personal communication with Prof. Abraham, Feb. 2012). See also *Be-Mareh Ha-Bazak* 9:46, end of n. 7, who notes that in a specific more recent case, R. Elyashiv ruled that the egg donor was considered the mother. However, R. Gideon Weitzman reports that even in his later years, R. Elyashiv ruled that the birth mother should be considered the mother; see "Egg Donation and Gestational Carriers," 72. Prof. Steinberg reported to this author that R. Elyashiv never changed his mind on this issue, but always felt that it is a case of doubt with no clear sources proving either position (which is why he ruled that a case with a non-Jewish surrogate requires conversion), even though his inclination was that the egg donor is the mother.

14. *Teshuvot Ve-Hanhagot* 5:318. Some have argued that according to this ruling, it is more precise to say not that both women are the mothers, but that neither is the mother; see the comment of A. Steinberg in *Ratz KaTzvi*, 98. See also Prof. Ze'ev Lev, *Emek Halakhah*, vol. 2, 165–9, based on the laws of the *omer* (*Menachot* 69b).

15. *Nishmat Avraham*, EH 5 (162 in 3rd ed.); R. Zalman Nechemia Goldberg, *Assia* 65–66 and *Techumin* 5. R. Asher Weiss concludes his responsum on this topic (available at http://www.medicalha lacha.org/ and *Ratz KaTzvi*, 55, 93–6) by stating that since we have no clear answer and never will, we must be strict and consider both the gestational mother and the egg donor to be the mother.

16. See n. 27 below regarding those who sometimes permit utilizing non-Jewish surrogates in certain situations.

17. *Nishmat Avraham*, EH 5 (163 in 3rd ed.) in the name of R. Shlomo Zalman Auerbach and R. Elyashiv. R. Zalman Nechemia Goldberg similarly writes that one would have to convert the baby out of doubt so that there would never be a question about the status of the child (*Assia* 65–66, 45). Many of the authorities who rule that the egg donor/genetic mother is the mother still require conversion when a non-Jewish surrogate is utilized just to be certain (*Be-Mareh Ha-Bazak* 9:46, n. 19).

18. *Shulchan Arukh*, EH 6:8; R. Zalman Nechemiah Goldberg, *Techumin* 10, 280. For this reason, some authorities (R. Yaakov Ariel, *Ohalah Shel Torah*, EH 70, quoted in *Be-Mareh Ha-Bazak* 9:46, n. 20) have suggested that when PGD is also being utilized, it is preferable to select a male embryo to be impregnated into the surrogate. He will then be able to marry any Jew. (However, if the father is a Kohen, he will only be a possible Kohen; if the non-Jewish surrogate is the halakhic mother, then the baby is not Jewish, and therefore not a Kohen, whereas if the Jewish genetic mother is the halakhic mother, the baby is a Kohen. Due to this doubt, he would not be allowed "to *duchen*," but he must keep the restrictions of Kohanim. See *Nishmat Avraham*, EH 5 [162 in 3rd ed.].)

19. *Be-Mareh Ha-Bazak* 9:46.

20. New York Stem Cell Foundation Research Institute FAQ sheet: https://nyscf .org/pdfs2/FAQ_on_Mitochondrial_Rep lacement_Therapy.pdf.

21. Responsum of R. Asher Weiss, available at http://www.medicalhalacha.org/.

22. R. Bleich argues that like IVF, mitochondrial DNA replacement is problematic in that it presents issues of potentially wasting seed, as well as problems of sperm

procurement, determining parental identity, potential need for fetal reduction, and dilemmas regarding what to do with defective or excess embryos, as well as the concern of who is the mother, like in surrogacy, including the potentially problematic possibility that a person will have multiple mothers. See Bleich, "Mitochondrial DNA Replacement: How Many Mothers?" *Tradition* 48(4) (Winter 2015), 66 (also published in Bleich, *Contemporary Halakhic Problems* VII [Maggid Books, 2016], 273).

R. Bleich rejects R. Asher Weiss's contention that it is impossible for a person to have multiple mothers or fathers, based on a statement of Tosafot that a child can indeed have multiple fathers (67, n. 16). R. Bleich thus opposes this intervention because it blurs maternal identity and potentially comingles male sperm with genetic material of the wife of another man, which is prohibited by Jewish Law (84). Furthermore, R. Bleich contends that at the current time, the safety of mitochondrial DNA replacement is not certain, and it thus poses significant health risks to the yet to be conceived fetus (72).

23. Bleich, "Mitochondrial DNA Replacement: How Many Mothers?", 84. R. Bleich argues that we cannot rely on the fact that one mother provides the vast majority of genetic material, since the minority provided by mitochondrial DNA can have a significant, perceivable, stabilizing impact on the offspring, such that it would not be subject to nullification (77–78). R. Bleich thus rejects R. Asher Weiss's contention that the mother who provides the vast majority of the DNA should be considered the mother by Jewish Law (n. 32).

24. An unmarried surrogate is preferable because this avoids some of the potential halakhic problems related to forbidden marital unions that may arise if a man's sperm is inserted into a married woman's womb. This is especially problematic according to those who rule that the ges-

tational carrier is considered the baby's halakhic mother, since the child is related to her and a man she is not married to. However, some argue that this still would not transgress the Torah prohibition of adultery (see n. 26 below).

25. This is suggested by R. Zalman Nechemia Goldberg and R. Yaakov Ariel in order to avoid concerns related to conversion (*Be-Mareh Ha-Bazak* 9:46, n. 16). Utilizing a Jewish surrogate is especially recommended for individuals who are not Torah observant, as it would be more challenging for them to convert the baby in a manner acceptable to all Jews (*Be-Mareh Ha-Bazak* 9:46, n. 23).

26. R. Amar in the name of R. Ovadia Yosef, since they rule that the egg donor is the mother according to Jewish Law and the surrogate mother has no relation to the child (*Be-Mareh Ha-Bazak* 9:46, n. 21). There are a number of problems with using a married surrogate, such as the concern that the baby will be considered one born of a forbidden relationship with a married woman (*mamzer*), which is especially problematic according to those who rule that the gestational carrier is the halakhic mother of the child. However, some authorities note that this prohibition only arises when there is actual prohibited intercourse (*Bach*, YD 195:5; *Taz* YD 195:7; *Beit Shmuel*, EH 1:10; *Iggerot Moshe*, EH 1:10, 71; 2:11; *Yabia Omer*, EH 2:1). However, others are concerned with the possibility that simply mixing the man's seed into a woman other than his wife is forbidden and can cause illegitimacy (the Satmar Rav in *Ha-Ma'or* [Av 5724]; *Minchat Yitzchak* 4:5; *Minchat Shlomo, Tinyana* 124; *Tzitz Eliezer* 13:97; see also *Bnei Ahuvah, Hilkhot Ishut* 15:6; *Otzar Ha-Poskim* 1:42, and the discussions in *Be-Mareh Ha-Bazak* 9:46, n. 21 and R. Shilat, *Refuah, Halakhah, Ve-Kavanot Ha-Torah*, 238–9). However, in the case of surrogacy, a previously fertilized egg is inserted into the surrogate and she

simply allows it to grow, so it should not be subject to this concern. Accordingly, some authorities have ruled that one may utilize a married surrogate in a case of great need, since it is often difficult to find an unmarried surrogate (R. Yaakov Ariel; R. Shlomo Amar with the agreement of R. Ovadia Yosef, quoted in *Be-Mareh Ha-Bazak* 9:46, n. 22).

Those who maintain that the biological mother/egg donor is the mother according to Jewish Law tend to permit a married woman to serve as a gestational carrier, since there is no concern of adultery according to their view. However, others have nevertheless counseled against using a married surrogate, even if the child would not be considered illegitimate, since there are some authorities who will rule that the child is illegitimate (R. Zalman Nechemia Goldberg, *Assia* 65–66, 47). For some other concerns with using a married surrogate, as well as possible resolutions, see *Be-Mareh Ha-Bazak* 9:46, n. 22.

27. *Be-Mareh Ha-Bazak* 9:46, n. 18. It has also been reported that R. Amar has permitted using a gestational carrier who is not Jewish (Weitzman, "Egg Donation and Gestational Carriers," 75). Finding a non-Jewish surrogate is easier outside of Israel and has an advantage in that it reduces the concern of accidentally marrying a sibling.

However, utilizing a non-Jewish surrogate causes other problems. For example, those who rule that the gestational carrier is the mother according to Jewish Law will accordingly rule that this baby is not halakhically related to its father, and the act may therefore constitute wasting of seed, as well as raise the concern that putting a married man's seed into another woman is illicit (*Chavot Binyamin* 3:108). However, others argue that there is still value in bringing a baby into the world, so that this is not rendered wasteful, and therefore utilizing a non-Jewish surrogate

would not be forbidden. According to the opinions that the egg donor is the mother, this problem is of no concern (*Be-Mareh Ha-Bazak* 9:46, n. 18).

Others are quoted as simply feeling that utilizing a non-Jewish surrogate to gestate a Jewish baby is unseemly (R. Elyashiv, quoted in *Yeshurun* 21, 535; *Teshuvot Ve-Hanhagot* 5:318). However, some argue that since R. Moshe Feinstein permitted utilizing the sperm of a non-Jew in order to become pregnant (*Iggerot Moshe*, EH 2:11), he would certainly also permit using a non-Jewish surrogate (*Be-Mareh Ha-Bazak* 9:46, n. 18). Furthermore, some argue that when there is no organized registry of who the genetic mother is, it may be best to utilize non-Jewish eggs or a non-Jewish surrogate in order to prevent one from unintentionally marrying a sibling (R. Moshe Kurtstag, quoted in *Ratz KaTzvi*, 54). Utilizing a non-Jewish surrogate is permitted when one is unable to locate a non-married Jewish surrogate, as long as the family and the child are aware of all the halakhic issues involved (R. Zalman Nechemia Goldberg and R. Yaakov Ariel, quoted in *Be-Mareh Ha-Bazak* 9:46, end of n. 18).

28. *Nishmat Avraham*, EH 1 (42 in 3rd ed.) quotes R. S.Z. Auerbach and R. Elyashiv as forbidding a woman to be impregnated with another woman's fertilized egg, whether it is a stranger or a family member. Some of the challenges with utilizing a donor egg include the fact that egg donation is usually anonymous. A Jewish woman may therefore not sell or donate an egg unless it is ensured that it will go to a Jewish couple who will know her identity, and thus ensure that the child would not marry one of her relatives. Also, a married Jewish woman may not donate or sell her eggs, as the concern for *mamzerut* is greater in this case, as opposed to a married Jewish woman serving as a surrogate, which is

less problematic (personal correspondence with R. Carmel, Summer 2015); See fn. 26 above. R. Gideon Weitzman of the Puah Institute told this author that the Puah Institute permits egg donation, as R. Zalman Nechemia Goldberg has ruled that it is permissible, and that they follow the ruling that the gestational carrier (the birth mother) is defined as the mother according to Jewish Law. Accordingly, the child will be considered Jewish and not need a conversion even if the egg was donated by a non-Jewish woman.

29. The Knesset ethics committee on surrogacy (which was chaired by R. Yehuda Amital, Rosh Yeshiva of Yeshivat Har Etzion), argued that the gestational carrier should be protected because she is doing an altruistic act to help people in need and is the most vulnerable party in the relationship, undergoing a dangerous medical experience for the sake of someone else. Furthermore: (1) The surrogate is effectively renting out her body for money, which can be seen as a form of slavery; (2) There are concerns related to treating the gestational carrier as an "object" despite all of the emotions that might surround her pregnancy and subsequent severed connection to the child (including challenges that her other children may feel seeing their mother pregnant but not being able to have a relationship with a baby they view as their sibling); (3) The danger that the surrogate faces in the process of pregnancy and childbirth, including the chance of losing her womb and being unable to have children of her own in the future, must be taken into account; (4) Surrogacy can be viewed as a type of bigamy (the act of entering into a marriage with one person while still legally married to another), and if the surrogate is married, it is reverse bigamy. Despite these concerns, the committee argued that instead of prohibiting surrogacy, it is best to allow people to attempt to fulfill their desire to have a child if they have proven that they have no other option to have children, as long as significant steps are taken to protect all involved (see next note). See R. Yuval Cherlow, "*Ha-Haganah Ha-Etit al Ha-Pundaka'it*," in Gil Siegel (ed.), *Bioetica Kahol Lavan* [Hebrew] (Mossad Bialik, 2015), 193–224.

30. See http://www.health.gov.il/DocLib /pon_tofes18.pdf. The Israeli Law regulates that the gestational carrier cannot be younger than 22. Even though most societies treat anyone older than 18 as an adult, the committee felt that due to the severe physical and emotional risks involved in surrogacy, more maturity is required. The gestational carrier may not be older than 38 for health reasons. The surrogate cannot be undergoing a personal crisis, such as in the process of divorce or death or major illness in the family. If she is divorced, she must have been divorced for at least a year before serving as a surrogate, in order to prevent making such a major decision in a time of distress, when she may be under extreme emotional or financial pressure. The committee emphasizes that the arrangement must take place out of free will desire and that all parties involved fully understand all of the health and emotional risks and ramifications; there may be no pressure to agree to be a surrogate; the rights of the child and the parents must be clear; the surrogate mother must be in good physical and emotional health; and the surrogate must have at least one child already (to ensure that she fully understands the emotional and physical ramifications of what she is getting herself into, and because she will already have a child of her own in case of a pregnancy complication that will lead to the loss of her ability to have more children). One may not serve as a gestational carrier more than twice (even if one or both of the pregnancies do not result in a healthy baby), in order to prevent anyone from selling the use of their body excessively.

One who has had more than 4 children or 2 C-sections may not serve as a surrogate, and it must be more than a year since she had her last child (to ensure that she is in optimal health). The gestational carrier cannot be related to either of the parents of the child, for halakhic, medical, and ethical reasons (if this were permitted, it might lead to pressure being put on girls in the family to serve as surrogates, even against their will).

Other precautionary steps include allowing the gestational carrier to spend some time with the newborn baby if she would like before the baby is given to its parents, and she is referred to as the "surrogate mother" ("*eim ha-noseit*"), and not "surrogate woman" ("*ishah noseit*") or simply "surrogate" ("*pundaka'it*"), in order to express the idea that she is an important partner in a significant portion of the birthing process, not just an incubator, and that she has some form of eternal connection to the child born from her womb.

Although the primary goal of these restrictions is to protect the surrogate mother, they are also intended to protect the intended parents, the welfare of the child being born, and the strength of the contract between the parents and the surrogate. See R. Cherlow, "*Ha-Haganah Ha-Etit al Ha-Pundaka'it*", and, "Surrogate Motherhood – Halacha, Law and Ethics in the State of Israel" http://www.yutorah.org/sidebar/lecture.cfm/845135/rabbi-yuval-cherlow/surrogate-motherhood-halacha-law-and-ethics-in-the-state-of-israel/.

These restrictions have the disadvantage of limiting the total number of po-

tential surrogates, thus potentially leaving some without the ability to have children and placing those surrogates who are available in higher demand, which may raise costs and make it more difficult for people of insufficient means to have children in this manner. Furthermore, it is a positive Jewish value to have children and fulfill the commandment to be fruitful and multiply, and some may therefore argue that it is best not to institute these rules, which would limit the number of children born. Indeed, Jewish Law sometimes overrides some of these protections for the surrogate mother. For example, the committee ruled that the gestational carrier must be unmarried (unless the parents can prove that they were unable to find anyone unmarried, in which case a married woman may serve as a surrogate). This rule was included purely for halakhic reasons, since most Rabbinic authorities require it (because of lineage concerns for most and illegitimacy concerns for others). However, since there is some doubt about how strictly they require this, room was left to permit married surrogates in some cases (as many see an ethical benefit of utilizing a married surrogate in that she may understand the implications of pregnancy and childbirth, may already have children, and has support from her husband and family). Despite these concerns, the various restrictions listed above to protect the surrogate mother were instituted by the committee based on the perspective that ethics are always about balancing the various goods and that there is never one perfect choice.

E. LABOR AND DELIVERY:
Some Jewish Customs and Issues that Arise
upon the Birth of a Baby

Jewish law generally discourages medically inducing labor,[1] unless it must be done for a proper medical reason or to avoid other serious issues or problems.[2]

There are a number of blessings recited upon the birth of a child:

- Upon the birth of a baby boy, both of the parents should recite the "*HaTov VeHaMeitiv*" blessing immediately following the birth[3] (or as long as one still senses the joy of the birth[4]).
- Upon the birth of a baby girl, both of the parents should recite the "*SheHecheyanu*" blessing the first time they see the baby[5] (or as long as one still senses the joy of the birth[6]).
- Upon the birth of twins, of which there is a boy and a girl, the parents should only recite the "*HaTov VeHaMeitiv*" blessing for both of the children.[7]
- Once the mother has recovered from childbirth and feels that she has regained her strength, she can recite the "*Birkat HaGomel*" blessing with a *minyan*.[8]

It is customary not to tell anyone the name of one's child until the child is formally named in a religious ceremony. In a case of need, parents may record the name of their baby on a form, such as a birth certificate application, even before they have named their baby in the traditional manner. However, they should only write the name down and not say it aloud.[9]

If a baby boy is not medically stable enough to be circumcised on the eighth day, when boys are customarily named, we wait until the circumcision is performed to give him a name.[10] However, if it is known that a significant period of time will pass before the circumcision can take place, many give the baby a name right away, even before the circumcision.[11] When the circumcision of a baby boy will be delayed, it is nevertheless customary to hold the *Shalom Zakhar* on the first Friday night after the birth, as is usually done, even if the baby was born on that Friday night, if the parents are able to do so.[12]

If a firstborn baby is sick and unable to be circumcised on time, the *pidyon ha-ben* may still be performed on time, despite the fact that he is not yet circumcised.[13] This is true even if the baby is still in an incubator. However, some recommend waiting thirty days after the baby is out of the incubator if he was not born at full term.[14]

ENDNOTES

1. *Iggerot Moshe*, YD 2:74, 4:105; *Torat Ha-Yoledet* 1:1–2. R. Feinstein has been quoted as ruling that it is not forbidden to induce labor, but it is better not to do so, even if that means that one will have to use a different doctor (R. Aharon Felder, *Rishumei Aharon*, vol. 1, 71). *Nishmat Avraham*, OC 248:4 (1:2) and *Torat Ha-Yoledet*, 26 (2nd ed.) write that as a general rule, once a woman has reached the 42nd week of pregnancy, she may take medication to induce labor, but she should do so early in the week if possible, so that she would not have to violate Shabbat (unless, of course, waiting presents any danger to the baby or the mother, in which case it should be done even on Shabbat). See also R. Eliyahu Bakshi Doron, *Sefer Binyan Av: Refuah Be-Halakhah*, 3.

2. For example, one may induce labor in order to prevent danger to the mother or the baby, but not simply for the sake of convenience. Preventing birth from taking place on Shabbat or a festival would not be a valid reason to induce, but having access to superior medical care may be. See *Torah Ha-Yoledet* 1:3–6 for in-depth discussion and various examples.

3. *Shulchan Arukh*, OC 223:1. If a son is born prematurely but the doctors say he will survive, one still says this blessing at the time of the birth, even if the baby is placed in an incubator (*Sefer Refuah Ke-Halakhah*, 191). However, if it is doubtful that the baby will survive, the blessing should not be made until the baby recovers (R. Beigeleisen, *Eit Laledet*, 236). Some are not accustomed to say this blessing at all, even when the baby is born perfectly healthy (see discussion in

Eit Laledet, 233).

4. *Mishnah Berurah* 223:3.

5. Ibid., 223:2. *Torat Ha-Yoledet* 37:3.

6. *Torat Ha-Yoledet* 37:5.

7. Ibid., 37:4.

8. Ibid., 62:5. There are many different customs regarding making this blessing after childbirth. In some communities, women recite this blessing in the synagogue from the women's section after the Torah reading. In others, the blessing is said in the woman's home with a *minyan*. Others say it in the presence of other women and one man (*Mishnah Berurah* 119:3). In many communities, it is not customary for women to recite this blessing at all. See *Piskei Teshuvot*, vol. 2, 873–4, and *Eit Laledet*, 339 for a summary of the various customs and Rabbinic opinions related to this matter. It is also possible for the husband to recite the blessing for his wife when he is called up to the Torah (*Mishnah Berurah* 119:17), although some discourage this practice (see the sources cited in *Nishmat Avraham*, OC 119:[3]).

9. R. Yosef David Weisberg, *Otzar Ha-Brit* (Jerusalem, 1993), vol. 1, 329. See also *Teshuvot Ve-Hanhagot* 3:297, who explains that there is a prophetic element to the parents' choice of a name, which is why it should not be shared before the *brit* or naming; the listener's reaction might influence the parents to choose a different name, which had not been chosen under Divine inspiration. According to this reason, simply writing the name on a paper that will not be read by anyone in the par-

ents' presence should not be problematic. However, *Teshuvot Ve-Hanhagot* gives a second reason for not sharing a name until the *brit*, which implies a connection between the soul of the baby and the occasion of the *brit*, so that it is better for the baby to receive the name only once he has been circumcised. According to this reason, it is best to wait to share the name at all, if possible. Not only do most authorities rule that it is permissible to write the name of one's child before he or she has been formally named, such as for their birth certificate, a couple who is having difficulty deciding on a name for their child may discuss the matter with a rabbi or family members (though the final decision must be left up to the parents of the child). See discussion of this issue in *Eit Laledet*, 256–260.

10. *Otzar Ha-Brit*, vol. 1, 331.

11. *Nishmat Avraham*, YD 263:2 (7), writes in the name of R. Neuwirth that if the circumcision will be delayed more than two weeks, the baby should be named before the *brit*. Many are accustomed to name the baby beforehand only if the delay will be very lengthy. This frequently occurs in the case of baby boys who have a condition known as hypospadias, for example, who often cannot be circumcised until they are nearly a year old. Nevertheless, others (including many Chassidim) always wait until the circumcision to name the child, no matter how long it takes, unless he is the mother's firstborn child, in which case some have the practice of giving the name at the *pidyon ha-ben* (*Otzar Ha-Brit*, vol. 1, 331). See also *Masorat Moshe*, vol. 2, 405.

12. *Nishmat Avraham*, YD 266:11 (8). See also *Ve-Alehu Lo Yibol*, vol. 3, 239. In contrast, it is reported that R. Moshe Feinstein ruled that the *Shalom Zakhar* should be held the Shabbat before the circumcision, and not the first Shabbat after the baby was born (*Sefer Masorat Moshe*, 353, n. 336).

13. *Nishmat Avraham*, YD 305 11(2) (404 in 3rd ed.). *Nishmat Avraham* adds that if the baby will be circumcised on the 31st day, the circumcision should take place first.

14. Ibid., R. Moshe Feinstein is quoted as ruling that a *pidyon ha-ben* should not be performed for a baby in an incubator (R. Aaron Felder, *Rishumei Aharon*, vol. 1, 69).

APPENDIX

STORIES FROM THE FRONT LINES:
Confronting Complex Ethical Scenarios and
Dilemmas

It's 6 PM, and as I get into my car to drive home from the hospital, my cell phone rings. "Rabbi! Help us!" are the first words I hear. "We are up here in the ICU, and we know that Jewish Law demands immediate burial. Please help us convince the staff here and at the cemetery to expedite my father's burial arrangements so that he can be buried tomorrow, before Shabbos! Can you help us make that happen immediately?" As I jump out of my car, I ask, "Okay, when did your father die and where is his body now?" "Dead?" the caller responds, appalled. "He's dying, but he's not dead yet! But we have to be ready just in case, don't we?"

As the Jewish chaplain of a major medical center, I have learned to expect all kinds of questions. Since healthcare is a rapidly changing field, the questions that I am asked are becoming increasingly complex – and understandably, many of them involve issues of life and death. Furthermore, I often find myself serving as a rabbi to people with minimal Jewish connection and in situations of conflicting views amongst family members that must be navigated with caution, nuance, and sensitivity.

Not everyone is familiar with the role of a chaplain. I have walked into the room of many Jewish patients who expressed concern when I introduced myself as a chaplain. "Don't try it on us, buddy! We are proud Jews, and you won't be able to convert us!" When I explain that I am also Jewish, and in fact a rabbi, people sometimes respond, "Oh. I thought they only had chaplains here. I didn't know that they have a rabbi as well!" But when I introduce myself to patients as the rabbi, they sometimes respond, "So you supervise the kosher kitchen?" The fact that rabbis can also be chaplains who work with patients, their families, and the interdisciplinary healthcare team often comes as a surprise.

Some of the issues that arise in a hospital setting are seen by the questioner as halakhic issues, although traditional Rabbinic training and responsa works don't always provide sufficient guidance. For example, I once received an urgent phone call from a senior hospital administrator. Our facility was holding a "topping off" ceremony that day as they put the final steel beam on the hospital's newest building, and their plan was to observe the ancient European custom of placing an evergreen tree on top of the structure. Someone suggested they use a cedar tree, since our hospital is called "Cedars-Sinai," but the administrator wouldn't acquiesce unless the rabbi permitted this deviation from the accepted *minhag* (custom). Honored that he sought my guidance on this issue, I told him I would have to consult the holy books and get back to him with an answer. After waiting a few moments for suspense's sake, I called back to give him a special one-time *heter* (permission).

Indeed, I now field many questions that I never received when I was a pulpit rabbi. Like the time I received a call to perform a funeral. That seemed routine enough – until the caller explained that the person in question had already been buried. They weren't happy with how the rabbi performed the initial funeral and were wondering if there could be a do-over on the ceremony. But that didn't compare to the time I was called urgently to a very sick patient's room. When I arrived, the patient's daughter asked if I had a live chicken handy. I couldn't figure out why they wanted a chicken. "I could order you barbecued or roasted chicken, if you would like," I explained, "but I'm not so sure I could bring a living chicken into a hospital room. Why do you ask?" The patient's daughter looked at me with disbelief. "I would like to put it on my father's belly so that it can absorb his disease, and then we'll kill the chicken here in the room so that the disease will be gone!" I continued to be surprised by this request until a few weeks later, when I was visiting another very ill patient, whose son told me, "Rabbi, we've done everything we can. We gave *tzedakah*, changed his name, killed a chicken on his belly . . ."

Many of the questions that arise require in-depth learning, creativity, and intricate knowledge of the medical facts to be handled appropriately. I try to learn as much as possible about medical Halakhah, and I frequently consult with local and international *poskim* (authorities in Jewish law) and *gedolim* (great rabbis) to resolve matters that are particularly complicated. Unfortunately, although many rabbis are extremely knowledgeable, not all are well versed in this specialty, or their experience is severely outdated.

For example, we were once dealing with a religious patient who was rapidly declining. The medical team was unanimous that continuing aggressive care was not only medically inappropriate, but harmful, and they strongly recommended that this patient be extubated (disconnected from the respirator). Of course, this can be very problematic from a halakhic perspective, so we called in the patient's rabbi to discuss the options. The rabbi met me at my office, and as I began to walk him up to the ICU, I casually asked how he was going to navigate this complicated case. "This one is simple!" he nonchalantly responded. "I will just advise them to follow Reb Moshe's opinion that when it is time to change the oxygen tank, they don't have to put in a new one." I paused and then gently explained that oxygen is now supplied continuously through an outlet in the wall; oxygen tanks haven't been used in decades! The rabbi stopped in his tracks, gave me a quizzical look, and sighed, "Oh. Well then I have no idea what to tell them!"

Family members themselves are also often very confused about the decisions they have to make. Since most patients don't have advance directives and people are afraid of having conversations about their preferences at the end of life, family conflicts frequently ensue as relatives struggle over their own values and what they think the patient would want.

A particular experience brings us to some of the more challenging ethical and halakhic situations that chaplains face. I was called to say a blessing for a patient before she was wheeled in to surgery. When I arrived, the patient politely explained that she had not asked for a rabbi. Her daughter, sitting by the pre-op bedside, coldly explained that they had no need for a rabbi at this time and that I should find my way out of there. Just as I began to oblige, the patient's bearded, yarmulke-wearing son entered the room and said, "Oh, the rabbi arrived. *Baruch Hashem* (Thank God)!" His sister quickly got up and explained that I was just leaving. They had a brief argument over whether or not I should be there, and everyone finally agreed that it would be okay for me to say a very short, simple prayer that the surgery should go smoothly.

I did as asked and was trying to exit when the son said, "Actually, Rabbi, since you are here, it would be a perfect time for us to discuss something very important." At that very moment, the staff came in to wheel the patient into surgery, yet her daughter agreed. "Yes! Hold off the surgery for just a second so that we can resolve this issue once and for all." Her brother, the patient's son, then grabbed his mother's hand and said, "Rabbi, please tell my mother that if she is indeed cremated, as is her wish, that she will go to hell." I took a deep gulp, but before I could say anything, his sister chimed in, "Yes, Rabbi, tell us the truth about this. Can you really say that this poor woman's soul will be punished? After all, we plan to spread her ashes over Jerusalem!"

I tried to remain calm and collected, softly explaining that this might not be the best time to have this discussion, but that I would be happy to sit down with them later. With a nervous chuckle in her voice, the patient herself then said, "No, Rabbi. What if I don't survive this procedure? I have chosen to be cremated, and my son needs to know now." I knew that she was not having a highly risky procedure and I had no interest in getting triangulated into this family feud, so I tried to skirt the question. "I'm sure we will have plenty of time to discuss this later. For now, let me just assure you that either way, I do not believe that you are going to hell."

The patient seemed satisfied with this response, until her son blurted out, "Notice what he didn't say! He did not say that it is allowed! You won't get him to say that, isn't that right, Rabbi!?" The patient and her daughter began to cry, I began to perspire, and the staff stepped in to remind us that they needed to take the patient into surgery. I agreed that I could not say that cremation is permitted, quickly reassured the patient that she would be well taken care of and that we would have plenty of time to discuss this later, and then proceeded to the waiting room with her children to try to calmly mediate their debate.

This story highlights one of the more challenging roles that a chaplain plays. I am certainly opposed to cremation, for both halakhic and emotional/psychological reasons (see Chapter 5F), but my role as a chaplain is not to mandate religious doctrine, force individuals into specific choices, or even advocate a particular lifestyle or worldview. Rather, the focus of chaplaincy care tends to be on facilitating the ability of individuals to articulate their own goals and values, and helping them uncover, navigate, translate, and resolve some of the issues with which they might be struggling. On the other hand, I am also a committed Orthodox Jew. I feel strongly about my beliefs – which I have a unique opportunity to teach and share – and I certainly wouldn't want to be guilty of abetting a transgression (*mesaye'ah li-yedei aveirah*) or placing a stumbling block before the blind (*lifnei iver*).

In consultation with *poskim* and experienced chaplains, I have thus developed an approach to these issues that has been helpful both in cases like this, where there is family conflict, and in cases in which the family is unanimous on what they want to do, but their decision goes against my own religious values. Of course, every situation is unique and must be dealt with on a case-by-case basis in consultation with a *posek*. Without pushing in one direction or another, I can often gently ask why a family or patient is making a given decision. In the case of cremation, for example, I am often told that it is simply easier and cheaper. When I offer to help arrange easy and inexpensive proper Jewish burial, this tends to result in consent to conform with Jewish Law.

Another approach is to determine if a person is making a competent decision against Jewish Law as a *tzava'ah* (clear, explicit will) or if they are simply stating a preference. If one is merely sharing a preference that has not been thought out, there may be room for an open discussion. Once the patient has died, we can sometimes assume that they either didn't realize the extent of the prohibition or would want to be treated in accordance with the unanimous desire of all of their children or executors of their will, even if that is different from what their stated preference had been.

However, sometimes a person's wishes are definite and diametrically opposed to traditional Jewish values or practices, leaving us in quite a bind. Halakhah only binds us to undertake responsibilities that we are capable of carrying out. If one's patient or relative has made a clear-minded and informed decision to do something that violates Halakhah, the religious family members or chaplain will have to take the approach of *shev ve-al ta'aseh* (sit and refrain from action), simply explaining that they are unable to carry out these wishes, but allowing someone else to do so. The concept of *"mitzvah le-kayem et divrei ha-met"* (the obligation to implement the wishes of the deceased) does not apply to fulfilling desires of the deceased to violate Halakhah. However, American Law does require that their wishes be respected by the executor of their will, and there is a certain integrity involved in fulfilling this responsibility. If the religious values of one in a position of legal responsibility do not allow him or her to fulfill the wishes of the deceased, they should simply step aside and allow others to proceed as planned, rather than protesting when they know that their concerns will not be heard. This approach makes it clear that one is not supporting the transgression, but avoids creating the *chillul Hashem* (desecration of God's name) that may result when belligerent religious individuals make a protest that will be neither understood nor effective.

Furthermore, showing willingness to compromise often enables us to find a way to fulfill the patient's wishes in a manner that involves the least amount of transgression, and may possibly lead to some mitzvah observance down the road. For example, I have seen cases where one family member was not able to convince the rest of his family to bury their relative in the ground instead of interring him in a mausoleum crypt. However, instead of persisting to fight this decision, he allowed them to proceed, but with the provision that they at least perform a *taharah* and bury in *takhrikhim* (traditional ritual cleansing and burial shrouds), place *afar* (earth) in the casket, and observe *aveilut* (the laws of mourning).

It is also important to recognize the importance of relieving *tiruf ha-da'at* (acute mental anguish) as part of healing. We have a small *Sefer Torah* (Torah scroll) in my hospital's synagogue that was frequently taken to patients' rooms before I arrived on staff. When I began work-ing as a chaplain, I consulted two great *poskim*, one in New York and the other in Israel, because according to Jewish Law we must usually be careful not to remove a Torah scroll from the ark unless we are going to read from it. However, both of these authorities told me that even though it may not be traditional to bring a Torah to a patient's bedside, if it relieves their emotional suffering and helps them heal in one way or another, not only is it permissible, but it also can be considered *pikuach nefesh* (saving a life)!

Like doctors, chaplains are on call at all hours for emergencies. Thankfully, I have been able to work out a system whereby I have never had to violate the Shabbat for my job, but I asked a prominent *posek* in Israel if there could ever be a case in which a chaplain could override Shabbat for the sake of a patient. This Rav responded emphatically that if the patient is very ill and the chaplain knows for a fact that their presence can improve the patient's condition, then the chaplain should do whatever it takes to be there for the patient, just as a doctor would. There are limits to this principle and its application requires careful Rabbinic guidance, but it is crucial to bear in mind.

So what is my role as an observant Jewish chaplain? It is related to the role of a Jewish hospital in general. The institution I work for is a proudly Jewish hospital with a huge *Magen David* (Star of David) on its building, kosher *mezuzot* on every door and Shabbat elevators in every building. Does that mean we should force everyone who enters our hallowed walls to eat kosher food or that all medical decisions are made in accordance with Halakhah? We live in a society in which autonomy is a primary value. My job is not to undermine that autonomy, but rather to *enable* Jewish Law to be observed to the greatest extent possible whenever necessary – to make sure that our hospital is Jewish-Law-friendly, while respectfully tolerating those who choose not to abide by it. Everyone appreciates being respectfully informed of Jewish values and having someone ensure that those who want to obey them are completely enabled and encouraged to do as they wish. If a situation arises in which I can influence decisions in favor of Jewish Law or values, then I may opt to do so, but not in a heavy-handed manner.

Some have pointed out that in Israel there is a *chametz* law, prohibiting bread products on Passover, nevertheless, people all over Israel continue to buy and sell bread products on Passover. Israel also has a pork law, but similarly, pork is purchased and consumed throughout Israel. However, there is one law that is kept very scrupulously throughout all of Israel: the Yom Kippur law. On Yom Kippur even the most secular Jews in Israel don't drive their cars and would never eat in public. What is different about the Yom Kippur law? Many suggest that it is the fact that such a law was never actually passed!

Religious coercion doesn't work. Voluntary encouragement does. Not all food served in my hospital is kosher, but there is a state-of-the-art kosher kitchen cooking fresh food daily at no extra expense to patients who choose to order it. Similarly, when we encourage patients and their surrogates to narrate their own values and goals, if they choose to follow Halakhah despite its occasional divergence from standard medical practice, we invoke our "reasonable accommodation policy," which allows their wishes to be respected and upheld.

Actually, this is not always easy. Physicians sometimes declare aggressive end-of-life treatment to be "futile" sooner than I am comfortable with. The value that Judaism places on every second of life is not always shared by society at large. The concept that a person may choose to undergo a certain amount of pain in order to remain alive is not always appreciated, nor is the fact that certain decisions in a hospital are actually moral, ethical, and religious, not medical or scientific. Chaplains play a crucial role in navigating the crossroads of modernity and tradition. Attempting to balance my role of serving as an advocate for patients and their values at the same time that I remain a full member of the interdisciplinary healthcare team is complex, but it is also a privilege – and quite an opportunity, when done right, for positive influence and *kiddush Hashem* (sanctification of God's name).

Note: None of the above is to be understood as *halakhah le-ma'aseh* (practical rulings). As stated above, every halakhic issue must be decided on a case-by-case basis by one's own rabbi or *posek*. In the stories I have shared above, I have not included all of the issues involved, and I have changed some details to maintain the privacy of the individuals.

INDEX

Abortion, 15, 51, 217, 292n7, 293n9, 300n39, 301n44, 302n45, 319–24
D&C (dilation and curettage), 334n40
Due to Predicted Illness/Disability, 322
Fetal Reduction, *see* Multifetal Pregnancy Reduction
Multifetal Pregnancy Reduction, 307, 322
Psychological Factors, 330–1n31
Stages of Pregnancy, 321
Determining Stage, 327n20
Stem Cell Research, 301n44, 322–3
Abraham, Prof. Abraham S., 18, 58n5, 76n12, 76n14, 130n6, 132n18, 133n20, 149n17, 151n23, 151n28, 153n37, 344n13
Advance Care Planning, *see* Advance Directive
Advance Directive, 73–74, 113–7, 124, 357
Age to Prepare One, 120n12
Concerns Related to, 113–5
The Need, 113
Types, 115
Afterlife, *see* World to Come
Aggressive Interventions, *see* Prolonging Life
Agudath Israel, 115
Air, *see* Oxygen
R. Akiva, 19n2, 145n3
Alternative Medicine, 70
Amniocentesis, 332n35 *see also* NIPT (non-invasive pre-natal testing)
Anencephaly, 322, 331n34
Anguish, *see* Tiruf ha-da'at
Antibiotics, 43n26, 87, 124, 126, 129, 132n18
Artificial Heart, 154–62
Artificial Insemination, *see also* Assisted Reproductive Technology
Fatherhood, 314n30, 316n38, 341n9
From Donor (AID), 21n17, 307–8, 339n2
Adultery and, 315n35, 316n36, 317n42
Illegitimacy and, 316n39, 317n42
Secular Ethicists and, 315n34
Single Woman and, 308, 317n42
Sperm Bank, 317n40
From Husband (AIH), 21n17, 304–5, 313n25

Wasting Seed, 302n47, 304–5, 309n4, 312n19, 330n28 *see also* Assisted Reproductive Technology, Semen Procurement
Artificial Nutrition, *see* Nutrition and Hydration
Assisted Reproductive Technology, 304–8 *see also* Artificial Insemination; IVF; PGD
Coitus Interruptus, *see* Semen Procurement
Condom/Seminal Collection Device, *see* Semen Procurement
Fertility Testing, 304, 309n3
Halakhic Infertility, 304, 309n3
Masturbation, *see* Semen Procurement
Nida, 312n20, 316n39
Semen Procurement, 304–5, *see also* Artificial Insemination, Wasting Seed
Supervision, 308
Testicular Biopsy, 310n13
Varicocele, 309n5
Auerbach, R. Shlomo Zalman, 18, 19n1, 21n17, 42n17, 75n9, 81n7, 84n17, 84n27, 85n28, 94–95, 119n3, 129, 130n4, 130n6–7, 131n14, 132n18, 133n23, 134n23, 146n6, 149n13, 149n17, 150n19–23, 164n20, 166n39, 167n45, 167n47, 176n25, 194n22, 194n24, 209–10, 214n12, 215n31, 232n46, 234n81, 244n11, 245n15, 248n30, 297n31, 298n35, 302n50, 303n51, 309n6, 310n8, 311n16, 312n20, 315n31, 317n44, 331n31, 340n6, 341n9, 342n10
Autonomy, 15, 23n26, 45, 114, 119n3, 122, 157, 164n16, 170, 263n13, 319
Autopsies, 210, 221, 236–40
"Before Us" (*Lefaneinu*), requirement of, 237
Consent of Family, 239, 248n29, 249n32–3
Fetus, 221, 245n15
Financial/Inheritance Purposes, 238
History of Disputes Regarding, 241n1
Imaging, 221, 237
Legal Purposes/Cause of Death, 238, 246n21,23
Lengthen but not Save Life, 243n7
Minor Procedures (biopsy, blood draws), 237

Mourning, 248n29, 249n35–6
Observing, 246n26, 248n28
Scientific Research, 238, 248n27
Treatment of Body During Autopsy, 239
Ayin Hara, 117

Baby, death of, *see* Death, fetus or
   newborn
Bad News, *see Tiruf ha-da'at*
Be Fruitful and Multiply, 289, 290,
   298n35, 299n37, 303n51, 303n53,
   311n16, 312n21, 313n25, 333n38,
   348n30
   Desire for Children, 299n36
   Having Children in order to Serve as
      Donors for Others, 291
Best Interest Standard, *see* Surrogate
   Decision-Making, Best Interest
   Standard
Bick, R. Ezra, 21n18, 342n10
Bleich, R. J.D., 21n18, 40n4, 42n21,
   82n9, 83n11, 83n14, 131n15, 149n15,
   161, 166n36, 167n45, 177n30,
   193n17, 202n12, 249n38, 295n17,
   297n29, 297n32, 313n25, 333n37,
   337, 339n1–2, 342n10, 343n12,
   344n22, 345n22–3
Blood Pressure, *see* Vasopressor
   Medications
Bone Marrow Donation, *see* Organ
   Donation, Bone Marrow
Brain Death, *see* Death, Brain Death
BRCA, 287, 290, 294n13, 295n17,
   295n19, 297n32, 302n48
Broyde, R. Michael, 35, 60n21, 300n38,
   303n51–53
Burial, 204, 213n9, 222, 242n3, 246n25,
   248n30, 250, 251, 254n2–3, 255n8–9,
   266–70, 272, 275
   Coffin, 266, 267, 270, 275
   In Israel, 278n28
   Mausoleum, 266–76

Cancer, 29, 44, 45, 46, 49n10, 287, 288,
   289, 291, 295n15, 296n19, 331n32
Capacity, *see* Mental Illness, Capacity;
   Pediatrics, Age of Capacity
Cardiac Arrest, *see* DNR
Cardiac Defibrillator, *see* Defibrillator
Cardiopulmonary Resuscitation, *see* DNR
Casket, *see* Burial, Coffin
Cassel, Dr. Eric, 31
Chayei Sha'ah, *see* Dying Patient
Chaplaincy, 17, 18, 173, 195, 197, 226,
   251–3, 355, 357–61
Chazon Ish, 13, 20n13, 21n18, 96,
   181n11, 232n43, 233n53, 244n11,
   245n14, 311n17
Chemotherapy, 46, 124, 129, 142,
   311n16

Children, *see* Pediatrics
Cloning, 19n2, 20n16, 21n17
Coffin, *see* Burial, Coffin
Comfort,
   Comfort Care, 88
   Comfort Measures, *see* Pain, Medical
      Pain Relief
   From Observing Jewish Law, 15
   Nursing Care and, 196
   Via Prayer, 97
Compelling Treatment, *see* Mental Illness,
   Compelling Treatment
Confidentiality, 260, 288–9, 296n21,
   296n26, 297n28, 308
Consent, *see* Pediatrics; Mental Illness,
   Capacity; Surrogate Decision-Making
Continuous Sedation, *see* Permanent
   Sedation
Cremation, 250–3, 276, 358
   Ashes, What to do with them, 251,
      256n9
   Reasons for Prohibition, 250
Crypt, *see* Burial, Mausoleum

Danger, *see* Risk; Triage
Death
   Bodily Fluids, treatment of, 199
   Brain Death, 34, 35, 101n1, 160, 187,
      188, 189, 216n31
   Declaration of, 189–91
   Extubation and, 150n19–20, 189
   Organ Donation and, 205, 207, 209,
      216n31
   Customs after Death, 197–8
   Definition of, 160, 185–91
   Definition vs. Criterion, 33–34, 187,
      188, 192n7
   Fetus or Newborn, 217–27, *see also*
      Autopsy; Death, watching over body
   Burial, 222, 233fn53
   Circumcision, 221
   Distinction Between Death of Fetus
      and Baby, 219–20
   Funeral, 222–3
   Holding the Baby, 220
   Incubator, 228n1, 350, 351n3
   Kaddish, 224
   Naming, 221
   Pictures, 220
   Reasons Not to Engage in Mourning
      Rituals for, 217–8
   Reasons to Engage in Mourning
      Rituals for, 219
   Shiva, 223
   Reasonable Accommodation, 35, 189
   Removal of Pacemaker from Corpse,
      245n17
   Resurrection of the Dead, 102n8, 218,
      232n51, 242n2, 246n25, 249n32,
      249n35, 250

Prayers Before, *see Viduy*
Preparing for, 117
Shabbat, 198–9
State vs. Status, 34–35, 186, 192n7
Treatment of the Corpse, 197, 207, 221, 241n2, 255n5
Watching Over Body, 199, 233n54
Decision-Making, *see* Surrogate Decision-Making
Defibrillator, 142, 166n39
Dentures, 200
Depression, 47, 51, 57n3, 58n5, 171, 172, *see also Yom Kippur*
Dialysis, 142–3, 154, 158, 165n23, 166n39, 177n29
DNA, *see* Genetic Testing
DNI (Do Not Intubate) Orders, 121, 141 *see also* DNR; Intubation;
DNR (Do Not Resuscitate) Orders, 37, 43n25, 80, 121–3, 127, 205
Do Not Stand Idly By, 40n3, 79, 174n8, 206, 211n3, 303n52, 326n18
Dopamine, *see* Vasopressor Medications
Down Syndrome, 58n9
Durable Power of Attorney, *see* Advance Directive
Dying Patient, 49n11, 66 71fn5, 86, 87, 89, 94–6, 105, 121, 122, 124–5, 139, 159, 171, 195–6, *see also* Pediatrics, Dying Children; Hastening Death; Triage
  Alone, 196
  Definition of Terminal, 125–6
  Respect for, 196
  Tearing Clothing, 196, 221

Eating Disorders, *see Yom Kippur*, Fasting
Ectogenesis, 342n9
Egg donation, *see* Surrogacy, Egg donation
Elderly Patients, 42n19
Emergency, *see* Triage
End of Life Option Act, *see* Physician-Assisted Suicide
Euthanasia, 156–8, 170, *see also* Physician-Assisted Suicide
  Passive Euthanasia, 170
Experimental Treatments, 70
Extubation, 122, 138–40, 158–9, 189, 200, 206, 357

Face Mask, *see* Oxygen
Faith, 94, 97,
Feinstein, R. Moshe, 18, 19n1, 20n11, 22n22, 42n17, 58n4, 60n17, 65n43, 71n7, 72fn11, 75n7, 76n9, 102n5, 109n19, 130n3–7, 133n19, 133n23, 135n38, 136n42, 145n2, 146n6, 152n31, 152n33, 153n37, 181n11,

212n6, 216n31, 228n1, 231n31, 233n53, 234n74, 280n58–9, 281n72–3, 294n13, 295n17, 310n11–2, 311n15, 311n17, 316n39–40, 329n26, 330n28, 332n35, 339n2, 346n27, 352n12,14
Fertility Testing, *see* Assisted Reproductive Technology, Fertility Testing
Forensic Medicine, *see* Autopsies, Legal Purposes
Fox, Dr. David, 59n16, 60n18, 103n14, 108n12
Freedman, Benjamin, 11, 42n22
Funeral, 197, *see also* Death, Fetus or Newborn, Funeral

Genetic Testing, 285–7, *see also* PGS
  Diagnostic Genetic Testing, 286
  Direct to Consumer Testing, 292n4
  Preconception Testing, 286
  Premarital Genetic Testing, 286–7
    Breaking Engagement/Divorce, 292–3n9
    When in Relationship to Test, 294n10
  Prenatal Genetic Testing, 286
  Revelation of Carrier Status, 287–8
Glick, Dr. Shimon, 23n26, 43n26, 50n18, 145n3, 241n1
Goldberg, R. Zalman Nechemia, 40n3, 75n8, 76n10–1, 134n23, 148n13, 182n12–3, 249n36, 295–6n19, 342n9–10, 344n17–8, 345n25, 347n28
God, 15, 19n2, 23n26, 36, 39n3, 41n9, 45, 52, 59n10, 62n26, 62n27, 63n30, 64n33, 64n34, 64n35, 70, 71n3, 94, 96–7, 99, 103n17, 147n10, 218, 250, 263n13, 290
Gossip, *see* Mental Illness, *Lashon Ha-Ra*
Guilt
  And decision-making, 12, 15, 37, 73, 113

Hastening Death, 45, 88, 89, 127, 157, 170, 204, 214n15
Holocaust, 256n11
Heart Disease, 155
Heaven, *see* World to Come
Hemophilia, 298n34
"Heroics," *see* Prolonging Life
Hope, 36, 50n20, 94–6, 100, 105, 106
Hospice, 86–90, 128 *see also* Pain; Pain, Medical Pain Relief
Huntington's Disease, 297n28
Hydration, *see* Nutrition and Hydration

Infinite Value of Life, *see* Value of Life, infinite vs. relative
Intubation, *see* DNI; Oxygen

Practice on a Corpse, 248n30
When is it Required, 138, 146n6
IV Feeding, *see* Nutrition and Hydration
IVF (In Vitro Fertilization), 289–90,
299n37, 301n44, 302n48, 306–7,
313n25, 314n26, 339n2

Jewish Law
Consequences of not observing, *see*
Reward and Punishment
Multiple Approaches/Conclusions, 15
Who is fit to rule, 14–15
Jotkowitz, Dr. Alan, 22n18, 22n25,
241n1, 262n7

Kashrut, see Mental Illness, non-kosher
food
Klapper, R. Aryeh, 22n18, 215n23
Kria, see Dying Patient, tearing clothing

Labor and Delivery, 349–50
Blessings Said Upon Birth, 349
Circumcision, 349
Inducing Labor, 349
Pidyon Ha-ben, 350
Revealing Name, 349
Shalom Zachor, 350
Lashon Ha-Ra, see Mental Illness,
Lashon Ha-Ra
Last Rites, *see Viduy*
Lichtenstein, R. Aharon, 15, 325n1,
328n23
Lies, *see* Truth Telling
Living Will, *see* Advance Directive
Love Your Neighbor as Yourself, 40n3,
131n14, 176n25
Lubavitcher Rebbe, 48n9, 317n44

Mausoleum, *see* Burial, Mausoleum
Medical Aid in Dying, *see* Physician-
Assisted Suicide
Medical Pain Relief, *see* Pain, Medical
Pain Relief
Meier, R. Levi, 36, 44
Mental Anguish, *see Tiruf ha-da'at*
Mental Illness, 51–66
Birth Control and, 58n5
Capacity, Determining, 55–56
Compassion Towards, 55–52
Compelling Treatment, 55
Informing Potential Spouse about
Mental Illness, 288–9
Lashon Ha-Ra (Gossip) to Therapist,
52–53
Lashon Ha-Ra (Gossip) to Therapist
about one's Parents, 53
Name Change and, *see* Name Change
Non-Kosher Food and, 58n5, 59n11,
61n23
Nechpaz, 56

Obsessive Compulsive Disorder (OCD),
54–55
Prayer and, 63n32
Prevalence in the Observant Jewish
Community, 61n24–25
Peti, 55, 78
Shoteh, 55, 59n10, 181n11
Yichud with Therapist, 53–54
Yom Kippur, see Yom Kippur, Fasting
Mental Retardation, 58n9
Miracles, *see* Prayer, Prayer for a Miracle
Miscarriage, *see* Death, fetus or newborn
MRT (mitochondria replacement
therapy), *see* Surrogacy
MOLST, *see* POLST
Morphine, *see* Pain, Medical Pain Relief
Mortuary, 197, 240, 251, 257n13, 271
Moses, Dr. Naftali, 34, 216n37
Mourning, *see* Death, fetus or newborn;
Autopsy, mourning

Name Change, 58n4, 102n5
Narcotics, *see* Pain, Medical Pain Relief
Nasal Canula, *see* Oxygen
Natural Law, 11, 19–20
NG Tube (nasogastric tube) *see* Nutrition
and Hydration
NIPT (non-invasive pre-natal testing),
332n35
Nutrition and Hydration, 87, 124, 124–5,
129
PEG vs. NG Tube, 133n22
Nutrition vs. Hydration, 135n33

OCD, *see* Mental Illness, Obsessive
Compulsive Disorder
Oophorectomy, 288, 295n19
Opioids, *see* Pain, Medical Pain Relief
Oral Torah, 12–14
Organ Donation, 203–10, 236, 291
Blood, 203, 212n5, 258
Bone Marrow, 81n7, 83n17, 84n17,
84n19, 211–2n3, 212n5, 291,
303n52
Cornea Transplantation, 213n10
Dead Donors (Cadaveric), 204
Definition of Death and, 189
Donation after Cardiac Death (DCD),
205–6
Forcing a Minor, 79–80
Heart Transplantation, 204, 212n6
Kidney, 204, 212n6
Living Donor, 203–4
Organ Donor Cards, 207
Prolonging Life for the Sake of, 41n12
Sale of Organs, 258–61
Skin Banking, 213n7, 213n10
Taking but not Giving, 207–10
Treatment of Corpse and, 207
Ovum Donation, *see* Surrogacy, Egg

donation
Oxygen, Requirement, 122, 124, 129,
    138, 158 see also DNI; Extubation

Pacemaker, see Death, Removal of
    Pacemaker
Pain
    Medical Pain Relief, 32, 86–90, 123–4,
        128, 131n15, 157, 172, 177n26
    Nutrition and Hydration and, 133n23
    Pain vs. Suffering, 31–33
    Pain Reduction via Risky Surgery, 70,
        132n17
    Palliative Care, 86–90
    Presumed Desire to Avoid Pain, 74,
        130n3, 131n8, 146n6
    Value of Suffering, 41–2n16, 157
Palliative Care, see Pain; Pain, Medical
    Pain Relief; Hospice
Palliative Sedation, see Permanent
    Sedation
Passive Inaction, 133–4n23, 144, 152n29,
    161, 167n47, 359
Peace of Mind, see Tiruf ha-da'at
Pediatrics,
    Capacity, Age of, 78
    Consent, 77–78 see also Surrogate
        Decision-Making, Best Interest
        Standard; Children and;
    Surrogate Decision-Making, Substituted
        Judgement, Children and (felt the
        need to clarify in this or some other
        way)
    Dying Children, 71fn4, 80, 101n1, see
        also Death, fetus or newborn
    Organ Donation, see Organ Donation,
        Forcing a Minor
    Parents Authority, 77, 78
    Risky Procedures and, 71fn4Trisomy 13
        or 18, 85n28
PEG (Percutaneous Endoscopic
    Gastrostomy), see Nutrition and
    Hydration
Permanent Sedation, 172
Persistent Vegetative State (PVS), 34,
    101n1
PGD (Pre-Implantation Genetic
    Diagnosis), 286, 289–91, 298n35,
    299n38, 301n40, 301n44, 302n45, 48,
    322, 344n18
    To Choose Gender, 290
    Ethical Issues and, 300n39
PGS (Pre-Implantation Genetic
    Screening), 300n38
Physician Aid in Dying, see Physician-
    Assisted Suicide
Physician-Assisted Suicide, 146n3,
    169–73
    Burial in a Jewish Cemetery and,
        175n15

Clergy and, 171–2
Compassion for, 171
Root Causes, 171–2
Placebo, 72fn13
POLST forms, 117–8, 124
Prayer, 41n9, 41n10 see also Mental
    Illness, Obsessive Compulsive
    Disorder; Viduy
    Efficacy of, 93–104
    For a Miracle, 93–104
    For Death, 171
    Upon Death, 196, 201n5, 220
Prenatal Testing, see Genetic testing,
    prenatal genetic testing
Procedure, see Risk
Prolonging Life, 89, 121, 170
    Prolonging Life vs. Prolonging Suffering,
        121–2, 127–8, 136n43, 138
Proxy, see Advance Directive
Peru U-revu, see Be Fruitful and Multiply
Psalms, 93
PTSD, 57–8n3
"Pulling the Plug," see Extubation

Rabbi
    Role of, 13–15
Rabbinical Council of America, 115
Radiation, 124
Refusing Unproven Therapies, 70
Religious Coping, positive and negative,
    32, 41n9
Research on Corpse, see Autopsy,
    Scientific Research
Respirator, see Extubation; Intubation
    Timer, 141, 143, 151–2, 182n12
Resuscitation, see DNR
Revealing Painful Information, see Truth
    Telling
Reward and Punishment, 15–16, 23n27–
    28, 41n9
Right to Die, see Physician-Assisted
    Suicide
Risk, 69–72, 203–4
    Levels of Risk (i.e. Percentages), 71fn7,
        204, 211n3, 212n4
    Medical Trials, 72fn13
    Prayer before Danger, see Viduy
    Pregnancy and, 301n40
    Surgery for Patient with Intermittent
        Illness, 136n42

Salutogenesis, 41n11
Sanctity of Life, see Value of Life, value
    vs. sanctity
Schachter, R. Hershel, 21n16, 76n9,
    120n12, 129, 134n23, 147n6, 176n15,
    257n15
Science vs. Religion, 42n22
    Religiosity of Physicians, 43n28
Seclusion with Opposite Gender, see

Mental Illness, *Yichud*
Sedation, *see* Permanent Sedation
Segulah, 117
Self-endangerment, *see* Risk
Self-Wounding, 263n16
Shabbat, 41n15, 49n11, 58n5, 61n24,
  62n27,29, 106, 139, 145n1, 147n11,
  198–9, 224, 245n17, 255n5,
  295n17, 305, 311n14, 323, 327n18,
  328n21,23,24, 334n43, 351n1–2, 360
Shabtai, R. Dr. David, 148n12, 150n20,
  153n37, 166n39, 167n45, 192n9,
  193n11–2,15–6,18,20, 194n21–2,
  212n6, 214n13–8, 215n23,29
Shev ve-al Ta'aseh, see Passive Inaction
Shomer, *see* Death, Watching Over Body
Sirus, 288, 310n13
Soloveitchik, R. Joseph B., 14, 21n17, 31,
  96–8
Steinberg, Prof. Avraham, 18, 119n6,
  131n10, 132n18, 133n21–2, 135n33,
  135n40, 136n43, 137, 145n3, 149n17,
  150n22, 151n23, 153n35, 166n43–4,
  193n20, 194n23, 194n27, 295n19,
  300n38, 331n31, 332n35, 343n12–3,
  344n13
Stem Cell Research, *see* Abortion, Stem
  Cell Research
Substituted Judgement, *see* Surrogate
  Decision-Making, Substituted
  Judgement
Suffering, *see* Pain, pain vs. suffering;
  Pain, Medical Pain Relief; Prolonging
  Life, Prolonging Life vs. Prolonging
  Suffering
  Comatose Patient, 130n7
  Of Family, 130n7
Suicide, 23n28, 133n23, 164n16, 170,
  171, 331n31
Sulmasy, Dr. Daniel, 40–41n6
Surgery, *see* Risk
Surrogacy, 335–8
  Concealing Identity of Surrogate, 339n1
  Ethical Issues and, 347n29–30
  Egg Donation, 21n18, 335, 338
  MRT (mitochondria replacement
    therapy), 337
  Who is Considered the Mother, 336–7
  Who Should Serve as a Surrogate, 337
  Permissibility of Surrogacy, 336
Surrogate Decision-Making, 73–76
  Appointing a Surrogate Decision-Maker,
    114, 116
  Best Interest Standard, 73–74
  Children and, 77–79
  Harm Principle, 77
  Substituted Judgement, 73–74
  Children and, 77–79

Tehillim, see Psalms

Terminal, *see* Dying Patient
Terminal Sedation, *see* Permanent
  Sedation
Tiruf ha-da'at, 43, 181n11, 106, 196,
  302n45, 360
Torczyner, R. Mordechai, 57n3, 61n23,
  62n27, 65n39, 75n6, 147n6, 176n18
TPN (Total Parenteral Nutrition), *see*
  Nutrition and Hydration
Tracheotomy, 141–2
Triage, 21n17, 152n28, 178–9, 201n2
Trisomy, *see* Pediatrics, Trisomy 13 or 18
Truth Telling, 44–50

VAD (Ventricular Assist Device), 155–6
Value of Life, 137, 207, 215n24, 260, 319
  Infinite vs. Relative value, 30–31
  Value vs. Sanctity, 30
Vasopressor Medications, 132n19
Ventilator, *see* Extubation; Intubation
  Timer, 141, 182n12
Viduy, 50n19, 59n12, 105–9

Weiss, R. Asher, 18, 21n17, 57n3, 59n11,
  60n21, 62n29, 63n32, 65n37, 76n9,
  108n19, 135n39, 146n6, 149n17,
  151n23, 152n30, 153n33, 161, 163n1,
  166n39, 167n52, 175n15, 182n12–13,
  211n3, 212n6, 230n19, 265n28,
  292n8, 295n19, 298n35, 302n48,
  311n14, 314n26, 314n28, 318n44,
  337, 341n9, 343n11, 344n15, 345n23
Withdrawal of Life Sustaining
  Treatments, 127, 133n23, 135n32,
  137, 138, 142, 143
Withholding vs. Withdrawing, 122–3,
  127, 137–8, 145n3
World to Come, 16, 23n28, 52, 95, 106,
  164n20

Yichud, see Mental Illness, *Yichud*
Yom Kippur, Fasting
  Depression Medications, 57n3, 58n5
  Eating Disorder and Force Feeding,
    65n37

Zohn, R. Elhanan, 109, 201n1, 256n10,
  257n15
Zilberstein, R. Yitzchak, 42n19, 49n14,
  58n10, 59n15,17, 60n19, 61n22,
  71n7, 82n7,10, 83n12, 84n23,
  85n29, 101n1, 129, 133n19-20,
  134n23,26, 135n38, 146n6, 147n9,
  152n28,30, 153n34, 161, 166n35,39,
  180n1,4, 181n7-11, 182n12, 243n6-7,
  244n11, 245n17, 263n16, 295n14,
  296n25, 297n28-9, 298n34, 299n36,
  302n45,48,50, 315n31, 326n14,
  328n21, 329n26, 331n31,34, 332n34,
  333n37, 339n2